The Way or the Black Messiah

*The Hermeneutical Challenge of Black Theology
as a Theology of Liberation*

Theo Witvliet

MEYER
STONE
BOOKS

Translated by John Bowden from the Dutch *De Weg van de Zwarte Messias: De hermeneutische uitdaging van zwarte theologie als een theologie van bevrijding*, copyright © Uitgeverij Ten Have 1985.

First English edition published in Great Britain by SCM Press Ltd, 26–30 Tottenham Road, London N1 4BZ

and

published in the United States by Meyer•Stone Books, a division of Meyer, Stone, and Company, Inc., 714 South Humphrey, Oak Park IL 60304.

Photoset in Great Britain and printed and bound in the United States of America.

Meyer•Stone ISBN 0-940-989-04-2 Paperback
           ISBN 0-940-989-09-3 Hard cover

CONTENTS

Contents

FOREWORD

Black theology is too important to be left exclusively in the hands of the black theologians! This is one of the messages, perhaps the most important one, to come through loudly and clearly from this ground-breaking book by Theo Witvliet, a Dutch liberation theologian who teaches at the University of Amsterdam. How does a white scholar who lives in Holland come by such an intriguing conclusion about black theology in the United States? Before trying to answer that question it may be useful to reconstruct briefly the modern history of this African-American way of doing theology that has been the cause of both consternation and celebration on both sides of the Atlantic.

Between 1964 and the publication in 1969 of *Black Theology and Black Power* (Seabury Press, 1969) by a young, relatively unknown black theologian named James H. Cone, a theological and cultural earthquake of major proportions rumbled across the black communities of the United States. Perhaps it would be most accurate to say that it was the most recent tremor, an after-shock of an eruption that began many years ago in the dark bowels of the slave quarters. It started as a muffled explosion under an overturned pot (believed to keep down the noise of worship) in the secret meetings of an "invisible institution" in the eighteenth century. It gathered velocity under the pressure of white racists and segregationists, until in the late 1950s it broke through the surface of the rural slums of a demoralized and impoverished South and expelled its volcanic lava of rage and black consciousness through the dilapidated tenements and storefronts of the Northern ghettos. It was both violent and nonviolent, and it was impossible to contain it by the usual proscriptions of orthodoxy, civil or religious.

At the vortex of the tornados of revolutionary thought and action that accompanied the upheaval at the end of the 1950s was a group of black church folk led by a young Baptist preacher named Martin Luther King, Jr., who organized a movement, mainly in the

South until 1965, with the help of a courageous cadre of preacher-leaders like Ralph D. Abernathy, Fred Shuttlesworth, Charles K. Steele, C. T. Vivian, Wyatt Tee Walker, and Andrew Young. In the North there were other religious leaders who greatly influenced the struggle that involved the total black urban population of the nation: Malcolm X, Adam C. Powell, Jr., Albert G. Cleage, Vincent Harding, Stokley Carmichael, James Cone, Herbert B. Shaw, Benjamin Payton, Anna Arnold Hedgeman, Edler G. Hawkins, and J. Deotis Roberts. This latter group, along with others too numerous to be mentioned here, molded an intellectual framework for a radical revision in black culture and religion that gathered its greatest momentum following the assassination of Dr. King in 1968. Before the end of the next decade this highly diverse, loosely-affiliated core of Northern leaders and thinkers gave impetus to a new black theology of liberation — the most significant theological development to disrupt the placid and largely irrelevant surface of Western Christendom since the First World War polemics of Swiss theologian Karl Barth.

In the United States this development of black theology was entirely in the hands of the descendants of African slaves — a small group of church leaders and theologians. The first white American theologian to confront the new movement in a full-length book was Frederick Herzog, a professor at Duke Divinity School, whose *Liberation Theology* (Seabury Press, 1972) was the occasion for more astonishment than appreciation among white American theologians. Herzog, in his Preface, remarks that in 1970 when Cone first published his second book, *A Black Theology of Liberation* (Lippincott, 1970), he, Herzog, had come to the very same conclusion, namely, that the mandate of liberation was at the center of the gospel message, and, at least for our time and place, black theology forced the white Christian to struggle with the same truth that Cone had discovered: "a new grasp of history as liberation history." Using the Fourth Gospel as the interpretive key to unlock the concept of liberation, Herzog then proceeded to define what it means to "think black" theologically, in the sense that Cone proposed primarily for blacks, and how to relate such thinking to the originating event of the life, death, and resurrection of Jesus Christ as taught by the Scriptures.

But one looks in vain in Herzog's book for an interpretation of black theology as it was evolving in the writings of James Cone and others by the end of 1972. Herzog's courageous initiative was to dare to announce that the new way in which blacks were doing theology was an analog of the radical challenge that the Fourth Gospel throws down before the bourgeois subjectivity, privacy, and "religiousness" of white Christianity. He saw the Gospel of John and the new theology of a militant black church forcing all who belong to the dominant church and society to recognize Jesus among the poor and oppressed of the earth, and to hear him calling all of us to that same identification.

Herzog played a major role in organizing a symposium on black theology, which was reported in the January – February 1974 issue of *Evangelische Theologie* in West Germany. The articles were reprinted in the *Union Seminary Quarterly Review* in late 1975. In that same year a conversation between white North American and Latin American theologians was challenged by black theologians in Detroit under the auspices of a new coalition called Theology in the Americas, but after an auspicious beginning and a second Detroit conference in 1980, Theology in the Americas collapsed. Because of the dynamism of its ideas and the influence in the black church of the people who were involved in it, the Black Theology Project continued to operate, but it carried on what was virtually a monologue with itself.

A young white theologian named Peter C. Hodgson, having come out of the Student Christian Movement in the U.S., had an early acquaintance with Christians in the worldwide social revolution. Black theology posed no threat to Hodgson. Two of his books, *Children of Freedom* (Fortress Press, 1974) and *New Birth of Freedom: A Theology of Bondage and Liberation* (Fortress, 1976), demonstrated an uncommon comprehension of black culture and an appreciation of the importance of black religious thought for white Americans. Similarly, Benjamin Reist wrote a positive commentary on black theology in his *Theology in Red, White and Black* (Westminster Press, 1975). Helmut Gollwitzer, Jürgen Moltmann, and Bruno Chenu in Europe, and Paul Lehmann, Rosemary Ruether, G. Clarke Chapman, Jr., and Glenn Bucher in the United States have each written sympathetic and helpfully critical articles dealing with the positions of black theologians.

James Cone, in an introduction to several of these writings in *Black Theology: A Documentary History* (Orbis Books, 1979), acknowledged his debt to the serious responses of a few white the-

ologians to his work. But anyone who has been the least bit aware
of what has been going on in American theological seminaries and
church circles these past twenty years would have to admit that,
generally speaking, the basic rejoinder of whites to black theology
has been a strange and sullen silence. Actually there has been
considerable scholarly and programmatic reaction to Latin American liberation theology and some (only mildly enthusiastic, for the
most part) to white feminist theology. But since about 1975 almost
nothing has been written by white theologians on black theology
in the United States and South Africa. Thus, the tantalizing question for me, as one who finds the suppression of the black-white
dialogue on theology sadly unaccountable, is what is so different
about Theo Witvliet to make him recognize the universal significance and ecumenical relevance of black theology when so many
others find it unspeakably taboo?

Frederick Herzog has ventured the opinion that white American theologians have always been preferential to the universal
note in Christian theologies and are confused when it is missing
among black thinkers. But that seems an unsatisfactory solution.
Witvliet, as we shall soon see, finds the impassioned particularism
of black theology precisely grounded in a universal consciousness
of injustice and the fundamental orientation of the biblical witness
to human liberation, not just the liberation of black people. So the
reason for the strange and sullen silence must be found elsewhere.
Several other questions come to mind. First, one cannot help but
wonder why this particular book was so long in coming. Secondly,
is Witvliet's relative geographical isolation from the place where
black theology is being done an explanation for his perspicacity
in grasping the intellectual and emotional content of the subject
about which he writes? Thirdly, is institutional racism so endemic
in ecclesiastical and academic circles in the United States (as compared, for example, to the European continent) that there is little
likelihood that a book such as this would be written by a white
American theologian?

I have no intention of wandering around in the marshy wilderness of those speculative questions, except to make the observation that scholars in the field of religion are by no means the
first African-Americans to discover that prophets, theologians, and
artists can gain respect not only among brothers and sisters who
speak the same language of non-white inferiority and subjection

and share the same unhappy history of three hundred years of African slavery. We remember that the Fisk Jubilee Singers, Richard Wright, Marian Anderson, and Paul Robeson — to mention only a few — all won greater acclaim abroad than at home. Recognition by white Americans came to many blacks after they had been wined and dined by the patrons of high culture in the artistic and intellectual centers of the continent (and in the nineteenth century the centers of England and Scotland would have to be included among them). This does not mean that racism in the arts and theology exists only in North America, but there is *something* afoot that would bear careful study. Whether race prejudice, intellectual snobbery, the failure of nerve incident to the last stages of capitalism, or just the dullness of American wit, I cannot say.

In any case, this Dutch theologian, Theo Witvliet, is evidently outside the pale, figuratively if not literally. He has not only taken pains to try to understand the theology that erupted from the dark underside of the English-speaking world, but is sensitive to its peculiar sins and considerable virtues as a theology of human liberation to a degree that seems not to have been the experience of more than a tiny minority of white theologians in this country. Now that this book, the first thorough analysis of black theology by a white scholar, is finally available in the United States, it will be interesting to see whether black American theologians will experience today the same increased attention that black concert artists, jazz musicians, poets, and novelists received upon returning home from Europe some years ago. I seriously doubt it. All pretensions to the contrary notwithstanding, the world of music and literature is characteristically more egalitarian than the world of religion and theology.

Be that as it may, such matters are not the primary concern of this Foreword. The main question (which could not be asked by a black reader without the aforementioned considerations) is what has Theo Witvliet accomplished here that deserves the attention of American Christians in general and black Christians in particular?

It seems to me that *The Way of the Black Messiah* breaks new ground in at least four ways. First, as I have already suggested, by demonstrating that a white theologian who has the correct instincts, inspiration, and information can do black theology as critically and constructively as those who claim African descent. Secondly, by propounding the thesis that the epistemological break

provoked by James H. Cone in the 1960s can be compared in theological momentousness to the one provoked by Karl Barth in the
1920s. Who would have dared to hypothesize as Witvliet, second-
ing a statement of Klauspeter Blaser (in *Wenn Gott Schwarz ware*),
"It is not illegitimate to suppose that here [in Cone's black theol-
ogy] perhaps for the first time in American theology Karl Barth
is really accepted and incorporated"? Thirdly, by using three key
concepts: liberation, context, and ideology, or ideological criticism,
Witvliet validates black theology as a theology of liberation that,
even more than Latin American liberation theology, provides an incisive hermeneutical and methodological challenge to the dominant
white, patriarchal, and bourgeois theologies of the West. That is,
of course, what some white American Christians expect to hear
from dependent and decadent Europe, but it does not make them
any happier. And finally, this book breaks new ground by being the first full-length treatment by a white theologian that not
only defends black theology against the accusation of being "mere
ideology," but moves the conversation to a stage beyond even ideological justification by blacks by recognizing its "pneumatological
basis" — its focus on the power of the Spirit within black history
as a persuasive testimony to God's freedom, and the power of the
Spirit in the universal struggle between "the living God and the
idols of death" as a kairotic expression of God's love in these closing
years of the twentieth century.

It is not my purpose in these remarks either to attack or defend
the several fascinating positions that Theo Witvliet advances in
this book. It should be obvious from the above that I am delighted
with what he has written and find myself in almost complete agreement with his basic contention that the theology of James H. Cone
is the most important (and in my opinion, the most neglected) example of liberation theology to arise out of the North American
context. Its challenge to the majority's way of doing theology has
enormous consequences for the ecumenical movement. The content of this second of Witvliet's books in English on liberation
theologies (the first was *A Place in the Sun*, Orbis Books, 1985)
should be given high priority on any reading list in contemporary
religious thought and stimulate black theologians (particularly but
not exclusively!) to engage in more vigorous debate and writing
that will build upon and correct the work of Cone and others that
this perceptive Dutch theologian discusses in these pages.

I first met Theo Witvliet when he was a young theologically-
trained journalist covering the study conferences and consultations
of the World Council of Churches. Perhaps it is because he has a
reporter's ear for a hot story that he is more sensitive than most
to the way the biblical story comes alive again in the black story.
That is why he can understand so clearly the way Cone, in *God of
the Oppressed* (Seabury Press, 1975), appeals to the proclamatory
charisma and authority of the story about Jesus for anyone who
has lived through suffering and struggle, an appeal that is Cone's
ultimate argument against the allegation of ideological corruption.
"Theologians," writes Witvliet, "must become aware that however
indispensable the formation of concepts and analysis, argumentation and abstract summary may be, the story is the basic material
and basic structure of theological reflection" (p. 258).

It is because he has this astonishingly empathetic "feel" for
the story of our journey and the way it is captured by and reca-
pitulates the saga of the Messiah, whose blackness is his identity
with dehumanization, misery, and oppression, that Theo Witvliet
writes like a black theologian. He senses the salvific vulnerability of
black history as the story of damnation, survival, and resurrection-
liberation over against the dogmatic and philosophical invulnera-
bility of white theology. By being so open he gets in touch with
the power of *metanoia* in the black religious experience. For him
the renewing power of the Spirit in the praxis of the black church
and community since Richard Allen and the Free African Societies
forces us backward to the messianic praxis of Jesus and forward to
solidarity with the wretched of the earth in our own time, with their
justice-seeking praxis of social, political, and cultural revolution.
The black experience and biblical witness are given a hermeneutical
basis that is, in Chalcedonian terminology, "unconfused and undivided." By these considerations the reader is brought to one of the
central insights of the book and a new hermeneutical and methodological starting point for dialogue, only faintly adumbrated in the
most recent writings of the black theologians: that the hermeneutical foundation that fuses black theology with the biblical witness is pneumatological, or as Witvliet puts it, "the hermeneutical, methodological process that connects the liberating praxis
of Jesus of Nazareth with black history and culture is therefore a
pneumatological obligation" (p. 218).

That is why black theology cannot be simply left to the black theologians! The Holy Spirit is the Spirit of truth that gives us koinonia in the one church of Jesus Christ. This is the reason for Witvliet's agonizing concern for a reinstitution and intensification of the conversation between black and white theologies within the ecumenical movement. One wonders what, if anything, will come of this suggestion. This is certainly not the first time it has been made. As late as the summer of 1985 the Faith and Order Commission of the World Council of Churches received, without comment or even much interest, an ecumenical statement from black American theologians that attempted to incorporate a pneumatological emphasis in its explication of the relevance of black theology in the search for a common expression of the Apostolic faith today. Like much of black theology, this statement was given scant notice in the white religious press, but was — I am gratified to say — finally published in the United States, together with the accompanying study documents, in the journal *Midstream* (vol. 24, no. 4, October 1985). In any case, the lack of interest in what we are writing or saying does not make me very hopeful what Witvliet's plea for greater appreciation and dialogue will be heeded. Indeed, I can only hope that it will get a respectful hearing among black theologians!

As a black historian-theologian who has been in this fight for some time, what is my final word about this unusual *tour de force* by a Dutch journalist-theologian who has a nose for what we in the United States call "religious news" and an ear for the black story as a pointer to the universal narrative of human liberation? My final word is that he belongs with us.

Somewhere near the end of this book the author calls himself "an outsider" who is in no position to prescribe what black theologians ought to do. If he is suggesting that in the final analysis a theologian who is not black cannot expect to express the full impact of the black experience any more than a black theologian can hope to express the full impact of the white, or Hispanic, or Chinese, etc. experience, then I would agree with him. But who is worried about "the final analysis"? Also I must insist that he has already proven himself to be no outsider to the black theology movement in the United States. He has made a manifestly important contribution to the study of the black religious experience, albeit at a scholarly level that will place it, unfortunately, somewhat beyond the level of comprehension of most American clergy and laity. But as far as the black clergy and laity are concerned, it will be our responsibility to "make it plain," to ensure that black theology, which always stands or falls on the fact of being a theology of, by, and for black people, in the sanctuary and the streets, can make use of the insights of "outsiders" like Theo Witvliet in such a way that even Aunt Jane will say, "Amen!" and "Thank you, Jesus!" I dare to believe that if more white theologians would join us in this kind of enterprise in their own communities, they would hear — miracles of miracles! — the same words of affirmation from white people.

I am painfully aware of the thinness of our ranks on either side of the wall of separation that was supposed to have been abolished. Moreover, on our part, black theologians in this country are already disappointed by the indifference that their ideas have met in white academic circles. Some have been distracted beyond recall by the rewards of doing theology in conventional, majoritarian ways. James Cone, and a few of his best students who are now teaching, are almost alone in the day-to-day work of reflecting upon and reporting the black experience in religion. In response to his leadership, a few small groups like Partners in Ecumenism and the Black Theology Project are attempting to demonstrate the liberating praxis of the mode of doing theology that we learned again in the 1960s. But the going is rough. Few of us have Cone's creativity or his courage. I sometimes think that it is more likely our lack of guts than the lack of creativity or brain power that since 1980 has lowered a curtain of silence and inactivity down upon a movement that was so vocal less than a decade ago. But I live in hope and believe, as much as we hate to admit it, that our white brothers and sisters have much more to do with this condition of "going with the flow" than they imagine.

Perhaps the reasons for the silence are deeper than even I suspect. Perhaps it takes an "outsider" like my friend Witvliet to draw the attention, first of African-American theologians, to something that that old Negro spiritual (we are singing it during these December days when I am writing this Foreword) continually reminds us. He comes to us, this "sweet lil' Jesus boy, born in a manger," as the Black Messiah, "but we didn't know who you was!"

GAYRAUD S. WILMORE
December 25, 1986   Durham, N.C.

PREFACE TO THE ENGLISH EDITION

I am delighted that this book is appearing in an English translation. At least the people about whom I write, first of all the black theologians, can read what I have to say about them. For me it is very important to know (*a*) to what extent black theologians recognize their real intentions in the picture I give and (*b*) how they react to my questions and comments. Amazingly enough very little thought has been given to the ecumenical implications of the rise of contextual forms of theology. How do we deal with theologies from other contexts? In taking this question seriously, this study is of an experimental nature. It might be considered as an experiment in ecumenical dialogue. But as far as this goes the proof of the pudding is in the eating. Only if some of its readers feel obliged to participate in this dialogue in one way or another will the purpose of this book have been fulfilled.

Theo Witvliet

PREFACE

My desire to write this book goes back more than ten years. In May 1973, on the initiative of the World Council of Churches, a symposium took place in Geneva on black theology and Latin American liberation theology. About fifty European theologians had an opportunity to get to know these forms of 'contextual' theology, which at the time were still virtually unknown on the European continent. Those days, in which I was involved as a producer for Dutch Interchurch Radio (Ikon), were unforgettable for two reasons. In the first place I have rarely been at meetings where the emotional tension was so evident. The vigorous discussions which were occasioned by the reports given by Paulo Freire, Hugo Assmann, James Cone and Eduardo Bodipo-Malumba made it clear that, however difficult some people found it to reconcile with their view of Christian reconciliation, there was indeed a clash between opposed experiences of faith and thought-worlds.

Secondly, I became convinced that the gap which was opening up had far-reaching hermeneutical implications. Here the term 'hermeneutical' does not just refer to the art of interpreting biblical texts but also includes the connection (whether implicit or explicit) with the historical and social context in which these texts are framed and function in one way or another. Because the European participants were in fact unprepared for the hermeneutical challenge and criticism which the liberation theologians put to them, there were short circuits and defence mechanisms which ruled out any conversation that was open and critical on both sides. So the symposium went down in history as an instance of 'incommunication'.

Although this experience suggested that there was urgent need for reflection on the hermeneutical challenge of liberation theology, my work as a journalist provided virtually no opportunity for it. Things changed when I was appointed lecturer in ecumenical studies at the theological faculty in the University of Amsterdam. This book, along with its predecessor *A Place in the Sun*, is the result of my research over recent years. Both works are to be regarded as exercises in dealing with liberation theology from another context. Whereas *A Place in the Sun* provided an encounter with different forms of liberation theology in the Third World, *The Way of the Black Messiah* is an attempt to reflect on the significance of 'contextual' theology by studying one particular example of it, namely black theology in the United States. Each book supplements the other in form and content, though they can be read quite independently.

In 1969, after the long hot summers in the black ghettos and the murder of Martin Luther King, the young black theologian James H.Cone produced his provocative book *Black Theology and Black Power*, in which he launched a fierce attack on the white churches and on the hidden racism in dominant 'white' theology. This book marks the beginning of the black theology of liberation, which is meant above all to be a critical reflection on the theological significance of black experience and history. In this theology, which meanwhile has taken shape in many monographs, articles and declarations, the spirituals and blues come to life, as does the thought of great leaders like Martin Luther King and Malcolm X.

This study of the hermeneutical challenge of black theology consists of three parts. The first seeks to provide a theoretical basis for the conversation with black theology. My starting point here is that if black theology sees itself as a theology of liberation, *ipso facto* (i.e. regardless of whether individual black theologians have themselves seen or thought through these consequences) it sets out a specific 'programme' which relates to the three interconnected elements of content (liberation), structure (contextuality) and function (theology as ideology or ideological criticism). The force of any form of liberation theology stands or falls with the force with which these three elements are really thought through. As *fides quaerens intellectum* (the commitment of faith which calls for reflection) liberation theology must give an account of three things which are closely connected.

1. Although the liberation theology which has emerged in recent decades in different parts of the world breaks with a form of practising theology which it finds oppressive, it is not breaking with

the Christian tradition as such; here we have both break and continuity. This situation calls for constantly renewed reflection on the matter of content, what the Christian tradition has handed down in connection with liberation and the relationship between the eschatological reality of God and the historical struggle of human beings, their suffering and their revolt against the powers that oppress them.

2. As a critical reflection on a praxis which precedes it, by and on behalf of the poor, liberation theology deliberately puts itself in a specific historical context; here it faces the methodological question of how the context is to be analysed, and what function this analysis has within theological reflection as a whole.

3. The hermeneutical priority of praxis or commitment already provides the third element, namely that of ideological criticism: liberation theology is a criticism of any theology which in its method strives to be universally applicable and in so doing 'forgets' that any reflection is always already part of a particular historical context, which moreover must be explicated before it can be criticized and corrected.

Thus in Part One the three key concepts of liberation, context and ideology (or ideological criticism) function as pointers in the search for ways of testing the claim of black theology to be a theology of liberation. Here special attention is paid to the insight of Latin American theologians that in the end method is decisive for the liberating character of theology.

However, this does not answer the question why we need to engage on a conversation with black theology and what significance it has. How does this theology concern us? What is the framework or the context of such a conversation? Part One, Chapter 2, seeks to defend the view that this location must be looked for on the interface between two ecclesiological models which are current in contemporary ecumenical discussion: those of 'conciliar fellowship' and the 'church of the poor'; 'conciliar fellowship' defines the ecclesiological structure for dealing with liberation theology from another context, while the other concept, the 'church of the poor', indicates the direction and the issues in this conversation.

Part Two goes at length into the historical background to the origin of black theology. This middle panel of the triptych seeks to make it clear that this origin is not a historical coincidence but is as it were embedded in the specific 'logic' of the dynamic of the black struggle and black experience. There is a special reason why this historical part, which ends up in a discussion of the first publications of black theology, forms the heart of this systematic or dogmatic study: by giving the black story this central place I am indicating that narrative – history as narrative – needs to be the basic material and the basic structure of a theological system. The insight into the contextuality of theology rules out an abstract approach, i.e. one which omits the specific context of the black exerience. In other words, no dogmatic conversation with black theology is possible without a thorough knowledge of the history of black slavery and the opposition to it. However, this historical analysis has important implications for systematic theology: the analysis serves as criticism of existing positions in systematic theology and in this way makes a positive contribution to ecumenical reflection on the question of the structure and identity of Christianity.

In Part Three, the last part, on the basis of the insights which have been gained in the two previous Parts, there is an interpretation of the discussion about liberation, context and ideology (or ideological criticism) as this has been prompted and carried on by black theology. First of all the question arises whether the black experience of suffering and slavery justifies talking about God or Christ in terms of liberation. How can black theology be a theology of liberation if black history and experience shows nothing of this reality of liberation? This question is focussed on the historical question whether black religion has a liberating or an oppressive character. Investigation in terms of the history of religion shows that black religion is a phenomenon in which elements from African religion and revivalist Protestantism from the South of the United States have become fused in a unique way. How was the relationship established between the black religious experience and the biblical witness? Can black religion be interpreted in christological terms? The internal discussions of black theologians and historians of religion are concentrated on this problem. The question which I feel must be raised in this discussion is whether so far black theology has not paid too little attention to the significance of pneumatology. I shall try to show that only a pneumatological foundation for the relationship between the Word made flesh in Jesus Christ and the black experience provides a guarantee of dealing with the historical data in such a way that it is not fitted into pre-existing dogmatic frameworks and patterns and thus made innocuous.

Secondly I shall discuss the analysis of context. Over recent years this has become much more sophisticated. Conversation with Third World and feminist theologians has been of great significance for black theology in helping it to get beyond the picture of America as a closed society, as a white monolithic block, and seeing racism as a complex of networks of power which is closely bound up with other mechanisms of domination that are also evident within the black community (sexism, the increasing gulf between the black middle class and the hopeless situation of the black underclass). This state of affairs calls for an ecclesiology which sees the black church as a community in which both the particularity of black identity and the universality of King's 'beloved community' take shape.

Finally, I shall discuss the relationship between theology and ideology on the basis of the debate between black and white theologians. Each side accuses the other of being an ideology: if black theology criticizes the theological traditions because of their benign neglect (C.Eric Lincoln) of black history and experience, white conversation partners are concerned that God's freedom is threatened by the way in which black theology identifies God's will and work with the black struggle for freedom. The book ends with an attempt to give as clear expression as possible on either side to the 'hermeneutical challenge' which black theology has posed to itself and to white theology.

I am indebted to many colleagues for the patience which they have shown over the numerous attempts, verbal and written, which I have made to formulate clearly my ideas on this theme. Professor E.J.Beker, who was prepared to take responsibility for sponsoring me over this work, has stimulated me with his distinctive charisma in his involvement in the problem of 'contextuality' as an urgent dogmatic question. Professor J.H.Kamstra gave me valuable advice on the historical section in Part 4. Professor L.A.Hoedemaker and Professor A.F.de Jong spent a good deal of time on a careful reading of the manuscript. Earlier outlines and parts of the manuscript were studied and commented on perceptively by Dr Dick Boer, Professor H.B.Kossen, Dr L.Schuurman and, at an early stage, Professor J.Sperna Weiland.

Ineke Eisberg and Ton van der Worp have been lavish with their care in making this study ready for the press. Finally I must mention the warm interest and friendship that I have received from Gayraud Wilmore and James Cone. The involvement of all these people makes it impossible for me to write the cliché that I alone am responsible for the content of my book. *The Way of the Black Messiah* is dedicated to my parents in gratitude to them for sharing my life and my thought.

PART ONE

Challenge and Response

1 · Challenge

Liberation Theology and the Liberation of Theology

The black theology with which this book will be concerned is a liberation theology. That means that I do not regard black theology as a more or less interesting variant of the theology that we already know.

This comment may cause some surprise. What is the difference between black theology, as liberation theology, and the theology that we already know? Does that mean that we do not yet know about theology of liberation? Has not the term liberation slowly become established in our theology, too? That may indeed perhaps be the case. However, we must consider whether the word liberation is not as obsolete as it is established. Anyone who is concerned about this would do well to reflect on what Hugo Assmann once said: the language of liberation, which spread so rapidly through the world of church and theology, is in itself defenceless against annexation and manipulation: manipulation arises where the original revolutionary implications of this language are denied.[1]

Liberation theology came into being in what in retrospect was a historical context of hope and optimism, in the second half of the 1960s. Strikingly enough, the first contours of liberation theology could be seen at roughly the same time in various parts of the world: they showed up against the background of struggle and radical expectation which was symbolized by names like Franz Fanon, Che Guevara, Bernadette Devlin and Martin Luther King. Liberation theology was born in the context of the struggle for social justice in two-thirds of the world, for women's liberation, for racial equality.

Struggle is always concrete, material, physical, even where it is carried on at the level of ideology – for ideologies are not just worked out in human heads, but have a material existence. So it is senseless and indeed misleading to speak of liberation theology in the abstract, apart from the historical, social, political and ideological context in which it functions as a specific movement. For that reason this study is not about liberation theology in the abstract but about black theology in particular. The question is what significance this particular theology, in its time-conditioned situation, has for the theological tradition in which we stand. Although black theology is very much alive in South Africa and in other places where there is racial oppression, I shall limit myself to the place where black theology came into being, the United States. Black theology in South Africa needs to be analysed against the background of its own context, and that lies outside the scope of this study.

It is not easy to describe the significance of black theology in an accurate and unbiassed way. The conversation may be loaded with guilt feelings about black people, or a still latent sense of superiority. The fact that the theological tradition in which we share (whether we like it or not) is white is part of the discussion. Black people regard theology which claims to be just theology, i.e. to be universal, as particularistic, i.e. white, because the historical experience of people whose skin is a different colour finds no echo there. Black theology does not criticize the personal disposition of individual theologians, but the fact that they are part of a discipline which in principle does not put up any opposition to an all-embracing ideological practice which excludes blacks from culture and history. If we ask how it can be that theology which knows a God who has taken the form of a slave (Phil.2.7) has *de facto* passed over the history of oppression, hope and expectation of a slave people, then perhaps we should look for the answer in the fact that in this history we are confronted with our own history. There is no slave without a master, no oppression without domination. Our own history is reflected in the history of the slave people, and the picture which we get from that is not a pleasant one.

In dealing with black theology, sooner or later we come up against ourselves. The paradoxical thing is that the more we succeed in doing justice to black theology, the more we are thrown back on ourselves. There is therefore quite a temptation to keep a safe distance from it and at most to make some well-meaning or critical comments on the grounds that this theology is intended for black people themselves. Black theologians do not take such an attitude at all well. In 1972 one of them, William R.Jones, wrote an article in *The Christian Century* in which he expressed his view that any critical discussion of black theology must take account of the fact that black theology is a new discipline which criticizes the norms of the established schools. From this Jones drew the conclusion that these norms can no longer function as the critical apparatus by which the new discipine is judged until they have been shown to stand up to criticism which is evoked purely and simply by the existence of this *enfant terrible* and its nature. Anyone who writes about black theology must be well aware of his or her own position. According to Jones, to write about black theology makes sense only if we follow a procedure of first accurately charting what black theologians have in fact written (taking account of the fact that this is a discipline which is still at the beginning of its development), and in which, moreover, we use internal criticism, in other words criticism which measures black theology by the problems which it has itself raised.[2]

Jones here rightly passes over something which most writers (fortunately not all) regard as a problem. Internal criticism is the only legitimate criticism. Anyone who, for example, prematurely accuses black theology of failing to do justice to the biblical concept of reconciliation, of reducing theology to an ideology, of not being scientific, must realize that these critical remarks are being made on the basis of an academic theological position which is itself now being specifically questioned by black theology. This gives rise to the notorious lack of communication which was so evident at and after the symposium on black theology and Latin American theology in Geneva in 1973. Lack of communication is inevitable as long as the conversation partners of black theology are in this vicious circle in which one side has a keen eye for the historical and ideological position of the other but deludes itself that it is transcending history by deriving abstract norms from scripture or science and using them to judge black theology and find it wanting.

Anyone who takes seriously the question of the significance of black theology must be prepared to leave behind his or her own certainties and to take the step of moving into the circle of black discourse, where he or she will sooner or later have also to become an object of reflection. However, the crucial question is whether it is really possible for us to move within the black circle. Are we in a position to do so, and do we have the competence for an adequate description

and criticism from within? There are at least two serious obstacles.
The first is that the texts which black theologians have produced
since the 1960s are so numerous and so different in tendency and
level that a thorough process of sorting and selection is unavoidable.
Is it possible in this process to do justice to the specific intentions
and dynamics which make black theology one distinct movement,
despite the internal struggle between various theological and
political options? The second obstacle is that black theology was
born into a world which we do not know and cannot know from the
inside: the world of black experience, of racial oppression and the
struggle against it. The more we steep ourselves in black history,
the more occupied we become with black cultural expressions, the
more precisely we seek to unravel the texts of black theologians,
the more strongly we feel the gulf which separates us from the black
world. Just as James Baldwin describes in *Notes of a Native Son*
how at a crucial moment in his development he discovered that
Shakespeare, Bach, Rembrandt, Paris, Chartres Cathedral and the
Empire State Building were not his creations and did not contain
his history,[3] so conversely we come to realize that the spirituals and
the blues, Frederick Douglass and Martin Luther King, Richard
Wright and James Baldwin, Charlie Parker and Aretha Franklin do
not represent our world. Any annexation from our side is not only
undesirable but also impossible. That also applies to our concern
with black theology, and it is precisely for this reason that it is so
important for us to deal with it. Any conception of black theology
stands or falls with whether or not it accepts its otherness. The
experience of this otherness already denotes in itself a far-reaching
learning process, as long as we live in a world which in economic,
political and ideological terms is not prepared to recognize the
otherness of other men, cultures and peoples.[4]

Nor is this the whole story. Without detracting from anything that
I have said above, but by way of a counterpoint, we must also be
aware of the danger of regarding the hermeneutical circle of black
theology as a closed circle which does not have a single point of
contact with that of so-called white theology. These are certainly
not two monolithic blocks which can only smash against each other.
In *A Black Theology of Liberation* James H. Cone describes white
theology as the theology which passes over the victims of oppression.
In this sense Dietrich Bonhoeffer and Karl Barth are not white
theologians, and according to Cone Reinhold Niebuhr's *Moral Man*

and Immoral Society moves in the direction of blackness.[5] There is an underground connection between Barth and Bonhoeffer's struggle against the Fascism of the Third Reich and the struggle of black theologians against racism. This connection comes to light not when we generalize their theology and detach it from its specific context, but only when we see how their theological thought functions within this context. Functioning is in fact a key term here, since this verb expresses the indissoluble connection of theory and practice which is a prime hermeneutical principle for any theology of liberation. Bonhoeffer interprets this principle in his own way when in *The Cost of Discipleship* he writes, 'acquired knowledge cannot be divorced from the existence in which it has been acquired'.[6] His friend and pupil E.Bethge associates this with the conclusion that theological statements, too, do not hold for all times.[7] Human existence does not take its course in a vacuum, but in a given social constellation. What in one context is liberating theological insight can become the opposite in another.

From this perspective the breaks in the history of theology do not run one-sidedly along the boundaries of the different church confessions or theological trends, but these differences are all too often, especially in their origins, expressions of social oppositions and conflicts. This may be shown by one example out of many, which is particularly relevant in connection with black theology, namely the World Council of Churches' Programme to Combat Racism; the implementation of this programme has exposed political and ideological oppositions which cut straight through all trends and church denominations. Precisely as a result of experience with this programme the question of the ideological function of theological remarks and arguments has become an urgent one for the ecumenical movement, and in any case a sounding board has been created for the questions raised by the various forms of liberation theology, each in its own way.[8]

Black theology relativizes in a far-reaching way the familiar conflicts between the various theological schools and traditions by asking what the whole of this thought world has meant and still means for people who are victims of racial oppression. Rudely and unasked, it lays on the table (as one among others) the question how this world of ideas and discussions is related to the real world of hope and acceptance, of living and dying, joy and pain, knowledge and ignorance, possessions and lack of possessions, power and powerlessness:

> For some are in the darkness
> and others in the light,
> and you can see those in the light
> and you cannot see those who are in the darkness.
>
> Brecht, *Threepenny Opera.*

Black theology does not avoid the conclusion (one by which it legitimates its own right to existence) that the network of spoken and written words in theological discourse does not function in the service of or in solidarity with those who are in the dark, and that the rules, procedures and institutions that regulate and maintain theological production exclude those who are also wrongly excluded by society. In theological discourse there is no room for the world of faith, the historical experience and the struggle of black slaves and their descendants. Therefore a black theology of liberation cannot be simply a more or less interesting variation within the order of this same discourse, but tries to liberate itself from the network of 'white' discourse by creating a new theoretical sphere of black consciousness. No theology of liberation is possible without the liberation of theology.

However, I must hasten to stress that this does not mean that black theology is blind to fractures within white discourse which break through the closed circle. The undercurrent of radical messianic expectation is clearly visible at particular moments in the history of theology; the perspective 'beyond bourgeois religion' (Metz) breaks through at unexpected moments in the form of opposition to the humanistic, idealistic and rationalistic concept of science or indeed in any form of opposition. It does not seem too rash to claim that the presence of these fractures in theology formed the condition for the rise of black theology and other forms of liberation theology. For example in its first phase (I am thinking of Cone's first publications and Major J.Jones, *Black Awareness*), black theology made intensive use of the work of Jürgen Moltmann to set out its own argument. I do not point this out to the detriment of the originality of black theology, since this originality stems from the way in which the insights taken from Moltmann and others function within hermeneutical circulation generally. What I am doing here is to point to the existence of connections which are both visible and hidden. At the same time this comment leads us to conclude that the real presence of such ties makes possible both in theory and praxis the internal criticism called for by William R.Jones. Theologians like Bruno Chenu, Helmut Gollwitzer, Peter Hodgson and Henri Mottu have shown that this is not just an imaginary possibility.[9]

To this should be added a further consideration, which is of decisive significance for the approach and method which we are following in this study. However much it must be accepted that black theology can only be understood and criticized from itself, i.e. from its own context and the problems it raises, at the same time we must also take into account the striking fact that theological movements with a similar concern came into being at the same time in other places and in other cultures.[10] This common programmatic concern can be summed up in three main points.

1. The gospel is read as the story of a messianic praxis which is concerned with liberation in (and not from) history.

2. This story is experienced as reality in the context of the commitment to which the story itself is a summons: the battle against the domination of one human being by another.

3. The subject of theological reflection is not the individual professional theologian but the community (in the service of which the theologian has put himself) in which justice is done to those who stand outside the dominant theo-ideology.[11]

The connection between these three elements is what holds any theology of liberation together. Their mutual connection gives this way of doing theology its vitality and consistency, and is at the same time determinative of its open, provisional, fragmentary and contextual character. These elements make it possible to speak of a family likeness between different types of liberation theology. The real relations of black theology lie here.

When Latin American liberation theology emerged at the end of the 1960s, this movement specifically saw itself not as the left wing of the political theology of Metz and Moltmann,[12] but as 'a new way of doing theology' (Gutiérrez).[13] However, this new way is not a speciality of Latin America. Wherever there is talk of 'theology from the underside of history',[14] the need arises to break with the dominant theological tradition and to look for new ways. However, it is one thing to discover this new way and something quite different to realize it. At the first conference of theologians from the Third World at Dar es Salaam in 1976, Gutiérrez described any form of liberation theology (he specifically mentioned black theology or the theology of other minorities, theology in the context of Africa, Latin America and Asia, and feminist theology) as theology which in the first place comes from people who have no name in history. He added that in this theology it does not make much difference whose name stands on books and articles.[15] This comment indicates the level of liberation theology; it remains below its own level whenever it is only the work of an intellectual élite. That does not alter the fact that the actual presence at the level of the lowest group or class in society calls for intellectual dedication at the highest level! 'To stop thinking, as some seem to advise, is to betray the vitality of the belief of people who fight for their liberation. This would create a vacuum which would very rapidly be filled with a way of thinking in terms of quite different categories, questions and concerns.'[16] The new way of doing theology of which Gutiérrez speaks must be lived through and thought through – in that order. The process in which this happens is an ongoing hermeneutical challenge.

Here the word hermeneutical has a specific theological significance: it relates to living through and thinking through the proclamation of God's word as illuminating, liberating *dabar*, the Hebrew term used in the Old Testament (in other words as the praxis of liberation) in the darkness of history (cf. John 1.4f.; John 8.12). The hermeneutical challenge mentioned here leads into a landscape the ways through which still for the most part have to be made passable.[17]

Here some of the instruments in the baggage brought from home can be useful. Without doubt the landscape may show a familiar aspect here and there. But that does not alter the fact that the total perspective remains different. A fracture runs between theology of liberation on the one hand and the traditional or modern theology out of which liberation theology has grown on the other. The fact that this fracture exists is in the last resort connected with the social, political and cultural contrasts of the world in which we live.

We can define the hermeneutical challenge which faces any form of liberation theology more closely in terms of the three points mentioned above:

1. What is the significance of the story of God's liberating *dabar* (word/action) embodied in Jesus of Nazareth, for people who suffer

under injustice and exploitation? Who and where is Jesus for us today? Liberation theology does not give an abstract answer to the hermeneutical challenge which is included in this question, from the standpoint of an observer. Choang-Seng Song expresses a fundamental insight of liberation theology when he says: 'Since theology must be committed to God's acts in concrete historical situations, the life situations of men and women in particular, theologians must begin where they are.'[18] Even theologians cannot jump over their own shadow; they must begin where they are. The hermeneutical basis of any theology of liberation is that in its specific context (*a*) there is a struggle against the 'structures of sin',[19] and (*b*) Christians are involved in this struggle on the basis of their faith in the reality of the kingdom of peace and righteousness. Without the empirical fact that people can in fact be committed in this way on the basis of their faith, liberation theology ends up in a vacuum. It is a matter of *fides quaerens intellectum*.[20] On the basis of the reality of this faith it is possible to ask back towards its possibility; that is the way of theological reflection.

So the Bible is discussed as the book in which the good news of the poor is documented. But, we may ask, does this method not contain a hidden danger of tautology? That is indeed the case if liberation theology does what it accuses the dominant theology of doing: appropriating the biblical story. In my view it avoids that danger when it takes the particularity of the biblical story as seriously as the particularity of its own context.

2. Liberation theology is contextual theology. It has discovered that the historical and socio-political context determines not only the questions that we direct towards God but also the way in which these questions are answered.[21] That means that analysis of the social context has an important place alongside exegesis of the Bible and study of the church tradition. For this analysis people make use of models and theories of explanation which have been developed by economists, sociologists and political scientists. This theorizing is indispensable, though it only comes to consciousness in terms of the presuppositions from which people look at the Bible, church history and the surrounding world. However, theorizing is dangerous in so far as it has a tendency to reduce reality to concepts, categories and models. The considerable hermeneutical challenge here is to let social analysis function in such a way that on the one hand justice is done to the historical experience of the class, group

or sex for which liberation theology is concerned but that on the other hand this world of experience is clarified and deepened by reflection.

3. Liberation theologians, too, bear the burden of history, in this case the burden of the gulf which has grown up in history between theology and popular belief (the term popular being used here to contrast with that of a privileged group or class). However, in the last instance their theology remains an intellectual game for academics, if they do not succeed in bridging the gap which yawns here.[22] Biblical exegesis and social analysis are in a vacuum if there is no critical and creative connection with what the people with whom it is concerned really believe, think and expect. Here every liberation theology is in search of a way, in other words a method, of responding to this challenge; but the way cannot be the same in each case: the differences in context are too great.

If we limit ourself at this point to a comparison between the Latin American theology of liberation and black theology in the United States we see that if Latin American theologians are to be able to function as 'organic intellectuals' (this expression of Antonio Gramsci's is used often) they must penetrate a world which they do not know from their own experience, the religion and culture of the people; they do this both through participation and through study.[23] Participation applies not only to the people's struggle for social justice but also to the way in which it lives: a number of theologians live for a shorter or longer period in a basic community. At the same time through study projects they try to sound out the culture and religious sensibility of the people (two things which are difficult to separate) in such a way that they recognize the impulses towards liberation and the elements of alienation. By contrast black theologians know the historical and religious experience of black people from within: the world of spirituals and the blues is their world; the black church has always been a popular church, even where the hegemony of the white theo-ideology has penetrated deep into its soul. The hermeneutical challenge for black theologians is to bring to bear their own history and experience of faith which the prevalent theological ideology has declared to be dead, in the light of the praxis of liberation of which biblical writings tell – and do this in a way which is recognized by their own community.[24]

If in this respect the difference in position between black theology and Latin American liberation theology is clear, the similarity is also evident: in both cases liberation theology means liberation from a theology[25] which does not recognize the particularity of its context.

By means of the three crucial points mentioned above I have tried to indicate what I mean by the hermeneutical challenge with which any form of liberation theology is concerned. Does this challenge, however, apply only to liberation theology? Or does it apply just as much to the theology from which it is trying to detach itself?

The way taken by liberation theology and the hermeneutical-methodological reflection on it have the character of a 'farewell to innocence':[26] they imply a fundamental criticism of a naive theoretical practice. However, this criticism remains within the hermeneutical circle of theological reflection. It poses the problems of this circle from within. In other words, theology is criticized as theoretical practice on the basis of its own presuppositions. Liberation theology opens up a new theoretical sphere not by leaving the circle but by testing its force and inner consistency. The specific feature of theological practice is that its inner power and consistency is bound up with the person and the work of Jesus Christ, the way, the truth and the life (John 14.6). Here the way of knowledge is the way of discipleship. It is this discipleship that is the ultimate legitimation of liberation theology when it combines the theoretical practice of theology with the practical action of theologians. It is from this perspective that we must understand its criticism which has rightly been summed up by the Dutch theologian Leendert Oranje and others as 'the charge of ideology': 'Theology is criticized for its unreflective (this is what makes up its naivety, TW) connection with the totality of conceptions, world-view and practice which legitimates the personal and social action of a particular group of people. The theoretical practice of theology here coincides with the ideological practice of a group.'[27] This charge of being an ideology of course rebounds on liberation theology itself: its reflection is an attempt to look for new ways here. When it poses to the dominant theology the question how the universality of its discourse (about 'God', 'humanity', 'the world') is related to the particularity of its experience (whether bourgeois, Western, white or patriarchal), the counter question is how the particularity of its own discourse (Latin American, black, feminist) relates to the universality of the gospel. The hermeneutical challenge cuts both ways.

In this study we shall investigate how black theology, as a theology of liberation, deals with the hermeneutical challenge which it evokes through its concern. In the specific way in which within the bounds of its context it deals with the three key elements of the challenge that will be developed further in the following sections we find the answer to the question of its significance.

Black theology is a movement, a process of development. Its way is not ours, but we ourselves come up along the way. To ignore this movement by arguing that it is for the Afro-American community and not for us is in fact to continue a racist practice which has gone on for centuries. To appropriate black theology and overlook the fact that it has another subject bears witness, albeit from another direction, to the same racist attitude.

The hermeneutical challenge which black theology addresses to us only emerges when we follow this movement critically on its own way, which is not ours.

1. Liberation and redemption

I see following this movement critically as a two-sided process. On the one hand we try to test black theology by the three hermeneutical elements by which I am convinced that its character as liberation theology stands or falls. These elements, summed up in the words liberation, context and ideology, are the guidelines for sifting and assessing the texts at our disposal, which differ widely in direction and level.

On the other hand this procedure is possible and credible only when we also allow this critical testing to be applied to our own presuppositions and ideas. If we were to leave this out of account, then our approach would remain external and incomprehensible. So in this first part we shall limit ourselves to two things. In the first place, by means of short prolegomena, I shall try to show what hermeneutical questions and decisions are implied in the three key elements mentioned above. In this way I shall make explicit what in my view is involved in the discussion of black theology. Secondly, I shall clarify the context of this investigation by asking about the *Sitz im Leben* of a critical discussion with this theology. In the second part we shall then come to a description of its origins.

I am aware that the method used in this book runs the risk of keeping us within a closed circle. I began by noting that black theology is, or seeks to be, a theology of liberation; secondly, broadening the scope to other forms of liberation theology, I have indicated three elements which in their mutual interconnection form the hermeneutical challenge of any theology of liberation. In Chapters 4, 5 and 6 we shall consider how black theology relates to each of these elements. This way of arguing does indeed run the risk of being like a snake biting its own tail. In that case the hermeneutical circle is closed. However, in terms of method, there is no point outside the circle which can free us from this danger. No method can turn the hermeneutical circle into hermeneutical circulation (G.Casalis). That has always applied to theology and now it applies to liberation theology and our discussion of it. The content (God's liberating praxis, the living Word; the naming of it may differ but the reality to which it relates is not open to two kinds of exposition) is self-evident; in other words it can only analyse its evidence in its own terms. This is certainly not to ignore the fact that the connection between Word and history which precedes thought must constantly be thought out again (and that also means, be explained and accounted for). Methodological questions are important in so far as they serve to make room for this connection, but they come up against their limit in the prayer *Veni Creator Spiritus*.

What is the content of the liberation which is sought in the praxis of liberation? That is the first question that we have to discuss.

'It will not do for us to reduce world history as a matter of course to the historicity of human existence.'[28] This short sentence from the polemical work *Jesus Means Freedom* by the German New Testament scholar Ernst Käsemann which appeared in 1968 (!) formulates the protest against a practice in theology and the church in which the history of liberation, reconciliation and redemption is reduced to a matter between God and the individual and in which, to quote the well-known words of Adolf von Harnack, 'The kingdom of God comes by coming to the individual, by entering into his soul and laying hold of it... it is not a question of angels and devils, thrones and prinicpalities, but of God and the soul, of the soul and its God.'[29] This protest against a theology which separates the justification of the godless from the wider context of a radical renewal of creation in which those who hunger and thirst after righteousness receive their due was first expressed powerfully in the twentieth century by the religious-socialist movement of Ragaz, Kutter and others.[30] This contrary voice has never been silent since.

In the face of the completed anti-history of the death camps and the battlefields of two world wars, eschatological expectation has been reborn. The structure and content of Karl Barth's dogmatics make it impossible to see redemption simply as an act of God to the individual on which the individual looks back in a life of thankfulness; the connection which Barth makes between christology, pneumatology and eschatology (without neglecting their different elements) and the distinction that he draws within them between the three forms of the one *parousia* of Jesus Christ,[31] make room for a concept of redemption which embraces the universal consummation that the whole creation is to expect: despite everything the perspective of history is a perspective of salvation and liberation. Where in theology eschatology and apocalyptic are not just an appendix to dogmatics but run through theological reflection from beginning to end, not only does the confession of Christ as the lord of history take on new significance but so too does human action, directed towards a new order in which men and women will be free.

What new insights do the various forms of liberation theology add to this? The question is raised by people who in fact think that liberation theology is nothing but a more or less interesting variant of what was developed earlier in the European sphere. In itself this conception is understandable, since liberation theology in fact offers little that is new in connection with the concept of liberation itself. If it nevertheless regards itself as 'a new way of doing theology' (Gutiérrez) it is expressing the conviction that the conceptual insight functions in a different way: what is at stake is not a new Christian theory of liberation or redemption in itself but the practical perspective within which this theoretical insight functions.

The perspective that is intended here becomes evident when we realize that black theology in the United States arose in the context of black power, that feminist theology is inconceivable apart from the women's liberation movement, and that the various forms of liberation theology in two-thirds of the world form a modest part of the long inescapable struggle for the fulfilment of the basic needs of life and the realization of fundamental human rights. Here theology is indeed 'in the context of the struggle for liberation' (José Miguez Bonino[32]); even more, it is 'theology from the praxis of liberation' (Assmann[33]) and as such is a 'secondary affair' (Gollwitzer[34]).

It would work in a vacuum without the actual commitment of the messianic community in the struggle for a new world. As 'critical reflection on praxis'[35] it is a secondary activity: the process of liberation in which Christians are involved on the basis of their commitment of faith comes first – though of course the chronological sequence is less important than the hermeneutical hierarchy. Liberation is not primarily a thought in the minds of theologians but a movement in history, illustrated in an exemplary way by the exodus of Israel from the bondage of Pharaoh.[36]

Liberation theology differs from current theological practice not through a new insight into the concept of liberation but by making itself aware of the contextuality of its own reflection; as critical reflection it is just as limited by space and time as the historical praxis of liberation on which it reflects. The very awareness of its limitation imposes an enormous tension on the practice of theology: in spatial terms this tension is expressed in the relationship between particularity and universality; in temporal terms in the relationship between history and eschatology. My thesis is that the vitality and credibility of liberation theology depends on the degree to which it can clarify this tension and is in a position to maintain it: any premature resolution of the tension breaks the solidarity with the people with whom it is concerned.

(*a*) Particularity and universality. The term liberation derives its content from the context of the struggle in which the liberation theologian is willingly and knowingly engaged: in black theology this is the struggle for a world in which people are no longer oppressed and discriminated against because of the colour of their skin; at the beginning of Latin American liberation theology 'liberation' stood in marked contrast to 'development' because the Western idea of development in the 1950s and 1960s maintained rather than removed the dependent relationship of the Latin American periphery on the centres of power. Thus in each liberation theology liberation takes on a different tone and colour. But when the context at least plays a part in determining the content of liberation, the question arises whether the universalist tendency of the biblical story does not come under pressure. Does the particularity of the context relate to the evangelical perspective of the universal liberation of all human beings? In this way is not liberation unavoidably reduced to an exclusive privilege of a particular group or class?

Or is this an expression of the concern of the outsider, and are these questions essentially abstract and therefore dangerous? If universal liberation is not an abstract utopia but a real perspective in history, must not its *topos* then be real commitment, limited by place and time, but demonstrating itself precisely in this limitation?[37] Does not the insight that James Cone expresses as 'no man is free until all men are free'[38] emerge precisely in the struggle? That one's own liberation is related to that of the other is a belief which is deeply rooted in the history of the black struggle for liberation, as is evident from one of the spirituals:

> You say the Lord has set you free,...
> Why don't you let yo' neighbour be![39]

The creative tension between particularity and universality is seen very acutely and analysed by Gustavo Gutiérrez when he distinguishes three levels of significance in the concept of liberation which, though distinct, cannot be separated. These levels are: 1. socio-political and economic liberation, where liberation is an expression of the struggle and the desire of peoples, groups and classes who live in situations of injustice and oppression; 2. liberation of humanity in the course of history; this level, the cultural and anthropological level, is an indication of the way in which people are actively realizing themselves in the whole process of history and growing towards a new humanity; 3. liberation from sin and guilt and entering into fellowship with God; on this level, which Gutiérrez calls theological, it becomes clear how history and eschatology are related: liberation from sin also implies political liberation (first level) and liberation in the course of history (second level); however, it is not exhausted by this, for 'without liberating historical events, there would be no growth of the Kingdom. But the process of liberation will not have conquered the very roots of oppression, and the exploitation of man by man, without the coming of the Kingdom, which is above all a gift.'[40] By deriving each of the three levels from the work of Christ the liberator, and regarding them in their mutual contexts as an all-embracing process, Gutiérrez succeeds – at any rate on the theoretical level – in creating a fruitful, dialectical relationship between particularity and universality. Only in the eschaton in which God is all in all will the tension which necessarily exists here be overcome.

In his *Theology of Liberation*, by distinguishing the three levels of significance Gutiérrez has developed a concept of integral liberation[41] which since then has been current in Latin-American liberation theology – though in the course of further development it is possible to distinguish shifts in accent.

With some exceptions,[42] the sense of a link between one's own salvation and the liberation of all people is also present in other forms of liberation theology. However, no matter how important and essential this insight is in itself, it is not void of problems. If the insight is to become fruitful, then it must be able to function in the best possible way and that brings in the whole hermeneutical circle of theory and practice: the actual relationship between particularity and universality comes to be determined both by the use of scripture and the doctrinal statements of the church on the one hand and by social analysis and political practice (in other words the strategy and tactics of the struggle for liberation) on the other. The real difficulties begin on this level. At the first conference devoted to 'Theology in the Americas' in Detroit in 1975, Enrique Dussel raised the question from the Latin American context as to how far North American feminist theology and black theology are struggling for a liberation which in fact comes close to integration into the existing unjust system;[43] this question emerged out of the concern of the Latin American participants that feminist and black theologies, as a result of their preoccupation with male-female, or black-white contrasts respectively, overlook the fundamental class contrasts in their own land, and imperialism abroad. In their turn the feminist and black representatives asked the Latin American participants why in their writings they say so little about machismo and racism, although the situation on their sub-continent gives every occasion for saying something. Finally, the (predominantly white) feminist theologians and the (predominantly male) black theologians had some pithy questions to put to one another. I mention this discussion, to which we shall be returning in Chapter 5, in this context to indicate how the creative tension in the relationship between particularity and universality disappears when there is insufficient analysis of social relationships; in that case the universal dimension disappears and all that is left is particularist practice.

Something of the same kind happens in the relationship between text and context when the historical difference between the biblical narrative and present-day reality is denied and the interpretation of the text is tailored to the ideological and political practice of a people, group of class. There then happens what has so often happened in history: scripture – *tenach* (Torah, Prophets and

Writings) and gospel – has no chance of being heard and understood in terms of its own text and context. There are two possibilities: either theological reflection selects models from scripture which it thinks to be useful and important for its own practice – this essentially authoritarian treatment of the story then makes liberation theology a less interesting variant of the theology which we already know – or reflection on its own context makes room for the innate and constantly surprising power of the text to bless.

(*b*) History and eschatology. That theology is seen as a second element says something about its relationship to the first element, praxis. As *fides quaerens intellectum*, theological reflection can clarify, deepen or explain what goes before it, but it is not in a position to provide, nor is it capable of providing, a basis for the praxis of liberation in the real sense. This praxis has a degree of self-evidence which cannot be justified by any theory. What is the nature of this evidence? It is what we can see, feel, hear and touch: the hopelessness of poverty and wretchedness, of human life violated and shattered from day to day; and at the same time the evidence of rebellion against hopelessness, of the courage to be, of the struggle for the right to a human existence.[44] The praxis of liberation can mean organized political struggle or armed rebellion, but it is equally just the courage to survive in the mines of Bolivia, in Soweto or in the shanty towns of Manila. The evidence of the courage, hope and joy in life[45] which people allow us to glimpse in situations of extreme oppression is the breeding ground for the struggle for liberation and the basis of the optimism with which this is constantly carried on anew. There is no rational explanation for this future expectation and this optimism; they cannot in any way be reconciled with the irrationality of the 'structures of sin'. There is no natural transition from the empirical historical reality to the equally perceptible eschatological expectation. History – or better, the reality which in fact does not deserve the name history – does not provide any building materials for the expectation of salvation. The imagination of a new world does not find any basis in the old: it is not a natural transition, an organic process of growth.[46] There is a fracture between history and eschatological expectation.

Then has the courage to be no connection with the biological drive for survival? Without doubt this factor plays an important role, but it does not explain the religious portrayal of a new world in the spirituals of the slaves, or the values which people are able to preserve in situations of poverty and humiliation which oppress them, nor does it explain the stories, poems, sayings and rites in which the wisdom of the people is expressed.[47] Does this wisdom then exist? Is this wisdom not foisted on the people by romanticizing intellectuals? Anyone who finds this view *a priori* attractive might reflect that contempt for the knowledge and wisdom of the people is an important ideological factor in the process of oppression. This does not mean that the culture of the people is undamaged: on the contrary, oppression runs through all forms of life, as e.g. Paulo Freire makes clear in his *Pedagogy of the Oppressed*.[48] But although hope, too, is damaged and is certainly not without ambivalence, it nevertheless remains; it raises people up from the dust and keeps them going. Liberation theology is the hermeneutics of *this* hope. As the hermeneutics of hope,[49] theological reflection articulates the unbearable tension between history and eschatological expectation. However, it can only articulate 'hope against hope' (Rom.4.17) if it shares this, and a fruitful interchange comes into being between its expertise and the knowledge of the people. This expertise cannot be a matter of the theologian justifying this hope with the means at his disposal – and what other means could these be than reason? He cannot give a reason for this hope any more than he is in a position to give an honest answer to the question why this suffering occurs. He does not give a basis for hope, but hope gives him a basis and justifies him.

What theological reflection can and must do, however, is to point to the figure of the crucified Christ, like John the Baptist on Matthias Grünewald's Isenheim altar. Just as the structures of sin have become evident in the cross, so hope is founded in the reality of the resurrection. In the risen Messiah, the firstborn among many brothers and sisters, the opposition between Jew and Greek, slave and free, man and woman (Gal.3.28) is done away.[50] If 'all things are created by him and for him' (Col.1.16) there is a foundation and justification for the questionable expectation of the rejected of the earth. If it has become evident in the resurrection that God has used his freedom to be God with us, Immanuel, then what Choang-Seng Song says from the context of Asia is valid: 'The woman who looks down and feels the seed coming into life in her womb, the mother who fills the bowl with new rice for her son each day, each of them encounters God in her suffering.'[51]

However, the reality of the resurrection remains a completely eschatological reality: an intolerable tension remains between cross and resurrection. Sobrino rightly says in his christology that the reality of the cross puts an end to all natural theology.[52] There is no natural transition from cross to resurrection. The cross represents the end of our imagination of God: 'God on the cross explains nothing; he criticizes every proffered explanation' (Sobrino[53]).

What does it mean to say that the cross is the end of all natural theology? To follow Sobrino's argument: natural theology constructs God on the basis of what is positive in the world – creation as a good book, as article 2 of the Netherlands confession of faith puts it; it looks for an interpretation of reality. By contrast liberation theology seeks to change the world: it begins with the negative elements in the world, with the question of reconciliation between God and suffering. Its problem is theodicy, not as a theoretical problem but as a practical matter.[54]

In black theology the problem of theodicy is raised emphatically as a methodological problem by William R.Jones in his book *Is God a White Racist?*, which appeared in 1973.[55]

In Chapter 4 we shall go into the discussion which Jones sparked off in black theology. Here our question is how black theology articulates the tension between the history of its people and the vision of Gal.3.28.

2. *The problem of context*

In the previous section we established that in liberation theology the evidence of praxis has a hermeneutical priority over the formation of theory; only on the basis of the reality of the commitment to liberation can its possibility be thought through and put into words. This priority of praxis has far-reaching and profound implications for theological existence,[56] which must now be discussed, in however brief and elementary a way. Here the fundamental question of the relationship between thought and action or theory and practice is important.

It is striking – but no coincidence – that in the relationship between theory and praxis the same sort of remarks can be made as in connection with the concept of liberation in the previous section: the theology of liberation does not so much develop a new theoretical insight as confront us with a different perspective. In order to clarify this position it is perhaps meaningful to draw a distinction which, however obvious it may be, is sometimes neglected. I mean the distinction between praxis as concept and praxis as historical reality. When theological writings of recent years speak with some emphasis about the primacy of praxis, there is every occasion to ask whether this is the concept of praxis which the author hopes will become a reality or in fact a reality which is demonstrable in history.

An example of the former can be found in the well-known book by Johann Baptist Metz, *Faith in History and Society*.[57] In this outline of a practical fundamental theology Metz argues for a primacy of praxis. In distinction from earlier publications in which, following Kant, he still stressed moral praxis, he is now concerned with a social praxis the contours of which he draws with the help of the categories of recollection, story and solidarity. Here he does not refer in the first place to conceptions of theory and criticism developed outside theology and very effective today which indicate that any theory is situated in a context of action and can be understood only in connection with this context, but bases the priority of Christian praxis on the incarnation, on the practical basic constitution of the Logos of Christian theology.[58] God cannot be thought of without *metanoia*, repentance and exodus: thinking about this God is in itself already practical thinking: discipleship is part of theological knowledge: Metz's central thesis is: 'The faith of Christians is a praxis in history and society that is to be understood as hope in solidarity in the God of Jesus as a God of the living and the dead who calls all men to be subjects in his presence.'[59]

Thus this statement speaks of Christian faith as a specific form of historical and social action. The inescapable question here is where this praxis can then be demonstrated in present history. This problem cannot be avoided because Metz himself gives hermeneutical priority to action in history and society! However, the remarkable thing is that while he touches on the question he does not go into it more deeply.[60] Thus we get the impression that Metz cannot or will not give any description of a real movement in history which exists outside his consciousness, but that rather his book has the character of a demand: this must be so.

If this supposition is correct, then in Metz's argument there is a suspicious dilemma. In his outline he argues in deliberately apologetic terms for a practical fundamental theology. He sees the present situation in the world as being dominated by two theories or systems and interpretations of the world:[61] on the one hand there is evolutionary thought with its roots in the Enlightenment and in Western bourgeois civilization, and on the other hand there is historical and dialectical materialism. Both are characterized by a transcending without transcendence (E.Bloch[62]), and according to Metz that means a far-reaching reduction of human existence. Over against this, with his theological outline he wants to evoke and describe a praxis which can in fact resist the claims of these world theories. Moreover, in the last resort his theology finds its verification in this praxis of mystical-political discipleship. However, the praxis which Metz describes is in fact no more than a concept of praxis; it remains uncertain how far this actually occurs in contemporary history. Of course that does not make his apologia stronger!

Thus in methodological terms Metz ends up with a contradictory situation. On the one hand he is treading the old familiar way from theory to praxis: first he outlines a theory which then has to be applied to something; it must be as it were the stimulus for a new praxis. On the other hand the theory itself argues for the primacy of praxis – which in fact calls for a new way of theorizing.

In indicating this conflict I am aware that the old way can also be relatively meaningful. Without being able to give any precise facts, I get the impression that *Faith in History and Society* has had some effect as a summons to political praxis *ex memoria passionis*. Perhaps we should say that the writing and publishing of such a work is part of a personal praxis by which Metz reaches the boundary of what is still possible within the academic and church tradition in which he stands. To go further represents an irrevocable break with this tradition.[63]

The difference between Metz's political theology and liberation theology is that in the latter – notwithstanding all the continuity there is – a break has in fact taken place.

The way which Metz has laid down in his thought has brought him to a boundary. Where the boundary is can be indicated clearly. It lies on the other side of bourgeois religion where the world of the non-persons, the people without names, a world of living and dead with which according to Metz, Christians must show solidarity.

Liberation theology begins on the other side: its point of contact is this world of non-persons, the evidence of their struggle and their existence. The boundary between the two worlds indicates both the break and the continuity.

If the gods of bourgeois religion are silent, those without a voice certainly seem to have a voice: in and despite the deep alienation of the 'culture of silence' (Freire) there resounds the call for another world, the call for liberation. Without this call and without people who know themselves to be called by their faith to be the 'church of the poor', liberation theology is an impossibility. The praxis which here hermeneutically precedes reflection is not a concept but a demonstrable movement in history.[64] Theology functions as a reflective element not above or below but within this historical praxis. Its primary function is the creation of theological clarification in a situation of ideological, political and economic struggle.[65] As such it is a secondary element, not chronologically (at least it need not be) but hermeneutically. As part of this secondary element, theological reflection moreover is in search of an adequate concept of praxis. It is striking that in this respect chronologically, too, development has taken place only in the second phase. For example in black theology it was 1975 before the problem of context and the concept of praxis was discussed at length with the publication of Cone's *God of the Oppressed*.[66]

Thinking through the concept of praxis in the first place involves biblical-theological arguments, what Metz calls the practical basic conception of the Logos of Christian theology. The unity of thought and action, of theory and practice, is directly connected with the heart of theology: the *logos* or *dabar* by which it is guided is both the action that speaks and the word that intervenes. According to K.H.Miskotte this means that '*Dabar* is the power through which the world is removed from human explanation and disposal, which at the same time makes human beings able to discover themselves and as such seeks to have control over them.'[67] This gets to the heart of the matter. From this perspective it has become impossible to regard reality as a free space in which the human spirit can begin to apply its abstract truths; this space *has been* occupied – to the benefit of the nameless and the oppressed.

An enormous decision arises here for dogmatics. In fact pneumatology is involved here: God's word is a creative event which does not need our definitions, concepts and categories to make itself felt as a reality. This relativization of all theology in principle is necessary for the possibility of indicating its function: theology is a matter not only of reflecting on a reality which precedes it but also of imitation, for the truth of the gospel is not just said but also done. Here a surprising sentence from Calvin's *Institutes* is important: *Omnis recta cognitio Dei ab oboedientia nascitur*.[68] Truth is not a matter of autonomous thinking but shows itself in a praxis of discipleship. So this praxis has its own evidence which cannot be dominated by autonomous thinking.

It should be clear that this evidence does not have anything to do with any form of natural theology. That would be the case if it were abstracted from the creative power of the Spirit and the circle around the incarnation were left. Natural theology, as this theology in which 'nature' and 'history' function as media of revelation in one way or the other, died a violent death on Golgotha, and it dies a new death every day in the torture chambers of the Latin American military dictatorships or wherever in the world human life is violated and annihilated. This insight that we meet in the christology of Sobrino must also be applied critically to those tendencies in Latin American liberation theology which attribute to the poor or the people a kind of natural predisposition for the gospel.[69] Whenever the deep ambivalence of popular religion is neglected, a new and dangerous form of the sacralization of history threatens. That the poor do not form the object but the subject of the church's mission is an insight which must be kept intact. Only this growing sense cannot be based on any kind of anthropological or psychological characteristic intrinsic in the poor; it is based exclusively on God's free, partisan love.

The evidence involved here is connected with what Miskotte has called 'the form of existence of the Word in respect of time'.[70] God is, a black ex-slave bears witness, a 'time-God': 'He don't come before time; he don't come after time. He comes just on time.'[71] The urgency of this *kairos*, the urgent character of 'today is this scripture fulfilled in your ears',[72] breaks through any attitude which is that of the mere observer and makes the classical construction of preaching in accordance with the scheme of *inventio-explicatio-applicatio* a theological impossibility. The presupposition of this scheme, which determines not only preaching but also a good deal of theological practice,[73] is that the exposition or theory comes first and that secondly (!) its consequences or its application can be considered; in that case the exposition or theory itself is not situated and it can move in a free sphere; only in this last phase, of application, does the situation come within its horizons.

On some pages of *Om het levende Woord*, which cannot be read often enough, Miskotte has made it clear that the actuality of the word overturns this pattern. The evidence of the living word precedes our theological mediations. 'The immediacy may not be lost by the intermediary authorities of the exposition that is needed. Thus the Word comes up against the fugitives who unconsciously delight in all that leads them astray, in all that can conceal the fact that the Word was in the world and that the world was made by the Word and that the world did not know it (John 1.10).'

For Miskotte the unity of word and deed, of thought and action, of theory and practice is founded on God's partisan love. This love breaks through the illusion of a thought which seeks to stand above the parties and makes the well-known application of preaching a misconception which by-passes the *kairos*. 'So the Word takes sides in the struggle for liberation of the poor and wretched over against the arrogance of religious people who can permit themselves the luxury of ignoring their own state before God, only to see in the future how they will relate what they have heard to themselves and will to apply it to their lives. Preaching itself is the application of the Word which is the light of humanity.'[74]

I must resist the temptation to quote more from these pages of *Om het levende Woord*, but what I have quoted may be enough also to prompt some thinking among those who hitherto – often wrongly with a reference to Karl Barth – rejected the problem of context or of the relationship between theory and praxis as being secondary or inauthentic. That the immediacy of the Word or, as we can also say, of God's liberating praxis precedes our necessary meditations[75] has at least three important consequences for the character of theological reflection which we must not lose sight of in a discussion of black theology.

1. The urgency of 'today is this scripture fulfilled in your ears' compels theology, as *fides quaerens intellectum*, to understand this today with all the means at its disposal, and one means does not exclude another. So we can see Miskotte going through the work of poets and thinkers with a toothcomb looking for the essential tendencies and oppositions beneath the surface of daily events;[76] thus black theologians are concerned above all with the exploration of black experience; and thus for Latin American liberation theology Marxist analysis is an important means of discovering the reality and the possibility of liberation beyond the actuality of an unjust and oppressive system. The *kairos* defines not just the contextuality

of theological liberation but also the means of understanding time as *kairos* (fulfilled time). Any intermediary authority is welcome to be of service to the Christian community in its prophetic function between the times on condition that in one way or another it is a reflection of God's partisan love. For example a theory of society which is not outlined from the perspective of the poor is disqualified from the start. Here theology may not forget that it cannot in any way raise itself above antagonistic reality; its discourse, its words and concepts conceal in one way or another a particular view of society and it can only exercise its critical function when it becomes aware of this fact. Paul Tillich's comment applies here: 'Anyone who proclaims a *kairos* helps to create it.'[77]

2. When Miskotte writes that the immediacy of the Word must not be lost by the intermediary authorities involved in the exposition that is needed we can apply this statement not only to the exposition of scripture but also to the exegesis and analysis of the surrounding world. Neither scripture nor the situation come first. Both are necessary, but at the same time they are relativized by the prior reality of the messianic kingdom which is the foundation of the struggle and the hope of the poor and their allies. In this connection there can be no harm in stressing yet again that in Latin American liberation theology too social theory does not come first.[78]The relativizing in principle of the theory of both biblical exegesis and social analysis implies that the one cannot prevail over the other; in the praxis of liberation they do not stand over against each other as rivals, but help each other as allies in the struggle against complacency, fatalism and against the myth of human impotence. There may be a tension between the two, but if it is true that all things have their existence in Christ (Col.1.16f.), in the last instance there can be no question of opposition. On the basis of 'the practical significance of the simplicity of God' (Miskotte) and in the light of the presence of the Word in history theology may know itself to be released from the duty of connecting the Bible and the newspaper too closely together; this connection can only be thought because it is already present beforehand in the reality of God's action.

3. In liberation theology the priority is not related to any kind of praxis whatsoever, but to a praxis of radical change. In thinking this through the theological insights into truth and historical reality which I have indicated above converge with considerations of a theoretical scientific kind which are inspired by Karl Marx's well

known eleventh thesis on Feuerbach which is also much quoted by liberation theologians: 'The philsophers have only interpreted the world, in various ways; the point is to change it.'[79]

This position is not to be misunderstood in an idealistic way. It is evident from the preceding theses that with this eleventh and last thesis Marx did not mean that first a revolutionary theory had to come in order then to change reality. In the second thesis he wrote: 'The question whether objective truth can be attributed to human thinking is not a question of theory but a practical question. Man must prove the truth, i.e. the reality and power, the this-sidedness of his thinking in practice.'[80] In other words, testing of the truth is a matter for praxis: an interpretation of reality which does not change historical reality is untrue. There is no knowledge of truth above or outside the programme of changing the world in which human action is involved.[81]

Following the same line, in *Matérialisme et révolution*, an essay from 1946, Jean-Paul Sartre formulated some insights into a philosophy of revolution. What he brings up there about the function of the theorizing in the process of revolutionary struggle and change is very illuminating for determining the place of liberation theology. Sartre describes revolutionary thought as thinking in situation. It is a way of thinking by the oppressed, in so far as it is communal opposition to oppression; it does not come into being outside the revolutionary process but is taken up in it: any plan to change the world is indissolubly connected with a particular understanding that illuminates the world from the perspective of the change that people seek to realize.[82] According to Sartre a philosophy of revolution cannot therefore be a view of the world which precedes action or is added to it: 'because it arises from action and returns to the action that it needs in order to be illuminated, it is not contemplation of the world but it cannot be anything else or it is itself an action.'[83]

Liberation theologians will have no difficulty recognizing themselves in this description of revolutionary thought. For example we seem to have an echo of Sartre's words when Hugo Assmann describes liberation theology as 'a method from action, in action and for action' (his italics).[84]

However, Sartre takes the argument still further: not only is revolutionary philosophy an action; that is just as much the case with the thought of philosophers from the ruling class: the difference is that the thinking that seeks to keep the world the same instead of changing it tries to hide its pragmatic character and presents itself as pure contemplation of the world as it is.[85] In Sartre's eyes revolutionary thought is superior because in contrast to the dominant thought it is aware of being an action.

This thought too has its analogy in liberation theology. Here we can think of the way in which, as I recalled earlier, in his christology Sobrino puts natural theology and liberation theology. Natural theology is contemplative and interprets the world; liberation theology seeks to change the world. Sobrino's criticism of natural theology is that it does not do justice to the cross[86] and human suffering; it therefore suits the ruling classes. Perhaps by analogy to what Sartre says we should be able to see the advantage of liberation theology in respect of what is still the dominant pattern of theological thinking in the fact that liberation theology, if it does not want to fall short of its own expectations, itself reflects critically on the historical contextuality of its theory and thus its own context of action in theory – and that gives it the possibility of avoiding the pretension that its own theoretical framework has an application which makes it valid for all times and places.

However, with these last comments we have in fact already arrived at what must be discussed in the next section: the relationship between theology and ideology.

3. *Theology as ideology and ideological criticism*

In the course of our listing of some hermeneutical implications of liberation theology we have now reached the third of the three key elements.

This element contains a complicated set of problems to which I have referred so far by means of the term ideology; however, we can also say that it involves the significance of the term critical in the description of liberation theology as a critical reflection on a praxis of liberation. In other words we are looking for the ideological-critical content of liberation theology. Here the essential question is how a way (a method) can be found of avoiding what liberation theology criticizes in dominant theological practice: unreflective association with a totality of conceptions, interests and practices of a particular class, group or sex.

So far no individual liberation theologian has arrived at a worked-out theory of ideology. Of course there have been many attempts in this direction, most of which seek a connection with the Marxist tradition – Marx, Gramsci and Althusser; and also, like James Cone in *God of the Oppressed*, with the sociological knowledge of Karl Mannheim or Werner Stark. Again we must note that theoretical reflection – in this case on the concept of ideology – comes after what has already been achieved. The ideological-critical function of a particular reflection is not dependent in the first place on the presence of a balanced concept of ideology; the functioning of the theory as a whole determines its ideological-critical content and it is quite possible that the concept of ideology, in so far as it is used explicitly, is inadequate for this.[87] Here we must remember that theory as a whole is never static but by nature forms a process. That brings us to the conclusion that we may never fix the ideological-critical content of liberation theology at a particular phase in its historical development but must keep to its process of development as such and the intentions which it contains, in the awareness that this process is never finished. At all events, liberation theology cannot be a rounded system without contradicting itself; it forms an ongoing process of criticism and formation (to use the terms with which Paul Tillich describes the Protestant principle). Any kind of liberation theology must undergo a careful historical reconstruction before any judgment can be passed on its ideological-critical content (or the possible lack of it).

Of course a genetic reconstruction of this kind falls outside the scope of our study. However, where would we find an adequate analytical apparatus for it? It is nevertheless of crucial importance that, mindful of the principle of internal criticism, we should use a concept of ideology which at all events is not excluded by the whole theoretical framework and the actual course of development of a theological outline which understands itself as critical reflection on a praxis of liberation. Therefore here I shall venture to take a methodologically correct way, at least to begin with, by starting with a description – albeit in abbreviated, stylized form – of some common characteristics of the history of the origin of various forms of liberation theology. In this process of development I shall distinguish three phases. From the description of these phases I shall go on to distil some essential ideological-critical elements which are peculiar to liberation theology and which implicitly or explicitly come to light in the course of its actual historical development.

(*a*) First phase. Commitment of faith and crisis

A sense of acute crisis lies behind the origin of any theology of liberation. The nature of this awareness of crisis determines the later development which as it were lies within it in embryonic form. While on the one hand this crisis affects the individual subject deeply, on the other hand it also transcends the individual to just as great a degree: the whole culture or society is affected by it. What causes such a crisis of consciousness? In general terms: revolutionary upheavals at an ideological, socio-political or economic level with the understanding that although these three levels are interwoven, each has a relative autonomy and can be separated from the others in time. However, regardless of whether it is a question of decolonization, the crisis of patriarchy or black power – divergent processes in which the three levels are manifested in constantly changing relationships and degrees – a sense of acute crisis denotes a crisis in ideology.

Here it is not a revolt which brings the individual subject into conflict with his environment. More is involved: the crisis presupposes a revolutionary awareness of which the subjects are those who are non-persons in the prevailing system. Who other than the *anawim*, the anonymous have-nots, can ultimately have the idea of a completely different world, a longing for radical liberation? Of course, the pressure of the prevailing power and ideology can be so severe that precisely this picture leads to deep self-alienation and to a flight from reality. Nevertheless, the imagination has its origin in this reality, of which it is the mirror image. A potentially revolutionary situation comes into being when the imagination becomes aware of this change and as a result transcends itself: over against oppression, another reading of reality then arises which discovers the real possibility of radical change in the existing political, ideological and economic structures. For example Paulo Freire's method of conscientization relates precisely to this process:[88] the process of learning to read and write is so organized, in questioning terms and in a group context, as to enable oppressed people to see themselves and their world with new eyes. When that turns out well, learning to read and write amounts to demythologizing: the silent culture becomes a questioning, speaking culture in which people and things are called by their names, in which the sacrality of the natural order of things is broken through in a common process of learning; the eternal seems contingent, changeable; the obvious and natural seems extremely unnnatural; in this way there comes into being a new reading of reality in which the evidence of 'that is how things are now' gives way to the evidence of the historical connection of things discovered in community.

This last comment provides an opportunity for giving added precision to the term evidence that I have used a number of times in the previous section. What sort of evidence is involved in a praxis of liberation? There are different kinds of evidence. Every ideological practice has its own evidence. Suppose we take the history of Africa and America as an example. How has the systematic oppression of the black people been dealt with ideologically, on the one hand by white society and on the other by blacks themselves? Anyone who investigates how the series of acts of violence, as vast as it is unimaginable, which really embraces all the cruelty that the human brain can devise, has been incorporated into the dream of freedom and democracy and taken up into the American self-consciousness, inevitably comes up against the omnipresent negro myth. In his ideological imagination the white person knows the negro, and on no account will he allow himself to be robbed of his right to define 'the negro' and 'the negro problem'.[89] From the moment that the Dutch shipped men and women from Africa to America to sell them like cattle, 'keeping the nigger in his place' has never been just a matter of physical violence, but just as much a matter of the ideological violence of identifying, categorizing and defining. Woe to the slave, male or female, who did not correspond to the image which the master had created of him or her!

In the ideological imagination of whites the negro on some occasions appears in a stereotyped way as childlike, intellectually unstable, lazy and sensuous, and then again becomes subtle and refined; academics talk of his 'pathological involvement', as happens in the influential 1965 Moynihan Report.[90] But no matter whether the picture is primitive and stereotyped, or is supported by sociological statistics, theories of heredity, historical arguments or whatever, the result is always that the social wretchedness of the black population is given a 'natural' explanation in the quality and pattern of behaviour of the black people themselves. Resettlement projects, ever new welfare programmes, are in the eyes of well-meaning authorities the solutions to the 'negro problem' – and in the meantime white society and its 'pathological involvement' remains safely out of range. The negro myth would not be so tough if it could not find any support in the evidence of what can actually be seen. Are black people (especially) not mentally unstable? Look at the number of cases of suicide, at the high degree of criminality, at the slavery to drugs, at the alcohol problem! Are negroes not lazy? Look at the numbers of them on the dole! The negro problem is obvious.

It would be a serious underestimation of the psychological effects of oppression if we failed to recognize that the black slaves and their dependents have – to a certain degree – internalized the picture which the dominant group forced on them. In the history of Africa and America the childlike clown Sambo, prototype of 'the' negro in the paternalist imagery of the slave owner and his literary friends, indeed appears; but in contrast to what the historian Stanley Elkins says in his book *Slavery*, which appeared in 1959, he represents only a minority.[91] Nevertheless, there are blacks who have not been able to resist ideological pressure and who have 'spontaneously' shaped themselves by the doctrine which was presented in the negro myth. So the ideological imagination which finds its expression in this myth has its own evidence: eyes and ears can confirm it. The more the imagination corresponds to the actual perception, the greater the social consensus can be and the more powerful the hegemony of the ruling group or class.[92] However, the evidence with which we are concerned here has one weak point: it does not embrace all that can be perceived and experienced; in fact it exists by virtue of reduction: the dominant ideology, as an ideology of the rulers, does not tolerate the facts of exploitation and servitude (except when these are put in a past time; the lack of compassion in slavery is then made much of in order to demonstrate the pathological involvement in which the majority of black people have been involved up to now[93]). As Gramsci demonstrates,[94] the working and functioning of ideology is always dependent on the degree to which, as the 'cement' of the whole block of society, it penetrates to all areas of society, and becomes a factor of social cohesion by imaging the hostile reality as a unity.

But who knows better than the black that unity and social cohesion have never existed in American society? The slaves sang 'nobody knows the trouble I've seen',[95] and nothing in human existence is more evident than pain. Pain leads to consciousness; black consciousness is born out of pain – the pain of slaves' work, the pain of daily humiliation, the pain of an unjust existence in a hostile society. Black consciousness, as a deliberate attitude and philosophy, is rooted in an ideological imagination in which those things are evident which are not recognized in the dominant ideological practice: that there are black women and men in the plural, but there is no such thing as 'the' black; 'the' black or 'the' negro is an imaginary creation of the white person (who in the same process creates himself or herself as 'white'), in which black men and women in the plural have never believed and to which they have been opposed in a number of ways. It is equally evident that the 'negro problem' is a secondary problem; as James Baldwin has constantly stressed, the real problem is posed by white society and its lost identity. This evidence manifests itself in what black men hear, see and feel day in and day out. The collective historical experience which is distilled from this, namely black experience, is not however, paradoxically enough, simply characterized by its evidential character, but equally by its opaqueness;[96] it goes so deep that it is impossible to encapsulate it in a neat and visible conceptualizing and theorizing of the problem of race, in which the relationship between class struggle and racial struggle or between racism and sexism is formulated once and for all. If theorizing, necessary and indispensable in itself, is to function in the struggle against racial oppression, that can only happen in so far as the black experience is and remains its breeding ground.

This experience finds expression in black idiom, in the spirituals, the blues, stories about 'Brer Rabbit', the Sunday worship, and in all the other forms of life and practice which in their totality make up the anti-ideology in which society shows its other face. In the anti-ideology the dominant ideological practice appears in a mirror-image: success and progress appear as catastrophe, freedom appears as compulsion, development as dependence, happiness as trauma – the anti-ideology goes against the grain of history. Victims know other historical evidence; they see reality differently. Even more markedly, they live in another reality, in another land;[97] they are strangers, unknown, because they refuse to allow their existence to be defined and determined by the ruling powers, because they are opposed to an identity that has been forced on them.

> O nobody knows who I am,
> Till the judgment morning.

James Cone, who cites these lines at the end of an article about America's bicentenary (!), speaks in this connection of his people as an eschatological community, aware of its separation and its delimitation over against those who have a voice in a white society.[98]

This state of alienation, this retreating into oneself, is the only possible way in which a culture in which people are condemned, categorized and defined by the colour of their skin, sex, work and income can avoid suffocation. Alienation and captivity form the protection of their own subjectivity in a necrophilic world;[99] they form the opposition to an objectified reality in which human existence is submerged under abstract definitions and categories.

It is here that the essential, qualitative difference is to be found between the evidence of the dominant ideology and that of the anti-ideology; if the evidence of the dominant ideological practice owes its existence to objectification and reduction, in the anti-ideology a process of de-objectification takes place in which people appear as subjects of their own history. In the counter-culture, rooted in black experience, ideologically dead people, non-persons, are raised to life and called into existence: 'Hush! somebody's calling my name.'[100] They become soul brothers and sisters, 'bone of my bone and flesh of my flesh' (Gen.2.23). They become people of flesh and blood.

The anti-ideology is radical because it is the reverse of the dominant ideological practice; it is vital because it is the negation of the necrophilia of the dominant power and imagination. However, its radical nature and vitality never appear unbroken and unambiguous. Anyone who does not see that becomes guilty of a dangerous romanticism, just as on the other hand a failure to recognize the potential radicality and vitality of the anti-ideological imagination has everything to do with unbelief, rooted in resignation and pessimism. It is often not sufficiently recognized that the struggle in ideology is not simply a struggle between groups or classes but at all events also a struggle which takes place in the oppressed themselves. At all events, oppression is never just socio-political or economic by nature; on the contrary, as a political and economic expression it can maintain itself exclusively by penetrating deep into the feelings, experiences and thoughts of the oppressed themselves. In his book *The Souls of Black Folk* the great Afro-American leader W.E.B.DuBois described this war in the oppressed self in the famous passage in which he speaks of the duality which is always present – an American, a negro; two souls, two ideas, two unreconciled aspirations: 'two warring ideals in one dark body, whose dogged strength alone keeps it from being torn asunder'.[101]

Whether the radicality and vitality of the anti-ideological practice remains underground or comes to the surface depends on the historical situation as a whole, on the tensions and oppositions of both the economic and the political and ideological level. So in the 1960s in the United States a situation came into being in which the anti-ideology of the black experience became as it were flesh and blood in charismatic leaders like Martin Luther King Jr and Malcolm X (we shall return to the historical circumstances in which this came about in Chapter 3). White backlash, rivalry and division among black leaders and organizations, uncertainty over the strategy to be followed, and by no means least the economic recession mean that we must see this period as being past for good. Does this mean that in fact all the struggle took place for nothing and that everything has remained as it was? Nothing is less true. The 1960s are a turning point in Afro-American history, to be compared only with the historical moment at which slavery came to an end. The important legacy is the enormous process of conscientization that the struggle for civil rights and the Black Power movement brought into being. This process cannot be reversed. One sign of this is the vitality of the black theology which came into being in the period, a vitality rooted in the evidence of black experience which does not cease to put our sceptical pessimism to shame.

But what is the relationship between liberation theology and the conscientization that takes place in the revolutionary process?

The answer to this question can well be summed up briefly as follows: conscientization is inconceivable without the commitment of faith.

This view is not as amazing as it might perhaps appear at first sight. We saw earlier that in the process of conscientization another reading of reality comes into being which discovers in the contrasts and contradictions of the existing ideological, political and economic structures the real possibility of a radically different reality. Two things are involved here which we must distinguish clearly: (*a*) the real possibility; (*b*) the new reality. The first is a matter for common critical analysis, the second is a matter of faith. At all events, the new reality does not follow deterministically from the discovery of its possibility; it is not a matter of calculating chances, but of struggling.

In the process of the conscientization of the oppressed, however, belief and social analysis do not stand over against each other as rivals, as they do in bourgeois thought, but together form an alliance against fate. Anyone who thinks of Martin Luther King Jr and his dream, of Che Guevara and his faith in the new humanity, must come to the conclusion that the prophetic, conscientizing and mobilizing power of their life and struggle rests on their stubborn belief in another reality, as a real possibility here and now. This belief, which gave their career a specific character as *kairos*, requires to be established by critical analysis of the nature of contemporary reality. Should this latter be omitted, then the commitment of faith irrevocably dissolves into foolish dreaming, a distant and dangerous utopia. Then faith and reason, eschatology and history become completely estranged, with all the social and political consequences. Critical investigation into the historical connection of things and the commitment of faith presuppose each other in the process of conscientization.[102] Their mutual relationship can best be explained by the well-known christological formulation of Chalcedon: unconfused and undivided.

So it is certainly not by chance that three things coincide historically in the far-reaching Latin American process of conscientization in the 1960s: (*a*) revolutionary opposition to oppressive powers and structures; (*b*) the discovery of the dependency of the Latin American subcontinent and its theoretical foundation in the theory of dependence; (*c*) a new commitment of faith which among other things finds expression in the documents 'Peace' and 'Justice' of the second conference of Latin American bishops in Medellin, held in 1968. In itself the mutual connection between these three elements, which we can also note in other situations from the same period, already says a good deal about the nature of this commitment of faith. Its anticipatory character is typical. By that I mean that the commitment is an anticipation of the new, still invisible world, and that means that anticipation comes close to emancipation. The emancipatory longing for liberation is included in the anticipation through faith of a new world in which the last are the first and in which 'undermen' are the bearers of a new humanity.

Suspiciously enough for those for whom concern for Christian identity matters more than anything, it does not make much difference whether this new commitment of faith is deliberately inspired by the Jewish Christian tradition or whether it is actually opposed to it. In both cases it seeks a new creative organic connection of what has hopelessly fallen apart in the Western, Christian cultural pattern: the now and the hereafter, history and eschatology, life and death, body and soul, male and female, theory and praxis, thought and action, speech and belief. Its anticipatory and emancipatory structure is a fundamental protest against an anthropology, a christology, a doctrine of God which justifies this crippling dichotomy and thus in the end, whether consciously or not, at the same time justifies something else: the abiding dichotomy and hierarchy of classes, races and sexes.

There has been a breakthrough in a sceptical, pessimistic view of humanity in which human beings, bound by the chains of their sin, appear as beings who are simply in a state of evil; a concept of God has been criticized in which 'God' functions as one who maintains the existing state of things, as an omnipotent, omniscient and omnipresent potentate with whose predestination and providence people arm themselves against their inescapable fate; farewell is said to the pale, white figure of Christ whose reconciling and redeeming work forces them to patient acceptance of their suffering and betrayal of their historical task. But, we may ask, surely protest against such an image of God and man had been expressed long before the 1960s in church and theology? What great theologian would want to take account of such an unbiblical concept of God? That question is justified, and in itself it is important to add that the unmistakable new verve of faith in the 1960s found an echo both in the established churches and in academic theology – not to mention the theology of hope, the theology of revolution and political theology, and, as far as the churches were concerned, the 1968 Uppsala Assembly of the World Council of Churches with its stress on Christ as the new man, the man for others. Only if we want to understand the passionate protest which emerged in Black Power and in liberation movements in Asia, Africa and Latin America, we need other sources than the writings and statements of our great theologians and church leaders. In that case we must know how the gospel is preached in the cotton plantations in Virginia, on the high plains of Peru, on the gold coast of Ghana and in the Javanese *dessa*. We then come across mission tracts, catechisms, texts from gospel campaigns, and their content does not agree with the latest theological insights of Schillbeeckx, Jürgen Moltmann or the ecumenical movement.

Without failing to recognize the complications in these problems – mission and evangelization were not just instruments of colonialism and imperialism but at the same time contributed to emancipation and liberation[103] – we must realize that conscientization contains a development in which a new commitment of faith goes hand in hand with discovery of one's own situation as alienating, imposed from outside; here exploration of one's own identity, own culture, own history goes together with the expulsion of foreign ways of life, of thinking and cultural patterns which are introduced by, among others, mission, church and theology. However, oppression would not be oppression if one's own culture and identity were not distorted and violated beyond recognition; real oppression means that ways of thinking and forms of life were not simply forced upon the oppressed but were also deeply internalized by them. If we realize that, we become aware to some degree of the acute crisis of awareness which, in at first sight a paradoxical way, was produced by the process of conscientization and liberation. It is this crisis which lies at the basis of this new hermeneutics which we denote by the term liberation theology.

As a supplement to what I have said above and by way of preparation for Part Two, I would like to pause over two articles by the black American historian Vincent Harding, 'Black Power and the American Christ' (1967), and 'The Religion of Black Power' (1968).[104] Harding interprets the Black Power movement which arose in 1966 as a commitment of faith. Here he caused a healthy disturbance among black church leaders and theologians, and in particular the challenging questions which were put in the second article inspired the rise of black theology.[105]

'Black Power and the American Christ', written in fierce, heavy language, stands out against the background of the psychosis of anxiety which the slogan 'Black Power' brought about, and the beginning of the nostalgia, not only in the white churches but also in the black churches, for the time of non-violence and integration, when blacks and whites could still join together in singing 'We shall overcome'. Harding sees Black Power as a radical repudiation of this culture and religion (I would say ideology) of which the American Christ is the symbol. At the same time he affirms that it was precisely this American Christ who called Black Power into being, for this movement 'is a repudiation of the American culture-religion that helped to create it and a quest for a religious reality more faithful to our own experience'.[106] Who then is this American Christ? He is imposed on the blacks, this white, blue-eyed Christ – and from the beginning the attitude of the black person to him is characterized by deep ambivalence: 'He condemned us for our blackness, for our flat noses, for our kinky hair, for our power, our strange power of expressing emotion in singing and shouting and dancing. He was sedate, so genteel, so white. And as soon as we were able, many of us tried to be like him.'[107] However, this Christ not only called forth imitations but also the wrath which manifested itself in Black Power. This wrath is thus the product of the American Christ and his followers. Granted, now that this Christ does not simply live but also ultimately seems to be righteous, can this wrath not be interpreted as a sign of his presence in Black Power? 'May he not be attempting to break through to us with at least as much urgency as we once sensed at the height of the good old "We Shall Overcome" days? Perhaps he is writing on the wall, saying that we Christians, black and white, must choose between death with the American Christ and life with the Suffering Servant of God!'[108] In this statement put in the form of questions is to be found the challenging focus of Harding's argument in this short essay.

In the much longer second article, 'The Religion of Black Power', Harding goes more closely into the nature of the commitment of faith which is manifested in this movement and the questions which are evoked by it. He notes that a religious process of fermentation is under way, in which everything is moving: the most important questions are involved, questions of God, of humanity, of the universe, questions of hope and faith, questions about eschatology and the nature of the kingdom – all this and much more. If the church earlier fulfilled an essential function in the life of the black community, the new movement is in a position to take this over; for its many followers Black Power is 'likely to become as fully church as the earlier phase was for others':[109] it satisfies the need for personal involvement and for community feeling with other black people engaged in a similar way; it embodies an impressive sense of social responsibility, a call for ultimate justice, and thus a struggle to stand alongside those in society who suffer. If this new movement is characterized on the one hand by eclecticism (the gods of Africa are in rivalry with Yahweh, Jesus and Buddha, says Harding[110]), on the other hand it brings about deep ambivalence in the black consciousness. Harding himself is also ambivalent about concepts like black self-love, black glory, black power. So he says: 'Now, if it is possible that the fullest stature of man was found in one who honestly and sharply opposed his enemies but finally faced them with his cross, then Black Power may have chosen far less than the best available way. If it has chosen a bondage to death, the mistake is completely understandable.'[111] Harding recognizes the same ambivalence in the attitude of a number of black church leaders who took a stand behind Black Power in a courageous advertisement in the *New York Times* of 31 July 1966:[112] he asks them whether they in fact are not maintaining a doctrine of two kingdoms: 'Do these leaders seek the Kingdom of the weaponless, defenseless, homeless King at certain times, and the Kingdom of the armed, propertied, politically powerful, American white (soon to be technicolored) King at another time? Where do the kingdoms meet?'[113] Vincent Harding's concern is that the black church leaders allow themselves to be determined too much by the one whom they oppose: the American Christ. Here he makes himself the spokesman for a problem with which Martin Luther King also wrestled: can a new, better society be fought for with the same means of power as those with which the ruling powers maintain and defend themselves?[114] This problem forms the background to Harding's critical question to the church leaders, namely what their relationship is to the life and work of Jesus of Nazareth, in whose person a completely different power is manifested, namely the power of God which is expressed in weakness and humiliation.[115]

To sum up, we can say that Harding had a keen eye for three things: 1. he saw that the Black Power movement is more than a radical political movement with a homogenous vision of society and a homogeneous strategy; for him Black Power is a process of conscientization, by which a commitment of faith is expressed; 2. however, he raises the question how far this commitment of faith is still supported by the same American Christ against whom it was directed; in other words, he asks about the presence of the ruling ideology in the anti-ideology; 3. he demonstrates that the process of conscientization as a whole raises urgent and fundamental theological problems, which call for a response on the basis of distinctive black experience.

Gayraud Wilmore, one of the people responsible for the advertisement in the *New York Times*,[116] once acutely observed that the strength of Vincent Harding lay more in raising questions than in giving answers. The gentle rebuke that can be heard here may possibly be justified; but it remains Harding's merit that he raised the right questions at the right time. Without earlier questions no new hermeneutic is possible. Of course Harding was not the only one to pose the urgent questions which underlie the rise of the black theology of liberation. However, through the level on which he posed the problem he gave a vital impulse to new theological reflection.

(b) Second phase. Break and continuity

With these last observations we have arrived at the second phase of our historical reconstruction. This phase is decisive for the origin of liberation theology. There is no question that the process described here leads as it were automatically to liberation theology. The first phase simply provides so to speak raw material from which in certain conditions a theology of liberation appears. However, the development can also move in another direction. If we stylize complex historical processes, we can distinguish three possible developments: 1. the new commitment of faith leads to a complete break with the Jewish-Christian tradition; in this case the result is not liberation theology, at least not in the usual sense; 2. the opposite takes place: the continuity with this tradition is not made a problem and continues to be taken for granted; in that case too the result is not a real theology of liberation; 3. there is both break and continuity; discontinuity arises because the new commitment of faith definitively breaks with the world of the current Christian tradition of faith; the continuity lies in the fact that the break comes into being on the basis of what nevertheless is handed down by the same tradition. Only in these circumstances does the dialectical tradition come into being which leads to a new way of doing theology.

Let us look at these three possible developments more closely for a moment. The first we can deal with briefly. When there is a total break the tension disappears. The field of Jewish-Christian tradition is no longer in dispute but is abandoned and written off as a whole. Although a separate question can emerge, namely how far the commitment of faith which led to this break is still living on the basis of this tradition from which it seeks to free itself, nevertheless this break is a deliberate choice. The criticism and practice of mission, of church and theology, is meant to be understood as criticism from outside. This blocks a development in the direction of liberation theology – because this theology derives its tension precisely from the fact that its criticism remains within the sphere of the Christian tradition of faith. However, that is not the whole story, since indirectly external criticism can at the same time contribute to the formation of liberation theology. The history of black theology provides a good example of this: the vehement criticism by Malcolm X and his angry children, the Black Panthers, of the hypocrisy of white American Christianity had a deep influence on the process of the conscientization of black church leaders and theologians, to which black liberation theology owes its existence.

If tension disappears with a total break, there is similarly no tension when the element of discontinuity is completely lacking. This development comes about when the process of conscientization does not embrace the whole but concentrates on the question of cultural authenticity in a way which leaves the socio-political and economic conditions vague. Thus at present many churches in the so-called developing countries are looking for forms of expression which find a point of contact in their own cultural and religious tradition: here they are striving for 'indigenization' or contextualization of the Western theological heritage. The starting point of theologians who are occupied with this usually lies in the question 'What does the gospel mean for people in our situation?' At first sight this question seems completely legitimate, but unfortunately it conceals a dangerous snake in the grass. This is the suggestion raised by the problem that there are two entities, the gospel and the situation – and that the task of the theologian is to reconcile these two. Here 'the gospel' is used unconsciously as a theory which is not in itself 'situated', which in principle can be applied to all situations and which now still waits to be applied in a specific non-Western context.

If, however, contextualization no longer means adaptation and application to specific situations in Asia, Africa and Latin America, then this contextualization is a contradiction in itself. Its half-baked character lies in the fact that it takes over one of the most essential characteristics of bourgeois Western thought without reflection or concern: the myth of free, autonomous theorizing unrelated to situation. If there is no discussion of the relationship between theory and practice, and contextualization is indeed only adaptation and application of a theory which has been stripped of its specifically Western garb, then there is no need for a break with the dominant theology. However, if there is no discontinuity, then this form of Third World theology is no more than one variety of already existing theology which may or may not be interesting. If this conclusion is correct, then it is appropriate to issue an emphatic warning against the tendency to identify Third World theology with liberation theology. Most theology which comes to us from the Third World is not liberation theology – yet!

In particular, forms of African theology which find the source of their inspiration in nostalgia for the intact culture of a time which is gone for good suffer from a certain degree of hermeneutical naivety. The problem of theory and praxis (and thus the problem of ideology) lies outside the field of vision and in this way the intrinsically legitimate interest in cultural authenticity becomes separated from political and economic reality. In that case it can happen that there is idealistic talk about 'the' African culture, in which the disintegration of old tribal cultures by the irresistible processes of urbanization and industrialization is certainly indicated, but not analysed on the basis of the perspective of many Africans who suffer under dependence and poverty. So this variant of African theology has rightly come under the suspicion that it is in fact a cultural resacralization[117] which serves to conceal the new social conflicts in African countries. In that case it is the ideological expression of the new native bourgeoisie, and the cultural emancipation which is its concern remains limited to that of a new élite. It is clear that such an African theology clashes with the black theology of liberation in (South) Africa and North America, as is evident from the polemic from both sides.[118] Here we need to be cautious against drawing over-hasty conclusions. The limits of the two movements are not clearly marked. Different tendencies can be indicated both within African theology and within black theology on both sides of the ocean. Thus in African theology there are tendencies in the direction of liberation theology, while conversely there is a black theology which is no more than a cultural variant of the existing dominant theological practice.[119]

What development must take place if we are really to be able to talk of liberation theology?

A development in this direction is possible only if there is in fact a break with the Christian practice of faith and the Christian tradition without leaving the ground to which they owe their existence. The continuity is as important as the discontinuity. The dialectic between the two elements produces a tension which leads to 'a new way of doing theology' (Gutiérrez).

As we saw, a process of radical conscientization underlies this dialectic. In this process there is manifested a commitment of faith which cannot be separated from the Jewish-Christian tradition because – despite all the injustice that this tradition has perpetuated, justified or suppressed on its way through history – it is aware of being supported by the subversive recollection of the slave people who were freed from the servitude of Pharaoh and of the righteous one who was crucified as a criminal but rose from the dead. The resurrection is the perspective in which the three basic Kantian questions are posed anew: what may I hope for, what can I know, what must I do?[120] So this commitment of faith leads to new questions which do not have an abstract and idealistic concern with the relationship between the gospel and a particular culture but have a specific materialist concern about the presence of the Risen One in the desire for liberation and the struggle of the oppressed.[121]

Simultaneously with the emergence of these fundamental questions, however, suspicion arises about existing theological practices in church and scholarship. How is it possible that precisely these questions do not now form the content of theological discourse, or scarcely do so? How can we explain that in this discourse all kinds of other matters are thought to be much more relevant than the question what the suffering Servant of the Lord means for the life and the struggle of the poor and insignificant? Theological practice is trapped in the 'deadly sin of omission' (C.Eric Lincoln[122]). The suspicion arises that this omission has nothing to do with a fortuitous and regrettable coincidence of circumstances, but that it is closely connected with the social function which theology fulfils. So this suspicion inevitably leads to the shocking discovery that, as Juan Luis Segundo put it, 'anything and everything involving ideas, including theology, is intimately bound up with the existing social situation in at least an unconscious way'.[123]

On the basis of this discovery current readings of biblical texts are looked on with new eyes. The existing exegesis of Hebrew and Greek texts is investigated with a view to its relationship to the praxis from which it emerges. Here, sooner or later, the means which were provided for this investigation by 'the two modern masters in the art of suspicion' (José Miguez Bonino[124]), Marx and Freud, prove indispensable. Thus the Jewish-Christian tradition as a whole forms the subject of an ideological struggle in which radical criticism of the self-understanding of this tradition forms the negative side of the positive: a new reading of scripture and a new concern for neglected aspects of church history. This new reading in turn calls for a thorough hermeneutical reflection, and in this way gradually a new way, a new method, a new hermeneutic opens up.

To sum up, we can therefore distinguish four elements in this process (which of course in practice can overlap chronologically): 1. conscientization, in which the new questions arise; 2. ideological suspicion; 3. the new reading of scripture and tradition; 4. a new hermeneutic. Here the second and third elements presuppose each other to such a degree that they are treated as one phase (the second) in our reconstruction. Of course it is no coincidence that the four elements mentioned virtually coincide – though the terminology is somewhat different – with the four factors which in his book *The Liberation of Theology* Juan Luis Segundo regards as being indispensable for the vitality of any theological hermeneutic.[125] If one of the factors is absent, then according to Segundo the hermeneutical circle is not complete and no vital theology can come into being. In order to support his argument he chooses four examples, three in which the hermeneutical circle is broken in one way or another, and one in which it is complete. As an example of a theology in which the four vital factors are indeed all present, Segundo takes Cone's *A Black Theology of Liberation*, and that is not a coincidence either.[126]

(c) Third phase. A new way

The term 'hermeneutical circle', which is taken from Bultmann, Tillich and others, is not really a very happy one. It conjures up the picture of a static event going round in itself. Therefore it is better to follow George Casalis in speaking of hermeneutical circulation, because this expression gives the suggestion of movement, of the circulation of blood between the four vital elements.[127] But what sets this circulation of blood going? This question was related to our reconstruction of the first phase. Under what conditions can the circulation keep going? When does it become blocked? That was the problem of the second phase. The third phase of the process begins when the motive force reaches the point at which the need for a hermeneutical course (method) which has to be followed proves indispensable. If in this phase there is indeed 'a new way of doing theology', that does not mean, though, that the final point has been reached. Theology of liberation does not know an end point because – at least if it remains true to itself – it does not form a closed system. The circulation between the four elements continues, indeed it begins all over again, from the start, in the temptations of everyday life.

This word temptation denotes an essential element of liberation theology, which unfortunately is not expressed in the term circulation, useful though that is in itself. This picture can provoke the misunderstanding that the hermeneutical circulation of blood takes place in a vacuum. Nothing, however, is farther from the truth. The movement of this hermeneutic is a counter movement. The sphere in which it moves is primarily a sphere which is occupied by the dominant conceptions and modes of thought. Its course is an expedition aimed at the liberation of territories under ideological occupation. The difficulty of this struggle and at the same time its temptation lies in the fact that from the beginning liberation theology finds itself on the ground of the occupying forces and therefore has no sanctuaries nor its own means of communication. It has to create and explore its own sphere, and this takes time 'since oppression always means that the communication skills of an oppressed community are determined to a large degree by the oppressors. That is precisely the meaning of oppression!' (Cone[128]). Liberation theology cannot detach itself directly from these communication skills; however radical its criticism may be, it remains dependent on them in the first two phases of its development. I myself have the impression that the dependence is greater, the more bitter and harsh the criticism is.[129] This situation is not without risks. How can liberation theology avoid its content being determined by the thought against which it opposes itself? Is not this mechanism at work when it is argued over against 'white' theology that God is 'black'? Is the theory of dependence with which Latin American theologians work not just as one-sided as Western thinking in terms of development which they reject? In the way in which it deals with biblical texts has not liberation theology always been just as selective as the theological tradition?

Questions of this kind do not simply come from tiresome outsiders, but form the nucleus of a problem: how does liberation theology overcome its dependence? As long as it is stuck in reaction, this dependence remains. As long as it is no more than the mirror image of the dominant theo-ideology, it is not a new way of doing theology. It is against the background of this insight that we must understand Segundo's statement that the only guarantee of the liberating character of any theology is not its content but its methodology. Only the method can avoid it being incapsulated by the existing system.[130] The search for this method marks the third phase of the development of liberation theology. Here we may not make Segundo say that the content of theology is irrelevant. What he means to say is that in the end the method is decisive for the content. Here the old wisdom, *methodus est arbitraria*, applies. According to Karl Barth[131] this principle does not mean that method is a matter of subjective arbitrariness: on the contrary, the arbiter takes a free decision though at the same time it is binding on himself and others. For Barth this arbiter is the dogmatic theologian. Segundo goes still further; he says in fact that the method itself is the arbiter, the decisive authority. Method, whether or not deliberately chosen, is decisive for content.

This last point, of course, also applies to the forms of theology from which Segundo and his followers want to part company. These forms, too, bring with them their own methodological starting points and presuppositions, and for liberation theologians it is a matter of establishing the connection between what is normative in this method and the functioning of theology in the context of church and society. It is a vital condition for liberation theology that it should gain insight into the way in which theological thinking and symbols function ideologically in what Castoriadis has called '*l'imaginaire social*'.[132] Ideological criticism is inherent in liberation theology. An analysis of theology as ideological practice is not a luxury which liberation theologians may or may not allow themselves: it is necessary in order to be able to arrive at a new way of doing theology. Without a thorough knowledge of the old way this new way cannot be followed.

This means that liberation theology cannot stop at the suspicion that the historical and socio-political context is determinative for the questions that we raise about God and our way of responding to these questions.[133] Nor can it be content with the discovery of the contradiction between the universality of theological discourse and the particularity of the underlying experience (middle-class, male, white, Western). It must press through to the question how this contradiction can be explained. How is it possible that this methodological contradiction has remained hidden for so long? What ideological imagination has made the 'natural' unreflective connection possible to theology 'with the totality of conceptions, world-view, practices that provides the legitimation of personal and social action for a particular group'?[134]

Developing thinking about these questions is still very fragmentary, leaning on the masters in the art of 'suspicion' whom I mentioned earlier. Moreover there are shifts in accent which have to do with the differing contexts of differing forms of liberation theology. However, we can clearly speak of a common trend in the search for an answer: the functioning of theology is connected with the academic milieu in which it often belongs as a specialist discipline. Determinative of this milieu is a concept of scholarship which begins from a subject with autonomous thought. Of course liberation theologians, too, know that the myth of the subject with autonomous thought who investigates in critical freedom the reality extending before him has been under attack for a long time both inside and outside the academic sphere. However, despite its theoretical refutation – which of course is far from being generally accepted – it lives on in practices, modes of thought and institutions, and moreover it is confirmed every day in a 'society which is losing its democracy to experts' (H.Gollwitzer[135]), in which the sense of dependence on experts, from technologists to auxiliaries, is steadily increasing.

The history of theology has some responsibility for the rise of this myth. Already in the early centuries of Christianity a division came about between clergy and laity, between an active *ecclesia* and a passive *ecclesia*, between a teaching church and a learning church. Theology was no longer the responsibility of the community as such (even the Reformation did not bring about any actual change here) but became the monopoly of an upper stratum: 'A stratum of those who know dominates those who are ignorant, an *ecclesia activa* an *ecclesia passiva*, the clergy the laity, who are freed from theological responsibility and kept immature.'[136]

We cannot go into the social and ecclesiastical causes of this development here;[137] however, the result has been that theology turns into a kind of theorizing which becomes independent of popular belief or community belief, with which it maintains only a one-way traffic. As an autonomous discipline theology raises itself above the expressions and practices of faith characteristic of the 'simple church people'. Its discourse organizes itself into a distinctive code of language and goes round its own autonomous circuit of questions, problems and answers which have their origin more in the privileged environment from which professional theologians come than in the specific experience of underlying groups and classes.

Precisely because theology as a science came to stand outside and over against popular culture and popular belief, a development could arise which had a detrimental effect on both theology and popular religion. Academic theology basked in the imagination of its own autonomy, and it did not feel it necessary - so obvious was and is this imagination – to raise the question, which is critical for itself and its own functioning, of its social and cultural conditions of production.[138] However, this omission made it possible for academic theology to conform to the prevailing ideas in education and scholarship without too much pain and distress. But is this involvement in prevailing academic practice so obvious? Should the recollection of its own origin and task not make Christian theology more suspicious and critical about what is felt to be evident in education and science? Having grown up in the academic tradition of teaching, liberation theologians inevitably come up against these questions on their way to a new way of doing theology. At the same time they see how little the questions are yet recognized in the established bastions of European and American theology; what Helmut Gollwitzer has to say about theological training in his own West German context does not seem strange to them: 'The question raised here, whether theological teaching must not be fundamentally different from the other disciplines which provide the experts needed in bourgeois society for its production and reproduction, is not recognized and discussed any more than one's own involvement in and service to this privileged society.'[139]

The myth of the autonomy of scientific thought also works its way into the relationship of theological theorizing to Christian praxis. Here, too, we have to do with a development in which theology as the work of thought makes itself independent of the historical contexts in which churches and individual Christians live and act. As a subject who has 'critical freedom' the theologian *qua* theologian

puts himself or herself outside the history of Christian praxis, even
though he or she may engage in theological activity emphatically in
the service of the Christian community and its proclamation. In the
latter he (or, of course, she) finds himself in an ambivalent position:
as a Christian he feels himself affected by the life and action of the
Christian community; by his critical freedom as a theologian,
however, he puts himself outside (or rather above) the historical
praxis of the Christian community in order to be able to judge and
comment on this on the basis of his autonomous position.[140] This
ambivalence is connected with our discussion in the previous section
of the relationship between theory and praxis: within the academic
tradition 'truth' is seen as the result of intellectual thought which
subsequently must be 'adapted' or 'transposed' into practical
action.[141] The thinking subject puts himself methodically outside
the field of historical conflicts and actions, codes of language and
ideological practices; the subject does not form any part of the
reality objectivized through thought since from a methodological
point of view the thinking subject is and remains in all circumstances
an onlooker. In so doing he or she 'forgets' that any theorizing,
however abstract, is always already 'situated', always already has a
place in a concrete ideological, socio-political and economic context
and always fulfils an ideological function within this context in one
way or another.

If theological reflection refuses to draw methodological consequences from the fact that it is impossible to avoid the power of
history – neither a concept of revelation nor a scientific theory can
authorize it to have the attitude of a bystander – then the result of
its work cannot be verified historically and as a result it is as elusive
as it is invulnerable; if the formation of theological theory does not
see itself as one ideological practice along others, it deprives itself
of the possibility of being addressed about its historical function; if
the already existing connection between the theoretical practice of
theology and the practical action of the theologian is not explained,
then the historical limitation which is intrinsic to any theological
discourse whatsoever is hidden and the contradiction which is
so problematical for liberation theologians emerges between the
objectivizing and apparently universal character of the discourse
and the limitations of the historical experience which underlies it.

It is of fundamental importance to see that at this crucial point
more is involved than the thought that orthodoxy must be guaranteed

by orthopraxis which has been taken up – but so slowly – thanks among other things to the political theology of Metz, Moltmann and others. However valuable it may be, the theoretical insight that orthopraxy is the criterion for theology is in itself no longer adequate. The primacy of praxis remains in a vacuum if the methodological consequences are not drawn: theology must be aware of the praxis in which it is already involved: as critical reflection it cannot leap over its own shadow in order to develop an ideal picture of what the praxis of the church and Christianity must be, but at least must connect this ideal picture with a critical analysis of the actual empirical praxis of which it forms a part. In the previous section we saw how J.B.Metz in his *Faith in History and Society* has not (yet?) taken this last step: his assurance of the situation is still a long way from a critical analysis of our own context in church and society. In my view at this vital point the ways of political theology in its present form and liberation theology part company.

A number of years ago José Miguez Bonino and Jürgen Moltmann had a theological discussion which is important enough to return to here. In this debate mainly hermeneutical questions were raised which ultimately focussed on the question of the need for a Marxist analysis of society. Liberation theology owes a great deal to Moltmann. Bonino is particularly complimentary about his christ-ology, *The Crucified God*: according to Bonino this work represents an essential deepening and correction of the *Theology of Hope* which was published earlier.[142] However, this work, too, causes Bonino to ask some critical questions which he poses – and it is worth pointing this out – in his discussion of the relationship between eschatology and history in his book *Doing Theology in a Revolutionary Situation*, under the heading 'Theology of the Oppressed'.[143] His criticism can be summed up in three points: 1. Moltmann contents himself with an impressionistic description of contemporary human alienation and misery without giving a coherent consecutive analysis of the vicious circle of death which he indicates (poverty, violence, racial and cultural discrimination, the industrial destruction of nature, meaninglessness or godforsaken-ness); 2. Moltmann speaks in idealistic terms about the church by allowing normative biblical-theological statements and empirical historical observations to stand side by side in his argument without demonstrating the connection between them; in other words

Moltmann describes what the church must be without taking account of actual practice in church history; 3. the identification with the oppressed does not become concrete: granted, Moltmann writes that 'the crucified God is in fact a stateless and classless God. But that does not mean that he is an unpolitical God. He is the God of the poor, the oppressed and the humiliated.'[144] However, because he fails to point to the specific praxis in which such a basic statement is grounded, Bonino asks: 'But the poor, the oppressed, the humiliated *are a class* and live in countries. Is it really theologically responsible to leave these two sentences hanging without trying to work out their relation? Do we really stand on the side of the poor and the oppressed if we fail to see them as a class, as members of oppressed societies? If we fail to say *how* we are "for them" in their concrete historical situation? Can we claim a solidarity which has nothing to say about the actual historical forms in which their struggle to overcome oppression is carried forward?'[145]

The question of the nature of social analysis, the question of the connection between ecclesiological statements and specific historical praxis, the question of the nature of solidarity with the oppressed – these questions relate to hermeneutics; they are concerned with the mode of theologizing. Therefore it is surprising that Bonino does not carry on his conversation with Moltmann in Chapter 5 of his book, which is about hermeneutics, truth and praxis. The nub of his criticism is that Moltmann does not give his theorizing a specific context in the field of historical conflicts and practices or, in other words, that praxis is not explained sufficiently in and after theory. However, Bonino has – in my view, wrongly – thought it was better to make room for discussion in Chapter 7, which is about the kingdom of God, utopia and historical commitment. This is connected with the fact that he sees the cause of the shortcomings he mentions in the 'eschatological proviso': in order to avoid the sacralization of any ideology or power structure, Moltmann – along with most of European theology – takes refuge in theology as a critical function, in other words a function which will not tie itself ideologically to specific socio-political options and analyses[146] but seeks to remain faithful to 'the critical freedom of the gospel'. Bonino retorts, 'We believe that the European theologians... must de-sacralize their conception of "critical freedom" and recognize the human ideological contents that it carries.'[147] It is striking that Bonino here associates the term critical freedom exclusively with the problem of the relationship between eschatology and history. He overlooks the fact that this term represents an important value in the scholarly tradition in which his German colleague stands as a professor in Tübingen. Jürgen Moltmann replied to the criticism of Bonino and some other Latin American theologians in an open letter.[148] This letter discusses many things which unfortunately we must leave on one side here. However, it is important for us that Moltmann vigorously rejects the charge that Metz and he misuse eschatological freedom in order to remain politically and ideologically neutral. Even more emphatically, Moltmann demonstrates that what Bonino himself has to say about the relationship between the eschatological kingdom of God and our political reality does not differ in any way from what one can already read in Barth, Bonhoeffer and Metz or Moltmann whom he criticizes! Therefore it is not clear to him where this sharp criticism is directed.

We cannot fault Moltmann here. In fact at this point the criticism of Bonino, Segundo[149] and some others is too sweeping to be convincing; it has too little eye for the heterogeneous character of the theological discourse on European soil (there is no such thing as European theology) and for the specific position occupied in it by theologians like Metz and Moltmann.

If the difference between the position of Bonino and that of Moltmann does not lie in the way in which the relationship between eschatology and history is envisaged, where does it lie? In my view we must trace the difference between the two on the three levels which together form someone's theological position: 1. on the level to which most attention is usually paid, that of the theological outline in the strict sense of the word; 2. on the level that is always involved in one way or another, that of a vision of society; 3. on the level that constitutes the unity of a theological position, that of methodology.

1. As to the theological outline in the strict sense, we must again return to the relationship between the kingdom of God and our historical reality. Precisely in order to avoid dualism, precisely in order to see that eschatological hope and historical expectation intensify each other, Moltmann cannot be content to talk in terms of anticipation, analogy or similarity. At the end of *The Crucified God* he speaks emphatically of 'materializings of the presence of God' and of reality as sacrament ('as a reality qualified by God's word which is made the vehicle of his presence'[150]). Now it is striking that these expressions go too far for Bonino – who in this respect is

more conservative than other Latin American theologians. He is troubled by 'mystical identifications': there is no place for theocratic dreams of any sort, either from right or from left'.[151] If I understand Bonino aright here, his concern is that in Moltmann the bewildering reality of history is overplayed in theological terms. He misses a clear and consistent recognition of the completely human, secular character of this reality and of the need for historical, analytical and ideological intermediaries. Without this recognition there can only be a 'new idealism of Christian theology',[152] in which the earthly reality is not done justice to in all its recalcitrance and godlessness. At this point, however, Bonino puts his thoughts in so abbreviated a form that at first sight his criticism seems illegitimate. Yet here he touches on the nucleus of what distinguishes him theologically from Moltmann, for all the agreement.

When Moltmann interprets the experiences of liberation from the vicious circle of death as real manifestations of God and as materializations of his presence he is not occupied with something incidental to his theological outline. On the contrary, these formulas express the heart of his theology: the doctrine of the Trinity. The experiences of liberation are taken up into the process of the trinitarian history of God. It is a pity that Bonino does not refer to this epistemological foundation. On the closing page of *The Crucified God*, Moltmann writes: 'In accordance with theological tradition it is possible to see the real presence of God pointing beyond itself, as the history of the Spirit which comes upon all flesh. We understand it here in the process of the trinitarian history of God.'[153] Earlier in his book Moltmann had already explained that the whole of human history, however much it may be determined by guilt and death, is 'taken up' into this 'history of God', an expression which, not by coincidence, is taken from Hegel.[154] Here a very important epistemological decision is made: according to Moltmann, to think of God in history always leads to theism and atheism and he rejects both these alternatives;[155] to think of history in God, however, transcends these two alternatives and leads to the new creation and theopoiesis.[156] However, Moltmann's theology of the Trinity is at the same time a *theologia crucis*: 'A trinitarian theology of God perceives God in the negative element and therefore the negative element in God, and in this dialectical way is panentheistic.'[157] This notion is carried through so consistently that even Auschwitz can get a place in the theological outline in the sense that, 'like the cross of Christ, even Auschwitz is in God himself. Even Auschwitz is taken up into the grief of the Father, the surrender of the Son and the power of the Spirit.'[158]

In search of what distinguishes him from Moltmann's theology, Bonino should not in my view have passed over the epistemological implications of Moltmann's doctrine of the Trinity. It is there, in strict theological terms, that the heart of the matter lies. It seems inconceivable that Bonino for his part could speak of the practice of torture and the other crimes of the former dictatorial régime in his country Argentina, in the way that Moltmann speaks here about the recent past of the German people. At least in such a case Bonino would have to go in detail into the human, i.e. the economic, political and ideological causes of fascism and dictatorship, poverty and oppression. Could the fact that he misses this interest in 'historical, analytical and ideological intermediaries in Moltmann have anything to do with the fact that for his German colleague history, even in its most cruel actions, is always taken up into the trinitarian 'history of God' – in other words, in Moltmann, thought about this history of God – even before its human, all too human, character is investigated?

2. Moltmann himself sees the main difference between Latin American liberation theology and political theology in Western Europe in the evaluation and assessment of the respective historical situations. Bonino sees his Latin American situation as a revolutionary one; however, in the European context, according to Moltmann, it makes no sense to speak of a revolutionary or a pre-revolutionary situation.[159] He also already thinks that there is considerable agreement over what is needed in terms of world politics; at the same time he affirms that separate countries, societies and cultures can experience situations which lie at different stages of history from one another. What is necessary and possible in the Latin American context can hardly be judged from Europe (although Moltmann thinks that he is justified in telling his Latin American conversation partners that to be occupied with a relevant analysis of the historically given situation of the people is a very different matter from offering a lecture about Marxism as a view of life).[160] As far as the European context is concerned, Moltmann opts for the way of democratic socialism.[161] In democratic socialism both right-wing and left-wing dictatorships are clearly rejected; the way to socialism may not be taken at the expense of democratic

liberties which have been gained (freedom of the press, the right to vote, the right to strike and so on) and therefore this way must not be passed over, but followed step by step.[162]

Whether the difference in social view is the most important feature which distinguishes Western European political theology from the liberation theology of Latin America is still open to question. However, at all events Moltmann is right to point out that there is an unmistakable connection between (*a*) the social context and the view of it and (*b*) the theological outline and the function assigned to it. Gutiérrez, Bonino and Assmann can see their theological activities as critical reflection on the praxis of liberation which is already present because in their direct surroundings they can see how fellow Christians, priests and laity on the basis of their commitment of faith are involved in social process, directed towards radical change. If they take the radical course, by contrast Moltmann takes the course of gradual change: in his context, that of the Federal Republic of Germany and Western Europe, he believes that radical revolutions are impossible. In the 1960s, at the time of the student revolts, the Vietnam movement and 'socialism with a human face', however, things seemed to be changing; at that time there was a situation with specific alternatives to the existing system, but 'it became clear that the most beautiful revolutionary theories found no basis in the people and therefore remained without a subject'.[163] Therefore all that remains is the way via the gradual democratizing of political institutions and socializing of economic conditions, though it remains an open question whether this democratic way to socialism will have results and also whether it will prove to be liberating for the countries in the Third World.[164]

We cannot go here into the complex problem of 'the contemporaneity of that which is not contemporary'[165] which Moltmann properly raises, and which emerges in connection with the relationship between Western Europe and the Latin American sub-continent; here we must also leave aside the question of the legitimacy and tenability of the various views of society. It is clear, though, that on the basis of his view of society Moltmann cannot give his theology the function of reflection on a praxis of radical change. At all events, he does not think that the conditions for this change are present in his context. He is therefore concerned to keep open the democratic way to socialism by being on guard against the threat of dictatorship from both the left and the right. That means that in his situation as a theologian he is concerned, following the Barmen theses of 1934, to safeguard the freedom of the gospel and to prevent Christian faith becoming identified with any kind of world view or specific political option. This caution about the inadmissible crossing of boundaries determines the 'critical function' of theology, and this function is therefore closely connected with the way in which his own social context is seen and experienced. Moltmann is right when he rejects the charge that in practice this critical function should amount to a neutral or liberal position. Such a judgment does not do justice to Western European political theology.[166] However, Bonino has right on his side when he asks Moltmann and other European theologians not to camouflage this 'critical function' as 'critical freedom of the gospel' but to analyse it and give it ideological expression on human, political grounds - just as the Latin American theologians do with their choice of socialism and Marxist analysis.[167] If this does not happen, then inevitably theological arguments are used to justify a political position and vice versa. In that case any conversation is doomed to failure from the start. The only way in which the argument can be kept pure is a strict application here of the 'unconfused' and 'undivided' of Chalcedon.[168]

3. The most serious accusation made by Jürgen Moltmann against his Latin American conversation partners is that in contrast to representatives of African, black and Japanese theology they in fact have little new to say. However, the remarkable thing is that in his open letter Moltmann completely passes over the hermeneutical claims of the Latin American theologians. In this sense, at any rate, Latin American liberation theology is 'a new way of doing theology' (Pablo Richard[169]) which is aware of being an activity 'in the second instance'.[170] Perhaps Moltmann has good reasons for disagreeing with this claim; perhaps he rightly doubts the liberating commitment of faith that forms the presupposition for this way of doing theology; perhaps he rightly does not believe in the conversion to the people of these theologians; perhaps in fact it is a gross exaggeration to speak of identification with the struggle of the people for its fundamental rights to life. However, we read nothing about this in the open letter:[171] just as the claim of Latin American theologians to be representing a new way of doing theology remains unmentioned, so too do the arguments for disagreeing with this view.

It is even more remarkable that Moltmann overlooks the degree to which all the questions raised by Bonino relate to hermeneutical, methodological problems. Nowhere in the open letter does he really go into questions of method. This omission is all the more striking when we see that Moltmann himself puts forward a political hermeneutic in *The Crucified God*, which aims among other things at recognizing the social and economic determination of theological institutions and codes of language and does not just ask 'what sense it makes to talk of God but also what is the function of this talk and what effect it has'.[172] Now this is precisely the matter with which Bonino is also concerned. The only question is how this function and effect can come to light. Does not such a hermeneutical interest argue for a far-reaching structural change in the nature of theological discourse? Is not a particular method needed for this?

However, Moltmann does not draw these consequences. True, he sees clearly that the critical solidarity with liberation movements for which he argues calls for a political hermeneutic that raises the question of the actual function and working of theology; but this important insight is in the last instance doomed to barrenness if this hermeneutical interest leaves untouched the nature of his own theoretical practice. There is no sense in putting the question of the socio-economic determination of theology in general terms; a political hermeneutic of the kind that Moltmann argues for must in the first place be concerned with investigating the real conditions of existence of his own theological production. At any rate, if 'systematic theology always consists of attempts by human beings to integrate their own story or that of their group, their culture, with a wider story about God' (L.A.Hoedemaker[173]), then we must not forget that throughout history hitherto the systematization of theological insights has almost always been the work of members of one particular sex, one particular class and one particular culture; to what degree was there room in systematic theology for other stories about God, deriving from people of different classes, races or cultures? To what degree is hermeneutical account taken of the limitation of the human experience which is involved in any account of God whatsoever? An investigation of the socio-economic deter-mination of theology only makes sense if it is in the service of a real ecumenical dialogical form of theology in which one's own experience and position is constantly under discussion. We can also put this last point in a different way by saying that ecumenical theology involves a way of theologizing which looks for ways of being able to analyse and bring to bear one's own ideological practice which is always already present.

This implies that the connection between the theoretical practice of theology and the practical action of theologians cannot be left out of account. It also means that the 'nonintellectual factors'(James Cone[174]) must come to light which, though kept silent and suppressed in the apparent rationality of the discourse, are often of decisive significance in the taking up of theoretical positions. If here theology makes room for historical materialist, sociological or psycho-analytical insights and theories, this is not an expression of an overbold quest for encyclopaedic knowledge, far less a misplaced nostalgia for times long past when theologians still thought that they had oversight of reality. On the contrary, these other disciplines serve in the first place to make known the boundaries of our own experience and the position of the theological subject in order to make room for the experience of others.

(d) Elements of ideological criticism

To return to the beginning of this section: no liberating theology is possible without ideological criticism; it takes its form as criticism – to use Tillich's terms once again – with its understanding that both the negative element, the self-criticism, and the positive element, the new way, are put under the sign of the form of grace.[175] The elements of ideological criticism in liberation theology only come into their own when they are seen as elements of a constantly ongoing movement of criticism and formation. In order to bring these elements to light I have therefore opted for providing as it were a running commentary by means of a descriptive reconstruction of liberation theology in three phases – a description which tries to trace the common tendencies in the history of the development of different forms of liberation theology.

If I now finally, for the sake of clarity, sum up the ideological-critical content of liberation theology in four points, it will be clear that these points only derive their validity from their function within the whole of the movement of which they form part and may not be abstracted from this movement in any way.

1. One of the most important passages in the final declaration of the first assembly of theologians from the Third World in Dar es Salaam, 1976, runs: 'We reject as irrelevant an academic type of theology that is divorced from action. We are prepared for a radical

break in epistemology which makes commitment the first act of theology and engages in critical reflection on the praxis of the reality of the Third World.'[176] According to the twenty-three theologians who made this declaration, theology can only be vital within the movement of discipleship; outside that it is irrelevant. Here the declaration expresses a main theme of liberation theology. What is criticized is that way of doing theology which does not recognize its own historical and ideological roots, whether because it supposes itself to occupy an autonomous position above ideological practices and institutions, or because it sets Christian faith and ideology over against each other.[177] This failure to recognize the historically limited and contextual character of its own discourse has serious consequences: its effect is a pseudo-universalism which leaves no room for the otherness of the other. This repression of reality means that the truth which is claimed on the basis of the critical freedom of the gospel or the autonomy of the subject *de facto* – given the actual social conditions – becomes the freedom to dominate others.

2. Criticism of the concept of freedom implies criticism of methodology. *Methodus est arbitraria*: the methodological starting points decide whether commitment, as the praxis of discipleship, in fact comes first in the hermeneutical order. Here that way of doing theology is criticized which is not aware of the conditions of its own existence and does not draw the methodological consequences from the insight that 'everything involving ideas, including theology, is intimately bound up with the existing social situation in at least an unconscious way' (J.L.Segundo).[178]

3. The epistemological break which makes the praxis of discipleship the first action of theology implies that the historical experience of oppressed groups, classes and peoples is taken seriously as the source of theological knowledge. This can happen in different ways. However, in itself the event already discloses a painful opposition in which any discourse is entangled, which speaks theologically in the name of the church as a whole, but in which in fact only a privileged upper stratum participates as *ecclesia activa*. No real contribution is expected from the *ecclesia passiva*, the people, the laity. In an assimilation to the world which is refused it on the basis of Rom.12.2 the church here reproduces the social conditions of a 'society which is losing its democracy and submitting to experts' (H.Gollwitzer[179]).

4. Taking the historical experience of the oppressed seriously in

theological terms implies an essential interest in the way in which they code and decode the surrounding reality. However, the discovery of these codings also brings something else to light: the quite inadequate character of the distinctions (sacred-profane, natural-supernatural and so on) and concepts (myth, animism, syncretism, superstition, etc.) which are currently used in academic writing. This terminology has a generalizing and domesticating effect.[180] But the question is whether things can be otherwise. Can intellectuals – and even liberation theologians are intellectuals – really understand the codes of the oppressed people from outside? This is the point on which the hermeneutical challenge is focussed.

4. 'Chalcedon' as a condition for a hermeneutic of liberation

So far we have been occupied in following the course of liberation theology and commenting on it. Now, on the basis of what has been said so far, I want to reconnoitre 'the new way' somewhat further for our purposes, so that it becomes clear from what perspective I approach black theology in the next two parts of this book.

In the previous section I stressed that insight into the limitations of one's own position is a necessary condition of an ecumenical and dialogical way of doing theology.[181] Systematic theology may not just consist of attempts by people to integrate their own story into an overarching story about God; Hoedemaker rightly points out that this process of integration must be 'interrupted, disturbed and stimulated afresh by the stories of others', time and again.[182] Perhaps we should go even further and say that of all the stories of others it is the biblical stories, with all their liberating recalcitrance, which form the great disturbance and interruption to the process of integration, undertaken time and again, into that overarching story in which 'God' functions as an omnipotent potentate, as the guardian of existence and the guarantor of human impotence. If the mystery of the biblical stories indeed lies in the wonder of God's incarnation and in the identification of the Son of Man with those who are humiliated and dominated, then the mystery of the incarnation of man should be connected with the refusal to dominate others. Theology, as a reflection on this mystery in the service of the apostolic function of the Christian community, is here confronted with the hermeneutical and methodological problem of how, in line with its messianic concern, it can prevent the other from being denigrated or annexed, objectified or declassed in it. If in fact the humanity of human beings is included in the incarnation of God, then this has far-reaching consequences for its hermeneutical structure: 'In this way theology becomes a science which asks and is asked from "the" human being to human beings, which can be "radically" historical – theology of existence – to the degree that it is conversation and leads to the conversation of human beings with human beings' (Friedrich-Wilhelm Marquardt[183]). However, such a structure calls for an ongoing self-critical caution over the effects of power, characteristic of any discourse that seeks for unity and consensus.[184]

As I have said, for recognizing its day-to-day functioning theology is directed towards means which lie in the sphere of the humane and social sciences. If this is the case, is theology not giving up its own identity, its *proprium*? This fear, which is constantly expressed, rests on a misunderstanding. The distinctive feature of theology is its relationship to the messianic story. This story is the cause in the service of which it is put. This cause does not lead into supernatural domains only accessible to those who have esoteric means at their disposal; its domain is ordinary, secular life – because of the radicalism of the incarnation; its instruments are not private means but public and accessible to all: in exegesis, history, praxis and dogma the theologian makes use of insights and methods which are also current in other disciplines. As to means, theology has no distinctive ones. Since God's Word has become human word and shares in the limitation and vulnerability of all human language, theological reflection can and must be open in principle to ideological criticism from the social sciences. It may not be evasive here with a reference to the critical freedom of the gospel. The detachment which is as crucial to theological reflection as to any other form of critical reflection may not distract it from the fact that Christian community and theologian are always already part of conflictual human reality in one way or another.[185]

However, ideological criticism does not serve to indicate the function and effect of theological reflection once and for all. On the contrary, this criticism creates the conditions for a practice of change. Theology too may understand itself in the light of the future liberation. That is where its critical freedom lies. Theology may give form to this freedom provided that it is at the same time aware of its limits. From a methodological point of view these limits lie with the 'unconfused' and 'undivided' of the Chalcedonian Definition. In the context of its time and at the same time in a normative way for later generations, this council laid down the limits by which the argument about the incarnate Word must allow itself to be determined. Transgressing these limits means irrevocable damage to the mystery of the incarnation. The freedom of theological dispute thrives on the grace of this healthy limitation. Outside this limit there is no order in theology, but *tohu wabohu*, chaos. Both the undivided and unseparated, the unconfused and unchanged, determine the order of theological argument.

The 'undivided and unseparated' implies the rejection of any dualism of Word and world. This reality, this earth, this history, is the concern of God's love and promise. 'Human beings, and the whole creation, live by the breath of God's declaration of love. Word and Spirit are not higher truths; they precede all things... A theologian is not one who delves deep into the galleries of the diamond mines, since the secrets lie on the surface' (G.F.ter Schegget[186]). The *arcanum* of the incarnation at the same time includes the mystery of the good creation. Despite bitter questioning, despite the overwhelming events of everyday, despite the complete unacceptability of what people can do to one another, this history is concerned with liberation and reconciliation and the *erets* (earth) is the place of peace and righteousness, love and happiness. Theology must reject the deeply rooted habit of thinking in two spheres: 'Just as in Christ the reality of God entered into the reality of the world, so too is that which is Christian to be found only in that which is of the world, the supernatural only in the natural, the holy only in the profane, the revelational only in the rational' (Bonhoeffer[187]). Therefore theology may not play Word and world off against each other, bathing the world in light and veiling the Word in conceptual darkness. It cannot declare itself competent in the sphere of *sacra doctrina* and at the same time be incompetent in the sphere of ordinary life and action.[188] As critical reflection on the proclamation and action of the Christian community it betrays the power and completeness of the biblical kerygma if it leaves the interpretation of this political and social event to the autonomy of the social sciences. This kergyma comes to be valid and plays a part in the ideological battlefield of conflicting experiences and interpretations of events in society.

However, such a partisan attitude can become dangerous and

suspicious if theology is not at the same time constantly aware of the 'unconfused and unchanged'. In fact what we have here are two aspects of the same thing: both the 'unconfused and unchanged' and the 'undivided and unseparated' mark the boundary line over against an unhistorical way of thinking which evades the radical character of God's humanity.[189]

Here the 'undivided and unseparated' is directed against the dehistoricizing of the Christian proclamation which emerges where God's holiness is separated from his love for humanity (Titus 3.5), where the act of faith functions as redemption from the world,[190] where historical reality may only be the scene for human failure and inability and where ultimately feelings of piety, the situation of the individual believer, remain as the only place of mediation between the world dominated by sin and God's kingdom as reality beyond this world.

However, the 'unconfused and unchanged', too, may be seen as a protest against a way of theology which does not give the necessary room to God's Word as the most specific historical factor.[191] No such area is present where a personal religious experience is uncritically confused with the story of Jesus the Messiah, political action with the proclamation of faith, the building up of society with the expectation of the kingdom of God. At this point we cannot go back behind Karl Barth's radical criticism of these tendencies in the practice of the church and theology – tendencies which have concentrated themselves in a powerful tradition which still has much to say for itself – in which the marvellous story of the human love which appeared in Jesus Messiah is applied to the rationality of modern, in other words Western, bourgeois man. In this tradition, which manifests itself most powerfully in forms of bourgeois religious feeling, but the roots of which reach into the early centuries of Christianity, there takes place a refined, complex interweaving of this messianic story with faith in progress, freedom and universal fellow humanity. Belief in the strange acquittal is appropriated as a spiritual possession to be handed on to others and functions as a world view alongside other competitive world views. The power of the stories centred on exodus and covenant, Son of Man and kingdom of God, which is constantly surprising and has many dimensions, is reduced to dogmatic formulae, annexed as ethical principles or put into operation as a political programme. The idealism of this tradition consistently denies the recalcitrant historical gulf which divides modern man from the appearance of God's love for humanity in the midst of a specific people (the people of Israel), in a specific person (the Jew Jesus of Nazareth); and where the sense of this gulf is present, the 'accidental truths of history' must give way to the evidence of the 'necessary truths of reason'.[192] An idealistic understanding of history – for that is the kind of understanding with which we are concerned here – tries in this way to transcend the hermeneutical problem of the historically limited, contingent character of God's love for humanity in the person of Jesus of Nazareth.

The question can arise whether the struggle to transcend historical limitations is not completely legitimate in itself. Does not theology stand in the service of the community? Does not the Christian community stand in the service of the apostolate? Does not the nucleus of its apostolic function lie precisely in those forms of crossing historical and geographical barriers which do not come to an end before they reach the ends of the earth? How else is it possible to do justice to the universal claim of the gospel than by crossing barriers?[193] Does not Karl Barth also emphatically assert that there is no theological justification for putting any limits from our side on the love of God which has appeared in Jesus Christ? Is it not rather our task to see and understand this human love 'as being still greater than we had seen before'?[194] However, there is a world of difference between the liberating philanthropy of the Son of Man who has come to serve (cf. Matt.20.28; Luke 22.26) and the crossing of boundaries by a dominant philanthropy of a bourgeois Christianity, extending to the ends of the earth, which knows no bounds.[195] In recent studies of the relationship between Christianity and the bourgeoisie attention has rightly been drawn to the revolutionary character of the mentality of the bourgeois class which transcends boundaries;[196] the 'capitalist revolution' (H.Gollwitzer) does not simply introduce an abstract rationality which makes everything that exists an object and subjects it to itself; it also introduces a restless concern for creation and the deployment of power.[197] D.Schellong goes back to the famous section on bourgeois society in Hegel's *Philosophy of Right* in order to be able to typify the bourgeois character as the personal aim of the individual in his needs as an end in itself over against whom other individuals are alien, indeed nothing, but are needed and used as means.[198] However short any indication of a bourgeois principle falls of the complicated

and heterogeneous character of its historical reality, the force of
Schellong's description lies in the fact that it corresponds to the
experience of those who live on the other side of the history of
democratic achievements, material prosperity and scientific technological progress.[199]

If an important element of truth does in fact lurk in the notion of
the 'aim of the individual in his needs as an end in itself', then
the question inevitably arises whether the permanent crossing of
boundaries by the middle class does not in fact amount to an equally
permanent approach to himself. The movement of expansion and
progress would then be essentially circular; there would be no
crossing boundaries in the sense of real confrontation with the
otherness of the O(o)ther. There would be no room for it. Anyone
who steeps himself in the history of colonialism and imperialism is
constantly confronted with the utter self-certainty to be found there
– it is even present where in the course of the nineteenth century
anxiety and uncertainty begin to attack the bourgeois self-awareness
– in which the bourgeois project themselves as human beings *par
excellence*, their culture as culture *par excellence* and their future as
the future *par excellence*. So one of the last great thinkers of the
educated middle class, Ernst Troeltsch, can defend mission as a
universal interest of European and American culture despite his
abhorrence of the practice of mass conversion and his respect for
Buddhism. Why does he see mission as a duty? Because nothing
more or less is at stake in it than the idea of cultured humanity; there
is a threat of large-scale racial war when the multiplicity of peoples
and states is not permeated by one spirit and one culture – and
Troeltsch does not doubt for a moment that this Spirit cannot be
any other than that which emerged from the fusion of Christianity
and ancient society.[200]

After 1914, however, since the decline of the educated middle
class, this conviction has ceased to be self-evident; but despite
Auschwitz, despite Vietnam, the end is not yet in sight of the
totalitarian tendency to go beyond bounds, which *de facto* excludes
the otherness of the other. More strongly still, this otherness of
others still poses the fundamental threat; it produces anxiety and
guilt feelings. That is evident, for example, from the forms of racism
which constantly raise their heads worldwide in modern history;
racism is far more than just an ideological factor of stabilization for
the economic and political subjection of others, it is (at all events

also) an expression of deep anxiety over the alien and the unknown that finds its all too specific physical symbol in a black skin.[201]

Where there is no room for the recognition of barriers between human beings, there is even less room for the otherness of the humanity of God. Where there is no longer any sense of the alien and unknown character of God's word, and where a sense has been lost of the eschatological and indeed apocalyptic tensions in the world of the Bible, privatization and domestication of Christian faith inevitably come into being. It is against this background that we must understand the great stress that Karl Barth laid in the second edition of his *The Epistle to the Romans* on the total otherness of God and the impossibility of natural knowledge of God. 'If I have a system it is limited to the recognition of what Kierkegaard called the "infinite qualitative distinction" between time and eternity, and to my regarding this as possessing negative as well as positive significance.'[202] This radical protest against the confusion of what must remain qualitatively different showed its historical strength in the struggle against the form of confusion of which the German Christians in particular were guilty. But Barth's criticism of religion did not do away with it; it continued to retain its validity where – whether out of apologetic interest, an urge for mission or a concern to explain theology before the forum of science – the hermeneutical rule of the 'unconfused' was violated. A theology of liberation, too, cannot escape this rule. On the contrary, I am convinced that the hermeneutical challenge which liberation theology has raised comes to a focus at precisely this point: it is only a new way of doing theology when it is in a position not to domesticate but to give room to the O(o)ther.

Apostolate indeed means crossing frontiers. However, this crossing of frontiers begins where the otherness of the O(o)ther emerges.[203] The characteristic thing about it is that it does not require room but makes room. The Hebrew word for 'liberate' is derived from a root which contains the notion of room:[204] liberation means making room, opening up space where things are narrow and constrained. Room is a fundamental category for a form of theologizing which puts itself at the service of those who are constrained and forced out of history. However, to make room so that the voice of those with no rights and no significance is heard is theologically impossible unless at the same time room is made for God as the 'concrete counter-reality' (Schellong[205]). God's humanity does not do away with his otherness; on the contrary, each presupposes and implies the other. The uniqueness of the name (Deut.6.4) determines the 'wholly otherness' of this God in the midst of the gods. No image can be made of this name. His otherness constantly escapes the domesticating effect of the formation of theistic, deistic, atheistic or pantheistic images and concepts. That does not mean that argumentative, discursive thinking that works with categories and concepts is completely disqualified. However, this thinking does disqualify itself if it is not sufficiently aware of its own inadequacy. It occupies an indispensable place in theology on condition that it is a dialectical way of thinking, i.e. thinking that is fully aware of its temporal limitations. What G.C. van Niftrik has observed in connection with dogmatics applies to any form of argumentative, discursive theology: 'The stammering and stuttering is so essential for dogmatics – is such an obvious, obstructive problem – that it must not surprise us in the least that its scientific character is misunderstood time and again.'[206]

Dialectic-discursive thought also needs constantly to relativize itself because, however indispensable it is and continues to be, it does not represent the basic form of theology. In biblical theology the right of the firstborn is reserved for the narrative. God's love for humanity only comes into its own as narrative history. Such different authors as J.B.Metz, J.Cone and E.Jüngel have drawn attention to this in recent publications.[207] They argue that justice should be done to the basic narrative structure of the biblical witness by means of a narrative theology: 'God's humanity introduces itself into the world as a story to be told. Jesus told about God in parables before he himself was proclaimed as the parable of God.'[208] In theology thought is constantly thrown back on remembering. Real remembering can only happen in the form of narrative: real remembrance implies both a temporal distance from the event and also a total involvement (not simply cerebral);[209] the structure of the story aims at this involvement and the necessary distance.

The preservation of the 'unconfused' is guaranteed only when theological reflection remains constantly aware of its basic narrative structure. At any rate, the story of God's love for humanity is limited by time and place: it became flesh in the historical person of Jesus of Nazareth. This story comes to us in the past; it comes to us from outside and determines our future.[210] As an account of what has happened and what is to happen it rescues us from fatalism, from the doom of the past; it affects us in the movement of the coming of the kingdom which is nearer to us than we are ourselves; it also puts us between the times.

The movement between the times requires that the capacity for human speech and thought shall be as mobile as possible. The dynamic of the kingdom cannot tolerate any incapsulation and fixation, any standpoints and certainties, and certainly not any preunderstanding.

No preunderstanding? In that case can thought be free of prior concepts? Can we interpret the kerygma of the Bible without preunderstandings always already being present? Have I not just argued that thought is always already situated in a particular context of action? Does not the theology of liberation require precisely that the theologian shall become aware of his social roots and make a clear choice in the ideological battlefield of social contrasts and interests?

The problem of preunderstanding is that thought fixes itself. A fixation to a particular preunderstanding of whatever kind irrevocably means a coagulation of hermeneutical circulation. Of course any form of critical reflection presupposes that one becomes as aware as possible of one's own presuppositions. However, if this process of becoming conscious is condensed into becoming the deliberate choice of a preunderstanding – of whatever conceptual content – then there is an enormous risk that the illumination of this one preunderstanding leaves obscure other ideological elements which are also present.

Preunderstanding has the character of drawing things to itself. The whole order of the discourse comes to stand in the light of this preunderstanding. By contrast the alien and unknown, the power of what is to be discovered, remains in the dark. This means that preunderstanding has a totalizing tendency which amounts to an essential attack on the dialogical structure of theological discourse in which the otherness of the O(o)ther comes into its own.[211]

The limitation which is inherent in this argument makes it necessary for everything to remain fluid and in motion. In this respect we can warmly agree with one of the concentrated sayings which are characteristic of Jüngel's book *God as the Mystery of the World*: 'Human speech corresponds to the being of God, which is coming, in that it moves any statement, each of which is as such unrenouncible, on into movement again, that is, it is not ashamed of its temporality, preferring instead some timeless concept, but rather carries out purposefully that temporality.'[212]

For Jüngel, the close connection between the mobility of a discourse that expresses God's humanity and its temporal limitation determines the hermeneutical significance of the story: 'Man can correspond in his language to the humanity of God only by constantly telling the story anew.'[213]

Sadly enough, Jüngel does not make any connection between the hermeneutical function of the story and the problem of ideology. He does not take any account of the fact that the story of God's humanity, as a story which comes to us from the past, is always already the cause of ideological struggle, always already the object of a struggle in which social interests are involved. Furthermore the concept of temporality does not fit well in Jüngel's book where there is mention of the need and the possibility of thinking of God's unity with perishability.[214] Jüngel fails to note that the limitation of our existence (at the least) lies in the fact that we do not for a moment stand outside the ideological struggle. For him it is the general 'human condition' which determines our limitation: specific social relationships and practices seem to have little to do with this.

Nevertheless it is striking that Jüngel argues that the discovery of God's humanity as history which is constantly to be narrated anew detaches thought from the autonomous subjectivity of the Cartesian 'I think'; thought discovers itself to be a consciousness entangled in history![215] 'Consciousness is structured in a thoroughly temporal way both by the stories which it always has in its past, which ontically mould it, and by the history which essentially lies before it, which ontologically moulds it.'[216] However, the difficulty is that Jüngel does not go into the nature of these stories in which human beings are entangled. Nowhere is it evident that he takes into account that these stories have a material basis,[217] that they form part of the complicated network of social associations, practices and institutions in which the individual is entangled.

It is impossible to reflect on the way in which the consciousness is entangled in stories without coming up against the problem of ideology. I feel that the approaches to a theory of ideology by Louis Althusser[218] demonstrate in a convincing way that ideology cannot be reduced to the level of images and ideas. Ideology is the expression of an attitude; this attitude concerns the reality in which people live; people imagine this reality in one way or another; they cannot live without such imagination. Thus according to Althusser ideology is the imaginary attitude of people to their real conditions of existence,[219] and each individual human life is impossible without it always already being in ideology.

The imagination, as the real sphere of ideology, is in the first instance supported by the stories in which it is involved. Far more than concepts, ideas and theories, stories have the power to image what has grown up in history (and thus can be changed) as being natural and evident: 'this is how it is and not otherwise.' At the same time, however, stories also have the capacity to preserve and keep the riddles and unanswered questions of human existence. Stories reach deep into the material sphere: every rite, every profession, every land has (or rather is) a story; stories at the same time reach deep into the unconscious: their signs and symbols are carried on until one day they appear on the surface of what is consciously known.

The mobility and many dimensions of stories determine their subversive power, but at the same time they are also the cause of their vulnerability to manipulation. Their ideological function and work depends on the context in which they are discussed. In stories people identify with one another.[220] Stories put people in a position to play their role, to insert themselves into existing social conditions and practices; they identify themselves and one another as the free farmer, the loving wife, the faithful slave. At the same time, however, it is in stories that another evidence, another possibility of humanity emerges: without story, without history, the revolt of an oppressed people, of a marginalized group or class against the existing powers, is impossible. The incongruous thing here is that the same story can both serve an ideological practice of oppression and also be a source of opposition and rebellion. We shall come up against a striking example of this in Chapter 4 below which discusses the history of black slavery: the story of redemption through Jesus Christ which was proclaimed by missionaries to the slaves on the plantations as a story of obedience to white masters – that same story was handed down and sung in the imagination of the slaves as a story of opposition and liberation:

> I'm a chile of God wid my soul set free,
> For Christ hab bought my liberty.

This one instance may be enough to indicate that the story of God's love for humanity shares in the vulnerability of any human story. It is defenceless against appropriation and the misuse of power – and this defencelessness is ultimately nothing other than the reflection of the helplessness of the Messiah himself who helps, not by virtue of his omnipotence but through the power of his sufferings.[221] At the same time, amazingly enough, this story constantly avoids the stifling pressure of the religious sensibility of existing powers; it seeks its own way and finds itself a hearing among the small and insignificant, among those who put their hope on the career of the *ebed Adonai*, the suffering servant of the Lord (Isa.53.5; Matt.8.17), as a way to righteousness and a good earth.

The story of God's humanity comes to us as one of many stories in which our consciousness is entangled. This historical and phenomenological datum defines the vulnerability of this specific story, and in this vulnerability the specific career of the *ebed Adonai* is reflected. However, this is only one side of the matter. There is also another side: hearing this story is hearing the name: 'Hear, O Israel, YHWH is our God, YHWH is one' (Deut.6.4); the uniqueness of the name gives the story its own context and therefore makes it a unique story, the only one of its kind. Therefore what Jüngel formulates in the following way is also valid: 'The definitiveness of divine revelation and the uniqueness of the God who reveals himself which make it impossible for God's story to be totally dissolved in stories.'[222]

Both elements of truth need to be maintained: the story of God's humanity comes to us as one of the many stories in which our consciousness is entangled ('undivided'!) and this story is a unique story because of the uniqueness of the name ('unconfused'!). A vital hermeneutical circulation comes into being only when justice is done to both elements in their reciprocal relationship of tension. Therefore narrative theology cannot work without a mobile dialectical way of thinking which derives its flexibility from the fact that it does not for a moment lose sight of its ideological limitation and partisanship. This last is only possible when the dialectical way of thinking is bound up with a materialistic understanding of history which confronts itself and others with the ideological question *cui bono?*:[223] what does theological reflection actually serve to do; where is its actual involvement, what social relationships and practice are furthered or undermined by it, to whom is it really addressed?

The fact that here dialectic is bound up with a materialistic understanding of history does not mean that a preunderstanding is being introduced secretly. Historical materialism is not a programme in principle but a method – or a way which is followed up hill and down dale – of bringing out social, philosophical and other preunderstandings that are present and expressing them. If this method functions as the framework into which the kerygma of prophets and apostles is inserted and to which it is added, then in fact it contradicts itself. By virtue of the ideological critical interest with which it constantly lays the question *cui bono?* on the table, however, it must be thought to be in a position to break through the objectivizations and fixations of abstract thinking in order to make room for the distinctive meaning of the story of the humanity of God.[224]

Historical materialism creates a distance: it is first of all a method which accentuates the difference in historical situation between us and the text in such a way that the text of the story is struck from our hands and restored to itself: 'Like the historical-critical method historical materialism is primarily a method of alienating the text from us' (H.Gollwitzer[225]).

This effect of alienation – and it is no coincidence that it is a central term in Bertholt Brecht's theory of tenets – makes room on two sides. On the one hand room is made for the way in which the total otherness of God's love is expressed in the biblical tradition – a love which is not caught up in general cohumanity but plays a part in the social oppositions in and around Israel in favour of those in the society of those days who represented the wholly other, the side of self: the poor, maimed and blind, children,[226] prostitutes and tax collectors:

> With righteousness he shall judge the poor,
> and decide with equity for the meek of the earth (Isa.11.4a).

On the other hand, the movement by which the biblical tradition is replaced in its own context also works in the way in which we experience and understand everyday reality; it forces back the gathering of religious clouds – the result of a disastrous centuries-long confusion of Christianity and culture – which veil from our eyes the hard, secular nucleus of social oppositions and conflicts. Life itself is the most pertinent criticism of religion. Auschwitz remains Auschwitz and its terrors cannot be fitted into any single religious or theological framework. However, this insight must not lead the Christian community astray to abandon reality to its fate. Social conflicts and problems can be analysed – their irrationality does not in any way stand in the way of a rational analysis. A sense of historical discontinuity between the world of the biblical tradition and the everyday world makes room for a sober, coherent (albeit transitory) analysis of the totality of social relationships. This latter does not mean that theology gives itself into the hands of the humane and social sciences; however, it does mean that these disciplines are not left prematurely aside by theology and that this rule is taken into account in order to criticize political insights or economic theories simply on political or economic grounds. Only on this condition is it possible to free the social language and action of the Christian community from an uncritical confusion of biblical or dogmatic notions with forms of contemporary social vision and analysis.

To create a distance, the effect of alienation, ideological criticism – of course these things are not ends in themselves. They are necessary as a means of making room for a distinctive context for the biblical tradition on the one hand and for a rational analysis of reality on the other. Both sides belong together. It is not a matter of playing off the Barthian concern for the distinctive logic of the Word against the call of Latin American theologians in particular for a rational analysis of structures of domination and dependence. On the contrary, each element needs the other and each is directed towards the other. The one does not go without the other. Only in their mutual connection can they give that mobility to theological reflection which puts it in a position to follow the movement of the messianic kingdom.

However, the movement of this kingdom does not take place *ad lib*, but is and remains the movement of God's *agape* (love) which goes out to those who are in the darkness. Hence the black slaves in the deep South of the United States, against all the empirical evidence, could sing:

> An' de God dat lived in Moses time
> is jus' de same today.

The different forms of liberation theology which arose during the 1970s have at least the merit of having laid on the table the urgent question of whether it is right and possible for a theology not to be rooted in a community where this *agape* is actually known. If love drives out anxiety (I John 4.18), is not the praxis of this love the only possible way of overcoming anxiety about the otherness of the other – an anxiety behind which our fear of death is concealed?

2 · Response

The Context of a Dialogue with Black Theology

In 1974 Jürgen Moltmann called black theology a new ghost going round in white societies and making theologians there uncertain.[1] Now we are some years further on, but this ghost still shows us its presence and we are to an increasing extent unavoidably confronted with the question what we must do about its appearance. Paradoxically enough, however, the threat that this appearance poses to established theology is the unavoidable reverse side of what it seeks to be in the first place, a theology of liberation. But who or what defines the liberating character of a theological praxis? The answer to this question is not simple. In the previous chapter we used three concepts – liberation (section 1), context (section 2) and ideology (section 3) – to look for ways to test black theology as a theology of liberation by its own claims.

We could only touch on an important additional problem in passing. This is the question of the context of the conversation with black theology that I am trying to carry on in this book. What is the framework, the *Sitz im Leben*, of such a conversation? Given the many difficult problems under which contemporary theologians are already submerged, is not a conversation with black theology a luxury rather than a necessity?

There is every reason to discuss these questions in a separate chapter. There is an unmistakable tendency to regard black theology at its best as a legitimate variant of existing theology – a variant which can have a necessary right to exist for black people but in which we do not need to become involved.[2] Is this theology not of limited local interest, precisely because of its specific concern for liberation from racial oppression in South Africa or the United States? Does not its link with a situation get in the way of its ecumenical character? Moreover, is not a real dialogue impossible because as whites we are already *a priori* under criticism? Using the three key concepts from the previous chapter, I shall try to show that 1. the universality of black liberation theology lies specifically in its particularity; 2. only contextual theology can really be ecumenical; 3. the *locus* of a conversation with black theology appears specifically on the surface of the two ecclesiological models which keep cropping up in ecumenical discussion at the moment: that of the church as a conciliar fellowship and that of the church as the church of the poor.

1. Black theology and liberation from racial oppression

Didn't my Lord deliver Daniel,
D'liver Daniel, d'liver Daniel,
Didn't my Lord deliver Daniel,
And why not-a every man?

He delivered Daniel from the lion's den,
Jonah from the belly of the whale,
And the Hebrew children from the fiery furnace,
And why not every man?

'And why not every man?' Sung aloud, shouted out in the bestial misery of a slave's life, this song is an exclamation of universal liberation. Here we have the ecstatic glow of the spark of new life in the black depths of a humiliated existence. In the incessant pain and anguish of everyday life the light of redemption and liberation breaks through irresistibly. A liberating history from God is celebrated here which goes completely against the fatal, natural course of things: the days and nights of oppression are numbered. The times are beginning to come under apocalyptic pressure:

The moon run down in a purple stream,
The sun forbear to shine,
And every star did disappear,
King Jesus shall-a be mine.[3]

However, this involvement in a liberating event of universal, indeed cosmic dimensions, this apocalyptic consciousness, does not make the black slave a passive onlooker; on the contrary, just as the three children of Israel refused to bow down before the golden idol

of king Nebuchadnezzar in captivity (Dan.3), so the black slave
refused to let himself be shut up in the servitude of Egypt:

> I set my foot on the Gospel ship
> And the ship it begin to sail,
> It landed me over on Canaan's shore,
> And I'll never come back any more.

Canaan is the promised land and redemption is essentially nothing
other than the liberation movement from God, from the house of
slavery to the land where all is different. The land of Canaan is
concrete utopia. It can be a designation of the free North or of
Canada; it can also point to the land on the other side of the river
of death; and with prophetic ambiguity it can bear both meanings
at the same time,[4] and thus be an expression of what an apocalyptic
view of life felt to be the almost intolerable tension between
history and eschatology, between particularity and universality. This
tension can never arise where the oppressed are no more than
victims without a will, softened by an inhuman system; but where
suffering is a form of survival and opposition this tension grows
against all oppression and bears with it an untamable hope and
expectation. In this struggle and expectation the prime concern
is for one's own existence, for the continuation of one's own
descendants, one's own people. But the universality of the 'And
why not every man?' is comprised in the particularity of this struggle.

Jean-Paul Sartre once wrote that the basis of every revolution is
the affirmation that we too are human beings.[5] As far as the history
of the black people in America is concerned this notion in fact gives
keen expression to the source of the ongoing struggle for black self-
awareness and identity. If for a moment we make use of the tripartite
Hegelian division into thesis, antithesis and synthesis to clarify the
dynamics of this struggle and its revolutionary potential,[6] it is clear
that the antithesis of black self-consciousness and black power was
brought out in the first place by the thesis of white racism. However,
that is not the whole story. More than the thesis of racial oppression
is needed for the antithesis 'we too are human beings'; black
consciousness is – and this is too little realized – more than simply a
reaction to white racism. The antithesis of black liberation is not
simply preceded by the thesis but also by the synthesis of the 'And
why not every man?' The synthesis which is its goal, its *telos*, is at
the same time its presupposition.

In the history of black experience in America the lines of particularity and universality cross one another in a complicated way. We also recognize this complexity, which is coupled with a degree of ambivalence, in the personal experience of black leaders like Booker T.Washington, W.E.B.DuBois and Marcus Garvey.[7] In the harsh reality of black experience the grand simplicity of the synthesis 'And why not every man?' can fall apart into the barren opposition between black nationalism and integralism. So we see how in the struggle of the 1960s the tension between universality and particularity was incorporated in the persons of Martin Luther King and Malcolm X.

However, we must be careful not to absolutize the contrast between integration and black nationalism. It is significant that in the last months before their deaths Martin Luther King and Malcolm X – one murdered in 1965, the other three years later – were undergoing a process or radical reorientation which without doubt would have brought them closer to each other:[8] both became increasingly aware of the deep structural and economic causes of racial oppression, and both felt themselves increasingly closely bound up with the struggle for liberation of colonized peoples all over the world. In this connection his journey to Mecca in 1964 was as significant for Malcolm X as King's attitude to the American involvement in Vietnam. It is no exaggeration to say that Malcolm X and Martin Luther King were occupied, each in his own way,[9] with transcending the element of antithesis, the struggle against racial oppression (without robbing it of its force – on the contrary![10]); there are remarks from the last period of their lives which point in a moving way to the synthesis of a universal community without class and race, a new heaven and a new earth where righteousness dwells. Shortly before he was murdered, King said in Mason Street Temple, Memphis: 'I've been to the mountaintop; I've looked over and I have seen the promised land.'[11]

Black theology, which developed at the end of the 1960s, owed a great deal to both charismatic leaders. It sees both as legitimate representatives of the black relgious and political tradition, and refuses to play off the integralism of King and his followers against the nationalism of Malcolm X. Precisely in the way in which these two supplement and correct each other, as Gayraud Wilmore points out,[12] they represent the broad spectrum of black experience.

Without question King represents the mainstream of black culture and religion, but in addition there was always another more radical proletarian line in black history which runs from the leaders of slave revolts like Prosser, Vesey and Nat Turner to Malcolm X. Black theology is concerned with the total spectrum of black experience, and here we come to the heart of its *raison d'être*.

The great presupposition with which black theology operates is that there is something like a unique, authentic black experience of faith. And the second presupposition which goes with this is that it is of vital importance for the survival of the black community to think through this experience of faith and articulate it again and again. Black theology does not regard itself as a *creatio ex nihilo*. It is a theological reflection on the distinctive and specific way in which black men and women give and have given expression to their belief in God, Jesus Christ and the Holy Spirit. This experience of faith is only indirectly to be derived from the distant land of their origin, Africa. However, it is very directly connected with a context of centuries-long slavery and racial oppression.

From the beginning the black slaves understood and experienced Christian faith in a radically different way from the white missionaries who preached it to them. The God who made himself known to them by night, during their secret meetings, who inspired their body and spirit and gave them the power to survive under the inhuman conditions of the slave plantations – this redeeming, liberating God could not be the God of their white master with his whip or the God of the white preacher with his 'show obedience to your master'.[13] During the traumatic history of the last three centuries the otherness of this God, the God of the slaves, is reflected in the otherness of the black experience of faith as this is expressed in the slave songs and popular stories, in the blues and the gospel songs, in the preaching style of Rev.C.L.Franklin and in the 'soul' of his daughter Aretha.[14] Certainly, powerlessness corrupts,[15] and the black church too has not avoided this corruption: passiveness, moralism, individualism – these things too are amply present, and they in turn form the reflection of the dominant white culture and religious feeling, sometimes as a caricature.[16] However, despite this deep ambivalence, the sense of the redeeming, liberating power of the God of the oppressed has remained alive in the black church. If there is anywhere that non-persons are addressed as persons, the nameless are given a name, and people who are humiliated and exploited day by day become conscious of their own identity, calling and value, it is in worship – and a black church service is above all a physical and spiritual event![17] 'Black theological reflection takes place in the context of this event.[18] It articulates the indissoluble connection of this experience of faith with the struggle for social justice – and it only succeeds here if it can bring out the specific historical roots of this connection. Therefore black theology is suspicious of any tendency to dissolve the particularity of the black experience in general ideas relating to the history of religion, theology or ecumenism world. It knows all too well how precisely a failure to understand the experience of faith, culture and history of people whose skin is another colour, or a slighting of it, is a subtle but essential part of that ideological system of oppression which is called racism. Hence we can understand why Gayraud Wilmore says, 'General theological propositions that cannot be rooted and grounded in the particular experiences of a particular people may have the value of broadness and universality to delight the hearts of ecumenists and synthesizers of comparative religions, but they have no power to save a people for whom a sense of special identity, vocation and destiny is the minimal threshold for survival.'[19]

However, as we have seen, the particularity of this experience carries within itself the synthesis of 'And why not every man?' If black theology wants to do justice to this universal dimension, then, however respectable this may be in itself in the light of traumatic events, it cannot simply be a theology of its own survival. Particularity and universality stand over against each other in a relationship of tension. Precisely the deep involvement in its own history impels black theology beyond itself to a commitment which is directed to the whole of human history – and precisely in this involvement in the whole lies the difference between liberation theology and survival theology.[20]

We find the universal dimension clearly expressed in the important declaration 'Black Theology in 1976', made by the theological commission of the National Conference of Black Churchmen:[21] 'Black Theology seeks to interpret the world-wide revolution against inhumanity, exploitation and oppression in which black people have played a major role and which is the work of Jesus Christ, and the mission of his church.' This world-wide perspective makes black theology an inclusive, ecumenical theology of liberation. It is exclusive in so far as it denies the right to exist of a Christian theology which trivializes, justifies the existing forms of oppression or keeps silent about them; for it the gospel is at heart a movement of liberation. Therefore it cannot accept – without contradicting itself – simply being regarded as a variant determined by a situation, perhaps legitimate or perhaps not – of another, obviously normative way of doing theology. Theology is only possible as a liberating science; the genitive in the expression 'theology of liberation' is not an indication of a particular variant but as it were an explicative genitive, which explains what any theology needs to be about. It is inclusive to the degree that in its specific struggle against racial oppression it anticipates a world in which the oppositions of race, class and sex are done away with, in the knowledge that no person is free until all are free.'[22]

2. *Context and ecumenism*

The tension between particularity and universality, so characteristic of true liberation theology, calls for space: it needs a place where it can manifest itself and, as Wolfgang Huber rightly asserts,[23] this place is ecumenism. Thus the relationship between particularity and universality can be transposed into the dialectic of context and ecumenism.

This statement calls for some explanation. The question of a 'contextual theology' came into being especially (but not exclusively) in the traditional missionary areas where Christians discovered the degree to which the communication of Western theology alienated them from their own culture, their own people and the struggle for liberation from (neo)colonial domination. However, contextual theology is not an attempt at the indigenization (domesticizing) of Western religious thought and concepts;[24] in this last case the Western tradition remains normative and it is always a matter of applying it to particular autochthonous cultures. By contrast, for contextual theology both the legitimation and the continuity of this tradition have become an acute problem; it discerns a totalizing tendency behind the claim to universal validity which comes close to a contempt for and marginalization of the experiences of others. Theology which is not aware of its contextual determination seems not to take account of experiences of faith from outside its own context, and to this degree does not arrive at real dialogue.

What does the contextuality of theology set over against this? At least mention needs to be made of an awareness of the determination of theological questions and positions by factors of a social nature. However, of itself that is insufficient. Contextuality is a matter of hermeneutics: it is a matter of integrating the structures of theological discourse in such a way that the conditions are present for mutual questioning and appeals.[25] Therefore a confrontation is needed between human experiences and practices from different contexts: without living dialogue theological dialectic comes to a halt, no matter how profoundly it is carried on, and becomes sterile rationalism.[26] However, the ability to take on and to integrate the experience of others is the task *par excellence* of ecumenical reflection,[27] – though it is important to note that the modern ecumenical movement, after seventy-five years, is still at the beginning of such a learning process. It is therefore a peculiar misunderstanding to suppose that the contextuality of theology forms a threat to ecumenism. The opposite is the case: only contextual theology can really be ecumenical, just a true ecumenical theology has a contextual structure.

In black theology the connection between context and ecumene is quite clear. Its context is the struggle against any form of racial oppression (cultural, psychological, economic, etc.) and in particular the struggle against racism that manifests itself in church and theology. This commitment makes black theology a contextual theology which is allergic to a cheap ecumenism[28] that is fixated on the dangerous illusion of an ecclesiastical ideal of unity in a divided world, and by avoiding the problem of the interweaving of theological and social conflicts reduces this ideal to the overcoming of the classical confessional differences. However, this allergy does not mean that black theology has no eye for the importance of the struggle for unity between church denominations; as the 1976 declaration mentioned earlier put it, this struggle is legitimate provided that it is in the service of a wider unity 'in which the restructuring of power relations in church and society and the liberation of the poor and oppressed will be recognized as the first priority of mission'.[29]

The connection between context and ecumenism in black theology is contoured. Different levels can be distinguished. From its position of conflict black theology must be very much on its guard against the danger of being incapsulated by white churches and Christians.

It cannot allow itself any unqualified ecumenical verve and therefore needs to choose its priorities clearly. This choice involves our being able to distinguish three different levels in its ecumenical activities. In the connection between these levels which I shall summarize below, the dialectic between context and ecumenism which I mentioned earlier comes to light.

1. The first level is black ecumenism. The 1976 declaration describes this primary form of ecumenism as the union of all black Christians, Protestant and Catholics, in one church which comprises the totality of the black religious experience and history.[30] However, black ecumenism is not only an affair of the institutional church; it extends over the whole of the black community and also over those who, while standing outside the institutional church, do not yet find themselves outside the sphere of God's revelation and grace. A characteristic of black theology is that at the same time it stubbornly maintains a close tie with Africa and with the descendants of black slaves in Latin America and the Caribbean. The communal experience of white racism and colonialism – black people in the United States often regard themselves as an 'internal colony' – is an important element here, but just as important is the conviction that black religion has its roots in Africa. Collaboration with colleagues on the African continent in investigating these communal roots therefore has high priority.[31] However, black ecumenism is not an end in itself. In 1972 Cone and Wilmore wrote in *Pro Veritate*, the paper of the now banned Christian Institute in South Africa: 'It is not too much to believe that God wills to use the churches of Africa and Black America to give the sublimity and spiritual depth to that historical process that will make it minister to the humanization and redemption of the world.'[32]

2. Closely related to black ecumenism is a series of activities which we could sum up under the term peripheral ecumenism.[33] This relates to the discussions and contacts, which are becoming increasingly intensive, both with church basic groups and theologians in Asia and Latin America and with marginalized minorities in their own land. Peripheral ecumenism is the reciprocal recognition of and bond between an alliance of groups of Christians who beyond the limits of divergent situations of poverty and repression form an alliance against the fate that is allotted them by the centres of power in this world.

It took some years before black theologians were in a position to look beyond the opposition between white and black in American society and see the wider context of their struggle. In this respect the 1975 Detroit conference is a small breakthrough. A number of projects arose out of this encounter between theologians from North and South America, of which the establishment of the Ecumenical Association of Third World Theologians (abbreviated to EATWOT) is the most important.[34] Since then the preoccupation of black theologians with white racism has certainly not diminished, but greater openness has developed towards the reality of the class struggle and sexism, and towards the associated questions of social analysis.

3. A misunderstanding as trivial as it is current sees ecumenical affinity and sharp polemic as incompatible. Anyone who holds this view will have difficulty in describing the relationship of black theologians with white churches and Christians as ecumenical. The approach of black theology was uncommonly aggressive: the 'Black Manifesto' (April 1969), expressly supported by black theologians,[35] is a fierce attack on the racism of the American churches, while the polemical force of Cone's *Black Theology and Black Power* was only equalled in the recent history of theology by some tractates from another born polemicist, Karl Barth. Can ecumenism be polemical?

In the first impression of *Romans* (1919) Barth writes the remarkable sentence, 'Polemic is love'.[36] Polemic as a way of taking seriously the specific action of another person is an expression of solidarity. This insight is not based primarily on psychological or sociological perception, but in Barth has an eminently theological character. The expression quoted comes in the context of his reading of Rom.9-11, which for him is the *locus classicus* of the doctrine of predestination![37] The church proclaims the partisan nature of God's love and grace as revealed in Christ. This electing and rejecting love is, however, directed against the church where this constantly forgets that God's love is concerned with the world and where in religious *hybris* it annexes God and plays him off against the world. The light of God shines from the darkness – but it is the predestined champions of God in particular who have all kinds of internal and external testimonies to themselves who are not its vehicles.[38] Where the church is constantly the grave of biblical truth, polemical solidarity with it is the only way. 'Everything that we perceive of the righteousness of God, of the victory of life, of grace, of freedom of the Spirit, is none other than the churches' own message, but it is the church which must feel that this message is directed against itself if it understands it at all.'[39]

These thoughts from *Romans* are extremely important if we want to understand how polemic can function as ecumenical activity *par excellence*. They have nothing to do with polarizing pedanticism; in the last instance it is a matter in which *all* are involved. Ecumenism as polemic is not a matter of playing off the one standpoint against the other, the one trend against the other, the one party against the other, the good guys against the bad guys, but expresses the fundamental contradiction in which all are involved (though not in the same way) and in which the *ecclesia catholica* is involved as a whole. We can formulate this conflict, using Barth's words from 1919, in the following way. 'That what the church means is something quite alien to the church.'[40]

The essential function of polemic in ecumenical dialogue is constantly to bring to light again the unpleasant truth of this fundamental contradiction, a truth which is constantly repressed because it anxiously relativizes and questions whatever ecumenical consensus has been reached (usually by means of the question *cui bono?*). However, this can never happen in general terms. Generalized criticism of religion and the church is meaningless and cheap. Real polemic is always concrete and specific. The criterion for its ecumenical content is whether it is essentially dialogical and gives its target room for manoeuvre; it disqualifies itself as soon as it shows a tendency to take its opponent's breath away, to force him out, to reduce him and make him an object. Ecumenism as polemic uses the vocative; it addresses, challenges, appeals, makes claims, gives responsibility – and here those who engage in polemic do not hide away in a bunker of church authority or academic status, but lay themselves open, make themselves vulnerable, put themselves alongside, not above, the opponent.[41]

Seen in this perspective the polemical dialogue of black theology with churches characterized as white and their theologians is an ecumenical action of the first order. Black polemic has a threefold function. In the first place it is a form of self-liberation. Above all Cone's first two books, *Black Theology and Black Power* and *A Black Theology of Liberation*, functioned in this way; black anger here functions as an affirmation of the courage to be in a theological world dominated by whites, as a process of purification to rid oneself of direct dependence on white theological teachers.[42] In the second place the polemic is a necessary means of bringing to light the heretical practice of hidden racism. By far the majority of theologians in Europe and America have no intention of being racist. On the contrary, they reject racist theories, and their attitude to blacks is in general not lacking in good will.[43] But it is precisely this good will that forms the great obstacle which can only be got out of the way through harsh polemic. At all events, it gives an excuse for washing the hands in innocence: for them racism is no problem! Here black theologians find themselves in a position which is comparable to that of women:[44] both groups see themselves confronted with what C.Eric Lincoln has described as the 'theology of benign neglect',[45] both encounter a failure to understand their spiritual right to existence, a failure which is not confessed openly but is deeply rooted in the structure of theological discourse.[46] Black polemic is therefore an instrument, a strategic weapon for breaking open the closedness of this argument and making room for the question of the theological relevance of black experience and history. The latter is the crucial point because on the basis of their experience of slavery and exodus, blacks should be able to have something to say theologically which has not yet got through to seminaries and universities.

However, the two functions mentioned above do not stand on their own; both are embedded in a third, specifically ecumenical task: black polemic is a means of bringing out the unity and credibility of the church as a whole. Wilmore rightly points out the significance of black theology for the mission of the whole church: 'The true significance of this theology for the mission of the whole Church of Christ is that it is unmasking the sin of Western Christianity…'[47] Far from sowing new divisions, black theology unmasks one of the most stubborn barriers on the way to unity, the colour barrier; far from stigmatizing white Christians and reducing them to the colour of their skin, it confronts Christianity as it is with its complicity in a centuries-long practice of white racism – a complicity which goes so deep that it cannot be dismissed as one of the unavoidable contradictions from which the church as a historical phenomenon now suffers. Black polemic confronts us with the truth – in its specific way, in connection with a specific matter – that Christianity is a contradiction, not only in terms, but really and historically.

Under the impact of the criticism of black and other liberation theologians, the British theologian David E.Jenkins has written an attractive if in some respects vulnerable study of *The Contradiction of Christianity*. In it he rightly argues that real Christianity is formed by what Christians do or are in reality; this historical-empirical reality may not be avoided by, for example, making an idealistic distinction between the invisible church as true church and the visible church institutions: 'If these historical existences, events and institutions are of such a quality that they contradict the claims, hopes and visions which are stated to be both the basis for and the aims of Christian believing, then Christianity is, in fact, contradicted.'[48] Seeing it from the perspective of this contradiction does not mean, according to Jenkins, playing with a verbal problem but the recognition of the real possibility of living with a lie.[49]

Does this sober pragmatism mean that contradiction must be the last word in theology? The basic thesis of Jenkins' book is that however seriously we take the contradiction of Christianity and in so doing use Marxist analysis and criticism, at the same time we must maintain that God, in and through Jesus, is at work and speaks precisely in and through this contradiction: 'The Transcendence is in the midst.'[50]

Of course the contradiction of Christianity cannot be the final perspective for any form of liberating theology. But despite his pragmatic intentions, does not David Jenkins express himself too much in speculative and philosophical terms when he says that God makes himself known in the midst of oppositions and conflicts? The problematical feature of his argument lies, in terms of biblical theology, in the unsophistiated use of the word 'midst'. If Moltmann is right in his observation that the sayings of Jesus about 'the least of my brothers' (Matt.25.31-46) belong in ecclesiology, despite their significance for Christian ethics,[51] then we are not referred to the midst but to the periphery, to the struggle for naked existence. There, on the underside of history where the Son of Man truly identifies himself with the least of his brothers and sisters, is the place where the contradiction is removed. *Ubi Christus, ibi Ecclesia*.

The confrontation with black theology here represents an enormous positive challenge. Its polemic has a positive side, 'Polemic is love'. In its unmasking of the contradiction of Christianity there is a plea for conversion, *metanoia*, for a radical transformation of perspective, which leads to the domain of the hidden history, the history which, judged by the usual church norms, belongs rather in the history of heresy.[52] Black theology wants to argue from this specific history extending from the invisible church of the time of slavery to the many-coloured variety of the black churches, cults and sects in contemporary America that here, despite all human ambiguity and misery, there is a glimpse of liberation, of the great light that shines over those who live in a land of deep darkness (Isa.9.1; cf. John 1.5).

During the Fourth Assembly of the World Council of Churches at Uppsala in 1968 James Baldwin, once a black preacher, gave an address in which more sharply than ever before he unmasked the complicity of the churches in white racism. However, he began with these words: '...though I may have to say some rather difficult things here this afternoon, I want to make it understood that in the heart of the absolutely necessary accusation there is contained a plea. The plea was articulated by Jesus Christ himself, who said, "Insofar as you have done it unto the least of these, you have done it unto me".'[53]

3. Ecumenism as a place of challenge and response

It has become clear from what I have just said that black theology, because of its own tension between particularity and universality, is directed towards ecumenism. By ecumenism I mean the structured mutual communication of churches and Christian communities at a local, national and international level. Ecumenism in its different forms is the place where the challenge of black theology must find an answer.

But it makes a difference whether we speak of ecumenism as an ideal or as concrete reality. Does ecumenism as it is provide room for the critical questions which black theology has to put about the complicity of church and theology in racial oppression? Is there within the different ecumenical organs room for the awareness that it is the churches themselves (always in new ways!) which, far from being a preliminary embodiment of the coming messianic reality, are an obstacle to ecumenism to come (Heb.2.5). Whether it makes sense to speak of the world (ecumene) as a place of challenge and response depends on the answer to these questions.

The ecumenical movement in modern times became concerned about the 'race problem' relatively early. In 1924, in his book

Christianity and the Race Problem,[54] which is still worth reading, J.H.Oldham analysed the racial question in terms of its moral causes – although the author was certainly not blind to the economic and political roots of racism. Oldham saw in the church as a universal brotherhood at least a potential counter force. We can find the ethical and church idealism of this ecumenical pioneer in the numerous declarations in which the ecumenical movement since the 1920s has condemned racial segregation and racial oppression.

Although there is certainly a concern for the church's involvement in all kinds of racism, the accent in the declarations lies on the importance of a unanimous and clear witness of the church towards the world. The formulations express what the church should do or be to outsiders without, however, plumbing to the depths the conflicts in which the churches themselves are entangled. Insight into the church's own involvement needed a lengthy process of growth.

However, the disappointing effect of the strategy of contacts, consultations and declarations has done its work as far as this is concerned. It is gradually beginning to penetrate through to the ecumenical consciousness how much the world church itself is riddled with and divided by racism. One bitter experience was the consultation in Cottesloe in December 1960 which was the occasion for the three Afrikaans-speaking churches in South Africa to leave the World Council of Churches.[55] However, it was above all the voices of those who suffer under racism which at the time of the Fourth Assembly in Uppsala in 1968 made the World Council of Churches resolve on the institution of a programme of action which was also prompted by the desire to take seriously and penitently the responsibility of churches and individual Christians for racial oppression.

Apart from the charisma of black leaders like Albert Luthuli and Martin Luther King, which worked as a catalyst on the resolution to go over to action, the direct confrontation with black anger and black power also had its effect. The words of James Baldwin in Uppsala cannot be blotted from the memory of those who heard them: 'I tremble when I wonder if there is left in the Christian civilizations (and only these civilizations can answer this question – I cannot) the moral energy, the spiritual daring, to atone, to repent, to be born again!'[56] The intervention of black militant leaders at the time of the Notting Hill consultation in 1969 made just as great an impression; their Declaration of Revolution in which the churches were asked for $500 million reparations (following the 'Black Manifesto' by James Forman) led after an intense and often heated debate to one of the most important undertakings of the Programme to Combat Racism which began in 1969: the institution of the special fund to support liberation movements in Southern Africa and elsewhere.[57]

The origin of the Programme to Combat Racism is an important sign that the ecumencial movement has understood how much racism devours the churches themselves, their unity and credibility, to the marrow. From the beginning the programme encountered fierce opposition within the member churches of the World Council, and that is in itself a sign that the struggle against racism is not just a struggle which the churches carry on outside themselves but a struggle which takes place right within them. Although in past years mistakes in judgment and communication have been made, the power of the programme lies in the fact that to an increasing degree, in the formation of resolutions, people have allowed themselves to be guided by those who experience racism every day of their lives. It is only because of this that since 1968 with relatively little money and personnel so much has happened, not only in terms of action but also at the level of theorizing (which some people underestimate). This theorizing relates both to the question of racism as a social phenomenon and also to theological reflection on it. It is worth going more closely into both these aspects.

In past years a deeper insight has arisen into the complex character of racism. The practical experience of the Programme to Combat Racism is in this respect a hard but thorough school. At the consultation over the struggle against racism in the 1980s, held in Noordwijkerhout in June 1980, clear suspicion could be detected of attempts to define the phenomenon of racism in general terms. In practice definitions all too often seem to be dangerous reductions. The Uppsala Assembly could still give the following description of racism.

By racism we mean ethnocentric pride in one's own racial group and preference for the distinctive characteristics of that group; belief that these characteristics are fundamentally biological in nature and are thus transmitted to succeeding generations; strong negative feelings towards other groups who do not share these characteristics coupled with the thrust to discriminate against and exclude the outgroup from full participation in the life of the community.[58]

If this description, which is akin to the 1967 UNESCO declaration, puts all the stress on the attitude and the relational behaviour of groups and individuals, the experience of past years has taught us that racism comprises much more. Uppsala limits racism to an ethical problem which takes place at the level of prejudice and deliberate discriminatory behaviour. Without doubt racism is also that! Although people in Uppsala also had an eye to the economic causes, that is not expressed in the definition. By contrast Noordwijkerhout saw racism first of all as a system of oppression and domination by which all social attitudes and institutions are affected. As the Noordwijkerhout declaration points out, however essential individual change and commitment may be, the greatest suffering of the greatest number of people day by day is caused by institutional racism.[59]

The term 'institutional racism' came into vogue as a result of a book by Stokely Carmichael and Charles Hamilton entitled *Black Power*, published in 1967,[60] which distinguishes institutional racism from individual racism. Institutional racism relates to the fact that racism is embedded in the structures of society, in education, housing, professional life and pronouncements of justice. In the practice of the struggle against racism the discovery was made that precisely this institutional character makes it an amazingly tough and almost ineradicable phenomenon which is constantly spreading on a world scale. Especially the experiences of people in South Africa have made it inescapably clear that racism has an economic basis.

All these experiences have led the Council to call member churches to base strategies for challenging racism on contextual analyses and theories. For the moment there is no all-embracing description of racism which does justice to its complex character.

Without doubt the lack of an accurate descriptive term raises problems. The risk is that the word racism begins by designating everything and ends up by denoting nothing. On the other hand the danger of the reductive affect of definitions is at least as great. The council of Noordwijkerhout tried to go between Scylla and

Charybdis by putting the emphasis on a contextual approach: making use of experience and knowledge gained in an ecumenical context, there will be a constant need to discover afresh in one's own situation where and in what forms racial oppression takes place.[61]

If in past years a growing sense has arisen of the world-embracing, all-permeating nature of racism, the Programme to Combat Racism has not left theological thought untouched either. At the beginning of the ecumenical movement theological statements about racism tended to be general and statements of principle: racial discrimination as such was put to shame and rejected as moral heresy; the unity of the human race founded on Christ was confessed, and in obedience to the gospel the churches were to banish the evil of racial prejudice and racial oppression from their midst. However, after 1968, in the emotional discussions over the Programme to Combat Racism, more specific ethical and dogmatic questions arose like that about the right to rebel, the use of violent means for liberation and the relationship between liberation and reconciliation.

Less spectacular, but no less fascinating or controversial, are the questions raised by the struggle against racism about the unity of the church, which when all is said and done is the basis of ecumenism. These questions concern 1. the relationship between cultural identity and identity in Christ (does Gal.2.20, 'I live, yet not I but Christ lives in me', leave room for a legitimate difference of cultural identity within the one church?); 2. the necessity of a church order which makes room for the tensions and conflicts within the church; 3. the urgency of a church discipline which is exercised not only over church doctrine but also over eucharistic practice (can a notorious racist take part in the eucharist?) and over the ecumenical community (can racist churches be members of the World Council?); 4. the need, given the limited value of theological generalizations, to get further via interdisciplinary collaboration.[62]

All these matters were discussed explicitly in Louvain, where in 1971 Faith and Order, the theological division of the World Council, held its assembly. It is important to note that there is reflection about these implications of the struggle against racism in the framework of the main theme of Louvain, 'The Unity of the Church and the Unity of Mankind'. Ernst Lange, the German theologian who until his death in 1974 was deeply involved in ecumenical affairs, wrote a fine book about this conference in which he noted that this theme was in fact presented to Faith and Order by a changed situation of the ecumenical movement in the modern world, 'in which the play with possibilities must be taken increasingly seriously, because serious attention is paid to this world and to the church in the world'.[63] The beginning of the Programme to Combat Racism, important though it may be in itself, is only one of the many symptoms from which this changed situation can be read.

The new thing about Louvain was that for the first time in the history of Faith and Order the old familiar questions of church unity and identity were put in the context of the oppositions and conflicts which cause havoc in the present-day world and set at risk the ongoing existence of humanity. As a result of these the theme of unity suddenly came to stand in a new and to some degree unusual light. Hitherto the questions and methods of Faith and Order had been 'strictly theological', in other words directed towards what was offered by scripture and tradition; in this approach 'the world' appeared in the first place as something 'over against', as the place where the church has to demonstrate its calling, witness and unity. To a large degree the fact that the churches are part of conflictual reality, indeed that they produce and reproduce it from day to day, remains outside the field of vision – and as a result so do the ideological-critical questions which churches and their theologians could put to themselves in this connection.

What brought about this shift in problems at Louvain? Ernst Lange makes some important comments here: 'The source of the compulsion to set the old theme in a new context was a changed concept of the Church. The question of the nature of the Church receded into the background and the question of the Church's *function* came to the fore.'[64]

This functionalizing of the concept of the church is a matter of far-reaching importance. It makes it possible, at least in embryo, to raise the ideological-critical question of the partisan involvement of churches and individual Christians in the conflicts and oppositions in the world. In other words, it makes these conflicts ecclesiologically relevant.[65] It takes account of the fact that – difficult though this may be for some traditions of faith to grasp – the truth and unity given in Christ comes to us shattered, broken and fragmented from reality and the real experiences that we have. If we follow Lange's interpretation, then this was the concern at Louvain. What seems such a static theme, 'The Unity of the Church and the Unity of

Mankind', in fact concealed a search for a much-needed theory of ecumenical action,[66] a connection between the soteriological existence of the church and its actual functioning, a creative combination of action and reflection, and a mutual relationship between analyses of contemporary situations of conflict and stories, insights and symbols handed down by Christian traditions. On a factual basis, at Louvain people looked for a way of doing theology in which context and ecumenism are dialectically related.

The ecumenical movement would not be itself had it not tried to capture this shift of perspective and awareness of the problem in a particular concept. The concept which was used here was conciliarity or conciliar fellowship. In fact this was not a new concept. Conciliarity functioned as a key concept in studies which Faith and Order had undertaken since 1961 of the ecumenical significance of the councils of the early church. Since Uppsala the word has had a double significance: on the one hand conciliarity refers to a constant structure in the life of the church; on the other hand this concept points to an 'event which perhaps will take place on a given day'.[67] This second line is stressed above all in Faith and Order by Eastern Orthodox and Roman Catholic theologians: for them conciliarity lies in a distant (utopian?) future; it is an aspect of the real consummation of unity; the ecumenical movement in its present form is at best to be seen as a pre-conciliar fellowship.[68]

At the Louvain gathering, however, for the moment the first line gained the upper hand. The tendencies towards democratization from the 1960s which did not leave even the churches untouched, the increasing criticism from the Third World of the Eurocentrism of theology and mission, the fierce discussions about the use of force by particular liberation movements and the churches' attitude towards them – these and other factors call for an ecclesiological model which leaves room for difference, tension and conflict. Wolfgang Huber expresses it in this way: 'The concept of conciliarity comes to a focus in the fact that it is to represent a model of the church's task of engaging in conflict which is in accord with the existence of the church.'[69] Conciliar fellowship is a structure of communication which cannot and may not be limited to questions of a confessional nature.

Sadly, the dynamic which the term conciliarity was given in Louvain was largely lost in subsequent years. At the moment conciliar fellowship is regarded above all as the continuation and restructuring of the unity given in Christ and in the tradition.[70]

However, that is far from being the whole story. An awareness of the problem, once aroused, cannot so easily be repressed. That the spirit of Louvain, as interpreted by Ernst Lange, is continuing, is evident for example from the report of a consultation on racism and theology which was held in Geneva in 1975 under the presidency of Gayraud Wilmore. At this consultation organized by Faith and Order and the Programme to Combat Racism people tried to think through the implications of racism for ecclesiology. In this report the church was seen as a fellowship which takes discipleship of Christ with radical seriousness and gives form to this discipleship in a disciplined life which constantly tries to group and regroup itself around suffering.[71] The venture of this new description of being the church is backed by a deep sense of church and theological involvement in racial exploitation.

The interesting thing about this embryonic ecclesiology is that the description of the church as regrouping around suffering to some degree continues what was said in Louvain about conciliarity: 'In the life of the church each human community must have the occasion to develop and express its own authentic self: the oppressed and exploited must be able to struggle for justice, the marginals of society – the spiritually and physically handicapped – must be able to make their own distinctive contributions.'[72] At the same time the ecclesiological approach of the Geneva consultation already seems to be moving in the direction of the concept of the 'church of the poor' which was developed at the end of the 1970s by the CCPD (Commission on the Churches' Participation in Development). Although the precise content of this concept is disputed – it would lead us too far afield to go into that now[73] – at all events in terms of the 1975 Geneva report there is mention of 'the Church's constant effort to regroup and reconstitute itself in situations of real suffering, where suffering is the deepest expression of the struggle for human freedom and reconciliation'.[74]

If this observation is correct, it would support Hoedemaker's view that the two ecclesiological models which at present are often played off against each other in ecumenical discussion – conciliar fellowship and church of the poor – can be related in a fruitful way.[75] Such a development is particularly necessary because within the ecumenical movement the theological reflection on racism has stagnated in recent years. Much can be pointed to in the 1975 report which still needs closer working out and support. To mention only one thing: the report speaks about the relationship between theological conceptions and racist practices: in this connection it mentions (*a*) the way in which notions like the people of God, election and predestination are taken over by the Western concern for expansion; (*b*) a fundamentalist doctrine of creation which presupposes inequality between races as natural; (*c*) the adaptation of Jesus of Nazareth to the picture of Western, white man; (*d*) an individualist conception of salvation.[76] However, it must be clear that such summary indications cannot be enough. To go further, thorough interdisciplinary investigations, i.e. investigations with a well-thought-out methodology, must be made into the way in which theological arguments have functioned and still function in the history of white domination. Neither Faith and Order nor the Programme to Combat Racism have so far started on such a study project.

Moreover the 1980 consultation in Noordwijkerhout, which I have already mentioned, does not provide any new perspectives on the relationship between racism and theology either. Certainly the working group which was concerned with this made a plea for contextual theology. Although the wording may not always be happy, this text demonstrates in an unmistakable way that the terms 'contextual' and 'ecumenical' presuppose each other.

> Contextual theology is pluralist by its very method. Since specific historical and cultural contexts will yield only partial theological reflections, they will need to be correlated with each other within the worldwide Church. This process of mutual learning and correction will yield a truly ecumenical vision.[77]

In this quotation two things are said which we must keep together anyway: 1. that contextual theology is a method of theologizing which is aware of the specific historical and cultural contexts in which it is involved, and senses that it is directed to the experiences and reflections of others; 2. that ecumenism is a communication structure of mutual learning and correction. The combination of both insights makes it possible to get through to the key question which has concerned us in this chapter: that of the *Sitz im Leben* of a conversation with black theology.

Beyond question black theology offers no more than a partial theological reflection. It makes no claims to totality. In this respect it is comparable to forms of regional theology (Asiatic, African, etc.) and to feminist theology. Black theology came into being in a specific situation born of a specific need, and in its reflections eveything turns on the specific question of the significance of the gospel for people who suffer under racism.

However, in the first part of this chapter we have seen how the partisan commitment of black theology is directed towards the whole: the particularity of its struggle includes the universality of 'And why not every man?' Like any other theology of liberation, black theology is an ecumenical theology *par excellence* which derives its vitality from the tension between particularity and universality. The *locus* of a dialogue with black theology is therefore ecumenism regarded as the conciliar fellowship in which tensions, oppositions and conflicts which really exist are stated, maintained and fought over in expectation of the presence of the Holy Spirit.

To find an answer to the question how far ecumenism in reality is the appopriate place for a dialogue with black theology I have gone into some aspects of the recent history of the World Council of Churches. Our conclusion must be that in this organization, as also in other ecumenical institutions and associations, conflicting tendencies are at work which mean that ecumenism can be the hermeneutical *locus* of real encounter with forms of liberation theology only on certain conditions. Laying down these conditions means that I would reject certain tendencies within present-day ecumenical practice and support others; in other words showing that ecumenism is a hermeneutical *locus* is in itself the choice of a position *vis à vis* the question of the identity of the ecumenical movement.

The conditions which in my view must be laid down are as follows: 1. ecumenism must be taken seriously as the world church 'by which is meant that in the building up of local communities people must also let themselves be guided by experiences and questions from elsewhere as these are communicated in the ecumenical movement';[78] 2. despite the statement of the Fifth Assembly of the World Council in Nairobi in which it is said, 'The one Church is to be envisioned as a conciliar fellowship of local churches which are themselves truly united', 'conciliar fellowship' must be a designation of an ecclesiological structure in which, as seems to have happened in Louvain, social oppositions and conflicts take on significance for the church; 3. although the concept of the church of the poor has raised questions from various sides, especially also in Asia, the perspective given by this idea must not be lost: that real unity – and at the same time that means real *koinonia* – must be initiated from the other side of history. Only on these conditions can the context of the dialogue with black theology be situated at the level of conciliar fellowship and the church of the poor.

PART TWO

Black Theology
and Its Historical Context

3 · Break and Continuity

Without doubt critics of black theology are right when they use terms like 'fragmentary' and 'one-sided' in their verdict. A superficial look at existing publications is enough to confirm this judgment. The one-sided preoccupation with the theme of suffering and oppression, liberation and reconciliation springs to mind, while there is no mention of any ecclesiology worked out to any degree,[1] or of trinitarian doctrine. The difficulty with this criticism does not lie in the observation of one-sidedness as such but in the motives which underlie it. All too often the one-sidedness, which is evaluated in a negative way, is measured by a tacitly presupposed normativity which is not discussed further, and which is derived from the direction or tradition to which the person himself belongs.[2]

This overlooks the fact that it is this very tradition which is put in question by black theologians because of its white one-sidedness! If this fact alone must give rise to some caution, in addition there is the fact that people *a priori* deny black theology a right which is granted without question to the great names in the history of Christianity. Who now objects to the one-sidedness of Augustine's *Confessions*, of Luther's polemical writings or Barth's *Epistle to the Romans*? In theology there seems to be something like a right to one-sidedness: there is room for thought which gives itself completely to the demands of the hour, to what must be said with all force and clarity in obedience to the gospel in a particular set of historical circumstances.

In itself one-sidedness cannot be a reason for distancing oneself from a particular kind of theological thought. More essential is the question whether and to what extent this thought is aware of its inevitable one-sidedness. If it really speaks to the historical moment of which it forms a part, then it has to give full account of its own historicity and the one-sidedness which is bound up with it – and this awareness is itself a condition of a truly dialectical way of thinking which stands under the sign of its own provisionality and realizes that other things need to be said at other times and places.[3] By contrast, what causes real problems is theological thought which does not recognize its own one-sidedness and provisionality; in that case one-sidedness simply means short-sightedness.

As we saw,[4] black theology represents a contextual form of doing theology which is aware of its 'one-sidedness'. 'The movement will be from the particular to the universal,' says J.Deotis Roberts,[5] who was himself involved in this movement from the beginning. Any attempt to place or criticize the phenomenon of black theology needs to take into account its contextual character. The movement does not take place in a vacuum but is part of a historical moment: the black struggle against racism in contemporary American society. This element determines its specific commitment and dynamic. Black theology does not tolerate an abstract and systematic discussion. Its 'situated' character calls first of all for a historical and biographical approach: it has a history which has to be known before analysis and evaluation of separate texts make sense. In other words, knowledge of the context is a first condition for understanding the text itself.

So in this chapter we shall first discuss the historical background of the civil rights struggle and the rise of Black Power; this turbulent period from the 1960s forms the direct context of the development of black theology. The story of this development itself, which took place between 1966 and 1969, forms the second part of the chapter. Finally, the third section describes the beginning of the exodus of black theology from slavery to what were experienced as 'white' ways of theological thinking, theories and symbols.

This account as a whole in fact itself raises questions which need further investigation: if theology is to be understood to mean this discipline which in some way expresses God, what experience of God is articulated by black theology? What epistemological and methodological implications does thinking through this specific experience have? What relationship does it have to the context of the black struggle? What are the ultimate consequences of the relationship for white churches and theologians?

Such questions will have to occupy us further, as they also came up in the first part of this book. This chapter in fact serves as the hinge which connects the first and last parts of the book. The formal and hermeneutical questions of the first part could not be done justice to here without constant reaching forward to the content of the black story; in the discussion in the next chapters of the various positions and discussions of black theologians, we shall constantly be referred back to the direct context of their story. The account of break and continuity therefore forms the centre between the more static, formal part which comes first and the more reportive part, focussed directly on a conversation with black theology.

1. Black revolt or revolution?

The origin of black theology goes back to the events of 1966 when the civil rights movement split and Black Power appeared. On 6 June of that year James Meredith was shot on his solitary demonstration, a march from the city of Memphis, Tennessee, to Jackson, Mississippi. The journey along Highway 51, in the deep South, was continued by a group of black leaders including Martin Luther King of SCLC (Southern Christian Leadership Conference), Stokely Carmichael of SNCC (Student Nonviolent Coordinating Committee) and Floyd McKissick of CORE (Congress of Racial Equality). In the evening, during a mass meeting in Greenwood, the underlying tensions of the past years finally came out: the younger leaders, above all of SNCC, rejected non-violence and racial collaboration and raised their fists for Black Power.[6] In a conversation lasting five hours, a disturbed King tried in vain to persuade Carmichael and McKissick to change their minds. Carmichael's reply was that the conflict between violence and non-violence was irrelevant; the real problem for blacks was the need to combine the political and economic resources at their disposal in order to gain power.[7]

From that day on there was a choice between 'Freedom Now', the slogan of King and his followers, and Black Power. Black church leaders were put under pressure from the white churches to condemn Black Power as conflicting with Christian belief. However, on 31 July a long declaration appeared in the *New York Times*, inserted by a group of representatives of the black churches who presented themselves as the National Committee of Negro Churchmen[8] which clearly, though in moderate language, backed Black Power. The historical significance of this whole-page advertisement lay in its deliberate farewell to the dominant white ethical and theological consensus over the racial problem in America: as such – as one of those behind it, G.S.Wilmore, could rightly say later – it created an ideological and institutional basis for what some time later, in 1969, was to be called black theology.[9]

In historical terms black theology thus originated from the break between Freedom Now and Black Power. As we shall see later, this origin deeply determined the nature of its questions, thoughts and arguments, at any rate during the first phase of its existence. Here we are confronted with the need first of all to understand the complex dynamic and the inner tension of a social and political movement which towards the middle of the 1960s grew to be the main force of opposition in American society.[10]

(a) White supremacy: power and powerlessness

The civil rights movement was born in the deep South: 'All my life the race problem had been as close as the beating of my heart, circumscribing my thoughts, my actions, my feelings.'[11] This sentence from the autobiography of Benjamin Mays, former President of Morehouse College, where Martin Luther King Jr studied, conveys the experience of anyone who had physically experienced the Jim Crow segregation.

This racial system of castes[12] had been introduced in all the Southern states at the end of the previous century and was based on two pillars: apartheid and terror. The earliest youthful memory of Benjamin Mays was a lynch party of a black man by a white mob. Terror lurked everywhere, and together with the all-prevailing system of segregation served the great purpose of 'keeping the nigger down in his place'. The separation of white and black was carried through to the most absurd details: different telephone booths (Oklahoma), different Coca Cola machines (Mississippi), different school books (Florida, North Carolina) and different Bibles for black and white witnesses in law courts (Georgia).[13] In retrospect and seen from outside it is inconceivable that this Manicheistic world should have been able to stand so long – inconceivable, until we think of South Africa where the inconceivable is still daily reality.

Paradoxically enough Mays' words convey not only the experience of black men and women but equally those of the white Southerner. If the white person dominates the life of the black, the converse is also true. Here we come up against the deep element of conflict which characterized the Jim Crow segregation. If this rigid system was a deliberate attempt to make the black an outcast and exclude him from political, economic and cultural life, the effect was in one sense the opposite: 'The negro stands in the middle, everywhere in the South, always recognizable, always present' (Schulte Nordholt[14]). The black politician and writer James Weldon Johnson wrote in 1912 of the white Southerner: 'his life as a man and a citizen, many of his financial activites and all of his political activities are impassably limited by the ever present "negro problem".'[15] Despite the strict segregation the white did not live for a moment without the black.

This contradiction was very much bound up with the rottenness of the myth on which the Jim Crow system rested, the myth of white supremacy. The excessive force, the segregation carried to absurdity, the endless discussions about the 'negro problem' should have been left behind had the black indeed been the inferior childlike being that myth made him. Of course the South had known its Sambos and Uncle Toms, and the system of oppression was strong enough for that; however, the much-discussed inscrutability of the negro[16] betrays the fact that black women and men opposed in every way possible the status of savage, the person without history and culture, which white racism wanted to impose on them – and it was precisely this inscrutability that disarmed the authorities who took refuge in the irrationality of terror and violence. However, any appearance of the Ku Klux Klan, any violation of a black woman, any brutality on the part of the police meant an open unmasking of the rottenness of the myth.

The virulent racism of Jim Crow had a social and psychological side which cannot be understood without taking into account this blatant contradiction in the system. It alone explains the permanent insecurity of the leaders, though they were apparently so powerful. The completely irrational outbursts of violence and lust for power which were not related in any way to the actions of black opposition to which they were usually a reaction betrayed a deep-rooted complex of guilt feelings and anxiety. The white South had a deep horror of the threat of the otherness of people of African origin and it could only rise above this horror by restraining the black way (segregation) or annihilating it (terror).

An illustration of this social and psychological mechanism is the absolute tabu on sexual relations between black men and white women. In his 'skyscraper' (J.Presser) *An American Dilemma*,

Gunnar Myrdal shows how this tabu formed the central element of the whole system of social inequality.[17] Infringement of it was the most serious offence imaginable and caused irrevocable mass hysterical agitation among the white population. Officially the tabu also held for relations between white men and black women; however it was a feature of the folkway of Southern life that many white men had black mistresses. This dual morality in fact amounted to the unequivocal confirmation of their male monopoly of power. Racism and sexism were closely intertwined in this patriarchal power structure – is that not always the case everywhere? – and this sexism affected not only the black woman but also the white. At all events, the romantic glorification of the purity of the white woman, a popular theme in the romantic but puritanical South, functioned in practice as a strait-jacket; she was subject to a strict code in her behaviour and feelings towards men whose skin was a different colour.[18]

This 'protection' of white womanhood was connected with a deep-rooted fear of the attraction of the negro. Even in the time of slavery his supposed sexual aggression and power were a source of constant anxiety and disquiet. How far this picture corresponded to reality was irrelevant; the fear of the black slave as a sexual partner was too deeply rooted in deep layers of irrationality. The historian Winthrop D.Jordan points out that the often excessive fear of slave rebellions had a sexual background: 'One has only to imagine the emotions flooding through some planter who had been more or less regularly sleeping with some of his slave wenches when he suddenly learned of a conspiracy among their counterparts; it was virtually inevitable that his thoughts turn in a torrent of guilt to the safety of his wife.'[19] From the time that white Western civilization created the savage and made the African a 'negro' it had a tendency to project its sexual longings – its suppressed sexual longings – on this figure to whom exceptional virility and promiscuity were attributed. At the end of the eighteenth century European scientific circles were certain that the negro had an abnormally large penis, and this conviction must also soon have found its way on to the plantations of the white colonists.[20] Against this background it become significant that in a number of colonies (North and South Carolina, Virginia, Pennsylvania and New Jersey) castration was the legally prescribed punishment for blacks who struck a white person or tried to escape.[21]

Ideas of progress and development, so characteristic of the still dominant view of history, show an ineradicable tendency to see the history of the black population in America as a laborious but gradual rise from slavery to freedom. In reality the course of this history is of a catastrophic freakishness which suggests the painting called *Angelus Novus* by Paul Klee which Walter Benjamin describes in his theses 'Über den Begriff der Geschichte (On the Concept of History)': where for us a series of events appears, the angel of history sees one single catastrophe which unceasingly heaps one piece of rubble on another.[22] While almost unparalleled inhumanity in history was represented by slavery in the South, studies by Leon Litwack and Ira Berlin[23] show that the free North was equally deeply infected by racism. When the end of the Civil War in 1865 brought the end of almost two hundred years of slavery, despite everything – despite the notorious Black Codes (1865-66),[24] despite the rise of the Ku Klux Klan (1865), despite the failure of Senator Thaddeus Stevens' plan to give land to ex-slaves, forty acres and a mule – a new time had in fact dawned with the Black Reconstruction (1867-1876);[25] however, the introduction of the Jim Crow laws put a drastic end to this illusion: a racist extremism came to power which was no longer curbed by the paternalism[26] of the old planters' class which had been eroded away. The system of segregation was strictly implemented, Schulte Nordholt rightly points out, 'when at the end of the previous century the planters' class lost its power to groups of small middlemen and farmers who were concerned for all kinds of reforms but who saw the negroes as dangerous economic rivals and even more dangerous sexual competitors. "Progressivism for whites only" came into being. The small people who came to power were more concerned, more miserly, more miserable than the planters; they left nothing to chance, but developed a network of laws to regulate every step the negro took.'[27]

However, the end of Reconstruction did not immediately lead to the introduction of segregation. On the contrary, when in the 1880s and 1890s the dominant class of planters and other owners came under pressure from a political movement from below, Populism, for a short time the white lower class sought to enter into an alliance with the black population to break the power of the plantation aristocracy. The recognition of common economic needs and interests seemed capable of overcoming white racism. It was no coincidence that *The Strange Career of Jim Crow*[28] was published in 1955, at the time of the rise of the civil rights movement; in it the influential historian C.Vann Woodward described this period as a time in which blacks and whites in all probability achieved greater political unanimity than ever before or afterwards in the South.[29]

However, from the beginning the Populism of the impoverished white farmers was characterized by two conflicting tendencies: one impelled the movement towards economic and political collaboration with the black farmers, who were equally exploited, and the other was based on white supremacy and led the white farmers to see the blacks as political and economic enemies. The latter tendency eventually gained the upper hand. Once the Populists had lost electoral support almost everywhere (only in North Carolina did they share power with the Republicans for a number of years) they allied themselves with the ruling class and excluded the black population from everything that they wanted to reserve for themselves: transport, education and political power. Frustration over the defeat was expressed in aggression, and the racist ideology of white supremacy seems to have succeeded in concealing and bridging the class conflicts among whites, at the expense of the blacks.

The episode of Southern Populism is a sad but very clear illustration of an experience which black people often had to undergo in American history. Racism, once brought to life, has its own social and political dynamics; it follows a course of its own and forms a social system of its own. Racism, as organized oppression on the basis of racial characteristics (whether supposed or real), is not simply a superficial phenomenon. In this respect an orthodox Marxist approach in which racism is regarded as an ideological by-product of the class struggle which disappears automatically in the dawn of the socialist revolution is inadequate. A static topology of the foundations (economic infrastructure) and superstructure (the legal, political and ideological situation) prevents Marxism from following Gramsci and Althusser(!) in noting the distinctive and underivable function of ideology and its material mode of existence. However, the current idealistic approach seems to fall just as short when it defines racism in terms of prejudice, belief systems,[30] or a set of interrelated values[31] in which groups or individuals rationalize, justify, maintain or further racial inequality. Since despite attention to economic and political factors the starting point remains unchangeably with the thought and action of (groups of) individual subjects who are regarded as autonomous, there is also a dangerous underestimation here of the material mode of existence of racism, and also of its deep roots in the collective unconscious (which is connected with this!).

Over against both these conceptions must be set the insight derived from Gramsci which is put like this by Eugene D.Genovese: 'Once an ideology arises it alters profoundly the material reality and in fact becomes a partially autonomous feature of that reality.'[32] Once an ideology, to use Gramsci's terminology, becomes the 'cement' of the whole block of society, then it exercises this hegemonial function above all through institutions, through education, religion and legislation, through terminology, customs and tabus.[33] In *The World the Slaveholders Made*,[34] Genovese has shown that as their class awareness grew, the slaveholders of the Old South were in a better position to exercise their mastery not just through brute physical oppression but by means of a specific ideology which Genovese calls paternalism. This ideology to a large degree performed what Gramsci sees as one of the specific functions of ideology: presenting reality as a unity and denying the existence of social conflicts. In the paternalistic view the relationship between master and slave is that between a father and his son who has not (yet) come of age: the father is aware of his responsibilities, strict but just. This paternalism developed above all after the end of slave trade in 1808 and was a stubborn attempt to overcome the fundamental contradiction in the system of chattel slavery. This contradiction arose because it was impossible for slaves to be the passive instruments, completely lacking in will, that the system recognized; it was implied in the impossibility of being at the same time both a human being and a thing. As such it posed an insuperable problem to the slaveholders.[35] However, paradoxically enough, it was precisely the stubborn attempt to overcome this contradiction which made it possible for Southern paternalism to develop into a separate life-style, a specific way of life which comprised the whole of life on plantations and outside and gave it its authoritarian and hierarchical stucture. This feeling for the distinctive power and dynamism of ideology makes it impossible for an eminent historian like Genovese *a priori* to discuss the relationship between class struggle and racial struggle. The way in which these two relate in a particular period can never be ascertained beforehand – except as an extremely complex problem in need of investigation. That also applies to the much-discussed historical question whether racism was the product of slavery or whether, on the contrary, black slavery was made possible by the already existing racism of the colonial powers. In his study *Capitalism and Slavery*, which appeared in 1944, Eric Williams argued that racism was to be seen as the consequence of slavery:[36] 'Here, then, is the origin of Negro slavery. The reason was economic, not racial; it had to do not with the color of the laborer, but the cheapness of the labor. As compared with Indian and white labor, Negro slavery was eminently superior.'[37] However, studies by David Brion Davis and Winthrop D.Jordan show that ethnocentrism and racialist prejudices already existed before the time of black slavery and indeed made its introduction easier. Therefore the one-sided view put forward by Williams cannot be maintained. On the other hand ethnocentrism and prejudice cannot be identified with racism, understood as a system of oppression and domination. Racism emerged when, in the framework of the formation of a world market and an integrated capitalist society, an archaic means of production like slavery was introduced in the New World which, as a system of oppression and domination, aimed at the maximum exploitation of people of another culture and with a skin of a different colour.[38] The transition from prejudice, ethnocentrism and so on to racism takes place by means of institutionalized mechanisms such as the régime on the plantations, the slave codes and the limitations of caste, imposed on free blacks.[39] In fact racism only developed completely in the second half of the nineteenth century; in this connection Genovese comments: 'it required the division of the world among the great Caucasian powers and the attendant vogue of Social Darwinism during the second half of the nineteenth century for a fully developed racist ideology to emerge and conquer the Western world. If scholars like Eric Williams, Marvin Harris, and Herbert Aptheker err in making racism a direct product of slavery, they err less than those who would simply invert the relationship.'[40]

It was the tragedy of the old South that the system of black slavery, introduced as an archaic means of production to further the original accumulation of capital,[41] brought to power a class of planters who developed their own ideology – paternalism – which increasingly clashed with the surrounding world of industrialization and the bourgeoisie. However, the paradoxical thing, in Genovese's view, is that it was precisely this paternalist ideology which tended to mitigate white racism. In the South it was a common observation that the planters had less aversion to the negro than those who did not have slaves.[42] The erosion of paternalism after the fall of the slaveocracy therefore did not mean any weakening of racism; on the contrary: 'The fall of the slaveocracy opened the way to new men in the postbellum era and brought to the top exactly those elements most infected with the racism radiating from slavery as a system permeating all of society and least influenced by the countertendencies inherent in the master-slave relation within the plantation community itself... In this sense, too, the triumph of the bourgeoisie in a society that had been originally shaped by slavery spelled the triumph of racist extremism.'[43]

If, then, on the one hand it cannot be maintained that black slavery was the historical product of an already existing racism, on the other hand the racial caste system of the new South must be seen as a direct consequence of the prevalence of racial conflict over other social conflicts. For despite all economic and political conflicts, what bound whites of different classes and sexes to one another was an ideology, an ideology of white supremacy. This ideology was far more than just a rational justification of black oppression; it formed a sphere of conceptions (myths, images, ideas or concepts), relatively autonomous of economic and political relationships, which derived its vitality (or rather, its mortality) from the institutional mechanisms in which it was entangled.[44] In this specific view of reality, which formed the 'world' of the white South, white supremacy and black inferiority were not experienced as injustice which had come about in history but as a natural world order which, if necessary, could find 'scientific' support from the Darwinist theories of evolution which were so popular at that time (though in fact they had little to do with the work of Darwin himself).

However, the deep and glaring contradictions of *Jim Crow* and the incessant black opposition saw to it that the utterly unnatural character of this natural order continually remained evident. Despite rigid segregation, the white never got rid of his *alter ego*, the negro: the negro, his own creation, followed him like a shadow wherever he went. Meanwhile, for the whites the black Africans remained the great unknown, the terrifying invisible element.[45] And so 'the racial question' was the dominant factor in the thought and action of both blacks and whites. The words of Benjamin Mays with which I began this section are an incomparable example of this: 'All my life the race problem had been as close as the beating of my heart...'

(*b*) The black courage to be

It is against this background that we must see the movement which emerged in the deep South half way through the 1950s. Was it the pronouncement of the Supreme Court of Justice on 17 May 1954 on the illegality of segregation in schools which brought the movement to life? Or did it in fact only begin on 1 December 1955 in Montgomery, when Rosa Parks refused to stand up in the bus for a white person and her arrest formed the occasion for a boycott of buses which lasted almost a year and which made the young local Baptist preacher Martin Luther King Jr world-famous? More important than the date of origin is the fact that the movement gained mass support and made conquests. The non-violent action for the right to vote, the sit-ins of black students, the freedom rides made an impression, also on the black population in the great industrial centres of the North who, inspired by the non-violent resistance in which blacks in the South offered courageous opposition to white terror and intimidation, also began to move. Thus the black people as a whole were seized by a militant hope which recalled the great expectations which were cherished after their liberation from slavery. A second period of reconstruction had dawned.[46]

The movement of the 1950s and 1960s had a much closer connection with the past than many of those involved realized. Everything seemed new and unprecedented. The historian Vincent Harding, himself deeply committed to the movement, blames this misleading impression on the great immediacy of the electronic media. Radio and television gave the impression that the black liberation movement had spontaneously arisen in Montgomery, Birmingham, Watts and Detroit, that in fact it had no history – and, Harding added, because it had no past many people also believed that it had no real future.[47] However, in the South the boycott of buses had been tried out earlier, and the same was true of the sit-ins; the massive marches, the impressive singing of groups of demonstrators in prison were old ingredients of black opposition. The strategy and tactics of the civil rights movement had already been anticipated during the war years, in 1941, by A.Philip Randolph, leader of a black association called the Brotherhood of Sleeping Car Porters who, by means of a march on Washington by between 50,000 and 100,000 people, sought to compel President Roosevelt to see to better working conditions for blacks; the march was called off at the last moment because Roosevelt yielded to pressure and issued a special order for a Fair Employment Practices Committee.[48] Similar historical victories prepared for and made possible the struggle of the 1950s and 1960s, and that is certainly also true of the patient political and legal work of organizations like the National Association for the Advancement of Colored People (NAACP).[49] The black struggle for justice and freedom did not begin in the 1950s; it already had a centuries-long tradition behind it. Harding does not exaggerate when he says: 'No word was spoken by Malcolm, Stokely, King or Fannie Lou Hamer which had not been raised earlier by Paul Robinson, W.E.B.DuBois, Garvey, Ida B.Wells-Barnett, Bishop Henry McNeal Turner, and David Walker in this country, and by a host of nameless spokesmen on the ships of the middle passage.'[50]

What was usually called 'the movement' for short by those who were involved in it is described in historical and sociological accounts with various terms like 'protest movement', 'black revolt' or 'black revolution'. Each of these terms is legitimate, but it is often a thing to distinguish between them. 'Black protest' should be applied to the first period of the movement (1954-1960) when it was supported by a vision in which racism was regarded as an accident of American democracy which, though serious, was nevertheless capable of being overcome, and acceptance and integration into a democratic and pluriform society was the aim of the protest. By contrast, 'black revolt' is a more far-reaching concept: it embraces not just the tendency to integration but also the black nationalism of the 1960s: this nationalism could be potentially revolutionary by nature – one need only think of Malcolm X, who was murdered in 1965 – but for the most part it was no real threat to the existing order – here one might think of Elijah Muhammad's Black Muslims or the cultural nationalism of a Ron Karenga or Imamu Amiri Baraka. The term 'black revolution' really applies only to the second half of the 1960s when the revolts in the ghettos of Watts, Newark, Washington and Detroit laid open the hard economic core of the racial conflict, when Franz Fanon's *The Rejected of the Earth* opened the eyes of young black leaders to the connection between racism, imperialism and colonialism, when the escalation in Vietnam and the invasion of the Dominican Republic led the same leaders to put their struggle in the context of revolutions in Asia, Africa and Latin America; when, in short, the question formulated by James Baldwin in 1962 became increasingly urgent: 'Do I really want to be integrated into a burning house?'[51]

However, this last revolutionary phase was only possible because from the beginning the black protest had had a deeper dimension than becomes evident from its political aims and strategy. In fact in the first phase the civil rights movement in the South concentrated on political rights. In one sense that was remarkable. Up to the Second World War most blacks in the rural South lived as smallholders and sharecroppers (a barely disguised form of slavery, in which blacks leased ground from white owners, were given equipment and in return were allowed to keep a small part of their crop for themselves); the mechanization of agriculture and agricultural reforms which were introduced on a large scale above all during and after the Second World War brought far-reaching socio-political and economic changes. These led to the great migration in which blacks, driven from their land and deprived of their means of existence, went off to the industrial centres of the North or to the southern cities.[52] In cities like Atlanta, Birmingham and Selma these deprived people formed the lowest level of society and it would have been 'logical' if structural improvement of their extremely vulnerable economic position had had the highest priority. In the first instance, however, their actions were directed not towards economic change but towards political change. They fought for the right to vote and the desegregation of their public life, and in order to achieve this they brought about great change in the power of the Federal Government which had increased above all since Roosevelt.[53] By this political route they hoped to build up sufficient power also to be able to bring about an improvement in their material circumstances.

Apart from demonstrating a confidence (despite everything!) in American democracy, this course of events also showed something else. The political rights were important enough, but they were not an end in themselves. The political and legal level was in fact the sphere in which a battle was being carried on that went much deeper, because nothing more nor less was at stake than black identity and humanity. The real struggle took place on the level of how reality was viewed, the level of ideology. Political rights were the appropriate means of carrying on this ideological struggle. How could things be otherwise? In a world in which everything was directed towards ignoring the humanity of the blacks – in the last instance for the sake of the maximum exploitation of black life and work as slaves, smallholders and sharecroppers, as 'last hired, first fired' in paid work – establishing one's own social and personal identity was the first act of opposition. Regarded and treated for three centuries as subhuman, 'the negro' was first of all forced to gain recognition as a human being. Here he could never deny his body. Therefore it was this corporeality which was the sign of his authenticity. Being black became his pride. And this assertion of black humanity, incarnated in a leader like Martin Luther King and his northern counterpart Malcolm X, was at the same time the unmasking of white power. Vincent Harding expresses this dynamic sharply: 'Indeed, it is part of the ironic realilty of a white racist society that even the simplest claims of black humanity – like the privilege of sitting where one pleases on a bus – have tended to become radical threats to those in power.'[54]

However much the civil rights movement also joined in the democratic play, however moderate its demands were, in a world of white supremacy this meant a radical break with the 'natural order'. From the beginning the protest of the 1950s therefore had a revolutionary dimension, threatening as it was to a racist view of reality which had found its institutional anchorage at almost every level of human activity.

If the manifestation of black humanity signifies the unmasking of white power, at the same time this 'courage to be'[55] is a first condition, a social and psychological necessity, for carrying on the struggle for radical economic and political transformation. If we try for a moment to sum up the specific dynamics of the struggle against racism in the Hegelian triad of thesis, antithesis and synthesis, and white racism is the thesis, then the particularity of black soul, of black identity and humanity, is the necessary element of antithesis which precedes the final synthesis which realizes King's vision of a world in which 'all of God's children, black men and white men, Jews and Gentiles, Protestants and Catholics, will be able to join hands and sing in the words of the old Negro spiritual: "Free at last! Free at last! Thank God almighty, we are free at last!"' [56]

(*c*) How long? Not long

However suspect it may be to hang history on 'great personalities', it is impossible not to have a few pages on Martin Luther King Jr. His paradoxical significance for the black struggle was too great for him to be left out: moderate in his political demands, ready to compromise, at the same time more than anyone else he contributed to the awakening of a black revolutionary consciousness.

I shall limit myself to explaining this paradox and leave aside much of what would be more than worth discussing in the life and work of King in conection with our subject.[57] We have an impeccable witness for the real existence of this paradox in Albert B.Cleage, preacher of the Shrine of the Black Madonna in Detroit, and, as a protagonist of black nationalism, certainly not a follower of 'De Lawd' (King's nickname among his fellow-workers).[58] After King's death, in the deep mood of penitence over the loss of the great champion of non-violence, Cleage made the following remarkable statement: 'In Washington, in Chicago, and throughout the country, the people who marched, who fought, who broke windows, who retaliated, are disciples of Dr Martin Luther King. His wife may not like it and his followers in the Southern Christian Leadership Conference may not like it, but Dr King played a bigger part in creating this situation than any man in America. The people who marched, the people who looted, and the people who burned were in a deep sense, his disciples.'[59]

The historian August Meier called King a conservative militant.[60] The secret of his success is said to have lain in his readiness to make tactical compromises with the established political order and in his combination of combativeness with conservatism and foresight, of rectitude with respectability. However, it is unmistakably part of King's paradox that this judgment is as just as it is unfair.

King was indeed conservative, in the sense that he had deep faith in the old American dream, in the great ideals of men like Lincoln and Jefferson, in individual freedom and democracy; he believed in the moral appeal to the white conscience and in collaboration with white people of goodwill; in fact he referred in his struggle to generally accepted bourgeois Christian values and ideals, and in the bourgeois sense he was respectable by origin and upbringing. Hence his calling as a preacher, his way of speaking and – it should not be forgotten – his impeccable dress. However, all this only tells part of the story. If King was really no more than a conservative, albeit a militant one, then it is impossible to explain how in the last period of his life he underwent a process of radicalization in which even his closest collaborators could not follow him.[61] Passionately and desperately he looked for new ways to banish the evil from President

Johnson's Great Society, the evil of poverty and unemployment in America's great cities, the evil in distant Vietnam, the evil of imperialism and militarism that he condemned in increasingly fierce terms. He discerned more and more clearly the injustice of economic structures, both national and international. He argued for a revolution, directed against structures which prevented society from 'lifting the load of poverty'.[62] His famous speech against American involvement in Vietnam on 4 April 1967, precisely a year to the day before his death – earned him the enmity of the White House, while leaders of civil rights organizations like NAACP and the Urban League rejected his action. Isolated from his former allies, simultaneously criticized for his non-violence by Black Power and the Black Panthers, who soon emerged, King decisively changed his strategy. He began to speak of massive civil disobedience, of a non-violent army. He no longer sought white progressive intellectuals but poor whites as his allies in the struggle against an unjust society. So arose his idea of a Poor People's Campaign, a campaign of direct non-violent action in Washington in 1968; however unconvincing this idea may have been, for the political establishment it was threatening enough in a city with a majority of black inhabitants in the tensions of 1968, certainly if King himself led the campaign. His murder in Memphis obviated this danger.

No one can say where King's vision of the beloved community would ultimately have brought him. However, it is certain that the winner of the Nobel Peace Prize was caught up by a revolutionary situation which had also come about through his making. Anyone who sees King simply as a conservative militant misses the point of his activity and strategy. In a sense being a conservative and being a revolutionary are not mutually exclusive. Revolutionary consciousness does not arise out of nothing, but is developed out of historical contradictions in existing social conditions. Revolutionary opposition begins where the gulf opens up between on the one hand the official ideal propagated and confessed by the state, of freedom, equality and democracy, and on the other the conditions of lack of freedom, inequality and injustice which actually exist. 'To begin with this discrepancy, to exploit the weak point of inner contradiction, in order to attack the moral integrity and legitimacy of the government was always an opportunity for action and argument which the opposition could seize.'[63] This formulation by the political theorist Cheryl Benard in her study of the international women's movement and the black movement in the USA is in fact an exact expression of the strategy of Martin Luther King Jr, who was a past master in exploiting the statements of American society against the reality of racial oppression. The very fact that he believed in the old dream of the new world made him completely credible and convincing in his unmasking of the hypocrisy of white power. Anyone who thinks that King was concerned for integration into American society and in so doing refers to King's own remark that his dream is deeply rooted in the American dream forgets how revolutionary this dream is...[64]

This specific link with the American tradition is expressed very tellingly in the breathtaking speech at the end of the march on Washington in 1963. Right at the beginning of his speech King recalled the memorable words which Abraham Lincoln spoke on 19 November 1863 in the churchyard at Gettysburg where the war dead were buried, in which he recalled that four score and seven years ago their forefathers founded a new nation, conceived in freedom and devoted to the view that all people were born equal:

> Five score years ago, a great American, in whose symbolic shadow we stand today, signed the Emancipation Proclamation. This momentous decree came as the great beacon light of hope for millions of Negro slaves who had been seared in the flames of withering injustice. It came as the joyous daybreak to end the long night of their captivity.[65]

This concern determined the direction of what followed. The opposition between light and darkness, dawn and daybreak, functioned as a stylistic means of stressing the blatant discrepancy between promise and reality. A century later there is still no freedom for the black, and therefore America is in debt to the black population. By interspersing his speech with quotations from the Psalms, from Amos and Isaiah, with allusions to Shakespeare, to the Founding Fathers, to the well-known hymn 'My country, 'tis of thee', King confronted American society with its own Western Christian tradition. At the same time, however, his audience was confronted with another tradition: the rhythmic cadence of his words, the heaping up of constantly changing imagery, the repetitions which heightened the atmosphere and made it almost unbearable, the dialogical response which he was able to evoke from the 'community' of demonstrators present, the purging ecstasy of the 'free at last' at the end – all this is not his personal property but belongs in the black church, a church born in slavery, with a tradition and a spirituality which go back to the land of its origin, Africa.[66] The confrontation between the two traditions produces an effect which was perhaps deliberate, perhaps unintentional. The white Christianity which has betrayed the dream sees itself confronted with the spirituality of the black church as a 'community' of those who are weary and heavy laden among whom the dream of a new world has remained alive. As a Baptist minister, as a preacher, King embodies this black spirituality and expectation. When at the end of his speech, in a trance, by means of the constantly recurring refrain 'let freedom ring', he conjures up the picture of the new America of peace and justice, he is not speaking as an individual but as the representative of an enslaved people that was borne up by hope for a new future. This produces a great change: the first seem to be the last and the last the first; a despised and humiliated people seems to be the vehicle of a new humanity.

This same revolutionary dynamic is present in King's strategy of non-violent resistance. This method of fighting inspired by the Sermon on the Mount and Gandhi's *satyagraha* also met with much criticism in his own circles. It ran contrary to the psychiatric insights of Fanon, who in the 1960 was gaining increasing authority among young black militants. According to Fanon the colonized person can only free himself by violence (counter-violence). The well-known black psychologist Kenneth B.Clark also thought non-violence an unnatural method which put black demonstrators under heavy psychological pressure.[67] Whether it was unnatural or not, the strategy was extremely effective, not only in political terms (think of the acceptance of the civil rights law in 1964 and the right to vote in 1965) but above all ideologically. The paradoxical feature of non-violence was that it provoked violence, white violence, symbolized in figures like Police Commissioner Eugene 'Bull' Connor in Birmingham and Sheriff Jim Clark in Selma. A black student put the paradox like this: 'I always love my enemies because it makes them mad as hell.'[68] Thanks to the electronic media all over the country and beyond pictures could be seen of black courage, dignity and self-control set over against white terror, hatred and anxiety. Supposed white superiority proved to be based on extreme violence. And the more sharply the white superiority of racist power structures came to light, the more black self-awareness increased.

However, one has not seen the real significance of the non-violent opposition if one has not recognized its eschatological overtones. Martin Luther King had the deep conviction that the new society, the beloved community, cannot be built up with means taken from the old. This is what lay at the heart of his criticism of Black Power: 'One of the greatest paradoxes of the Black Power movement is that it talks unceasingly about not imitating the values of white society, but in avocating violence it is imitating the worst, the most brutal and the most uncivilized value of American life.'[69] The impressive non-violent demonstrations had an eschatological dimension: they anticipated as it were a future in which people lived with one another without violence and oppression. They were an anticipation of the new life which dawned in Christ. And here too we see the unheard-of change: humiliated people prove to be the vehicles of a new humanity. King's eschatology has nothing to do with an escapist belief in the hereafter. It is present eschatology, directed towards the here and now. The biblical words, 'Behold, now is the accepted time, now is the day of salvation' (II Cor.6.2), resounded in Washington when King told his audience:

> Now is the time to make real the promises of democracy. Now is the time to rise from the dark and desolate valley of segregation to the sunlit path of racial justice. Now is the time to lift our nation from the quicksands of racial injustice to the solid rock of brotherhood. Now is the time to make justice a reality for all of God's children.[70]

Here a black preacher is speaking, from a tradition which attaches importance to the living, in other words to the sung and spoken, word; the content of the proclamation and the way in which it is expressed form a single whole, for in the black church the gospel is not a system of dogmas but an event, a happening, in which the believers are wholly involved. The rhythmic cadence of the swelling cascade 'Now is the time' makes the urgency of the moment physically tangible; in the spell-binding cadence of the stream of words – which really should be printed colometrically – the unknown possibilities of the conjuncture are captured and brought out as an effective antidote to the 'tranquillizing drug of gradualism'.[71] The fullness of the messianic time is at hand. The *kairos* has dawned. Justice is prepared for the poor, liberation for the captives, healing for those with broken hearts. In King's dream we hear the words of that part of scripture which he once called Jesus' manifesto, Luke 4.16-21, words which Jesus read in the synagogue of Nazareth from the book of the prophet Isaiah and of which he said, 'Today is this scripture fulfilled in your ears.'[72]

The evidence which the *kairos* gives of itself is not objectively verifiable; it is not based on scholarly insights, though it does not rule them out either. King does not speak as a cool, detached observer but as one who is himself caught up in the historical moment and is seized by it. He is in Washington, 1963, a prophet who dares to illuminate the opaqueness of historical events with the light of an ultimate reality. Because he does this his own appearance becomes a creative factor in the historical situation, for 'The one who proclaims a *kairos* helps to make it' (Tillich).[73] The expectation which King put into words in his dream resounds in the hearts of millions of people, of blacks who feel liberated from their daily humiliations, but also of white people who are seized by the vision of a humane society. This power of human imagination itself becomes an objective factor in the contemporary event with which any political analysis needs to reckon.

King's dream brought the imagination to power – with all the attendant risks. Where precisely is the boundary between prophetic inspiration and political naivety? With his dream King made himself extremely vulnerable, an easy prey to realists, sceptics and cynics. He encountered resistance even in his own circle; when he spoke of the need for a struggle for righteousness and truth to redeem the soul of America his colleagues had a tendency to smile blandly or to turn away in horror at such naivety. However, Vincent Harding, who tells this story, adds that over the years it has become increasingly clear to him that the naivety lay with the co-workers (himself included) rather than with King![74]

In one way or another King had fathomed the depths of the disease from which American society suffers. For him more was involved than what can be expressed in terms like racism or capitalism. The soul of America really was at stake, though as he went along he saw increasingly sharply that redemption of the soul is impossible without the abolition of existing economic structures. Perhaps we must conclude that the mysterious effectiveness of his career was due to the radical optimism of his imagination of a new reality, inspired by the story of prophets and apostles, recognizable in the ideals of the American revolution, kept alive in the black experience of suffering and oppression. Perhaps, we might add, this revolutionary imagination was ultimately the only remedy capable of withstanding the demonically exorbitant power of racism. Martin Luther King challenged racism on the home ground of this corrupting power, that of ideology, of the imagination of reality. Both by his non-violent strategy and his rhetoric he exposed the contradictions of the dominant ideology and in so doing at the same time opened up the perspective on another more humane reality. In this way, more than anyone else he contributed to the creation of a new consciousness, since the 1960s referred to as black consciousness.

There is a good deal of misunderstanding over this last term. From the white side it is regularly suggested that black consciousness is a form of racism in reverse. However, as long as racism has to do with power relationships, such a presupposition is by definition absurd. Black consciousness is the black courage to be, founded on an unshakable trust that domination and oppression do not have the last word. It is this combativeness which derives its verve from the profound belief that victory cannot be far off.[75] Only this expectation of the future makes sense of preoccupation with one's own identity, culture and history and gives it meaning.[76] Black consciousness – and this is insufficiently recognized – is impossible without a sense of *kairos*. And it was precisely this latter that King was able to express in a way which is unique in modern history. On 25 March 1965, after the successful march from Selma to Montgomery, King addressed the crowd for the umpteenth time. In an antiphonal exchange between him and his audience, so characteristic of the spirituality of black church services, King called to the crowd standing in front of him, 'How long?', and the massive jubilant answer came back: 'Not long!':

> I know some of you are asking today, 'How long will it take?'
> I come to say to you this afternoon however difficult the moment, however frustrating the hour, it will not be long, because truth pressed to earth will rise again.
> How long? Not long, because no lie can live forever.
> How long? Not long, because you will reap what you sow.
> How long? Not long, because the arm of the moral universe is long but it bends towards justice.[77]

King's theology was essentially eschatology. His ethical thought, inspired by Walter Rauschenbusch and his social gospel, Reinhold Niebuhr, Gandhi, Tillich and his direct teachers, found a deeper unity in an expectation of the future founded on the specific spirituality of black history and experience. Gayraud Wilmore has rightly argued that the life and work of Martin Luther King Jr must be put in the context of the radical tradition of faith in the black church.[78] The charisma of this black preacher was the charisma of Harriet Tubman, Sojourner Truth, David Walker, Henry Highland Garnet and Henry McNeal Turner, who together with many other black witnesses of faith form a tradition in which the daily struggle is grounded in the radical eschatological promise of a new heaven and a new earth. For King, too, history and eschatology stood in a creative relationship of tension to each other; he knew that God's kingdom may never be identified with any kind of political and social system,[79] but this knowledge could never lead him astray into separating eschatology and history. He lived by the same faith that had given black slaves the vital optimism to see light in the darkness of their everyday life and in an apparently hopeless situation to hold fast to the promise of a new future. In this connection it would be worth making a separate study of the way in which love (*agape*) functions as a central concept for him: love is in primarily an eschatological reality, but precisely as such it provides the basis and the revolutionary power for daily living and acting.[80] The specific utopia of the beloved community meant that from its beginning in Montgomery the movement inspired by King was more than a protest movement of a minority group against its repression. The term black revolution is not incorrect.

Black theology is inconceivable without Martin Luther King. Above all, it is the articulation of an experience of faith and a tradition of which he is one of the greatest defenders. It was King who restored to the black church the spirituality of struggle which speaks from the old slave songs, from David Walker's *Appeal* of 1829 and Henry Highland Garnet's famous 1843 *Address to the Slaves of the United States*. As such he can be regarded as the direct pioneer of black liberation theology.

The prophetic legacy of King's awareness of a *kairos* carries obligations with it. Black theologians who refer to him and honour him as a guide and pioneer cannot get round the radical nature and universality of his expectation of faith. Anyone who wants to remain faithful to his spirit will not practise survival theology but liberation theology in the full, inclusive sense of the word. Anyone who wants to keep his spirit alive will not bow down to the oppressive power of existing circumstances but hold fast to the imminence of a new future:

> We'll soon be free
> De Lord will call us home.
> We'll fight for liberty
> De Lord call us home.

(*d*) Dream and reality

In my interpretation of the life and work of Martin Luther King, so far I have put the emphasis firmly on the bright side of his career. We have not yet come to the darker side. However, we may not ignore the fact that despite victories and successes his political struggle was not without its tragedy. Here I use the word tragedy in an evocative sense as the 'greatness of humanity in failure' (Karl Jaspers)[81]. The *kairos* which King evoked and proclaimed did not become a reality. The promised land that he saw before his death from the mountain top seems further away than ever. The time has remained unfulfilled. Was he mistaken? Or is it true that no authentic prophetic word ever remains unfulfilled?[82]

Power and weakness, conquest and defeat, dream and nightmare are paradoxically bound up together in King's struggle. More markedly, it is precisely in power that we must seek the cause of weakness, in conquest the cause of failure, and in the dream itself (also) the cause of the nightmare, It is significant that at the unmistakable climax of King's career, during the march on Washington, the failure of his views and strategies was evident in the voices of some radicals and of Malcolm X, who was also present, and spoke of the 'Farce on Washington'.[83] 'The recollection of the March on Washington was very soon obscured by a tragedy of violence, and that violence would grow over the years. The Dream of Reverend King did not come nearer, but on the contrary seemed to get further and further away' (Schulte Nordholt).[84] Anyone who now, more than twenty years later, looks back on the films of the endless mass demonstrations and again hears King's heavy baritone summoning up the vision of the new America still feels – or at least

I still feel – the same wave of emotion as the first time, but the voice and the images seem to come from another age.

Paul Lehmann, Emeritus Professor of Union Theological Seminary, New York, pointed out that in the way in which King strove for the realization of the dream there was a deep ambivalence: 'In restrospect, it appears that every achievement of the Dream was shadowed by an incipient corruption, if not capture, of its vision and its goal.'[85] The events of 1963 in Birmingham, Alabama, are an example of this.[86] On B day, 3 April, a non-violent campaign which was impressive in every respect and strategically well thought out was begun for desegregation; after a vigorous struggle a month later a half-hearted, shaky compromise was achieved which King wrongly presented as a great victory; the day after the proclamation of the agreement, 11 May, bombs were set off in the home of King's brother and in the motel which the campaign leaders had made their headquarters; the black population, provoked by the extremely violent racism of Police Commissioner 'Bull' Connor and his followers, could no longer be restrained; a wave of black anger and rioting ran through the city. For the first time white violence was met on a large scale by black counterviolence. The historical significance of this becomes clear when we realize that this drama was played out on the eve of the long hot summers of violence in the great cities. The outburst of violence in Birmingham was not to be an incident but a harbinger of the massive lootings and burnings which were to follow all over America.

Unmistakably the non-violent strategy provoked reactions of violence, not just from the white side but also from the black side – one thinks of the feelings of those who on television had to see men, women and children in a peaceful demonstration being soaked with fire hoses, crushed against one another and attacked by police dogs. Here there is a paradoxical connection between the non-violent dream of Martin Luther King and the nightmare of violence which followed. Albert Cleage was referring to this when he described the rebellious looters among the ghetto inhabitants as followers of Dr King. In so doing he was well aware that this discipleship was in conflict with King's intentions.[87] He was well aware of the influence of Malcolm X and black nationalism. However, nothing brought the extreme violence of white racism to the surface as clearly as the non-violence of King and his followers. In retrospect, this unmasking of the arrogance of power which took on unprecedented force and significance in the second half of the 1960s after the escalation of the Vietnam war must be seen as leading to a radical rejection of the middle-class Christian foundations on which American society rested – however, this rejection, which came above all from the side of young black militants, at the same time represented the rejection of the views and strategy of King, who in his struggle always referred to the officially acknowledged values of freedom, equality and democracy. The power of King's impact – his credibility in the way in which he exploited the ethical, political and legal claims and principles put forward by those in power – was thus at the same time the cause of his failure – it was precisely because he held fast to the Christian heritage that he became alienated from the young radicals and began to lose his grip on events.

Here another factor was involved. In order to bring about social changes in favour of the black population King confronted the existing order with its own claims, ideals and pretensions. This strategy was effective by virtue of the moral pressure that it could exert on the political authorities to make conessions. At the same time it was risky since in fact in this way King was making himself dependent on the political establishment, dependent on authorities whose legitimacy he already recognized in principle, dependent on politicians who were out for compromise, delay and negotiation. King constantly found that in the political power game there is little room for moral considerations. When the Kennedy government finally sent Federal troops to Birmingham on 11 May 1963 after the outburst of violence it did so primarily to restore law and order as quickly as possible; it was hardly concerned with the legitimacy of the black demands.[88]

The most compromising thing of all was that King was used by political and church authorities in order to counter further radicalization of black opposition and knock it on the head. King himself was very well aware of this; even more, he allowed himself to be used.[89] In his letter from Birmingham Gaol he assured his white fellow-Christians that if they did not opt for him and his non-violent action they would be confronted with the violence of the Black Muslims and with millions of negroes who out of frustration and despair would seek refuge in the ideology of black nationalism.[90] This sort of appeal reveals the deep dualism of King's career: ideological radicalism which with its emphasis on the urgency of the historical moment conflicts with a policy of moderation, compromise and patience. If King was on the one hand the one who more than anyone else – thanks to his stubborn persistence in holding to the reality of the American dream – was able to demonstrate the contradiction between dream and reality, on the other hand he himself also remained trapped in this conflict. His dependence on compromises discredited the evocation of the dream and meant that over the years there was an increasing discrepancy between the expectations which he conjured up and his political strategy of achieving the achievable. The growing sense of this gulf underlies the deep spiritual crisis of the last years of his life; we must see the process of radicalization that he underwent in this period and of which the traces can be found in his posthumous *Trumpet of Conscience* as a stubborn attempt to bridge the gaping hole between the vision of the beloved community and the devastating chaos that he saw around him.

(*e*) Black power and powerlessness

The rift in the movement which became evident in June 1966 on Highway 51 and thus took on an irrevocable character is the logical result of both the success and the failure of the struggle for civil rights. Without the victories in Montgomery, Selma and elsewhere and the black consciousness which arose out of them, Black Power would have been historically inconceivable; without the defeats it would have been superfluous.

In her study *Die geschlossene Gesellschaft und ihre Rebellen (The Closed Society and its Rebels)*, Cheryl Benard has done important work in seeking to discover both the logic and the ambivalence of the process of changing consciousness which is characteristic of the rebellion of marginalized groups against the established order. At first glance, she comments, one might get the impression that the resistance of opposition groups which had a marginal position in the existing social system was determined by irrational arguments, conflict and the lack of a clear strategy; at one time the demands which are the goal of the struggle are realistic and conventional (equal pay for equal work), at others irrational and utopian. However, behind this fluctuation and confusion there is a system; 'a logical system for attaining new possibilities of thought, an ethical system for representing other values, a tactical system for setting short-term and long-term aims.'[91]

Benard reconstructs this 'logical system' through the thinking and argumentation in the international women's movement and the black movement in the United States – in which above all the movement seems to be a paradigm of the logic of opposition.[92] Marxist theoreticians who maintain the need for a strict model of class analysis and consider this a necessary condition for the establishment of a new social order are on their guard against opportunism, arbitrariness and destructive anarchy. The specific logic of this opposition escapes them because racial struggle and sexual struggle are only interesting for them as an occasion for correcting and perfecting their own theoretical model and thus 'renewing Marxism'.[93] As a political scientist and sociologist of a younger generation which has become allergic to the pressure of systems,[94] Cheryl Benard – in the footsteps of Adorno, Foucault, Luce Irigaray and others – criticizes the totalizing tendencies of a theoretical machine (idealist or Marxist) which skates over the ambiguous and opaque situations of extremely complex social relationships in the name of a truth which is far too simple and a model of thought which is far too monolithic.[95]

The often paradoxical dynamic of the discursive process in which marginalized groups try to make room for themselves and create their own identity cannot be understood in terms of an established model of social analysis but must be brought into the field of force of complex, strategic power relationships – here as a postulate there is a multiplicity of perspectives of truth which neither complement one another nor contradict one another.[96] The course of the polar relationship between centres of power and marginalized sectors of society is not, however, arbitrary or chaotic, but displays a particular recognizable framework: 'Certain modes of expression and developments of thought are characteristic of periods of resistance against the social order and point to basic stages of development in political consciousness among marginalized system positions.'[97]

The typological reconstruction which Benard gives of the different stages in the resistance of opposition movements is probably derived too emphatically from the black opposition of the 1960s to be capable of application to the struggle of other groups and movements. But that is no problem for our purpose, because we are concerned precisely with the specific dynamic of the movement. In the first phase the underprivileged movement protests against the fact that it falls outside social norms and is stigmatized. Those who belong to the group rebel against the fact that their sex, their race or ethnic origin determines their social status and their chances on the work market. People do not want to be seen as black or as gay but simply as human beings. They seek integration and try to achieve this by appealing to the democratic values from which the democratic order claims to begin. Tactically this strategy can be effective, but its weakness is that people in fact make themselves dependent on the goodwill of the centres of power; they would never publicly disavow the reference to human rights and the moral appeal but argue for realism, saying that changes must take their time and only come about gradually.[98]

However, it gradually becomes clear that the neglect and stigmatization is not just a technical fault in a democratic development which is otherwise sound but is intrinsically bound up with the existing economic, political and 'discursive' (Foucault) order. Integration into this order in fact means the continued oppression of those who are not yet on the programme.[99] This insight leads to a deep-rooted shift in thought and strategy. The discredited values of the existing order can no longer be normative for a human society, but the criteria for humanity are sought in the group itself. Its own culture and history, marginalized, suppressed and despised though it has been so far, now becomes the place where humanity is to be found. This conversion is expressed in the terminology: black, woman, gay, become symbols of a positive identification. Black is beautiful.[100] This new self-awareness which marks this second phase can go with a radical attitude, extreme formulations and an aggressive, irrational-sounding rhetoric which not only has a therapeutic function but is also meant to make breaches in an existing order which is experienced and presented by the group as a closed one.[101]

Unfortunately Cheryl Benard does not point out that as far as the movement is concerned the black nationalism which came to the fore after 1966 was a consequence not just of the failure of the strategy of integration but also of its success. The television pictures of the demonstrations in Montgomery, Birmingham, Selma and so many other places were particularly significant here: 'Black is beautiful' became visible in the sharp contrast between the impotence of white power and the disciplined dignity of the non-violent black crowds. What Benard describes with an expression taken from Adorno as 'reflection on the difference',[102] is here prepared for and made possible. In this sense black studies, black history, black theology and the formation of black caucuses (black groups in predominantly white churches, educational institutions and political parties) are an expression of a 'reflection on the difference' which is the paradoxical result of both the failure and the success of the previous first phase of the struggle.

There is a dialectical relationship between the two phases. The first brings about the second, and the second phase exists to some degree thanks to the first. Just as Martin Luther King in his Letter from Birmingham Gaol used (anxiety about) black nationalism for his own political capital, so on the other side we must not misjudge the sometimes extreme expressions of black nationalism or separatism: the rhetorical refusal of any communication with white institutions is in fact a demonstrative gesture the strategic aim of which is by means of a change in the distribution of roles (whites are excluded from black organizing structures) to communicate the historical experience of oppression and exclusion – and as such these forms of activity are, paradoxically enough, at the same time an attempt at dialogue.[103] In this dialectical interaction both tendencies, integralism and nationalism, point beyond themselves. Each in its own way points to the possibility and the need of a creative synthesis, which so far has not been found.

The conflict between integralism and nationalism does not date from the 1960s; it dominates Afro-American history and is given with the fundamental ambiguity of the black presence in the new world: the descendants of the Africans who against their will were introduced into the land as slaves, thus lost their home in Africa, but have not been accepted in their new homeland. Certainly they are part of the American nation as an ethnic minority in the midst of many others, but through the racism of this same nation they have been made a people apart, which found its negative identity in the lack of basic civil rights and human rights.

The ambiguity of this position is reflected in the thoughts and strategies of the leading figures which this Afro-American people has produced in the course of its history. The integralism of Frederick Douglass, W.E.B.DuBois and Martin Luther King is contrasted with the nationalism of Martin Delany, Booker T.Washington and Malcolm X. But in the biography of the most important of these people the boundaries of both directions are constantly broken: one might think of W.E.B.DuBois, who vigorously kept to integration and gave this belief form in his work for the National Association for the Advancement of Colored People (NAACP) which he also formed, but at the same time was the founder of the Pan-Africa congresses of the 1920s and, convinced of the need for black autonomy and self-recognition, as a scholar more than anyone else contributed to the reclamation of Afro-American culture and history.

One of the later leaders of the NAACP, Roy Wilkins, gave a speech in 1970 which is a good account of the nucleus of the philosophy of integration. 'Given the position of the Negro American population as a numerical minority of one-tenth and an economic, political and social minority of far less than one-tenth, the only tactical road for the black minority is integration into the general population.'[104] Black nationalism, by contrast, begins where the attempt at integration has come up against the harshness of an utterly racist society in which blacks are thrown back on mutual solidarity and group unity in order to be able to survive.

The historical reality of black nationalism is too complex for a sharp definition to be possible.[105] Certainly there are some essential characteristics which are constantly present: 1. A marked emphasis on mutual solidarity and unity rooted in the common fate of people who in a hostile environment are exclusively thrown back on one another and share with one another a specific culture of their own which in itself has been a means of surviving and opposing a racist world;[106] 2. a feeling of their own worth and pride in black culture and tradition (this black pride does not exclude a critical attitude towards their own commuity; on the contrary, the historian Sterling Stuckey points out that the ideologues of black nationalism sometimes couple their declaration of love for the black community with a bitter criticism of its weaknesses and failures);[107] 3. a deep bond with the land of their origin, Africa, and with all Africans in the diaspora; 4. the struggle for a particular form of autonomy which can vary from local community control to the formation of an independent nation in their own land;[108] connected with this is 5. the rejection of any form of political and economic dependence: collaboration and coalitions with other white organizations and parties may only be entered into on the basis of independence and their own power.

According to Sterling Stuckey, black nationalism as a comprehensive view and programme was first articulated around 1830.[109] What before this period could be found scattered and slumbering in the rebellion of the black slaves, in their very distinctive religious experience or in a song like the Hymn of Freedom, sung by slaves with a marked African awareness on an island on the coast of South Carolina, was expressed in concentrated form in Robert Alexander Young's *Ethiopian Manifesto* (February 1829), in David Walker's *Appeal to the Colored Citizens of the World* (September 1829) and in a number of texts of a rather later date, of which Henry Highland Garnet's *Address to the Slaves* (1843, but only published in 1849) is the most important. The striking thing about these texts is their universalist accent. In contrast to the picture that people often have, among most theoreticians of black nationalism there is a strong tendency 'to reach beyond themselves toward union with mankind' (Sterling Stuckey).[110]

This last feature derives from the deep religious and sometimes messianic character of this nationalism. In the *Ethiopian Manifesto* the coming of a black messiah is prophesied in dark language,[111] and in 1898, at the end of the nineteenth century, Henry McNeal Turner, bishop of the African Methodist Episcopal Church, caused a commotion with his remark that God is a negro.[112] On the basis of black nationalism there is intense wrestling with the question of the destiny of the black people in a hostile land: how is the absurdity of black wretchedness and damnation to be reconciled with God's plan of salvation and providence? In this connection Martin R.Delany formulated a basic notion which, although it hardly belongs within the walls of the churches, was deeply rooted in black popular religion: God helps those who help themselves.[113] The black community was directed towards self-help, and only in this way could it realize its destiny. However, Delany saw no possibility of the elevation of the black community to its real humanitarian destiny within the confines of racist America itself. Therefore according to Delany massive emigration is the only possibility of realizing the glorious future of the black people.

This emigration – not as yet in Delany but later[114] – was focused on Africa and was coupled with a strong missionary concern towards those who were still heathen inhabitants of the motherland. The same 'missionary emigrationism'[115] is also typical of the thought and struggle of other prominent nationalist leaders like Alexander Crummell, Edward W.Blyden and Henry M.Turner. There is no mistaking the fact that this missionary consciousness displays paternalistic and patronizing features towards those who in the eyes of missionaries were still uncivilized Africans. On the other hand it is a fact that this missionary activity was a great stimulus to the rise of the 'independent churches' in South Africa and elsewhere.[116]

During the last century nationalism never had much support among the small upper stratum of the black population in America and the black churches. The majority of the black élite, which in political terms could hardly make much of an impact, opted for integration and tried to extend their power base by recruiting support within the existing political and legal systems. However, by far the majority of the destitute black population in the country and later in the urban industrial centres was more sensitive to the nationalist appeal.[117]

In the period between 1900 and 1940 this broad nationalist substratum gained enormous support from two leading figures, Booker T. Washington and Marcus Garvey. Anyone who wants to condemn the maligned nationalism of the former must remember that this ex-slave, who became the most influential black politician in history so far, was working at a time when (*a*) an overwhelming majority of the black population was still tied to agricultural life in the South, and (*b*) in the South a rigid caste system was introduced which, supported by white terror, deprived blacks of all the political rights which they had won after the Civil War. In these circumstances Washington opted for an economic nationalism which was accommodated to Jim Crow and supported modest development in the context of a segregated capitalist society.[118] As leader of the Tuskegee Institute and inspirer of the 'Tuskegee Machine' (a group of white philanthropists and black educationalists and politicians) he supported the acquisition of agricultural and technical qualifications among blacks, the accumulation of private possessions, black businesses and the establishment of black institutions in the sphere of education, politics and economics.[119] He was fiercely against the emigration plans of Henry M. Turner and urged the black population to stay at home.

However much criticism Booker T. Washington may have provoked by his support of segregation, the ideas about self-help and increasing the black share of the market which he and his supporters put forward had a long influence: one might think of tendencies within the Black Power movement to identify black power with black capitalism and 'buy black', but above all also of the economic zeal of the Black Muslims.[120] During the 1950s and 1960s, this organization, the official name of which is The Lost-Found Nation of Islam in the Wilderness of North America, combined a vigorous religious radicalism with an economic realism.[121] Although its leader, Elijah Muhammad, taught that Allah had chosen the black people to inherit the earth and that the total annihilation of the white man and his religion was at hand, he was careful not to mix religion and politics. Muhammad was able to give form to the notion of self-help and autonomy by building up a substantial empire of private undertakings and businesses – restaurants, supermarkets, farmsteads, abattoirs and so on. In this way the Black Muslims succeeded in getting decent housing, clothing and food for their supporters, who were recruited from the criminal element and the unemployed in the urban centres of the North, and thus to give a material basis to the ideology of black pride and identity.[122]

However, during the second half of this century, even more than by Booker T.Washington, Black Nationalism was influenced by the person who was able to build up the greatest black mass movement in history, Marcus Garvey. Under the impact of Washington's autobiography *Up from Slavery*, in 1914 Garvey set up the Universal Negro Improvement Association (UNIA) in Jamaica, the land of his birth; in 1916 he came to America on the invitation of Washington, who, like Henry M.Turner, proved to have died the year before. Garvey arrived at a time when the black population both in the South and in the North was having a particularly hard time. Schulte Nordholt writes: 'He could hardly have come at a better time. The Great Migration to the North had begun, the tension between black and white had increased as a result of the revival of the Ku Klux Klan and the growing sense of resistance among the negroes, and in 1918 and 1919 the number of lynch parties and riots constantly grew. In this situation Garvey came to preach his negro nationalism, to proclaim his social ideas to these people who were piled on top of one another in cities. His success was enormous. In a few years this small stout man from Jamaica succeeded in doing what neither Washington nor DuBois, the NAACP nor any other organization had come anywhere near doing. He touched precisely the sensitive heartstrings of the masses, and they streamed to him, the thousands who wanted to hear specifically that their colour was not their shame, but their glory and their riches and their future.'[123]

Following Martin Delany and Henry M.Turner, Garvey preached mass emigration: 'To win Africa, we will give up America.' To achieve this end he set up his own shipping company, the Black Star Line. By then, 1919, the UNIA had grown into an organization which, according to Garvey's own estimation, which will not be far from the truth, numbered more than two million, and the Liberty Halls in the ghettos were centres of social activity for the unemployed and the needy. In 1925 Garvey was imprisoned on charges of fraud. It has never become clear whether he was really guilty. However, there is no doubt that he was cheated by those who sold him unseaworthy ships for the Black Star Line at extortionate prices. In 1927 Garvey was deported from America and had to return to Jamaica.

Garvey's nationalism, like that of his predecessors in the nineteenth century, was religious through and through. The motto of UNIA was 'One God! One Aim! One Destiny!' Although Garvey believed that God has no colour, he wanted to banish the white conception of God among blacks because it endorsed their oppression. In 1921 his fellow-worker, the episcopal priest George Alexander McGuire, was consecrated bishop of the newly established African Orthodox Church, which took seriously the worship of a black Christ and a black Mary.

What was the charisma of Marcus Garvey? Without doubt he was a potentate, with all the suspect features of such a figure. Opportunism, bombast and vanity were not alien to him. On the other hand, he put his gifts of rhetoric and organization at the disposal of a social programme which unerringly focussed on the needs of the uprooted black city proletariat. His nationalism was of an extremely complex radical kind; it coupled a humanitarian ethos with a belief in racial purity,[124] and despite his biting criticism of American society and its exploitation of the black population he embraced its economic system, capitalism, without reserve. Gayraud Wilmore gets to the heart of the matter when he writes: 'It was this subtle ambiguity that was intrinsic to Garvey's message – his love-separatism, his paramilitary pacifism, his conservative radicalism – that succeeded in grasping the complexity of black pyschology and the situation in the United States, the West Indies, and Africa.'[125]

The fiery followers of Marcus Garvey included an itinerant, illiterate Baptist preacher, Earl Little. In Lansing, Michigan, the

Reverend Little was butchered by a white mob because of his black self-awareness and his message of 'back to Africa'. That happened in 1931. Fifteen years after his death, one of his sons who had broken the law in every way in order to survive in the asphalt jungle of the ghetto, was imprisoned for ten years in Massachusetts State Prison, in Charlestown: he was then twenty-one. There he came into contact with the Black Muslim religion. After his conversion he changed his name from Little to X to express the fact that he had lost his African identity (name) but refused to bear the name of a white slaveowner any longer. From then on he became Malcolm X.

Richard Lester called the nationalist leaders of Black Power 'The Angry Children of Malcolm X'.[126]

About a year after the murder of Malcolm X in February 1965 there was a rift in the movement which meant that for the first time in Afro-American history the black élite began to think and act in a predominantly nationalistic way. It thus emerged as the voice of the mood which prevailed among the rebellious ghetto inhabitants during the long hot summers. Above all Black Power denotes a mood, a sphere. The term is specifically ideological; the slogan of the Paris student revolution can be applied to it: imagination of power. Black Power is the power of black imagination. In a sense that is logical: however deeply racism is rooted in economic exploitation, it is primarily an ideology, in other words it is a white view of reality which implies the negation of that kind of humanity which is comprised by the term blackness. As a negation of this negation Black Power is a view of reality in which blackness takes on a positive connotation; therefore in his first book, James H. Cone can describe black power as 'an attitude, an inward affirmation of the essential worth of blackness'.[127] In the struggle against white racism this positive affirmation is indeed a necessary first element, but in itself that is not enough to undermine the complex of power networks which is denoted by the term institutional racism.[128] Imagination alone changes power relations very little. An image which constantly emerges in these years is that of the Afro-American people as an internal colony.[129] Nowhere are the thoughts of Franz Fanon on colonial oppression and liberating power in his posthumously published *The Rejected of the Earth* discussed more passionately than among the new generation of black leaders. But what does liberation from the white power structure mean in a situation of internal colonialism? How must separation from the motherland and all the dependence that that represents be achieved? It was very significant that in March 1964 Malcolm X broke with the essentially conservative separatism of the Black Muslims and dissociated black nationalism from the struggle for an independent state. We cannot rule out the possibility suggested by George Breitman[130] that he was moving in the direction of a revolutionary socialism. He outlined increasingly sharply the connection between racism and capitalism.[131] But he saw the need for black unity and solidarity more clearly than anyone else. How the Organization of Afro-American Unity which he set up in June 1964 was to realize this unity was the central problem which occupied him in the last months of his life.

Malcolm's Angry Children saw no chance of solving this problem. Their militant rhetoric could not conceal the fundamental lack of unity in vision and strategy. All the fine words about self-determination and independence could not get round the fact that most of the Black Power leaders were tied hand and foot to white power structures – if only because they allowed the activities of their organizations to be subsidized by the business world. The contradiction of Black Power reveals itself painfully in these words of the Revd Nathan Wright, Chairman of the National Conference on Black Power held in Newark in 1967: 'Black Power in terms of self-development means we want to fish as all Americans should do together in the main stream of American life.'[132]

The American Federal government and the business world skilfully exploited the tendency of black leaders like Floyd McKissick of CORE (Congress of Racial Equality) to interpret Black Power as 'black business' and 'black capitalism'.[133] In his study *Black Awakening in Capitalist America* Robert L. Allen has given a convincing description of the ambivalence of Black Power and at the same time shown the strategy which the top of the American business world followed to undermine the revolutionary potential of the rebellion in the black urban areas: private enterprise had to be stimulated with the aim of cultivating an upper stratum of black entrepreneurs and managers who would be an inspiring example to the rebellious ghetto inhabitants of what the American way of life had to offer those who wanted to work hard and could discipline themselves;[134] alongside this people wanted to further the integration of blacks into the working world by tackling the problem of the hard-core unemployed;[135] for a number of reasons this was doomed to failure.

The incapsulation strategy of the business world and the Federal government in fact met with little resistance. This was due, at any rate in part, to the lack of a consistent and shared theoretical insight among Black Power leaders into the complex mechanisms of institutional racism. We only find the embryonic insight of Malcolm X into the historical context of racism and capitalism, still undeveloped, among the Black Panthers,[136] and in the *Black Manifesto* of James Forman.[137] For the majority of the new generation of black leaders the idea of American society as an open and pluralistic society remained the natural starting point. So the authoritative and often quoted formula of Stokely Carmichael and Charles V.Hamilton ran: 'Before a group can enter the open society, it must first close ranks. By this we mean that group solidarity is necessary before a group can operate effectively from a bargaining position of strength in a pluralistic society.'[138] The conviction that the black population is comparable to other ethnic groups and must like these others find access to the mainstream of American life dominates the approach of Black Power. Despite the flamboyant nationalistic rhetoric, integration, as before 1966, remains the aim of the struggle – only the mood and the means have changed.[139]

Perhaps the sense of *kairos* in the new black consciousness stood in the way of a sober estimation of the real power relationships. Looking back, Vincent Harding had to note:

> In spite of all the rhetoric about revolution, we were too American to believe that revolution in this country might take at least a generation of disciplined, organized, sacrificial struggle. At times it seemed as if we were more prepared to die on the streets than to struggle against long, hard odds, for long years – far from the appealing eye of the television cameras.[140]

Harding's assessment does not alter the fact that the black struggle of the 1960s did have results. On virtually every social field breaches were made in the walls of institutions where hitherto the white hegemony had prevailed. Political parties and local government organizations, businesses and professions, schools and universities, churches and synagogues had to make concessions when confronted with black anger. However, in turn Black Power had to pay for these concessions: the openings which were made were just big enough to let in a small minority, the new black bouregoisie. The majority of the black population was left outside.

This co-opting by the system of an élite could not but disrupt the unity of the black community. The 1970s were characterized by increasing contrasts and conflicts between the black middle class and the black underclass. There was a paradoxical and tragic element here: the nationalism of Black Power with its vigorous emphasis on the need for mutual unity and solidarity in fact helped to sharpen the class distinctions within the black community. Vincent Harding can even say: 'more often than not, Black Power became the power to exploit black people.'[141] And where the strategy of co-opting was not enough to restore the damaged hegemony of the ruling classes – in full accordance with the scenario of Antonio Gramsci - the power of the state was used with deadly effectiveness. The over-powering show of military strength on the evening after the murder of Martin Luther King in 1968 contained a threat which could not fail to have an effect on the black population.[142]

The longer substantial change for the majority of black people failed to come, the more the *kairos* ebbed away and mutual squabbling, frustration and resignation gained the upper hand. 1972, the year of Richard Nixon's great election victory, was of crucial importance. March saw the setting up of the National Black Political Assembly in Gary, Indiana, at the instigation of Imamu Baraka, Charles Diggs and the mayor of Gary, Richard Hatcher. This conference was an undoubted climax in the history of black nationalism. Despite all the opposition and ambivalence, despite the presence of integrationalist leaders like Jesse Jackson and Coretta King, there could be agreement on a basic programme, the Black Agenda, which contained all the visionary power of black nationalism:

> We come to Gary in an hour of great crisis and tremendous promise for black America. While the white nation hovers on the brink of chaos, while its politicians offer no hope of real change, we stand on the edge of history and are faced with an amazing and frightening choice: we may choose in 1972 to slip back into the decadent white politics of American life, or we may press forward, moving relentlessly from Gary to the creation of our own black life. The choice is large, but the time is very short...[143]

Gary saw the deep crisis of American society as a direct consequence of white racism and capitalism. Radical change is necessary, but it cannot be achieved within the existing party system. However, Gary was not only a climax; in some senses the assembly also marked the end of an era. After Gary the process of dismantling black nationalism began. Most of the politicians present did not really take the Black Agenda seriously. Many of them were nominated or elected to official positions within the existing political system. The subsequent meetings of the National Black Political Convention had fewer and fewer participants. One of the most important causes of this was internal division. Manning Marable writes:

> The internal crisis, the inability of competing black progressive political forces to agree upon a common social progranme and a black critical theory for social transformation was decisive in the destruction of the Movement as a whole. The lack of an adequate theoretical understanding of the meaning of class stratification within black America undermined the very programs and institutions which nationalists tried to create.[144]

The thorny problem of the relationship between racial struggle and class struggle underlies the internal crisis. This question had already come up in the 1960s. The Black Panthers in their radical period saw the class struggle as being more basic than racial conflicts and wanted to join other minorities in a socialist revolution; they rejected the cultural nationalism of Baraka and Karenga as bourgeois and conservative.[145] By contrast, for the cultural nationalists questions of race and culture had top priority; they rejected Marxist analysis as a white, Western way of thinking. In 1971 Pan-Africanism emerged, which stressed the cultural and historical unity of black people in the United States, the Caribbean and Africa, and the unity and continuity of the world-wide struggle against neocolonialism and racism. However, from 1973 on a polemic as vigorous as it was sterile began to arise within pan-Africanism between the cultural nationalists, who became increasingly opposed to Marxism, and left-wing nationalists. Imamu Amiri Baraka, the great protagonist of cultural nationalism, caused a great shock when between 1973 and 1975 he moved over to Marxist-Leninist-Maoism.[146] Others put even stronger stress on the need for the overthrow of the capitalist system. But this left-wing nationalism did not succeed in gaining a broad basis of trust among black workers, the unemployed and students.[147] In 1976, the year in which Carter became President with the support of the black community led by Andrew Young, the signals were finally set. The political initiative was again in the hands of moderate leaders, and radical black nationalism was put in an isolated position by virtue of its mutual divisions.

The powerful backlash of the 1970s inevitably casts its shadow on any survey of the turbulent period which preceded it. As a result the weaknesses and conflicts of the movement can be over-exposed in a way which does not do justice to its significance in American history. Following C. Vann Woodward, black historians interpret the 1950s and 1960s as the era of the Second Reconstruction. In so doing they rightly associate the importance of this period with the time of hope after the Civil War, the Reconstruction.[148] Both mark a point of no return: just as the first Reconstruction brought the end of slavery as a legal system, so the second put an end to the legality of segregation. And just as the first reconstruction was followed by the distress of sharecropping and segregation, so the second was followed by Richard Nixon's policy of benign neglect, economic recession[149] and the accentuation of class conflicts within the black community. But however great the reversal, the historical significance of the two periods still remains. The optimistic élan, the sense that a new day had dawned, to some degree points beyond itself. The possibility of another society in which people were not judged on the basis of the colour of their skin but on the basis of their character came into view, and with it also the prospect of a third definitive reconstruction.

The legacy left by Malcolm X and Martin Luther King imposed obligations. Both were murdered at a time when, each in his own way, they were occupied in leaving behind the old opposition between integrationalism and nationalism.[150] Work on the Third Reconstruction will have to build on the insights and intuitions which developed above all in the last period of their lives. But their thought did not develop in a vacuum; the 'historical situation', the specific conjuncture of circumstances, made them what they were. Especially after 1966, when King was confronted with the angry children, an enormous amount of violence arose. The birth pangs of black theology also come in this period – alongside all the other things that happened. If black theology, as we saw earlier, is inconceivable without Martin Luther King, its actual *Sitz im Leben* is formed by black nationalism, which in 1966 was all the rage. Three elements in this nationalism were of particular significance for the rise of black theology: 1. the trend towards a cultural revolution; 2. thought about power and violence; 3. bitter criticism of the church and Christianity.

1. In a first outline of the basic programme of the Organization of Afro-American Unity by Malcolm X, dated 28 June 1964, there is the following passage:

> We come from Africa, a great continent and a proud and varied people, a land which is the new world and was the cradle of civilization. Our culture and our history are as old as man himself and yet we know almost nothing of it. We must recapture our heritage and our identity if we are ever to liberate ourselves from the bonds of white supremacy. We must launch a cultural revolution to unbrainwash an entire people... This cultural revolution will be the journey to our rediscovery of ourselves. History is a people's memory, and without a memory man is demoted to the lower animals.[151]

Up to the 1960s the black population in the United States was usually seen as a group without its own culture, history and identity. From Ulrich B.Phillips to Kenneth M.Stampp and Stanley M.Elkins – to mention different approaches[152] – historians described white slaves as a people without identity. For generations social scientists recognized the existence of an Afro-American culture; at most they saw it as part of a wider culture of poverty or as a pathological version of American culture generally.[153]

On the basis of his own experience Malcolm X knew the devastating and demonic effect that this negation of identity had on the human psyche. But the image of the black person that racist society has created for itself cannot just be disputed with political means. Here is the heart of Malcolm's criticism of the struggle for civil rights. In his view what was at stake was not civil rights but human rights, the right to be, to think, to administer justice, the right to one's own destiny. 'How is the black man going to get civil rights before he wins his human rights?'[154] For Malcolm X the need for a cultural revolution basically meant the need for a new humanity, a new anthropology. As Paul Lehmann put it, he was looking for the human meaning of blackness.[155] But this new identity has to be grounded in the specific history of the black people. It cannot be otherwise. So Malcolm X and other nationalists could not detach thought about their own black destiny from the land of their origin, Africa. In African life-style and culture the potential for a black anthropology, for black pride and human values, survives. Origin and history are determinative of what distinguishes Afro-Americans from the dominant culture.

The image of Africa in cultural nationalism has emphatically idealized features. It is first of all a counter-image – not only in so far as it is a reaction to the image of dark Africa as a continent of savages and heathen but above all as a positive contrast to what people reject in American society. The most telling instance of the way in which Africa functions in cultural nationalism is the doctrine of Kawaida, a system of values developed by Maulana Ron Karenga and Imamu Amiri Baraka which goes back to African life-style, customs and usages.[156]

2. The construction of such a system of values is a form of power, ideological power formation. Power is the key problem in the black struggle of the second half of the 1960s. The clash between Martin Luther King and Black Power is essentially about the relationship between *agape* and power. In the vigorous polemic for and against this is often caricatured: King's vision is presented as a passive attitude of turning the other cheek, while on the other side Black Power is identified with hatred and violence.

King was vigorously opposed to contrasting the terms love and power. For him power was legitimate if it were a matter of the 'ability to achieve purpose',[157] of the power needed to achieve social, political and economic changes. If black power is regarded in these terms, or as a 'psychological call to manhood',[158] King was in agreement. However, it was vital for him that the *agape* which took form in Christ should remain the ontological basis connecting power with justice. For him power was love which brings the demands of justice to fulfilment. Because King failed to find this connection between power and love in the supporters of Black Power, he believed that the slogan was essentially a nihilistic philosophy born of despair: he was opposed not only to the separatist tendencies which he regarded as unrealistic but above all to the summons to avenging power; this last could only lead to misuse of power and destruction.

But within black nationalism there was more sophisticated thought about the use of violence than people might suppose from King's outbursts and the comments in the press at the time.

Alongside the thought of Fanon, that of Malcolm X was also to the fore. For Malcolm violence is a necessity where other means fail to realize basic human rights; in that case violence is always counter-violence, opposition to the violence of white power structures. However, he works out and expresses this basic notion in different ways: sometimes the stress is on self-defence as a right of any American citizen whose life is threatened, and sometimes in fact the idea of retribution can be heard – eye for eye, tooth for tooth; then again, following Fanon, he can see violence as an act of liberation and consolidation. These various elements return in Black Power: the SNCC leader H.Rap Brown and the Black Panthers adopted an extreme position, beginning from a *de facto* war situation and calling on the black community to arm itself; mostly, however, the stress is on the right to self-defence 'by any means necessary'.[159]

However, just as non-violent resistance is directly connected with King's deepest convictions, so more than strategic considerations are involved in the right to self-defence. In fact in a racist society the right to self-defence with all necessary means is a consequence of the concern of black power: self-determination, the right to determine one's own future. Self-determination was a concern that from then on blacks should refuse to let the white ruling powers prescribe how they must think and act – and therefore how they should oppose their inferior position.

If for both King and Black Power power is intrinsically a positive concept, the difference between them is to be found in the way in which this term is given content. *Agape* – serving love – which for King forms the link between eschatology and history, between the vision of the beloved community and the black struggle, sets a limit to the 'by any means necessary'. There may not be any discrepancy between end and means.[160] Is humanity really dependent on the need to defend one's own life? Is this American shibboleth in fact the source of human freedom? Following King, and the Mennonite tradition from which he himself comes, Vincent Harding has discussed these questions in his essay 'The Religion of Black Power' (1968), which I mentioned earlier.[161] With his vision of the beloved community Martin Luther King gave a clear direction to the question of black identity; here was his answer to the problem of the image of humanity. How is black nationalism related to that? That is Harding's key question. What image of humanity, what social structure, is the ultimate perspective of the black concern for self-determination?

3. One factor, however, is involved here which in this period cut right across the intrinsically legitimate questions of Vincent Harding and in fact made a sophisticated answer to them impossible. That was the hostility of the moment. The call for Black Power resulted in a direct change of strategy on the part of the authorities. Official bodies, and above all the church, which beforehand had never spoken out in principle against the use of violence, now suddenly recalled that violence is incompatible with the Christian conscience. The acts of violence in Watts, Harlem and the other black ghettos triggered off a deep anxiety which came to be expressed in the white backlash. The militant rhetoric of the new generation of black leaders, coupled with the outbursts of violence during the long hot summer, made the non-violent actions of King and his followers suddenly the only honest alternative to which white progressive Christians could in all conscience give their support. All of a sudden non-violence was propagated as the only possible way for Christians to resist racism.

This opportunist appropriation of King's deepest conviction blocked the conversation between King and Black Power and had a disturbing effect on the social and ethical equilibrium among the black leaders. The very authorities which once set up and justified the colour barrier now suddenly rejected any opposition between white and black and referred to the Christian idea of reconciliation to justify their view. On the basis of this approach the formation of black power was rejected in principle and Black Power was condemned as the gospel of hate.

This double morality aroused the bitter scorn of the black nationalist leaders. It was a confirmation of what has always been brought to the fore in the history of black nationalism: that Christianity is the white man's religion, and serves as an instrument to turn blacks into obedient docile slaves. In no period of American history has Christian hypocrisy been more broadly and more bitterly assessed than between 1966 and 1972. However, in this respect too Malcolm X preceded his angry children. No one understood better than he the art of unmasking the complicity of churches and missionaries in the terrors of slavery:

The blond-haired, blue-eyed white man has taught you and me

to worship a white Jesus, and to shout and sing and pray to this God that's his God, the white man's God. The white man has taught us to shout and sing and pray until we die, to wait until death, for some dreamy heaven-in-the-hereafter, when we're dead, while this white man has his milk and honey in the streets paved with golden dollars right here on this earth![162]

However, this unmasking of Chrisitanity also affected the black churches. In the nineteenth century black nationalism (Martin Delany, Henry M. Turner) still moved within a Christian framework, although there was also bitter criticism of white Christianity and the tendencies towards assimilation in the black churches. In the twentieth century things changed when the migration to the industrial, primarily northern centres came about and alienated the black proletariat from the institutional black churches which are often associated with the small black upper stratum,[163] the black bourgeoisie.[164] The violent intervention in the life and history of the black population represented by migration[165] did not leave the black churches untouched. In the rural South the church dominated the life of the black community. It functioned as a free place, as the only spot in society where blacks could be themselves and were relatively free from omnipresent white control. But in the period of rigid segregation the black churches lost the verve to freedom of the 'invisible church' of the time of slavery. Jim Crow exerted pressure towards accommodation, in other words towards faith in the hereafter, towards a fixation on the social status of the local church and its predecessor and a social ethos which was more concerned with prohibitions against smoking, drinking and dancing than with the struggle for social justice.[166] In a historical survey of the history of the black church James Cone writes of this period:

The black churches withdrew from the politics of society at large and became a small isolated society, serving as a haven for oppressed black people. They became centres for the circumscribed political, economical, and social aspirations of black people who had been denied participation in the overall social and political affairs affecting their lives. Ministers of these churches, to a great extent, were more interested in who would be elected bishop or president of a convention than they were in the social and political liberation of the black people.[167]

The proclamation of the gospel, the diaconate, education and – to a modest degree – mission, directed towards Africa and the Caribbean, were the four traditional tasks[168] which the black churches undertook not only in the South but also in the secularized, urban society of the North. For the uprooted migrants who seemed to have exchanged one wretchedness for another, these churches were a familiar home, a symbol of recognition in a completely new but equally hostile world. With their moralism and revivalist preaching they were in fact still pervaded by a rural ethos.[169] But this spiritual climate and organizational structure – remember that seventy per cent of the clergy had no specific education or training – made the black churches incapable of responding to the immense social needs and problems of a group of the population which on the labour market belonged to the category of the 'last hired, first fired'.[170]

Their answer to the situation was, with some important exceptions,[171] a dualism which kept apart faith and social reality, church and world, salvation history understood in individualistic terms and secular history. This retrogressive movement, which left to its own devices the difficult and complex reality of a racist society, was brought about by the fact that even within the black community an unavoidable process of secularization took place. The establishment of organizations like NAACP in 1909, the National Urban League in 1910 and black trade unions represented a lessening of the social-political function and responsibility of the black church, which in addition, in the life of the modern city, had to cope with the formidable competition of theatre, cabaret, sporting events and other forms of amusement and culture.

According to Gayraud Wilmore,[172] the third factor in this loss of function was the immense number of church divisions. In the black ghettos of Chicago, Washington, Los Angeles and New York the storefront churches mushroomed: empty shops and abandoned buildings offered a way out for all these nameless people who within the intimacy of the small group got a name and identity of their own which was denied them in the anonymity of the world outside. The traditional Protestant churches were too large, too respectable, too sophisticated for these people, for whom the presence of the Spirit was not an intellectual conviction but a physical experience. The fervent sense of religion among these saints who live by the ecstatic power of the Spirit and for whom smoking, drinking and dancing are from the Evil One, has been described in an unforgettable way by James Baldwin in his first novel *Go Tell It On the Mountain*.[173]

However, the world wars and the depression of the 1930s also saw an explosion of all kinds of cults which wanted to have little or nothing to do with the church and Christianity. The worse the economic situation got during the great depression, the more the blacks turned their backs on the churches and sought refuge in religious movements like Father Divine's Peace Mission, The United House of Prayer for All People, run by Daddy Grace, the Black Jews, for whom God is black, and the Moorish Science Temple of America, which regards Islam as the religion of the black.[174]

If in the nineteenth century black nationalism was still rooted in the specific spirituality of the black church, in the ghetto situation of the twentieth century it gradually detached itself from this. It rejected not only the 'Christian' civil religion of Uncle Sam but also the 'turn the other cheek' Christianity of the black churches. Above all, as a result of the Black Muslims and Malcolm X it moved increasingly more aggressively against the American Christ and all the oppression and humiliation which he symbolized. This aggression reached a climax on 4 May 1969, when James Forman presented the Black Manifesto in Riverside Church in New York;[175] it called on the church and synagogue for $500 million dollars as reparations for three centuries of racist violence. However, Gilmore comments that the target of the action was not just the white church but also the black.[176] That does not mean that the nationalism of the 1960s and 1970s rejected black religion as such. However, it did confuse the black church leaders and confront them with a difficult dilemma.

2. The dilemma of the black church leaders

The declaration of 31 July 1966 in the *New York Times* by the National Committee of Negro Churchmen (NCNC) was a response to the dilemma which pressed in on black church leaders. This declaration, which formed the ideological and institutional basis for the black theology that was about to come into being, derives from an *ad hoc* group of especially northern church leaders who sensed that a clear choice could not longer be avoided.[177]

The call to Black Power produced disquiet and anxiety not only among whites but also in the black churches. Black church leaders came under heavy pressure to condemn Black Power as incompatible with Christian love and reconciliation. In fact such a condemnation seemed obvious in a situation in which (*a*) Martin Luther King emphatically based his non-violent strategy on the Sermon on the Mount and (*b*) the black nationalists were lashing the churches with their harsh words about Christianity as the religion of the white authorities. So the choice between King and Black Power indeed seemed inescapable.

However, for the well-known church leaders who together made up NCNC the dilemma posed in these terms was a false one. A condemnation of Black Power would have meant betrayal of all the black youth who had rebelled in the ghettos against their powerlessness and against the hopelessness of their existence. It would have played into the hands of the white authorities who had chosen King as the lesser of two evils, but who in the end of the day wanted anything but essential change. Moreover, this group of church leaders felt deeply that the criticism by Malcolm X and his angry children of the role of the black church was in principle irrefutable. The regular churchgoers in the black population were among the least militant,[178] and for a great deal of the black church – one might think of Joseph H.Jackson and his National Baptist Convention, USA Inc, with its six million members[179] – even someone like Martin Luther King was far too radical. Therefore penitence and a confession of guilt were felt more appropriate than a condemnation of Black Power. But at the same time the church leaders knew that the criticism of Black Power was not the whole truth about the black church. Remarkably enough it was above all the controversial book by Joseph R.Washington, *Black Religion*,[180] which drew attention to this. Of course Washington thought that the contemporary black church communities were pervaded with a 'crass materialism, overlaid with a few theological generaliz-ations',[181] but at the same time he recalled the subversive radicalism of the black church from the days of slavery. A condemnation of Black Power would have been a rejection of this radical tradition, of the religiously inspired slave rebellions of Gabriel Prosser, Denmark Vesey and Nat Turner, of Richard Allen and James Varick who turned their backs on the white church and founded their own black church, and of the subversive liberating work in the Underground Railroad by women like Harriet Tubman and Sojourner Truth.[182] Betrayal of this tradition was impossible, all the more since this radicalism had not yet died out in the black ghettos, despite what Washington suggested. The repudiation of Black Power would have meant a condemnation of the work of Adam Clayton Powell Jr and his Abyssinian Baptist Church in Harlem, or of someone like Albert Cleage and the Shrine of the Black Madonna in Detroit. The only way of doing justice to this long tradition of dispute and opposition was to make a public declaration of solidarity with Black Power, directly against the pressure of the white backlash, which was also very tangible in the churches.[183]

On the other hand this witness to solidarity could not imply any condemnation of the position of Martin Luther King. Whatever criticism people might have of his Southern Christian Leadership Conference (SCLC), there was no ignoring the fact that preachers like King himself, Ralph Abernathy, Wyatt T.Walker, James Lawson, Andrew Young and many others had given the black church a new militant image both nationally and internationally. It was impossible for the *ad hoc* group which met for the first time at the beginning of July 1966 on the initiative of Benjamin F.Payton[184] to dissociate itself from this. Of course King's position could, indeed had to, be relativized. The non-violent stategy of SCLC could no longer be regarded as the only possible Christian option in all circumstances. The black church had the moral right not to condemn the rebellions in the ghettos.[185] Therefore it had to be made clear in the declaration that the real dilemma did not lie in the opposition between violence and non-violence nor even in the contrast between agape and power, far less in that between Christian conscience and black power. The church leaders felt that the key problem lay in the unfair distribution of power, in the confrontation between power without a conscience and conscience without power.[186]

Like King in his book *Where Do We Go from Here?*, which appeared in the same year, the *ad hoc* group refused to accept a contradiction between love and power:

> We regard as sheer hypocrisy or as a blind and dangerous illusion the view that opposes love to power. Love should be a controlling element in power, not power itself. So long as white churchmen continue to moralize and misinterpret Christian love, so long will justice continue to be subverted in this land.[187]

There is an important shift in accent between King and the NCNC which is not explicitly stated in the declaration. For King love is the fundamental ground of human existence and is therefore in fact an ontological category; by contrast, for him power is an instrumental notion, necessary to make love effective and give shape to righteousness. In the Black Power declaration by the NCNC it is the other way round. There power is the fundamental category and love as the controlling element in power is an instrumental concept necessary to protect the formation of power from misuse and corruption. We can see simply from the way in which the declaration is constructed that for the compilers power is the connecting link between freedom, love, justice and truth. For them power is essentially the organizing principle to make the black population participate with equal rights at all levels of society. Without political and economic power the blacks are powerless, and powerlessness produces a people of beggars. Therefore power also has an important psychological dimension: it is necessary for reconciling the black person with himself and givng him a view of himself in which there is room for a normal feeling of his own worth. 'As long as we are filled with hatred for ourselves we will be unable to respect others.'[188] Power is a condition for reconciliation between white and black.

However, by shifting this concept into the place which for King is occupied by *agape*, something happens which will prove to be very important for our discussion of black theology – especially for the problems which are discussed in the last chapter of this book – so I must refer to it specifically here. As we have seen, for Martin Luther King *agape* formed the connection between the vision of the beloved community and his political strategy, or, to put it in a more abstract way, between history and eschatology, particularity and universality. The more clearly he began to realize that far-reaching structural changes would be necessary in American society to make visible something of the beloved community, the more his belief in *agape* came under pressure. But despite all temptation he never abandoned his vision of faith. In the last period of his life his thought was characterized by a dialectical tension between history and eschatology, particularity and universality, which made him a liberation theologian before his time.[189]

Now since the church leaders united in the NCNC, in obedience to the demands of the hour, opted for power as the central notion, one would expect that for them this concept would become the culminating point of the dialectical tension between historical reality and the kingdom of God. However, this did not happen, and it was

Vincent Harding in particular who had already raised far-reaching questions at an early stage over this point.[190] In fact the 1966 declaration was far from being as radical as those who made it themselves supposed. The eschatological tension characteristic of King's view is absent. Whereas for King *agape* is both a historical and an eschatological category, in the NCNC declaration the eschatological dimension of the concept of power does not appear. Nowhere in the declaration is power connected with the reality of the kingdom of peace and justice; nowhere is power used in connection with the power of the Spirit which makes all things new and makes non-persons the subjects of their own history.

This theological deficiency is closely connected with the superficial view of society which emerges from the declaration. A superficial view of society leads to superficial theology, and vice versa. Strikingly enough the declaration is addressed in the first place to the political and church leaders of the American people with an appeal to their moral conscience. In accord with the prevailing ideology America, referred to as 'our beloved homeland',[191] is seen as a pluralistic society consisting of different groups. The call for black power is just what other ethnic groups have done and still do: a summons to join forces and exercise power as a group in order to be able to participate at all levels of society. No account is taken of the fact that racism is deeply anchored in the capitalist organization of society, still less is any connection made between domestic racism and external imperialism (Vietnam). In this sense the declaration falls far short of the radical insights at which both Martin Luther King and Malcolm X arrived at the end of their lives.

Although solidarity with Black Power comes first, the declaration can be read as an attempt to mediate between Martin Luther King and the young black nationalists.[192] With their reference to the conscience of political and church leaders those who made it are in fact more in the integrationalist line than in the nationalistic line of Afro-American history. What we noted earlier also applies here: the moral appeal to the prevailing order necessarily makes use of predominant values and conceptions. The vocabulary of the NCNC declaration alone is sufficient proof of this dependence.[193] Here we come upon a remarkable contradiction: while on the one hand there is a plea for self-determination and for the power which that calls for, on the other hand there is dependence on the good will of the political and church authorities. This paradoxical situation manifests itself at a theoretical level in the fact that the starting point is a 'reflection on the difference' which has not yet come about. This reflection which is still to come will soon be called 'black theology'.[194] So as must slowly become clear, the rise of this theology is anything but a historical coincidence. Looking back on the crisis of the long hot summers it is fascinating to reconstruct after the event the historical logic behind the birth of black theology; at the moment when at least a small part of the black church refused to give a hearing to white definitions of love and power and with as much shortsightedness as expectancy began to look for a way of bridging the gap between Christian faith and black existence, black church and black power, Martin Luther King and Malcolm X, the epistemo-logical break[195] was a fact, as was the hermeneutical crisis with which the birth pangs of a new way of doing theology were unavoidably coupled.

In *Black Religion* (1964), Joseph R. Washington had put his finger firmly on the sore spot. He asserted that blacks were excluded from the white churches and their theological tradition. Therefore, Washington said, the black churches are religious organizations rather than churches in the true sense of the word, because a church without theology is a contradiction in terms.[196] In a sense Washington was right. In fact theology as an academic discipline was a discourse closed to blacks and was so in two respects: (*a*) black theologians were barely represented in university institutions; (*b*) it did not occur to anyone in academic circles that experiences of God in black history and the black struggle could be of theological importance. James Cone has repeatedly described - at greatest length in *My Soul Looks Back*[197] the deep alienation which a theological education meant for a black student who was given nothing which connected his theological knowledge with his situation as a black person. There was no explicit, deliberately theological, reflection on the history, situation and struggle of blacks, and this state of affairs meant that the preaching and life of the black churches was characterized by a dualism which J. Deotis Roberts describes as follows:

> Some black preachers who are well trained and who are deeply involved in social causes preach only priestly sermons and sing and pray about spiritual comfort here and in the afterlife. Those members who work in the educational and social programs of the

church do not worship, and many of those who do worship see religion as a means to personal peace and salvation.

Evangelicalism and social gospel are present, but because the minister does not operate out of a conscious theological understanding of the black situation, he is not able to relate the black rite on Sunday with programs of black liberation during the rest of the week. He needs an understanding of man which will bring wholeness to his people. This theology will have to emerge out of the black religious experience. This is where ethnicity and theology meet.[198]

However, the need to, as Roberts puts it, connect ethnicity and theology is only felt at the moment when black church leaders and theologians refuse to respect the claims to universality of theological discourse which is closed to blacks. Washington had not yet got that far in 1964. On the contrary, the white theological tradition remained normative for him and his book is a plea for the abolition of black religion by integrating it into the mainstream of American Protestantism.

In a period in which the ideal of integration was becoming increasingly dubious, the provocation of Washington's view led to a considerably sharpening of the hermeneutical crisis which was already present among black church leaders. It was true that all kinds of classical and modern theological questions and problems were barely alive in the black churches. But did that mean that the black churches were thus starved of biblical theological insights? Had white Christians then the right to define what had to be understood by true church and theology? Or had they in fact forfeited this right by virtue of their complicity in slavery and white racism? Was it not rather, despite all the ambivalences and shortcomings, the black community which was the scene of authentic biblical proclamation, because for it the God of Moses and Jesus had always been regarded as a companion of those who had been humiliated and trapped in their struggle for freedom and justice? Was there not still a quite distinctive spirituality alive in the black community which was essentially different from the spiritual climate in the white churches and which was a challenge to a separate theological articulation, independently of the thought patterns and definitions of white theology?

Such questions and insights were close to the hearts of the black clergy at a time when black nationalism was taking over hearts and minds. In the black churches this nationalism was interpreted in a radical way by figures like Albert Cleage, pastor of the Shrine of the Black Madonna in the heart of the black ghetto of Detroit, where in June 1967 there were very serious outbursts of violence. For Cleage, who had close connections with Malcolm X, Jesus was the black messiah and belonged to the black nation of Israel: according to him it was impossible for the biblical people to have been a white people judged by the definitions of black and white which held in America; on the contrary, Jesus was the black leader of a black people which was struggling for its national liberation against the domination of Rome, a white nation. A white person who took part in one of the many meetings where Cleage spoke, a consultation arranged in November 1967 by the Urban Training Centre in Chicago, gave the following impression of him:

> The black interpretation of Christianity is heard in silence, in a room full of church leaders, without any discussion. The main points are roughly as follows: Christianity was originally a revolutionary religion. Moses was charged to keep the people of Israel in the wilderness for forty years until all who had the sign of slavery had died. After that they went to take possession of the land given by God, with all the means that they needed. Jesus was a revolutionary leader the essence of whose activity can only be understood from his attempts to lead his people out of oppression into freedom by rebuilding the nation. Christianity was a good religion until the time of the crucifixion; from that moment on the falsification began and through Paul's letters the Bible became a Bible for whites.
>
> In America Christianity as it had been accepted by the negroes was a religion which Ol'Massa commended. It was a slave religion, but for centuries it fulfilled a necessary function: on Sunday the black slaves went to church for strength to endure oppression from their white masters for the next six days. Now, however, the new black church has to teach black people to love and forgive one another and to work together for mutual support; every Sunday black people have to be given strength to fight against white oppression in the six weekdays.[199]

Although this Christian nationalism in which skin colour has a dominant theological function did not get much support from black church leaders and theologians, it did compel attention to the question whether and on what conditions it is theologically legitimate to speak of a black or a white Christ. Albert Cleage was probably the first to give blackness a central position in his pastorate and his theology and to connect it with liberation.[200] That was also the significance of his collection of sermons, *The Black Messiah*, which appeared in 1968.[201]

Once brought to life the NCNC was quickly swept away in the turbulent nationalistic current in which the movement had got caught up. 'Swept away' is the right term here, for as Vincent Harding critically notes,[202] while the church leaders reacted to white racism in increasingly more radical statements, they lacked organization,[203] and the creative capacity to take the initiative and give actual impetus to the radical changes of which the declarations speak. Nevertheless a prophetic fire glows in them, a sense that there is no evading the *kairos*. It is still not too late to show that the churches are really present in the ghettos and are working for justice 'in the places of social change and upheaval where our Master is already at work'.[204]

A decisive moment was the conference arranged by the American Council of Churches in Washington, DC, in September 1967 on the urban crisis. The black participants insisted that the assembly should be split into a black and a white caucus, each of which would come out with its own declaration. Barely a year later there were black caucuses in nine of the predominantly white church denominations in the United States,[205] which provided as it were a material basis for the 'reflection on the difference' that was beginning. This reflection was in turn very deliberately stimulated by the Theological Commission Project of the NCNC under the presidency of Gayraud S. Wilmore. This commission came into being because the NCNC no longer wanted to be dependent on a theology which was felt to be white; its task was to investigate whether a consensus could be reached among black theologians and historians of religion over the fundamental theological questions and dilemmas which the church leaders saw before them. After widespread consultation,[206] on 13 June 1969 the commission came out with a declaration which was meant as a kind of Barmen declaration, a confession to provide support in the struggle. The declaration, which was produced by theologians like James Cone, Preston Williams, Henry Mitchell and

Deotis Roberts,[207] is simply entitled *Black Theology*; the most important passage runs,

> Black Theology is a theology of black liberation. It seeks to plumb the black condition in the light of God's revelation in Jesus Christ, so that the black community can see that the gospel is commensurate with the achievement of black humanity. Black Theology is a theology of 'blackness'.[208]

Those who produced the declaration based the theological relevance of blackness on the incarnation of the Word. The partisan presence of Jesus Christ as the liberator of the dehumanized and those without rights was confessed on the basis of Luke 4.18, the *locus classicus* of liberation theology. This living presence is not, however, a discovery of some theologians trained in exegesis but a historical experience which the black community has had in its struggle for survival and which has found expression in the slave songs, in the revivals of black preachers and in all kinds of other forms of black spirituality. So black theology does not bring any new insights of faith but is an articulation from the past in a language which speaks to the contemporary situation in which blacks find themselves. One sentence is of great hermeneutical importance: '*All* theologies arise out of communal experience with God.'[209] Theology is not a private affair but the affair of a community. Black theology serves the black community in its struggle for liberation, and this liberation is described in terms like achievement of black humanity, affirmation of black humanity, or affirming the dignity of black personhood.

But however much black humanity is also the subject of black theology, liberation is very much seen as a two-sided process in which both whites and blacks are affected. However, the recognition of Jeuss Christ as the liberator calls on whites to put an end to all forms of a sense of superiority and misuse of power. That can only come about by concrete repentance. So the declaration supports the demand for reparations which James Forman had put to the churches a month earlier in the *Black Manifesto*. With a reference to the remark of the publican Zacchaeus in Luke 19.8, 'if I have extorted anything from anyone, I repay it fourfold', the need for reparations is seen as an essential element in penitence:

The church which calls itself the servant church must, like its

Lord, be willing to strip itself of possessions in order to build and restore that which has been destroyed by the compromising bureaucrats and conscienceless rich. While reparation cannot remove the guilt created by the despicable deed of slavery, it is, nonetheless, a positive response to the need for power in the black community.

In this way the declaration gives theological legitimation to the support by NCNC – in the meantime, significantly enough, rebaptized as the NCBC, National Committee of Black Churchmen – of the *Black Manifesto*, which was hotly disputed even in the black churches.[210]

It is time to round off this account of the historical and socio-political background. On the basis of what has been said earlier I would mention three points which are important for understanding the context of black theology.

1. Although black theology became known thanks to publications by individual theologians like Cone and Roberts, its real *Sitz im Leben* was provided by the activities and position of the NCBC and some related organizations.[211] Black theology is a product of the creative imagination of those representatives of the black church who, confronted with the revolt in the black ghettos, recalled the subversive praxis of the 'invisible church' of the time of slavery and the revolutionary preaching of Henry Highland Garnet and Henry McNeal Turner. The real subjects of black theology are not, or at any rate not in the first instance, the professional theologians, but those black Christians who, in obedience to the command of the hour, ventured into the boundary territory between integration and separatism, non-violence and self defence, black church and black power.[212] The basis of black theology is therefore the black church – which must be taken to include both the separate black churches and black Christians in predominantly white denominations. Here we must remember that the black church occupies such a dominant place historically in the black community that even now the one is unthinkable without the other.[213]

Only secondarily is black theology a matter for theological faculties and seminaries. That was also the case chronologically. Both Gayraud S. Wilmore[214] and James H. Cone[215] distinguish three phases in the development of black theology: whereas the first phase was supported by the NCBC, from 1970 the arena moved to the college lecture room. The establishment of the Society for the Study of Black Religion (SSBR) made an important contribution in getting black religious experience on to the agenda at university level. However, the danger of this period was that black theology became too much of an academic affair without influencing the daily practice of the black church. The third phase, which begins in 1976,[216] is characterized by the struggle to take black ecumenism seriously and in a sense is to be regarded as a return to the church commitment of the first phase.

2. The history of the rise of black theology was determined by a struggle on three fronts. The first relates to the struggle within the black church; here it was a question of detaching black churchgoers from their ties to the American Christ and pointing them to this other, the black Messiah Jesus, who has left his traces in the black experience of slavery and segregation. Thus black theology implies criticism of the church, criticism of the way in which black Christians have internalized the white Christ and allowed themselves to be alienated from their own culture, history and situation.

However, confronting the black church with its own subversive past – a past which King took up in a particular way by his ability to combine political struggle and eschatological expectation in a prophetic proclamation of a *kairos* – also had the aim of making clear to the young nationalists who blamed the black church for an Uncle Tom syndrome that they did not know the history of the black church properly and were mistaken about its potential power as an instrument of liberation. Black theology is therefore also an appeal to a younger generation not to write off the black church.

The third front is directed against the closed discourse of white theology; this theology is unmasked as white because it has committed the deadly sin of omission (C.Eric Lincoln) in respect of black experience and in so doing has contributed to the subtle mechanisms of domination of which blacks are the victims. The vehement polemic, especially that of James Cone, is a means of breaking open this discourse and making room for theological theorizing which relates to this 'blackness'. Although polemic carries with it the danger that one is determined by what one opposes, the conquest of this theological sphere is a condition for any further development.

3. The history of the origin of black theology is indissolubly

connected with both the movement for civil rights and Black Power, with Martin Luther King and with Malcolm X. It is a stubborn misunderstanding to·think that black theology backed Black Power against King.[217] The first books of black theology in fact cover the whole field from integration to separatism. If Albert Cleage represents an extreme nationalist position, over against this are both *Liberation and Reconciliation: A Black Theology* (1971) and *A Black Political Theology* (1974), by J.Deotis Roberts, and *Black Awareness: A Theology of Hope* (1971) and *Christian Ethics for Black Theology* (1974) by Major J.Jones, which are concerned to stress the universal outreach of the gospel. In so doing they come close to Martin Luther King, and this also holds for Joseph R.Washington's *The Politics of God* (1967), which interprets the theme of the representative suffering of the black people. In 1969 Washington, not bothered about revising his thinking, discussed the theology of Black Power in *Black and White Power Subreption* and argued for violence as the only strategy that would lead to victory.[218] Black Power was also embraced by James H.Cone in *Black Theology and Black Power* (1969) and *A Black Theology of Liberation* (1970), though his nationalism is considerably more sophisticated than that of Cleage.[219]

It is clear that these publications do not just stand side by side in communal wrestling over a theology to serve the liberation of the black community but partially also stand over against one another. The gulf between the extremes of separatism and integralism is too great to be bridged. One of the important controversies is about the relationship between liberation and reconciliation. In the polemic between James Cone and Deotis Roberts on this point, for the former liberation precedes reconcilation, whereas for Roberts the two are indissolubly interwoven.[220] Were this an abstract dogmatic discussion, one might soon get the impression that it was an empty play on words. However, when one remembers the specific historical context of the debate it certainly is an important argument over the strategy to be followed. This latter point also applies to Preston N.Williams' criticism of Cone's position. In an article 'James Cone and the Problem of a Black Ethic' which appeared in 1972, Williams accuses Cone of irrationality;[221] Williams is looking for a rational basis for action 'by reliance upon some prima-facie duties acknowledged by the generality of mankind';[222] for ethics stands or falls with honest consideration and free choice; black theology may be under no obligation here, but, as Williams says at the end of his article, blacks know better than anyone what are the fruits of irrationality and emotionalism.[223]

So if the views of James H.Cone are certainly not undisputed, the publication of *Black Theology and Black Power* made him in a very short time the leading figure among black theologians. Gayraud S.Wilmore, himself more than ever the coordinator and inspirer behind the scenes,[224] writes in his *Black Religion and Black Radicalism*:

> In the midst of the crisis [over the Black Manifesto] a little-known scholar with a doctorate in systematic theology from Northwestern University joined the faculty of Union Theological Seminary in New York City and made a singular contribution to these developments. James H.Cone's first book, *Black Theology and Black Power*, appeared during the height of the debacle over the Black Manifesto. Before its publication date, advance notices made it something of a sensation among black religionists. In 1969 Cone was the youngest of the new theologians and the first to suggest the broad outlines of what the NCBC theological commission was looking for – a theology that took the black experience seriously, including the search for countervailing power, while based upon an essentially classical interpretation of the Christian faith.[225]

If the publications mentioned above by black theologians in their totality cover the whole field of tension between the particularism of black power and the universalism of King's beloved community, James Cone is undoubtedly the one who has most sharply put into words what he experienced in the circle of the NCBC and who uses the sharpest weapons in the battle on the three fronts that I have indicated. Therefore there is every reason to pay special attention to his *Black Theology and Black Power* and *A Black Theology of Liberation*.

3. Black theology and black power

When at the end of his life Karl Barth looked back once again at his career and remembered the deep hermeneutical crisis in which he had landed in 1914 as minister in Safenwil, Papageno's words from Mozart's *The Magic Flute* went through his head: 'My child, what shall we say now?' As is well known, the answer was, 'The truth, the truth, even if it were a crime.' 'But,' said Barth, 'that was easier said than done.'[226]

We have to remember that the catastrophe of the First World War meant no less for him than the final collapse of the bourgeois Christian world and the complete bankruptcy of a theological science which had sought and found the locus of the divine revelation in the history, and especially in the intellectual history, of this society.[227] But the 'epistemological break'[228] with the liberal world of his theological teachers did not of itself provide the 'wholly other' foundation that Barth and his friend Thurneysen thought necessary![229] Where were the building bricks for this new foundation to come from? It could be argued that only with the completion of Barth's study of Anselm's proof of God, *Fides Quaerens Intellectum*, in 1931 did the epistemological break really become a fact. In his view only then had he sufficiently thought through the epistemological implications of the discovery of the 'wholly other' God in Jesus Christ.[230]

In 1967 and 1968 James H. Cone found himself in a similar position to Barth and Thurneysen in 1914. Experiences of the racism (mostly latent) in his theological training, the refusal of white theologians to take the black experience seriously in theological terms even in the explosive situation of the violence in Watts, Newark and Detroit and the murder of Martin Luther King, led Cone to an intuitive feeling of theological bankruptcy.[231] Everything that had been communicated to him in his theological study became incredible in the light of the situation in the black ghettos. What had the story of Jesus Christ to do with the black struggle for survival? What relationship did the black religious experience have to the theology of Luther, Calvin, Barth and Bultmann?

These questions tormented him, and the words, 'My child, what shall we say now?' also applied to him. But it was not Mozart that ran through his head, but the spirituals and the blues with which he had been familiar from his earliest youth. For the small black community in Bearden, Arkansas in which Cone grew up, this music was an essential part of the daily struggle for survival. In his third book, *The Spirituals and the Blues*,[232] Cone tells how on Saturday evenings men and women, weary from their daily humiliations and from work in the sawmills and factories, could get vent their feelings in the rhythm of the blues:

If de blues was wiskey,
I'd stay drunk all the time.[233]

Others sought their salvation in singing spirituals and gospel songs on Sunday in the Macedonia African Methodist Episcopal Church. The roots of Cone's black theology lie in the spirituality of this community. In *My Soul Looks Back* he writes about the black church in Bearden:

> After being treated as things for six days of the week, black folk went to church on Sunday in order to affirm and experience another definition of their humanity. In the eyes of the Almighty, they were children of God whose future was not defined by the white structures that humiliated them. That was why they called each other Mr and Mrs or brother and sister. The value structures in the society were completely reversed in the church. The last became first in that the janitor became the chairman of the Steward Board and the maid became the president of Stewardess Board Number One. Everybody became somebody and there were no second-class people at Macedonia.[234]

These experiences proved a decisive factor in the crisis period of 1967 and 1968. Recollection of his father's pride and his mother's piety[235] made it impossible for Cone to accept the gulf between Christian faith and Black Power. So the crisis became the beginning of a new way which had to lead to a dialectical connection between the (hi)story of Jesus and the story that black people in America tell of themselves. But in order to make room for this connection and this story, by means of the razor-sharp polemic into which he transformed his pent-up anger, Cone had violently to break into a theological discourse in which there was no place for the black experience. However, the striking thing is – and we shall have to get back to this later – that the 'epistemological break' with the dominant white theological tradition came about on the basis of a counter image provided by the same tradition. That means that however much this tradition might have passed over the black experience of God, it was in itself heterogeneous enough to provide room for conflicting voices. In fact Jürgen Moltmann, Paul Tillich, Dietrich Bonhoeffer and Karl Barth were the theologians who provided the ammunition with which Cone opened fire on white Christian praxis and tradition.[236] There is still little of specifically black culture and history in his first two books.[237] Obviously first of all the battering ram had to be set to the closed door of the theological academy before room was made for the theological exploration of blackness. But this does not alter the fact that right from the very beginning it was not Tillich or Moltmann but the spirituality of the black church which proved the distinctive breeding ground for the passion with which James Cone put his intellect to work – *fides quaerens intellectum!* – in order to seek a theological answer to the burning question what Jesus Christ has to do with the black struggle for power and identity.

The analogy between Cone's epistemological break in the 1960s and that of Barth in the 1920s is intriguing – all the more if what Klauspeter Blaser says in his book *Wenn Gott schwarz wäre* is true: 'It is not illegitimate to suppose that here [in Cone's black theology] perhaps for the first time in American theology Karl Barth is really accepted and incorporated.'[238] Cone himself also gives occasion for making the comparison with Barth when in *My Soul Looks Back* he gives a retrospective survey of the prior history of *Black Theology and Black Power*:

I decided to write a brief manifesto identifying Black Power with the gospel of Jesus. I knew that a persuasive presentation of that thesis would cause the theological hairs on the heads of white theologians and preachers to stand up straight. From Barth and others I knew all about the ideological dangers of my procedure. Identifying the gospel with historico-political movements was anathema to anyone who bases his theology on divine revelation. But I purposely intended to be provocative in much the same way that Barth was when he rebelled against liberal theology. As Barth had turned liberal theology up-side-down, I wanted to turn him right-side-up with a focus on the black struggle in particular and oppressed people generally. No longer would I allow an appeal to divine revelation to camouflage God's identification with the human fight for justice. I was angry not with Barth but only with European and North American Barthians who used him to justify doing nothing about the struggle for justice. I have always thought that Barth was closer to me than to them. But whether I was right or wrong about where Barth would stand on the matter, the truth was that I no longer was going to allow privileged white theologians to tell me how to do theology.[239]

However, the great question remains whether Cone, regardless of how provocative he wants to be, has not crossed theological boundaries which from Barth's perspective have to be taken into account no matter what. How is the *diastasis* between God and humanity which lies behind Barth's rejection of any form of natural theology to be reconciled with the identification of the black revolution with the work of Christ?[240] Is there no irreducible contrast between Barth's discovery of God as the wholly other and Cone's confession of God's blackness? Has Cone not lost sight of the 'infinite qualitative difference' between God and humanity when he describes Black Power as a manifestation of God's ever ongoing activity in the liberation of humanity from slavery?

Here we are touching on a vital point which most critics of Cone's work think very important. Even those among them who completely recognize the right of black theology to exist have the fear that Cone has succumbed to the very *hybris* of which he accuses white theologians. Does not the *eschatological proviso* also apply to black theology? Does Cone not run the risk of claiming God's revelation for a particular group or race – and in so doing make the same mistake as the white theology which he rightly attacks at this point? In the last resort does not theology ultimately become ideology for him, the justification of specific human interests and concerns? Does not Cone forget that black people, too, fall under the judgment of God? Klauspeter Blaser expresses the concern of many people when he says of black theology: 'The true God who shows himself in the new and true man Jesus Christ is the judge who judges the perversions of white and black human beings.'[241] And Helmut Gollwitzer points out that God's partisan intervention in favour of the oppressed cannot mean that black people are better or that the *metanoia* that is necessary for every person is easier for them. God's partisanship for the oppressed is not a yes 'to everything they do in various enterprises'.[242] In the last chapter of this book we shall return to the charge of being an ideology that black and white theology mutually level against each other. But in order to be able to do that well we must first ask whether God's otherness can be combined with his blackness. Then we must show that in the criticism I have mentioned above the weak spot of *Black Theology and Black Power* and *A Black Theology of Liberation* is located in the wrong place because this criticism takes too little account of the specific dynamics of a movement of thought of which Cone's first books mark the beginning.

(a) God as alien and partisan

In his lecture 'Biblical Questions, Vistas, and Prospects', given in 1920, Karl Barth describes religion as a phenomenon which, while it is related to and knows of God, truth and worldly matters, at the same time constantly corrupts its own involvement and knowledge.[243] Religion forgets that she only has a right to exist when she continually does away with herself. Instead of that she regards herself as indispensable. She cannot bear waiting, being a stranger and a pilgrim. Her problem is her wealth 'of sentimental and symbolic associations, of interesting nooks for the soul, of dogma, cultus and morality, of ecclesiastical circumstance'.[244] She gives the impression of being in possession of a gold mine and in so-called religious values actually pretends to give out chinking coins. 'She takes her place as a competitive power over against other powers in life, as an alleged superior would over against the world. She sends missionaries as if she herself could give them a mission.'

In fact in doing this the religious person appropriates to himself both God and the world. He sacralizes reality. Without a blush he speaks of 'Christian' morals, clubs and organizations. Prayer – 'that last possibility grasped at by spirit-imprisoned souls in their deepest need or joy' – becomes a more or less recognized element of bourgeois housekeeping or church-keeping. Over against this religious *hybris*, which simply allows itself everything, including talking about God in us – I in you, you in me – over against this religious objectification Barth sets the piety of the Bible, which is aware of its own limitations and relativity. This piety points beyond itself and lives by the object to which it is related. It hardly takes any account of its own religious experience: 'In biblical experience nothing is less important than experience as such.'[245]

Barth finds this attitude symbolized in the figure of John the Baptist as Matthias Grünewald depicts him on the Isenheim altar, with an excessively long finger pointing to the wretched figure of the crucified Christ. By him are the words *Illum oportet crescere, me autem minui*: 'The object, the reality, the Divine Himself takes on new meaning; and the meaning of piety as such, of the function of the church as such, falls away. We may call that the characteristic insight of the Bible.'[246]

Grünewald's figure of Christ has nothing of the *Christus trium-phans* about it. In fact we see nothing but a wretched human being, one of the rejected of the earth. And of this figure it is said: *illum oportet crescere*! This abhorrent figure is certainly no projection of the self-understanding of bourgeois man. Rather, he represents the other side of the historical progress of this person, and all the religious values he bears. And it is ultimately with an eye to this outcast that as early as 1914 Barth can speak of God as someone who has become alien to us,[247] as a stranger.

Dieter Schellong has rightly pointed out that talk of this kind of God as a stranger, as a specific counter-reality,[248] must be understood in the historical context of theology after 1914. For Barth the First World War was a symptom of the deeper fundamental crisis for the political and economic system which even religious experience could not escape. In his essay 'Theology after 1914' Schellong says:

> We appreciate the depth of the problem if we become aware of the reversal of progress into self-destruction, if we understand 1914 as a sign set over all the subsequent years and thus also as the manifestation of the principle of a lengthy development; where the failure to heed the victims of progress which has been practised for so long and the trampling down of these victims as a necessary element in progress comes to an end.[249]

The decisive question is whether the context of the modern world described here, in which God can be mentioned only as a concrete counter-reality, extends so far that the infinite qualitative difference between time and eternity in fact applies without qualification to all people in the same way. Doing 'contextual theology' would then be superfluous and dangerous. For in that case it is universally true that 'all have sinned and fall short of the glory of God' (Rom.3.23).[250]

Now it would be far too easy to exclude the victims whom Schellong mentions in the above quotation from this historical context by drawing a neat line between oppressed and oppressors. To be oppressed in fact means that one cannot avoid the world of the oppressor, far less his religious values. That also applies to black history and culture. Here the white God, whose power is the projection of the powers that be, is emphatically present. Blacks have not been able to avoid the worship of all that this idol represents, and that is precisely why Cone, in contrast to what some critics think, relates God's judgment firmly to black history and the black church.[251]

But black history is a history of struggle – also at the level of religious imagination. Black slaves have been aware of God's otherness, of the fact that he is a stranger in a world of death and oppression. They have recognized this otherness in the crucified one, and in him they have recognized their own fate and struggle. So they counted Jesus one of them, a friend and ally in the struggle for life.

> They nail my Jesus down
> They put him on the crown of thorns,
> O see my Jesus hangin' high!
> He look so pale an' bleed so free:
> O don't you think it was a shame,
> He hung three hours in dreadful pain?[252]

Black history confronts theology with a fundamental epistemological insight: God's otherness or exteriority ('the vertical from above') is not a theological metaphysic but is indissolubly connected with the fate and struggle of those for whom there is no place in his world. Their otherness represents his otherness. And in a society which is dominated by the conflict between white and black, this means that God is black.

When James Cone confesses God's blackness, in a world of white racism his theology is *ipso facto* polemical theology – but this polemic takes place in complex ideological power relationships where 'white' or 'black' are not simply determined by the colour of someone's skin.[253] In this theology God's blackness is expressly based on the biblical witness.[254] For Cone, Jesus Christ, the living Lord, remains the norm of any theological and anthropological statement.[255] But as *living* Lord, Jesus will not be imprisoned in the first century. He is our contemporary, who proclaims deliverance to the captives and condemns all those who tacitly accept injustice. He is present where people live on the periphery of existence, and in the America of the 1960s this means that he can be found in the ghetto.[256] 'Thinking of Christ as nonblack in the twentieth century is as theologically impossible as thinking of him as non-Jewish in the first century.'[257] Where in a history and culture going back centuries blackness is associated with the dark side of existence, with not-being – with all the anxiety, self-hatred and fascination which go with this, as a theologian Cone cannot interpret black power, i.e. the black courage to *be*, otherwise than as the work of Christ.[258] And where history shows an indissoluble connection between blackness and suffering, the theological assertion that God has no colour is a legitimation for passing over the causes and experience of racism and slavery. Over against this flat pseudo-universality black theology sets as it were a vertical universality which in the depths of blackness looks for the universality of a God who has chosen what is weak in the world to put to shame the strong (I Cor.1.27).

Of course there are risks in talking of God's blackness. Whether the predicate 'black' may be used to denote God or Christ depends very much on the specific historical context where that happens. But does not the same thing apply to Barth when he speaks of a God who comes to human beings from outside, a 'vertical from above'? Cone thinks,

> To be sure, as Barth pointed out, God's Word is alien to man and thus comes to him as a 'bolt from the blue', but one must be careful about which man one is speaking of. For the oppressors, the dehumanizers, the analysis is correct. However, when we speak of God's revelation to the oppressed the analysis is incorrect. His revelation comes to us in and through the cultural situation of the oppressed. His Word is our Word; his existence, our existence.[259]

Although the last sentence is dangerous if it is not understood in dialectical terms, here we come to the heart of the matter. What sense does it make to tell destitute people who have to experience their inferiority every day, that God is a stranger in their existence? The reality of the incarnation forbids an undifferentiated discussion of 'the' human situation as if this is the same for all human beings in the light of God's revelation. The biblical stories are a challenge to a 'reflection on the difference': the poor are blessed and woe is called down on the rich. The situation and social position in which people find themselves does make a difference.

Therefore it can come about that the 'epistemological break' which compels Barth in his situation to speak of God as the wholly other does not conflict with Cone's confession of God's blackness in the America of the 1960s. Where Barth fought against identification and appropriated God from his religious (including his religious socialist) contemporaries by describing him as the wholly other,

Cone dares to confess Christ's real presence in the black struggle. In both cases there is a reflection on the difference, which is meant not in dialectical and idealistic but in ontological terms: God's being is in no way to be thought of along with and identified with the existing powers; God's omnipotence as the absolute extrapolation (and thus legitimation) of the powers that be is radically rejected – it is here that confessing God's otherness has its significance. In both cases we have an epistemological break with a bourgeois reason which undertook 'to produce from itself the order which it had negated outside' (Adorno[260]).

Dialectic as the awareness of non-identity is distinctive of both Barth's and Cone's theology. However, the difference is that for Barth in *Romans* God's otherness comes as a vertical from above – God's revolution has no social surface in history, no historical subject, while Cone sees blackness as the embodiment of God's otherness. Is this distinction essential? In Barth's later work God's otherness seems increasingly clearly to be the other side of his humanity: the *totaliter aliter* of God's divinity becomes visible in his actual solidarity with the least among human beings in the person of the work of Jesus Christ. For Cone, too, there is a strict christological concentration, but since he lives in a different context and stands in a tradition in which everything depends on the bodily experience of the presence of the Spirit, Cone's theology tends towards a christological pneumatology which draws the consequences of the dialectical relationship between God's humanity and his otherness by identifying God in Jesus Christ with what in a racist culture represents otherness, namely being black.

(*b*) The 'epistemological break' as the beginning of a new way

However, it is legitimate to ask whether there are not greater tensions between Cone's theology and that of Barth than I suggested above. Does the difference ultimately amount just to a difference in context? Or is there more to it than that? It is clear that both confess a God who has made the cause of the oppressed his own. But is the presence of the messiah among the rejected of the earth given the same theological basis and thought through in the same way?

There is certainly a conflict between Latin American liberation theology and Barth in this respect. Among Latin American liberation theologians there is a tendency to think of the relationship between Jesus and the poor in ontological terms: we see Christ in the faces of the poor; there is a mystical ontological bond between the crucified one and the crucified people in El Salvador or anywhere else in world history.[261] This solidarity of Christ with the poor, understood in ontological terms, makes it possible to see the poor as a medium of revelation. However, for Barth, for whom the cross and resurrection of Christ form a unique and unrepeatable event, this solidarity is purely factical: so in para.18 of his *Church Dogmatics* he writes about 'The Life of the Children of God':

> In what Jesus says about the last judgment in Matt.25.1f., both those on the right hand and those on the left declare quite definitely that they did not know that they had or had not given Jesus to eat and drink and sheltered and clothed and visited Him. This must be a warning to us that it is not a question of seeing Jesus in our fellow man. The text does not say that he is to be seen in these 'least' as His brethren, but that He actually declares Himself to us in solidarity, indeed in identity with them.[262]

Where does Cone stand in this discussion? Does he see the identification of Christ with the most insignificant in factical or ontological terms? It is striking that nowhere does Cone attribute to blacks a natural disposition to salvation. Blacks do not have anthropological properties which make them a medium of revelation. In this sense Cone is concerned for a factical presentation which does not infringe God's freedom.

However, things are more complicated, at least in his first two books. In *A Black Theology of Liberation*[263] he calls blackness an ontological symbol and in so doing refers specifically to Paul Tillich's description of the symbolic character of any theological terminology. Tillich draws an important distinction between symbol and sign. A sign does not necessarily have a relationship to that to which it points; by contrast a symbol participates in the reality for which it stands. Religious symbols do the same thing as all other symbols: they open up a level of reality which otherwise would remain hidden. We can only talk of God in symbols, but these participate in the reality to which they point. This implies an *analogia entis*,[264] an analogy of being, between God and finite reality. But participation is not complete identity. God's reality transcends any symbolizing.[265]

When Cone speaks of the black Messiah, 'black' is not 'just a symbol'. As long as the 'colorline' marks a basic conflict in society, the expression black theology cannot simply be replaced by the more general 'theology of the oppressed' without damaging the concreteness called for by God's word. But the identification of Christ with blackness is not exclusive. Other symbols can be legitimate, depending on the context.

I would maintain that for Tillich the use of religious symbols implies an analogy of being and I assume that in this Cone follows Tillich. This impression is confirmed when we look at the methodology of *A Black Theology of Liberation*. As Tillich says, 'since the method is derived from a preceding understanding of the subject of theology, the Christian message, it anticipates the decisive assertions of the system'.[266] What are the sources and norm of Cone's theology? The distinction between sources and norm which Cone uses in Chapter 2 of his book also appears in Tillich, in the introduction to his *Systematic Theology* in which he discusses the method and structure of his theology.[267] Tillich draws a distinction between three sources from which the theologian draws his knowledge: 1. the Bible; 2. church history; 3. the history of culture and religion. But these sources are only accessible to those who really take part through experience; experience is thus not itself a source, but the medium through which knowledge of the sources comes to us.

The question then remains: what is the criterion by which what is given through the sources is tested? Tillich describes this criterion or material norm as the 'New Being in Jesus as the Christ'. Only now do we come into what according to Tillich is an unavoidable hermeneutical circle, since we only know the norm through the sources. 'Since the norm of systematic theology is the result of an encounter of the church with the biblical message, it can be called a product of the collective experience of the church. But such an expression is dangerously ambiguous.'[268] At any rate, it could mean that the collective experience produces the norm! Precisely because of this danger it is extremely interesting to see how the third source, the history of religion and culture, functions in Tillich. This question is all the more important because, according to Tillich, we are always dealing on the one hand with the message of the gospel and on the other with the human situation. The danger is that when the one pole of the human situation is related to the other pole, the gospel, the substance of the latter is lost.[269]

Tillich wants to remove that risk by giving an autonomous place independent of theology in the narrow sense to the philosophical, psychological or sociological analysis of the situation. The 'self-interpretation' of man in his culture then provides the existential questions to which theology must give the answer. Tillich calls this method the method of correlation; the questions which the human situation calls forth correlate with the answer that is given us by the gospel. Question and answer are dependent on each other. Thus Tillich's hermeneutical circle in fact has the form of an ellipse with two foci: the one is philosophical (psychological, sociological) and analyses the human situation in an autonomous way; the other is theological and interprets the Christian symbols as an answer to the one great question to which all the others point; that of oneself, of the true Reality from which human beings are alienated.

The difficulty with this method – at least one of the difficulties – lies in the impossiblity of an autonomous analysis of reality: 'Are not the questions which are brought to light involuntarily the negative of the answers that we immediately get?'[270]

In *A Black Theology of Liberation* Cone leans somewhat heavily on Tillich in his methodological and hermeneutical approach. Although he is well aware of the dangers of the method of correlation, his conviction is nevertheless that 'Black people need to see some correlations between divine salvation and Black culture.'[271] The gospel comes to us in and through the cultural situation of the oppressed.[272] On the basis of this gospel Cone begins his summing up of the sources of black theology with black experience, culture and history. And Holy Scripture? The Bible, too, is a source of revelation, but that does not mean that this book is a sort of guide that makes decisions for us; the significance of scripture does not lie in the words of scripture as such but in its power to point beyond itself to the reality of God's revelation.[273] Scripture itself is not the norm. Cone formulates the norm as follows:

> The norm of all God-talk which seeks to be black talk is the manifestation of Jesus as the Black Christ who provides the necessary soul for black liberation.[274]

In comparison with Tillich's method of correlation it is striking that Cone takes his anthropological point of reference from the situation of the oppressed black community. Cone can justify that because in his view the oppressed person is the point of reference for Christ himself. In a remarkable passage from *Black Theology and Black Power* which is concerned with teaching authority, he attacks fundamentalism, liberalism and neo-orthodoxy by stating that another authority precedes that of scripture, which unites all blacks and which transcends the differences between the three directions mentioned above. This authority is the common experience of oppression: 'Black theology knows no authority more binding than the experience of oppression itself.'[275] Here we are back to our question of the *analogia entis*. If we take seriously what Cone writes here, it is clear that the two focal points of the ellipse, the gospel and the situation, find their connection in the experience of oppression. This experience gives black people, on the basis of an analogy of being, the possibility of speaking about God with authority.

Anyone who breaks with the dominant theological tradition must begin from the beginning. But how? The 'epistemological break' is in itself only the beginning of a movement of thought which cannot but be extremely difficult. Cone's black colleagues have accused him of still being very dependent on white theology, at least in his first two books. Is Cone really doing black theology, or is this in fact no more than white theology with a black veneer?[276]

However, these critics have failed to indicate where this dependence most takes its vengeance on Cone. In my view, in this respect the hermeneutical and methodological starting points are decisive. The method of correlation is incapable of doing justice to black theology as contextual theology. Because the two focal points of the ellipse are so closely related, this method has a remarkable unhistorical element: justice is not really done either to the specific history and situation of black people or to the specific nature of the biblical witness. The method of correlation is fundamentally too transparent to do justice to the opacity – a term used by Charles Long – of black history and experience. If it is indeed the task of theology to show what 'the changeless gospel means in each new situation',[277] then this theology in fact can no longer do justice to the mobility of the Spirit, far less to the problem of contextuality which only emerges in Cone's later work. The formulation itself already betrays the fact that the old scheme of *inventio-explicatio-applicatio*[278] still plays a part here. In methodological terms Cone still has not avoided being the prisoner of the dominant tradition of thought from which he wants to detach himself. And it is a direct consequence of the essentially abstract dialectic of the method of correlation that above all in *A Black Theology of Liberation* the tension between eschatology and history, particularity and universality, which is so vital for liberation theology, does not sufficiently come through.

Therefore Cone's first two books raise critical questions on three fronts. These are 1. the question of the content of liberation as a historical and eschatological reality, a question posed by the circle of black theology itself, formulated as it has been in different ways by Gayraud Wilmore, Cecil Cone, William Jones and Charles Long; 2. the structural question of the problem of contextuality, a question raised particularly by Latin American liberation theologians; 3. the functional question of the ideological content of black theology, a question which appears above all in the conversation with white theologians like Paul Lehmann and Helmut Gollwitzer.

In formulating these three questions we are in fact back at the three core concepts of liberation, context and theology which functioned in the first part of this book as pointers to the constitutive elements of a real theology of liberation.

In the third and last part, which will discuss the further development of black history, these terms return in reverse order. Here the question of the content of liberation (Chapter 4) leads to christology (the dialectic of cross and resurrection); the structural question of contextuality (Chapter 5) leads to ecclesiology (the dialectic of particularity and universality); and the question of its ideological functioning (Chapter 6) leads to the hermeneutic of the black story (the dialectic of power and love).

PART THREE

Black Theology
as Theology of Liberation

4 · Liberation

Black Theology in Dialogue with its Own Tradition

1. Historical liberation as a problem

Black theology is conservative in the literal sense. It conserves the past of slavery and segregation and does so in the knowledge that the quality of its commitment to liberation is dependent on the depths to which its own historical experience is plumbed.

But why must black people continue to carry the traumas of their past around with them? Does this not stand in the way of their social acceptance and their working towards a better future? Black theology is well aware of the enormous suction with which the one-dimensional tendencies of modern technological society pull the growing black middle class away from its own history and culture. However, at the same time it is aware that the saying of the great industrialist Henry Ford, 'History is bunk', is fatal to the identity and the self-awareness of black people.

No authentic future is possible without assimilating the past. But this past is not an open terrain, accessible to anyone who wants to enter it. Rather, it can be compared with an impenetrable wood, through which people have to hack a way. The black past is occupied by ideas and images which are cut to the measure of those who 'make' history. And who makes history if not the ruling class, the strong sex, the noble race? Therefore stories are still going the rounds about Africa as the continent without history, about black slaves as people without true religion and culture, about these same slaves as the passive objects of their masters with no will of their own, about the 'pathological entanglement' in which they are caught up as a result, about their inability to unite among themselves, or about their emotional religious feelings and the belief in the hereafter in which they take refuge. All these myths and images have two characteristics: 1. they have enough points of contact in reality to be able to cling tenaciously to existence as absolutized partial truths; 2. they explain situations of oppression which have grown up in history in such a way that the reason why blacks are backward is subtly laid at their own door and the white history-makers are given a philanthropic task to perform towards their black fellow human beings.[1]

The black nationalism of the 1960s sensed the importance of the struggle for the past as an essential part of the struggle for the future. Black studies, black history, black sociology and also the Society for the Study of Black Religion (SSBR) were the result of the efforts made on the level of the historical depiction of reality which is so essential for the struggle against racism. Here people did not always resist the temptation to make the historical investigation subordinate to what was thought necessary for the black struggle for liberation. Thus it could come about that the pitiful Sambo of the white historian Stanley Elkins turned into a black resistance hero, and that what was earlier regarded as a history of assimilation was now transformed into a history of violent opposition.

However, liberation is not served with absolutized half historical truths on either one side or the other. The interpretation of the black past in heroic terms is essentially a bad imitation of the historiography from which there is a desire to get free. Romanticizing nationalism, precisely because of its exclusivist interest, gets caught up in the dense web that the dominant portrayal of reality has spun around the reality of blackness. One does not make any changes in the structure of the web simply by changing the roles. The texture of historical fabrications is only broken apart when the realization dawns that coping with a past which is hard to get at and even harder to accept is a task to be shared between whites and blacks. This inclusive interest in historical truth resounds unmistakably through Vincent Harding's essay 'The Uses of the Afro-American Past', written in 1969:

> It is my thesis, and partly the motivation for my work, that an American history which cannot contain the full story of the black pilgrimage is no more worthy of life than an American society that cannot bear the full and troublesome black presence in its midst... The urgency some of us feel for the creation of such a

new American history is no less critical than the pressure that impels us to seek for the lineaments of a new American society. Obviously, the tasks are not unrelated. For there will be no new beginnings for a nation that refuses to acknowledge its real past.[2]

Since Harding wrote these words much has happened in Afro-American historiography. An imposing cavalcade of historical studies written by black and white scholars has shed new light on the world that the black slaves created for themselves. Some of the most important are: George P.Rawick, *From Sundown to Sunup*, Greenwood Press, Westport 1972; John W.Blassingame, *The Slave Community. Plantation Life in the Antebellum South* (revised and enlarged edition), Oxford University Press 1979; Eugene D.Genovese, *Roll, Jordan, Roll. The World the Slaves Made*, Random House 1974; Herman G.Gutman, *The Black Family in Slavery and Freedom 1750-1925*, Random House 1976; Lawrence W.Levine, *Black Culture and Black Consciousness*, Oxford University Press, New York 1977; and Vincent Harding, *There is a River. The Black Struggle for Freedom in America*, New York 1981. The world which is mapped out in these publications still has a good deal of *terra incognita*, of impenetrable areas, in it. Particularly in these publications it emerges that black history is in two senses a silent history: not only concealed by the white feeling of guilt but also removed from the eye of the beholder by the black self, which refused to hand over to the oppressor its deepest experiences and feelings:

> Got one mind for white folks to see
> 'Nother for what I know is me;
> He don't know, he don't know my mind.[3]

The reality of blackness is never simply a given; to a degree it is hidden, invisibly present in the womb of history. It tolerates only a dialectical approach which takes account of the ambiguous reality of the slave: if on the one hand the existence of the slave is fully determined by the will of the white master who robbed his slaves of their language, land, religion and history, on the other hand, as Gutman has shown, at the same time there was in the slave community a definite family structure of African origin which put slaves in a position to pass down customs and patterns of behaviour from generation to generation: if blacks on the one hand had largely to adapt to the dominant forms of American society in order to be able to survive, on the other hand they remained aware of their African origin and thus of their otherness. This twofold awareness about which W.E.B. DuBois wrote in his *The Souls of Black Folk* – 'two souls, two thoughts, two unreconciled strivings'[4] – characterizes the dialectic of black history and experience. Black history is a history of adaptation and rebellion, of opposition and surrender, of resignation and revolt. Nowhere is that expressed more evocatively than in black religion, which came to have a central place in the life of the slave community. The two-sidedness of daily reality – determined by oppression but not exhausted by it – is expressed in the two-sidedness of a religious experience in which the 'promised land' or 'Canaan' which is celebrated in the spirituals points to another reality which can be located either in the free North or in Canada or in a world beyond.

How does black theology deal with the dialectic of black history and experience? How does this history relate to the theme of liberation which dominates the theology of James H. Cone? Is the talk in black theology about 'liberation' really compatible with the historical experience which blacks have had of 'God'? Or is this term simply a label which is stuck on this experience from outside for apologetic reasons?

Very soon after the appearance of the first publications these questions came to have a central place in the debate among black theologians and historians of religion. What is the relationship between black theology and the black religious experience? Does black experience justify our talking about the experience of God in terms of liberation?

While recognizing that James Cone has been foremost in pioneering theological argument in his first books and making room in it for black experience, Gayraud Wilmore nevertheless thinks that Cone has made himself too dependent on classical or traditional Christian theology. In his view black religion is a unique historical phenomenon which, while being closely bound up with the Christian tradition, is not exhausted in it.[5] The traditional African religions and even Islam have left their mark on black religious experience. The African perception of reality did not disappear during the harsh existence of slaves, but African religious feeling with its belief in the power of life, in the 'living dead', in magic and witchcraft, has left its mark on the 'collective unconscious' of black people. It forms the spiritual reservoir on which the black community, and especially its lowest layers, have constantly drawn in order to be able to survive in times of bitter need and repression. This black popular religious feeling is certainly to be found in the black churches, but not only there: it lives and flourishes in the charismatic movements, in the countless sects and cults, and in the various expressions of black nationalism. Therefore the locus of black theology cannot just be the black church. Black theology has to do with the life of the black community as a whole, and above all with its lowest strata.

> Black theologians must learn to appreciate and understand these roots before turning to white scholars for the substance of their reflection on the meaning of God, human existence, and freedom. Folk religion is a constituent factor in every significant crisis in the black community. We ignore it only at the risk of being cut off from the real springs of action. When the black community is relatively integrated with white society, the folk religious elements recede from black institutions to form a hard core of unassimilable nationalism in the interstices of the social system – biding its time. When the black community is hard-pressed by poverty and oppression, when hopes are crushed under the heels of resurgent racism, then essential folk elements exhibit themselves and begin once again to infiltrate the power centers that ignored or neglected them. This is the significance of the developments of the 1960s that Vincent Harding called 'the religion of Black Power'.[6]

The stress that Wilmore puts on the African origin of the black religious experience is also present in Henry Mitchell and Cecil W.Cone. In 1975 the latter wrote *The Identity Crisis in Black Theology*, in which he derived the identity crisis of black theology from the fact that it has no right to determine the unique character of black religion. Two factors got in the way of that: 1. dependence on white European theology, whether as a result of the appropriation of its methodology (James Cone), or as a result of a wrong emphasis on the universality of reconciliation (Deotis Roberts); 2. dependence on the political liberation motif of Black Power (James Cone, Joseph Washington). For Cecil Cone black religion is the starting point and norm (!) of black theology.[7] The concept of the Almighty Sovereign God has a central position in this. According to Cone, this concept of God, present in African traditional religion, survived the terrors of the traumatic crossing of the Atlantic and has governed the black experience of reality in the violent absurdity of slavery. If one can say that the three main sources of black religion were African tradition, the experience of slavery in America and the biblical proclamation, the factor that holds them together is a personal encounter with the Almighty Sovereign God. The deep experience of conversion and vocation with which this encounter is associated certainly gives men and women freedom, but this freedom transcends any form of social and political liberation. Political liberation cannot therefore be the starting point of black theology. Its beginning and end can only be encounter with the Almighty Sovereign God.[8]

In a review of Cecil Cone's book, Gayraud Wilmore showed that his attitude is problematical in three respects: 1. the character of black religion is described in a simplistic way; 2. there is a narrow view of the content of black religious experience; 3. Cone misunderstands the task of theology in general and that of black theology in particular.[9] Wilmore's criticism is justified. Because Cecil Cone has no eye for the ambivalence of black religion, and still less for the critical function of black theology, he runs the great risk of encouraging conservative trends in the church with his views – all the more where, as James H.Cone has observed in connection with his brother's book,[10] there is no political and social vision. However, none of this criticism does away with the fact that in his book Cecil Cone has touched on a vital problem: did the theme of liberation as articulated by James Cone and others really arise out of black history and experience? Or was it imposed from outside?

Two years before the appearance of *The Identity Crisis of Black Theology* these questions were discussed in depth from quite a different perspective by William R.Jones. In his book *Is God a White Racist?*, which appeared in 1973, theodicy was introduced as a problem which must dominate black theological argument. The unimaginable suffering of black people compels us to ask how it is possible to speak of God's liberating action in the face of this history of suffering. Whenever black theologians associate God with black liberation, in terms of method they in fact face the need to regard theodicy as a vital problem in their argument. At all events, does not the holocaust of black history point rather in the direction of a divine racism? Do historical events and misdeeds in any sense point in the direction of God's liberating intervention in favour of black people? What basis is there, then, for the claims of black liberation

theology? Is there a basis without which the existence of an 'exaltation-liberation event' can be demonstrated in black history and
experience in one way or the other? On the basis of this perspective
from the philosophy of religion Jones accuses black theologians like
Washington, James Cone, Roberts, Major Jones and Cleage of each
in his own way getting on the band-wagon: their starting point is
what they want to stress.

Jones goes on to say that this criticism is not external criticism but
internal criticism. The programmatical concern of black theology is
simply to refute the allegation of divine racism. As long as this does
not take place, the only possibility which remans open without
involvement in conflict is the option for a 'humanocentric theism'
which no longer counts on God's partisan intervention in history
but begins from the 'functional ultimacy of man'.[11] William Jones,
as a philosopher of religion, looks for a black humanism which will
find a place for itself alongside the now familiar texts of black
theology.[12]

In one sense the black historian of religion Charles H.Long stands
at the opposite extreme from William R. Jones. In this sense
the latter is a child of the ·Enlightenment, in that he calls for a
transparency of history which makes it possible in all honesty to
verify statements about God as the liberator in historical and
empirical terms. Long's starting point, by contrast, lies in the
opaqueness of the black historical experience – and this concept is
deliberately chosen as an indication of the other, dark side of
the Enlightenment. What does the period of the Enlightenment
represent to the colonized people among whom Long also includes
the black population of America?

In some senses all modern colonized peoples are products of this
period, for within the heteronomous context of the Enlightenment
the basis for modern racist theory, capitalism, humanitarianism
and Christianity may be located. The Enlightenment, true to
its name and symbolic reference, attempted to overcome the
opaqueness of the concrete forms of human life and nature. Its
analytical methods dissected reality for the sake of knowledge
and relegated the sheer depths of the real to the arena of
unknowability. It is this seeing through rather than 'standing
before' and 'coming to terms with', which is the hallmark of this
cultural orientation.[13]

However, by using the term 'opaque' as a symbolic concept for the situation of the African slave in America, Long is not only describing the social position of the slave on the other side of the modern history of the Enlightenment but also indicating a specific structure of consciousness which finds its origin in the opacity of blackness. In this blackness is manifested an otherness which, seen from the world of the Enlightenment, is infected, defiled and laden with guilt.[14]

> The otherness of Blackness hit us so hard that we hated that life could be this way. This Black reality took us down, down, way down yonder where we saw only another deeper Blackness, down where prayer is hardly more than a moan, down where life and death seem equatable. We descended into hell, into the deepest bowels of despair, and we were becoming blacker all the time. We cried like a Job and we laughed to keep from crying and we wanted to curse God and die.[15]

But black experience is a dialectical experience. In the impenetrable depths of blackness in one way or another a reversal takes place – here Charles Long refers to Hegel's paradigmatic description of the dialectic of master and slave in the *Phenomenology of Spirit*.[16] Blackness, as a symbol of inhumanity, anxiety, meaninglessness, cruelty and death, contains the germ of a new humanity, of a new meaning, of freedom, beauty and life. Those who have lived in cultures under oppression know something about freedom which the oppressors will never know. However, only the careful deciphering of the secret writing of one's own history can prevent the oppressed being doomed to imitate the power-structures of the leading classes and repeating the destructive circle of events.[17]

If black theology really seeks to work for a break in this destructive circle, then it is confronted with the task of becoming a 'theology of the opaque'. However, as Charles Long asks, is it in a position to achieve this? Is not black theology, in so far as it really seeks to be theology, burdened with a tradition which makes it impossible to penetrate to the depths of blackness? Is this tradition not so permeated with the spirit of Western Christianity and the Enlightenment that 'black' and 'theology' are at odds with each other? With these questions Charles Long raises, perhaps more radically than anyone else, the question whether black theology is not impossible.

Here we have in fact returned to the key question of this

chapter: does the black experience justify talking about Christ as the liberator? However, before we go further into a discussion of this we need a closer reconnaissance of what concepts like black experience and black religion represent as a historical experience of reality. To this end, in the next section we must look at the sphere of the history of religions.

2. The black experience

The specific experience of faith which is known as black religion was born in slavery. What was baptized by E.Franklin Frazier as the 'invisible church' came into being in the plantations during secret meetings of the slave community between sundown and sunup – though we have indications that the invisible church can be seen earlier in history than the famous black sociologist assumed.

Black theology refers back to this time of slavery, when it makes a connection between black religion and liberation. But is it right to do this? Did the faith-experience of the slaves really have a liberating effect? For a long time black religion was seen above all as a belief in the hereafter, as a flight from harsh reality and as compensation for the inhumanity of everyday existence. In past decades a large number of studies have been published which have changed this picture fundamentally – and this change cannot be detached from the rise of the black self-awareness of the 1960s.

Within the scope of this book it makes no sense to repeat what has already been described very well elsewhere; indeed that would be impossible. In pointing to the rich harvest of the research of past years I shall limit myself to indicating the essential elements in the experience of faith among the black slaves. So I shall begin with a brief bibliographical survey in order to stress the indicative character of this section.

One pioneering work was the article by Vincent Harding, 'Religion and Resistance Among Antebellum Negroes, 1800-1860', in August Meier and Elliot Rudwick (eds.), *The Making of Black America* 1, Atheneum Publications, New York 1969, 179-97. Harding in particular questions Benjamin E.Mays, *The Negro's God As Reflected in His Literature* (first impression 1938, reprinted with a foreword by Harding, Negro University Press, New York 1968), a book whose collection of texts is still valuable. Mays describes the religion of his people as 'otherworldly' and 'compensatory'. By contrast Harding stresses that the black experience of faith has two sides: protest and subjection.

The question of the function of black religion as opposition and/or opiate is closely connected with another question: how far were the black slaves capable of retaining their African heritage? Is black religion permeated by African spirituality or is it a product of Christian mission and evangelization? Scholars who stress the latter usually interpret black religion as belief in the hereafter, whereas those who argue for the influence of the African perception of reality accentuate the otherness of black religion over against the dominant Christian tradition and thus also its character as opposition.

There is a classic difference of opinion between E.Franklin Frazier and the anthropologist Melville J.Herkovits. Whereas in *The Myth of the Negro Past*, Peter Smith, New York (1941), Herkovits saw African survivals present in virtually every aspect of black life in the USA, Frazier wrote in *The Negro Church in America* (posthumously published by Schocken Books 1964, 6): 'It is our position that it was not what remained of African culture or African religious experience but the Christian religion that provided the new basis of social cohesion.' Wilmore pointed out that this view of Frazier's (who died in 1959) was connected with the 'attitudinal-change integrationism' which flourished in his time: a stress on the differences between white and black damaged the desired integration.

In *Slave Religion, The 'Invisible Institution' in the Antebellum South*, Oxford University Press, New York 1978, Albert J.Raboteau made a careful evaluation of the Herkovits-Frazier debate. If Herkovits went too far in pointing to African elements in the life of the slaves, Frazier was wrong when he thought that the systematic oppression of the slaves was so harsh that traditional beliefs, values and patterns of behaviour were totally obliterated. Raboteau's view is that, 'While it is true that Africa influenced black culture in the United States, it is also true that African theology and African ritual did not endure to the extent that they did in Cuba, Haiti and Brazil. In the United States the gods of Africa died.' According to Raboteau, this difference between the situation in the USA and that in the Caribbean and Latin America is connected with the fact that Catholicism offered more points of contact for African rites and customs than the Protestantism of the USA and further with the fact that there were relatively fewer whites on the plantations in Cuba or Brazil than in the South of the USA, while in addition in the USA more slaves were born in the country, which made recollection of their land of origin vaguer.

Raboteau's *Slave Religion* is essential reading for anyone who wants to study the black religious experience. Alongside this mention must also be made of Gayraud S.Wilmore's *Black Religion and Black Radicalism*, second revised and enlarged edition, Orbis Books, Maryknoll 1983, which deals with black religious history up to the present and succeeds even better than Raboteau in giving the reader a feeling for black experience. The analysis of spirituals and slave stories offered by Olli Alho in *The Religion of the Slaves*, Helsinki 1976, is also important: one small doubt about this Finnish study is that the distinction drawn in the analysis of the spirituals between messianic, eschatological and millennial elements hinders rather than helps any view of the inner connections and dynamic of the black experience of faith. New source material is worked on in Mechal Sobel, *Trabelin' On. The Slave Journey to an Afro-Baptist Faith*, Greenwood Press, Westport 1979. Among other things Sobel has been able to discover that already between 1758 and 1822 at least thirty-seven independent black churches were in existence, each with a name and nickname: the earliest is the African Baptist or Bluestone Church in Mecklenburg, Virginia. The 'invisible church' was more visible than has so far been assumed! Henry H.Mitchell probably goes further than any other black theologian in stressing the African character of the black experience of faith in America. In *Black Belief*, Harper and Row 1975, he discusses the effect of the African view of life and life-style on Afro-American popular religion, and in so doing comes to this conclusion: 'At the bottom of all African and Blackamerican belief is an unshakable affirmation of the goodness of creation and of human existence, under the rule of a powerful and benevolent Creator.' Other studies which deal with the process of acculturation of Africans in the new American world are: Roger Bastide, *Les Amériques noires: les civilizations africaines dans le Nouveau Monde*, Paris 1967; Sheila S.Walker, *Ceremonial Spirit Possession in Africa and Afro-America*, Leiden 1972; Leonard E.Barrett, *Soul-Force: African Heritage in Afro-American Religion*, Doubleday 1974. It goes without saying that one cannot form any judgment on these problems without knowledge of African traditional religion; a general introduction is John S.Mbiti, *African Religions and Philosophy*, Heinemann Educational 1969; id., *Concepts of God in Africa*, SPCK 1970. Most slaves came from West Africa which, however great the differences, forms a geographical and cultural unity; see Geoffrey Parrinder, *West African Religion*, Epworth Press 1970; E.Bolaji Idowu, *Olodumare, God in Yoruba Belief*, Longmans 1962; id., *African Traditional Religion*, SCM Press and Orbis Books, Maryknoll 1974: Kofi Asare Opoku, *West African Traditional Religion*, Singapore 1978.

The other component in Afro-American spirituality is the Protestant Evangelical tradition of faith which took hold in the Old South from the period of the first Great Awakening (1739-1742). The best study on the religious world of the South with its itinerant preachers, revivals and camp meetings is Donald G.Mathews, *Religion in the Old South*, University of Chicago Press 1977; other valuable studies are Milton C.Sernett, *Black Religion and American Evangelicalism*, Scarecrow Press, Metuchen 1975, and Erskine Clarke, *Wrestlin' Jacob. A Portrait of Religion in the Old South*, John Knox Press, Atlanta 1979, in which much attention is paid to the work of the Presbyterian preacher Charles Colcock Jones, the 'Apostle to the Negro Slaves' and author of *The Religious Instruction of the Negroes in the United States*, Savannah 1842, reprinted Negro University Press, New York 1969. For the attitude of the churches to slavery see Donald G.Mathews, *Slavery and Methodism*, Princeton University Press 1965; H.Shelton Smith, *In His Image, But... Racism in Southern Religion, 1780-1910*, Duke University Press 1972; Lester B.Sherer, *Slavery and the Churches in Early America 1618-1819*, Eerdmans, Grand Rapids 1975.

However powerful the effect of African origin may have been, and however much impression the Christian missionary message may have made, a third factor underlay the growth of Afro-American popular religion, namely the situation of slavery. It must never be forgotten that black religion is the product of a slave people. However, it was not until the 1970s that historians sufficiently recognized the dialectical interaction between slave community and black religion: as black religion is the product of the black community, so conversely it can be said that the black experience of faith was constitutive of the slave community. Examples of studies in which justice is done to the place and function of black religion in the framework of a general description and analysis of the world which the slave community made for itself are: John W.Blassingame, *The Slave Community*, revised and enlarged edition Oxford University Press 1979; it is also worth reading the discussion prompted by the first edition, Antony Gilmore (ed.), *Revisiting Blassingame's The Slave Community: The Scholars Respond*, Greenwood Press, Westport 1978; George P.Rawick, *From Sundown to Sunup. The Making of the Black Community*, Greenwood Press, Westport 1972, and Eugene D.Genovese, *Roll, Jordan, Roll. The World the Slaves Made*, Oxford University Press, New York 1974, which puts the accent on religion as 'resistance within accommodation'. In the black community it is difficult to make a distinction between religion and culture: Lawrence W.Levine, *Black Culture and Black Consciousness*, therefore makes an important contribution to the understanding of black religion; here this historian investigates what is primarily oral black culture: hymns, popular stories, sayings, aphorisms, jokes, word-plays and toasts (long narrative poems). In addition to *Black Culture and Black Consciousness*, Oxford University Press, New York 1977, see also Sterling Stuckey, 'Through the Prism of Folklore: The Black Ethos in Slavery', in *Black and White in American Culture*, ed. Jules Chametzky and Sidney Kaplan, University of Massachusetts Press 1969, see esp. 186f.

Secondary literature like that by Levine and Stuckey is admirably suited to make one want to get to know the primary sources. However, it is difficult for anyone who has not specialized in this area to estimate the true worth of the various sources, see above all 'Critical Essay on Sources', in Blassingame, op.cit., 367-82, and, with a focus on the religion of the slaves, Alho, op.cit., 11-42. For the autobiographies, recollections and letters of slaves see the following collections: Gilbert Osofsky (ed.), *Puttin' On Ole Massa: The Slave Narratives of Henry Bibb, William Wells Brown and Solomon Northup*, Harper and Row 1969; Robert S.Starobin (ed.), *Blacks in Bondage: Letters of American Slaves*, Watts, New York 1974; John Blassingame (ed.), *Slave Testimony: Two Centuries of Letters, Speeches, Interviews and Autobiographies*, La State University Press 1977. In the 1930s many interviews were held with ex-slaves about their recollections of slavery in the context of the WPA (Works Progress Administration); of the 31 volumes edited by George P.Rawick under the title *The American Slave. A Composite Autobiography*, Greenwood Press, Westport 1972-8, Vol.19, *God Struck Me Dead*, is particularly important for understanding black religion; here former slaves tell of their ecstatic conversion experiences. There are further valuable selections of interviews in: Benjamin A.Botkin (ed.), *Lay My Burden Down*, University of Chicago Press 1954; Norman R.Yetman (ed.), *Voices from Slavery*, New York 1970; Charles L.Perdue et al. (eds.), *Weevils in the Wheat: Interviews with Virginia Ex-Slaves*, University of Indiana Press 1980. Zora Neale Hurston, *Mules and Men*, Philadelphia 1935, reprinted University of Indiana Press 1978; Langston Hughes and Arna Bontemps, *The Book of Negro Folklore*, Dodd, Mead 1958, and Harold Courtlander, *A Treasury of Afro-American Folklore*, Crown Publications, New York 1976, are fascinating collections of popular stories.

No account of black religion can pass by one of the most evocative forms of black popular culture, the spirituals. There are numerous editions and interpretations of these slave songs. The classic is W.E.B.DuBois' interpretation in the last chapter of *The Souls of Black Folk*, 1903, reprinted 1961. Perhaps the best introduction to the world of spirituals is the little book *The Negro Spiritual Speaks of Life and Death*, Harper and Row 1947, by Howard Thurman, who died in 1981; see also *Deep River*, Harper and Row 1945, reprinted Kennikat Press, Port Washington 1969, also by this profound thinker and mystic. The thorough studies by Miles Mark Fisher, *Negro Slave Songs in the United States*, Cornell University Press 1953, and John Lovell, *Black Song: The Forge and the Flame*, Macmillan, New York 1972, interpret the spirituals as songs of resistance with deliberate double meanings. James H.Cone similarly lays considerable stress on the liberation motif in his theological, or rather christological, account in *The Spirituals and the Blues: An Interpretation*, Seabury Press 1972. Spirituals, gospel songs and social change are similarly covered in *Somebody's Calling My Name. Black Sacred Music and Social Change*, Judson Press, Valley Forge 1979, by Wyatt Tee Walker, who was at one time one of the closest of Martin Luther King's colleagues and is now preacher at the Canaan Baptist Church of Christ, New York City.

If there is a wealth of literature about the spirituals, in other areas of the expression of black faith that is much less the case. An important gap has been filled by Harold A.Carter, *The Prayer Tradition of Black People*, Judson Press, Valley Forge 1976. For black preaching see Henry H.Mitchell, *Black Preaching*, Lippincott 1970, and *The Recovery of Preaching*, Harper and Row 1977. Anyone intrigued as a result of reading e.g. the studies by Genovese or Wilmore mentioned above by the unique but also ambivalent position of the black preacher in the black church and community will find Charles V.Hamilton, *The Black Preacher in America*, Morrow 1972, a good sociological study. The gaps also include a thorough up-to-date historical and theological study of the black church. Until this appears, see: Carter G.Woodson, *The History of the Negro Church*, The Associated Publishers, Washington, DC 1945, or E.Franklin Frazier, *The Negro Church in America*, supplemented by C.Eric Lincoln, *The Black Church since Frazier*, Schocken Books ²1974; see also W.E.B.DuBois, *The Negro Church*, Atlanta University Press 1903; Benjamin E.Mays and Joseph W.Nicholson, *The Negro's Church*, Institute of Social and Religious Research, New York 1933; M.Nelson, R.Yokley and A.K.Nelson, *The Black Church in America*, Basic Books, New York 1975. Special mention should finally be made of the biography, by Charles H.Wesley, of the founder of the African Methodist Episcopal Church, *Richard Allen: Apostle of Freedom*, The Associated Publishers, Washington DC 1935, reprinted 1969.

(a) Conversion and community

It is incontrovertibly true that for the slaves in North America the break with their African past was more complete and drastic than elsewhere in the New World. If –as Raboteau puts it – in Jamaica, Cuba or Brazil the gods whom the African slaves brought with them were forced to live in captivity, in the slave system of the Old South they were doomed to die out. But even there this twilight of the gods did not mean the end of the sacred world (Levine) of the uprooted Africans. 'Sacred' in this connection does not stand in opposition to profane but denotes that experience of reality in which sacred and profane, spirit and matter, the supernatural and the natural cannot be separated. What we tend to call religion is not a separate sphere alongside others but permeates all spheres of life. The songs of the slaves and their ritual customs, proverbs and stories, their magic and their morality, voodoo in New Orleans and the funeral rites, can only be understood in the context of this sacred world which they brought with them from Africa.

This world represents a specific life-style and sensibility which are also present where specific elements of African culture have disappeared. It is misleading to call African only those elements in the black slave community which were for the most part taken over directly from Africa. That gives a wrong idea of what culture implies. Culture is not static by nature, but is an ongoing process in which past and present interact on each other. Levine rightly points out that the toughness and resilience of a culture are not determined by its capacity to withstand change – something of that kind is more a sign of stagnation than of vitality – but by its capacity to react creatively to the reality of a new situation.[18] In the case of the black slave community in North America we are therefore dealing with a process of acculturation in which three elements interact on one another in a complex and dynamic way: (*a*) the life-style and sensibility which were brought from their land of origin, and which have an effect at the conscious as well as the unconscious level; (*b*) the dehumanizing situation of the daily existence of a slave; (*c*) constant confrontation with the religious and cultural world of the white oppressors.

What is called black religion or black Christianity eventually grew out of the interaction of these three elements after a long historical process. In her study *Trabelin' On*, Mechal Sobel has paid a good deal of attention to this development. She distinguishes three phases which, schematically, look like this. The first period is that of the first generation of African slaves who, in contrast to what was assumed for a long time, were able to maintain much of their culture, language and religion. In the new environment the great variety of African cultural expressions grew together into what Sobel calls a neo-African consciousness. Despite the great and traumatic changes, belief remained in the life force of which every living thing is a part and in the powers which control this life force: the Supreme Being (God), the spirits, the 'living dead' (the ancestors) and the magical power or power of witchcraft which resides in particular persons and objects. Soothsayers, priests, medicine men and above all exorcists were never far away on the slave plantations. It is striking that the new slaves showed no respect for the religion of their white masters; the Anglican Society for the Propagation of the Gospel in Foreign Parts had little success with its missionary activities, since the rationality and formality of Anglican expressions did not speak to the imagination of the slaves.

Whereas the first generation of Afro-Americans spoke a broken English which was called Pidgin English (Pidgin is defined as an auxiliary language alongside the mother tongue), in subsequent generations this English became the first language and was then called Creole English. In its structure this Creole reflects the second period which was characterized by assimilation to white, partly Christian, values which differ from or even conflict with the African life-style. The actual power of the white over the life of the black slave – a power against which all too often rites of exorcism or amulets were of no avail – brought about a crisis in the consciousness of the exiled Africans. A growing dichotomy and incoherence arose in the experience of reality among these people, who had lost any direct prospect of liberation from slavery.

But just as black English gradually arose out of Pidgin and Creole English as black people's own language, so under the enormous pressure and misery of their life as slaves the blacks arrived at their own coherent and integrated experience of reality which Mechal Sobel calls the Afro-Christian world-view. The Protestant-evangelical faith movement which reached a climax in the Great Awakening around 1740 offered blacks the possibility of a creative synthesis in which crucial elements of African sensibility are associated with Christian beliefs. This faith took institutional form in the black Baptist church, the origin of which goes back to 1750. Sobel writes:

> In the melding of the African and Baptist Sacred Cosmos that occurred both in plantation congregations and in more accultu- rated urban areas, the core of the African and of the Baptist world views united to form a new whole. Blacks became Baptists. This

union of the two world views was occasionally delayed, in part because of the many African folkways retained... As suggested, the African High God and the Christian God became one – a God close to man, but one who still sent messengers to lead his black people home. Spirit force or power was still recognized, but it was exerted by God, Christ and the Holy Ghost, as well as by holy men.[19]

There should be no mistaking the fact that this periodization, as Sobel herself stresses, has mainly heuristic value and does not do justice to the complex historical reality as such. However, its merit is that it becomes clear that black religion is neither a creation of Western Christianity nor a pure product of Africa but is a unique phenomenon, as the result of a long process of acculturation. The term 'acculturation process' in this connection is an academic euphemism for what in reality was an intense wrestling to survive as a human being in an inhuman situation, to discover light and warmth in the grim darkness of a cruel and absurd world.

Why did the evangelical faith of Baptists and Methodists have so much attraction for black slaves? Why did the evangelical summons to conversion speak to them, while the mission of the Anglican church made so little impression?

From a sociological point of view the evangelization movement which penetrated the South as an extension of the revivals that had taken place throughout British territory formed a movement 'from below', from the underside of society. Personal relations with God, the decisive conversion experience and the life of self-discipline and sanctification – these three characteristics of the new experience of faith represented a break with the hierarchically structured society that was sanctioned by church preaching and morality. In the inhospitable colonial world it had not escaped the notice of the authorities that religion had an essential function in the building up and stabilizing of a new society; compulsory churchgoing, uniformity in worship, catechesis and moral codes of behaviour were appropriate means of achieving this. But the small and insignificant, who experienced in their bodies the harshness of daily existence, felt frustrated by a formal liturgy and a rationalistic preaching which made God a distant, detached entity. The summons to repentance and conversion issued by the itinerant evangelistic preachers therefore fell on fertile soil; many thousands of men and above all women felt affected to the depths of their souls by preaching which, while stressing the total corruption of humanity, at the same time was able to imbue believers with God's very personal and salutary concern over the cares and needs of ordinary people. The irrational sides of daily life, which the enlightened thought of an intellectual élite had so particularly managed to banish, came out at the revivals and day-long camp meetings, where there were marvellous visions and healings through prayer, where the emotions could be unloaded in collective barking exercises, where conversion was an ecstatic experience and where moaning and lamentation about one's own corruption were mingled with tears of joy over the overwhelming experience of God's presence and his grace.

A misleading commonplace would have it that evangelicals are concerned only with the salvation of the individual soul. The personal experience of conversion and grace is indeed of decisive significance, but as Donald G.Mathews stresses,[20] the New Birth is at the same time the basis of a new community. The radical experience of conversion did not isolate the believer but provided access to a community in which the old social differences had disappeared. The new life of sanctification to which people had committed themselves represented a break with the 'world' and all the corruption of the world – horse races, dancing and frivolous clothes. In contrast to worldly people, in the community there was a life of common discipline, mutual respect and social intimacy: people touched one another in many ways; brothers and sisters in Christ were greeted with a kiss; during prayers they threw their arms around each other, and among the Baptists they often washed one another's feet.[21] In the evangelical community of faith poor, restless people found warmth, security and self-confidence.

That in its first phase the evangelical movement certainly had a radical social potential should be clear from the hostile reactions of the ruling class. Itinerant preachers often met with crude and aggressive behaviour. In addition, the insight that God has no respect for persons (Acts 10.34) led some radical evangelical leaders to reject slavery. Sadly enough for black slaves this attitude changed as the evangelicals themselves began to gain prestige and power. The egalitarian implications of the gospel faith were then elevated to a purely spiritual level, detached from existing social relationships. The missionary task was not seen to be the abolition of slavery but the conversion of slaves with the aim of making them better slaves.[22] According to Mathews this dubious development involved a grudge against the non-evangelical slaveholding class: there was a desire to demonstrate that one was in a better position to integrate slaves into the community.[23]

Despite this later development it is not surprising that black men and women felt attracted to evangelical faith.[24] It was the slaves who most powerfully sensed and experienced the liberating force of evangelical faith. That God has no respect for persons was good news.

Anyone who wants to explain the success of the evangelization movement among black slaves must take into account the elements of both continuity and discontinuity. The discontinuity lies in the experience of conversion itself. Conversion and baptism mark the break between life and death. We cannot imagine that in sufficiently concrete terms. In a world overshadowed by a system of domination which reduced the blacks to being anonymous objects over which the master had complete control, the story of Good Friday, of suffering and death, was a tangible reality. The transition from this world to the new life in Christ was not experienced by the slaves as a 'natural' transition, but as an ecstatic, miraculous experience. In the conversion experience the discontinuity between death and life was experienced physically – and this experience of resurrection from the dead meant liberation from the house of slavery and entry into a community in which God knows everyone by name.

Outside this break between death and life, cross and resurrection, on another level there is also an element of continuity with the past: what happened during religious services was not strange to people who came from Africa. Ecstasy and possession (by the spirits) are common in African religion, and the rites of initiation there, like the evangelical conversion experience, had the character of a new birth.[25] Baptism by immersion or by sprinkling also shows an affinity with particular rites of initiation, while in the ring shout, the birth song and the dialogue between preacher and community there are recognizable parallels with African forms of song and dance.

It is incontrovertibly true that in the first twenty-five years of the evangelical movement there was a strong interaction between white and black. So it could come about that a white community had a black preacher. But as the ethnocentricity and racism of the white evangelicals gained the upper hand – in connection with their growing prestige and their interest in maintaining the slave system – the gulf between black and white churches became larger. But in fact from the beginning the difference between the black and the white experience of faith was tangible. The difference in social position and cultural background meant that blacks experienced the evangelical faith in a different way from white Christians. This can be demonstrated from a concept like sin. Genovese points out that the African view of life is not familiar with the idea of original sin; even after black slaves had accepted Christianity this doctrine remained essentially alien to them.[26] Here black theology denied the only doctrine which could have reconciled the slaves to their lot at a spiritual level.[27] If in Western Christianity original sin is bound up with feelings of guilt and a pessimistic view of the world, the African tradition gave the slaves an irresistible joy in life which could withstand the severest trials, Paul Radin aptly described the difference by his observation that whereas whites asked Jesus for forgiveness, blacks in the first place asked for recognition.[28] Were blacks then unaware of sin? Certainly not, but sin for them was not so much connected with feelings of guilt as with transgressing moral commandments and injustice. So Mathews can write: 'For blacks, slavery was both the metaphor and the actuality of sin; and present salvation was metaphor for the liberty that was to come.'[29]

One can also see from the conversion stories collected in *God Struck Me Dead* that blacks appropriated evangelical faith in their own way. Here is one story as an example:

I got troubled. I just felt worried for two or three days... I wanted to send for my mother to see me die. I couldn't eat. I just sat down and folded my arms and when I died I was sitting in the chair.

Suddenly, in a vision, I saw myself at hell's dark door. There was a deep gulf and when I saw myself, I was standing in a pretty little path. I was trying to fix my feet in the path. I said, 'Lord this road is so narrow and my feet so big.' There appeared a little man and he said, 'Follow me.' He kept a little distance from me. We journeyed on eastward and came to a wall. The little man had left me. I said, 'Lord, I can't climb this wall.' When I saw myself I had passed over the wall and was in a beautiful white snow house and inside was a lot of half-moon shaped fruit. I thought it was snow but a voice said, 'This is manna; that is healing for the nations.'

When I came back here, I did not want to tell but the voice said to me, 'Go and tell the people.' I started to tell my mother but the spirit directed me to the Baptists...[30]

Intensely personal though this story is, it follows a particular pattern which constantly recurs in these spirit travels. At least three clear phases can be distinguished: it begins with a restless, anxious, heavy feeling; then the crisis of death and rejection appears, which suddenly goes over into the third phase of the experience of being accepted by God, of peace, freedom and joy. This pattern also occurs elsewhere in the Christian tradition, and in this respect the black conversion stories are not unique.[31] However, the figure of the 'little man' who constantly appears is remarkable. Many scholars have already puzzled over this mysterious figure, and the general conclusion is that he must be of African origin. He appears only in the visions of black people, and in them we also find references which occur strikingly often to 'the man in the man', 'the little me in the big me', 'the little Mary in the big Mary', and similar expressions. Mechal Sobel connects this kind of statement with the West African philosophy that 'in each thing there is another thing' and 'in every man a little man'.[32] This would mean that every person or thing has a 'nature' ('soul') which hides itself behind the external manifestation; the 'soul' is not part of the person but the person himself or herself, the 'little man', which existed before birth and which will go on existing after death. In that case, according to Sobel, the 'little man' in the story would be an example of the way in which African elements are integrated into a Christian view of faith. Unlike Legba, who functions as a messenger of African deities, the little man is trustworthy and as a guide shows the convert that his or her name is written in the book of eternal life: 'The name, the essence, is thus given a renewed Christian meaning, symbolizing this chosenness by God and tying the individual to his new Christian clan for eternity.'[33]

In some stories the 'little man' is also called 'little white man', and this fact brings us to the striking emphasis which is placed in black conversion stories on the whiteness of heaven, God or Jesus. The snow, which also occurs in this story, is used in other stories to indicate how white God or Jesus is! The question inevitably arises whether the God of these stories has not taken on the features of the white oppressor. However, Sobel's view is that here, too, there is an African background. She points out that in the West African view of life white is a symbol of purity and goodness, whereas black symbolizes evil. This symbolism goes back to before the time of white enslavement in Africa. According to Sobel, as a symbol of evil black has deep roots, which are perhaps universal and have to do with anxiety about night and darkness and the loss of the sun.[34] Although Sobel is probably right in this respect, that does not alter the fact that the social context of black slaves and ex-slaves was so determined by the opposition between white and black that it was impossible to make abstractions from it. Who can fail to see that the idea of a white God or Jesus confirms the dominant ideology? Anyone who misses this deep ambivalence runs the risk of idealizing the religion of the oppressed.[35]

But although there are ambiguous elements in these stories, they have nothing to do with a flight from reality. On the contrary, the story quoted above ends with a mission charge. However intensely personal the experience of spirit travel is, the convert is referred back to the community. Just as in Africa the rites of initiation are made possible by the community and in turn make possible the continuation of this community, so the community created the framework and the possibility of individual experience for slaves. Cecil Cone comments in this connection: 'When a person became a leader in the community it was by virtue of his unusual experience with the knowledge of God, but as sanctioned by the community.'[36] More than any other factor the religion of the slaves was decisive for the origin of what Genovese has called a 'protonational consciousness'.[37]

(b) The world upside down

That black religion was the factor that bound the slave community together is also attested by the spirituals. A strong sense of community emerges not only from their content, but above all from the way in which they were sung. Wherever they could be heard, at work in the fields, rowing on the river, or at night in the secret meetings in the hush harbours, where a pot hung upside down had to serve to damp the sound of song and ecstasy[38] – they were sung antiphonally, and according to Lawrence Levine this structure brought the individual singer into constant dialogue with the community.

In fact, the form and structure of slave music presented the slave with a potential outlet for his individual feelings even while it continually drew him back into the communal presence and permitted him the comfort of basking in the warmth of the shared assumptions of those around him.[39]

The slave songs certainly did not come into being in a vacuum. There are many parallels to Methodist and Baptist hymns from the eighteenth and nineteenth centuries, and on the basis of this some (white) scholars have doubted the originality of the black songs.[40] On closer inspection, however, the salient differences emerge, in both form and content.

That the slave songs are the creation of members of the black community is formally evident from their inexhaustible capacity for improvisation. As a community people felt free constantly to recreate songs; words and melodies were constantly adapted and changed. Different versions of many songs have been handed down. Their multi-dimensional character makes them in a sense capable of bearing many interpretations: they cannot be limited to a particular situation or a particular meaning. Therefore as a mutual means of communication they were also used all too often to mislead the whites. One thinks for example of the well known 'Steal away to Jesus', by which the slaves let one another know that there was to be a secret meeting that night.

This last feature at the same time also says something about the function of these hymns. It gave slaves a certain detachment from their masters and saw that there was the social and psychological living space which they desperately needed. In this sense the spirituals in their totality are only open to one interpretation. But we must in fact go still further and say that in terms of content these songs conjure up a reality which is the denial and the reversal of existing reality. They sing of heaven ('When I get to Heaven, gwine to be at ease; Me and my God gonna do as we please'), of a house ('We'll fight for liberty, when the Lord will call us home'), of a kingdom ('Gwine to sit down in de kingdom, Gwine to walk about in Zion'), of the promised land ('Brethren, will you come to the promised land'), of the land of Canaan ('Canaan is the land for me') or of Jerusalem, new Jerusalem or the city ('I been to Jerusalem', 'Patrol around me', 'Tank God he no ketch me'). All these expressions relate to a 'beloved community' – to use Martin Luther King's favourite expression – in which the existing social relationships are reversed.

Many interpretations of the spirituals suffer from the flaw that they begin from the opposition current in Western theological thought between an experience of faith which flees the world and seeks salvation in a life after death, and a belief that has marked social and political content. The question is whether this is not an interpretative framework that was alien to the slave community. If Levine is right in speaking of the 'sacred world' in which the black slaves lived, then Western dualism is alien to their experience of reality and their imagination of it. It is therefore misleading to speak in terms of belief in the hereafter, but also to regard the language of these hymns as a secret political code of opposition. Here it emerges that the black slaves can in one sense still be reckoned among the illiterate peoples – they were forbidden to learn to read or write – who cherish a way of thinking which never abstracts from reality but always remains concrete.[41] Without doubt the slaves of white Christians had heard of God, creator of heaven and earth, of Jesus Christ his Son, and of salvation history. But the African slaves integrated these stories and testimonies into their own experience of reality and transformed them into something what was tangible and concrete. 'In this way,' Olli Alho perceptively observes, 'they created a unique land of freedom which was not characterized by being either "this-worldly" or "other-worldly", but by the absence of slavery...'[42]

Thus the term 'heaven', as a concrete symbol of the land of freedom, has nothing to do with abstract speculation on an *eschaton* that is far away. Heaven is a reality which is described in extremely evocative terms, in which above all the stress is on what no longer occurs:

No more hard trial in de kingdom; no more tribulation, no more parting, no more quarreling, back-biting in de kingdom, No more sunshine fer to bu'n you; no more rain fer to wet you. Every day will be Sunday in heaven.

Heaven is before all else the place where there is real community. That applies to the familiar relationship with Jesus and God the Father: 'Gwine to argue wid de father and chatter wid de son'; 'I'm going to walk with (talk with, live, with, see) King Jesus by myself, by myself.' The relationship with other biblical figures is intimate and direct:

Gwine to sit down in de kingdom,
Gwine to walk about in Zion,
Gwine to see my sister Mary,
Gwine to see my brudder Jonah.
Gwine to talk wid de angels,
Gwine to see my massa Jesus.

But heaven is above all also the place to see kindred and friends again. The importance that the slave attached to this is doubtless connected with the constant threat of being separated from loved ones, whether through sale to another slaveholder, or through death, which was never far away. This interpretation is strengthened by the fact that Herbert Gutman has shown that in contrast to what has been assumed so far, the black slaves in North America were in a position to keep more or less the African 'extended family' structure; in those cases in which, for example as a result of a move, there was no mother or father, the children were brought up by relatives in the way that is customary in African countries. Moreover, we must certainly not rule out the possibility that the desire to see dead members of the family again expresses feelings connected with the African belief that ancestors are part of the family and as living dead are involved in the ups and downs of everyday existence.

That for slaves heaven is as it were a historical category and not an idea of a metaphysical reality is evident from the connection which the spirituals constantly make with the exodus story. For them this story is an experienced reality: they are the chosen people ('we are de people of de Lord', 'we are de people of God') on the way to the promised land ('To the promised land I'm bound to go'). Freed from the servitude of Pharaoh, they go through the Red Sea:

My army cross over
O, Pharaoh's army drowned!

It is interesting that in the spiritual from which these lines are quoted the river Jordan is identified with the 'mighty Myo', the West African river of death:

We'll cross de mighty river,
My army cross over;
We'll cross de river Jordan,
My army cross over;
We'll cross de danger water,

My army cross over;
We'll cross de mighty Myo,
My army cross over.

The river can both represent the ice-cold water of death and be an
indication of the rite of baptism. The direction of the songs does not
change essentially: on the other side of the experience of death
(slavery, physical death) is life. The elements from the exodus story
can express the personal conversion history of an individual, but
also the history and the future of the black slave people as a whole.
The one significance can go along with the other. Canaan or the
promised land can be the land on the other side of physical death,
but it can also be a reference, as Miles Mark Fisher thinks, to Africa,
or to the free North or Canada – the last is certainly the case in the
well known 'O Canaan, sweet Canaan; I am bound for the land of
Canaan'. The one does not exclude the other. The decisive thing is
that these songs depict a reality which is the specific opposite to the
complete dehumanizing of the slave society. In a period in which
Western Christianity showed a tendency to neglect the Old Testament and detach the gospel from it, the African slaves in North
America expressed a marked preference for the stories of the Old
Testament. They identified themselves with Joshua who brought
down Jericho, with little David who defeated the powerful Goliath,
with Daniel who was saved from the lion's den. Levine points out
that it is important to remember that all these Old Testament figures
about whom the slaves sang so joyfully were redeemed in this world
and in a way which spoke to the imagination of slaves.[43] Moses
occupied a special place, as the leader and liberator of the people.
And the realism of the slave's imagination is expressed in the fact
that Moses is not experienced as a figure from the distant past but
is identified with contemporaries who emerged as popular leaders:
Harriet Tubman, the famous woman who through the underground
railroad brought her fellow blacks to the free North, was such a
Moses.

However, most attention was paid to Jesus. The Old Testament,
and especially the exodus story, forms the framework in which his
appearance as messiah and liberator is set. Here the slaves had a
biblical-theological insight which elicited from a white contemporary
the scornful observation that they looked on Jesus Christ as a second
Moses.[44] Little could this camp preacher in 1865 imagine how much

the insight of these 'primitive' people anticipated what in the twentieth century a 'theology after Auschwitz' was to discover again, after much pain and grief!

But as the one who frees his people from slavery Jesus in the slave songs is at the same time also the divine king who comes to redeem the world. The images of exodus are supplemented and sometimes confused with those of the Revelation of John. Jesus is both the captain on the ship that goes to the promised land and the one who sits on the white horse as in Rev.6.2; 19.11:

> Meet, O Lord, on de milk-white horse,
> An' de nineteen wile in his han';
> Drop on, drop on de crown on my head,
> An' roll in my Jesus' arm.

As king of kings and lord of lords he comes on the day of judgment to pronounce judgment on living and dead, white and black. But this powerful figure who successfully fights against old Satan is in fact none other than the humiliated and crucified man in whom the slaves could recognize their lot so well. They, too, are beaten and tortured. They can identify all too easily with the anguish, the pain and the shame of the cross:

> They nail my Jesus down,
> They put on him on the crown of thorns,
> O see my Jesus hanging high!
> He look so pale an' bleed so free:
> O don't you think it was a shame,
> He hung three hours in dreadful pain?

If the slaves can put themselves in Jesus' painful position, conversely he is also the one to whom they can entrust their deepest cares and needs. Jesus is their friend and helper:

> I'm troubled, I'm troubled, I'm troubled in mind,
> If Jesus don't help me, I surely will die.
> O Jesus, my Saviour, on thee I'll depend,
> When troubles are near me, you'll be my true friend.
> When laden with trouble and burdened with grief,
> To Jesus in secret I'll go for relief.
> In dark days of bondage to Jesus I prayed
> To help me to bear it, and he gave me his aid.

The collection in which this song is included tells in a touching note how the father of the singer sang it after he had been whipped: '...he always went and sat upon a certain log near his cabin, and with the tears streaming down his cheeks, sang this song with so much pathos that few could listen without weeping from sympathy, and even his cruel oppressors were not wholly unmoved.'[45]

Jesus, as he appears in the spirituals, is above all an intimate friend who through his help enables the slaves to bear the pain of their daily humiliations:

> Sometimes I hangs my head an' cries,
> But Jesus' goin to wipe my weep'n eyes.

His complete identification with the pain of the poor and helpless makes him the helper *par excellence*. But his living presence, as it was experienced by the slaves, means that Good Friday is not the end of history. The crucified is the one who rises from the dead:

> Weep no more, Martha,
> Weep no more, Mary,
> Jesus rise from de dead,
> Happy Morning.

The slave songs do not offer a rounded christology, a theological system – far from it. Their poetic force lies precisely in the fact that they express something that cannot be contained in any single system – not even in that of the 'dialectic of cross and resurrection'. That there is life from death, conquest in defeat, joy through all pain is sung and confessed in the songs of the slaves, but not explained. That does not mean that this mystery can simply be accepted as an abstract truth of faith dictated from above. It does mean that their concrete mode of thinking was opposed to the form of knowledge which cannot be experienced and lived through. Their knowledge of faith was a knowledge from the heart. Deep in their hearts the slaves knew that they did not match the humiliating names given to them by their oppressors. Deep in their hearts they knew that they were not created in the image of their oppressors. They were aware of their otherness, and in the last judgment this otherness would be manifest:

> O' nobody knows who I am, who I am,
> Till the Judgment morning.

The insight of Charles Long, that the oppressed know something about freedom that their oppressors will never know, is applicable here. And it is in fact possible to introduce here the Hegelian dialectic of master and slave, which Long does as a historian of religion – of course not as a thought-pattern which is imposed on reality, but as an attempt to penetrate into the depths of the black soul. Perhaps – and we shall return to this later – this dialectic is none other than the dialectic of cross and resurrection, a pointer to the conversion of which the songs and stories of the black slaves bear witness. Levine says that the world of the spirituals is a black world in which there is not a single reference to white contemporaries,[46] whereas in social reality the white presence is dominant and blacks are non-persons. In this sense these songs form a world upside down, in which non-beings are called forward to be recognized, and the last are first!

Genovese points out that the black slaves saw heaven primarily as a place of reconciliation with one another, and only sometimes did they view it as a place of reconciliation with whites.[47] Many slaves refused to believe that their white masters would get to heaven after their deaths. Levine quotes a number of comments to this effect. One of the aptest is the reaction of a slave to the news that as reward for his hard work he would be buried in the same grave as his master: 'Well, massa, one way I am satisfied, and one way I am not. I like to have a good coffin when I die (but) I fraid, massa, when the debbil come take you body, he make mistake, and get mine.'[48]

(c) Have I got a witness?

If their religion put black slaves in a position to find the social and psychological room they needed in order to survive and keep their human dignity, that was not least thanks to the leadership which the black community received from the black preacher. Anyone who senses the degree to which black religion shaped the slave community will understand why the preacher was given a leading role not only in spiritual but also in political terms – a tradition which has been continued right down to the present day in figures like Jesse Jackson and Andrew Young.

He inherited from his African forebears – priests, prophets, medicine men – a deep sense of the mysterious powers in the universe and a charismatic capacity to unleash these powers, as a result of which he could transport his audience to the extreme limits of ecstasy. Anyone who has taken part in even one 'old-style' black church service will be aware of the essential difference from an ordinary white Protestant service. The black preacher proclaims the word of the Bible just as, if the sermon is good, his white colleague does. But he does so in such a way that the presence of the Spirit in the midst of the community becomes physically tangible and is expressed in the response of those present, in the shout, the groan and the ecstasy. The style of preaching is characterized by a quiet, well-considered beginning which gradually gives way to a more rhythmic way of speaking that comes to a climax in which the speaking becomes *Sprachgesang* and then song. As has often been remarked, it is characteristic of black worship that importance is attached not only to what the leader says, but above all to how it is said. Everything depends on the interchange between the preacher and his congregation. The preacher needs to be empowered by the Spirit, but the verification of this empowering is the endorsement of it by the congregation. The congregation determines whether its leader is in a position to 'tell the story'. So it is not just empty words when during his sermon the preacher asks the congregation, 'Are you with me?', 'Have I got a witness?', and on Sunday morning there is certainly something missing of the presence and help of the Holy Spirit if the 'Amen, Yes Sir, Sho' 'nough, So true', does not ring out loudly through the congregation.

In the time of slavery the black preacher had an extremely responsible and delicate position. He functioned as a mediator not only between God and his people but also between the white masters and the slave community. He knew that he was dependent on the protection of his master, and certainly after the slave revolts of Vesey and Turner the white slaveholder had every reason to be suspicious of the effect of Christian preaching on the black slave. The preacher also knew that the white ruling class was trying to use him to make the slaves obedient by holding out to them the prospect of a reward in the hereafter. And there were certainly preachers who did the bidding of their masters. Ex-slave Charley Williams, who lived in Mississippi, Louisiana and Texas, said: 'We had meetings sometimes, but the nigger preacher just talk about being a good nigger, and doin' to please the master.'[49] But most of them knew their people well enough to realize what they expected: a medicine that could still their longing for freedom, an antidote to the daily humiliations and the assurance that all human beings are equal in the face of God.

Gayraud S.Wilmore devotes some sound and moving pages in his *Black Religion and Black Radicalism* to the emergence of the black preachers.[50] He comments that these often uneducated but extremely shrewd men were capable of bringing their audience to a frenzy which could have devastating resutlts. However, that sort of thing rarely happened. The preachers held themselves back at the right moment. They knew that violent revolt could mean collective suicide for the flock entrusted to them. The régime was simply too strong and stable. But they also knew that the day of God's justice and freedom would certainly come. However, they did not see that day as yet being very near.

Therefore they followed what Wilmore calls an interim strategy:

> It was the deliberate choice of the preacher to give his people something to which they could attach their emotions – something to substitute for the immediate, uncontrollable, and probably illfated decision to strike, then and there, for freedom. He, therefore, gave relief from the tragedy of slavery, a modicum of comfort in the presence of the overwhelming reality of defeat and despair. Black religion may have been otherworldly, but it was not otherworldly-quietistic, but otherworldly-disruptive. Oppressors have never been able to relax in the presence of this kind of otherworldliness.[51]

Given the sacred world of their holistic view of life the preachers could never exclude the social and political sphere from their spiritual and moral leadership. But they did not feel themselves in a position to overcome the dominant social system and carry through radical social and political changes. So they bided their time. They could not bring about the kingdom of God with violence, nor did they want to. We find few chiliastic tendencies among them. However, their sermons are not pessimistic resignation. Joy in life and optimism prevail, and without doubt their African background also has a role here. The day of God's judgment will certainly come, but only faith and prayer can bring this liberation nearer.

But is what is said here not contradicted by the fact that the great slave revolts clearly had a religious inspiration? Was Gabriel Prosser not convinced that he had been predestined from his youth to be the liberator of his people? Did he not apply the deeds of Samson as related in Judges 15 to himself? Was Denmark Vesey not in turn fascinated by the story of the fall of Jericho in Joshua 6? And finally, was not Nat Turner, the leader of the most famous slave revolt, himself a preacher?[52]

These prophetic figures indeed cannot be excluded from the history of black religion. Nat Turner, with his outspoken preference for the gospel account in Luke, saw Jesus as the liberator of the poor and those without rights and regarded the eclipse of February 1831 as the sign of Christ's second coming and the signal for violent revolt. He thus belongs in a (proto-) nationalistic tradition to which David Walker, Henry Highland Garnet and Henry McNeal Turner also belong.[53] But these voices have never been normative in the history of the black church, even in the time of slavery. The militant and aggressive tone was an exception. The emergence of black preachers from this period is characterized by a precarious equilibrium between resistance and surrender, adaptation and subversiveness. Both elements are dialectically interconnected and belong indissolubly together. The subversiveness is grounded in the fantastic imagination of another reality, in which the otherness of the slave will be manifest; but this faith in another reality in turn finds its basis in a stubborn refusal to accept the existing reality of slavery and domination as the ultimate reality.

(*d*) The dialectic of resistance and adaptation

The combination of resistance and adaptation makes it difficult to describe the popular theology of the hymns, stories and prayers of the black slave community without qualification as liberation theology. Rather, one can speak of a 'theology of survival'. Henry Mitchell's comments in his *Black Belief* seem to me to be correct: 'Black folk theology, despite its record of highly liberating activity, cannot properly be labeled exclusively a theology of liberation... It is more likely a theology of existence or survival, whose affirmation of selfhood logically denies all hindrances to full being, including slavery and oppression.'[54]

Their religion gave slaves the possibility to survive and to avoid the deliberate dehumanizing process which the slave system represented. The word survival expresses both the idea of resistance and the element of adaptation. In their religious meetings the slaves found a sphere out of reach of their white oppressors, a place of security. But their powerlessness prevented them from extending this sphere into the political and social field. In political terms the slaves and their preachers had no choice: it was impossible for them to arrive at a well-considered strategy of change.

For liberation a certain form of power is needed – at all events powerlessness produces a people of beggars. It is therefore understandable that in the second revised edition of *Black Religion and Black Radicalism* Wilmore comes to distinguish two traditions in the history of black religion: a survival tradition and a liberation tradition. He locates the survival tradition above all in the South and the liberation tradition in the North, and in southern cities like Charleston, Richmond and New Orleans. The liberation tradition was handed on by people who could command a degree of power, for example by being free instead of slaves or having a certain level of education. If the survival tradition, which in the twentieth century was continued in the heterodox sects and cults, focussed on the will to survive, the liberation tradition was about more than that, namely the education, social welfare, cultural and moral progress of blacks within the American political and economic system. In Wilmore's view this tradition begins with the historic decision of Richard Allen and Absalom Jones in 1787 to set up the Free African Society in Philadelphia – similar organizations of free blacks existed in Charleston, Boston and Newport – and was continued in the Negro Convention Movement, in the black press, in the struggle for the abolition of slavery and in organizations like NAACP and the National Urban League which supported the struggle for civil rights. If the survival tradition was alive among the lowest classes in their struggle for self-preservation, the liberation tradition was to be found among blacks who, freed from the primary concern to remain alive, could address themselves to society as a whole and claim the place blacks should hold in it.[55]

Although the distinction that Wilmore makes between the two traditions is in itself right and meaningful, I wonder whether the labels do not cause misunderstandings. The connection between survival and liberation is more dialectical and at the same time more ambivalent than Wilmore's distinction indicates. If we regard the term liberation, in contrast to survival, as an inclusive term that relates the particular social and political struggle to the aim of a society in which everyone is free, then we have to say that the tradition to which Wilmore gives the label 'liberation' has all too often worked within the existing economic and political power-relationships without asking how far the struggle for racial equality really attacks these power relationships. So too this tradition is characterized by the ambivalence of opposition – to racial oppression – and assimilation. By operating within the social system it adapts itself to the norms and values which exist there.

On the other hand, at the same time there is a liberating dimension in the slave religion of the Old South which points beyond mere survival. As I have said, survival is characterized by two elements which determine each other: rebellion and adaptation. Adaptation in itself can lead to fatalism and quietude. In that case a division comes into being between faith and social life, and the kingdom of God is transposed to the eschatological distance of the hereafter. In the course of history the black church has not avoided this danger. But in the spirituals the vision of heaven is nourished by a refusal to accept the existing reality of domination and slavery as the ultimate reality. Here these hymns contain a liberating potential – survival, the will to live, is based on a further perspective, on the expectation of another reality. Precisely because they bear witness to this new reality, even today these slave songs are a source of inspiration for the struggle against racism and other forms of injustice. In the gospel train of which they sing there is room for others, and there is no difference in class:

> De fare is cheap, an' all can go,
> De rich an' poor are dere,
> No second class a-board dis train,
> No difference in de fare.

3. Towards a black christology. The dialectic of cross and resurrection

It is time to return to the question with which the chapter began. How does contemporary black theology relate to black history and experience? Can black theologians refer to this history when they speak of God and Christ in terms of liberation?

On the basis of what has emerged in the previous section, at all events one important conclusion emerges: that black religion as a distinct Afro-American way of believing, speaking and thinking does indeed exist! Black slaves appropriated in their own way the Christian gospel which was brought to them by white missionaries and preachers. They saw a chance of integrating the good news of God's incarnation in Christ and his redemption into the sacred world which they brought with them from Africa, and, contrary to the intentions of their white masters, understood the biblical story as an exodus story, as a story which made it clear that they were not destined to go through life as slaves.

In slavery black religion was born as an independent tradition of faith. People in the slave community were very well aware that there was an essential difference between the black and white experience of faith. Ex-slave Katie Sutton from Evansville, Indiana, put this feeling like this: 'We's different in color, in talk and in ligion and beliefs. We's different in every way and can never be spected to think or to live alike.'[56] Black people have reflected critically on this difference – as is evident from numerous statements and stories. To this degree black theology as 'reflection on the difference' is nothing new.

The new thing is that black theology has become an academic discipline. From popular theology it has become an object of scientific study, something about which people hold conferences, write books and give lectures. But this development at the same time causes a problem: is it possible within the framework of what is called 'theology' to do justice to the unique character of black religion? Is it possible to do the intellectual work which is needed in systematic theology to arrive at a christology, ecclesiology, pneumatology, without in so doing using an apparatus of concepts and ways of thinking, in conflict with the experiences which have been undergone in black history?

James H.Cone has expressed the hermeneutical challenge to black theology which seeks to be a theology of liberation with a biblical inspiration in his own sharp and terse way:

> If the struggle of the victims is the only context for the development of a genuine Christian theology, then should not theology itself reflect in its speech the language of the people about whom it claims to speak? This is the critical issue.[57]

In this connection Cone accepts the criticism of his first two books by Long, Wilmore and his brother Cecil Cone. The result of his assimilation of this criticism is *The Spirituals and the Blues* (1972). But Cone's christocentric interpretation of black religion and culture has not convinced everyone. He is suspected, to some degree rightly, of having imposed a theological dogmatic scheme (with a strong stress on political liberation) on black history, and thus of having done violence to the reality of the history of religion.[58] The underlying question here is whether and how far it is possible to interpret black religion as a special expression of the Christian tradition of faith. Is the framework of this tradition too narrow and too bound to Western forms of thought to do justice to the specific African character of black religion? Moreover do not the Black Jews and the Black Muslims also belong to the broad spectrum of black popular religion – not to mention the many other sects and cults? Must it not be remembered that from the very beginning Islam was present on the slave plantations because among the West Africans who were transported to America there were certainly many who had been converted to Islam in the land from which they came? All these factors make it impossible to incorporate the black religious experience just as it is into the Christian tradition of faith.

The urgent question then arises as to whether black theology can and must be a specifically Christian theology. However, one certainly cannot say that black theologians and historians of religion have become sufficiently clear about this to reach agreement. As I have already pointed out, for Charles Long Christian theology is so burdened with a tradition of Western ethnocentricity and imperialism that its language is incapable of doing justice to the experience of faith among oppressed peoples and cultures.[59] By contrast Henry Mitchell puts more stress on the convergence between African traditional religion and the Christian concept of God; in his view the incarnation of God was the really new element to which the Christian mission introduced black slaves, but this new element could be integrated into their experience of reality, which remained specifically African.[60] However, Mitchell so overlooks the ambivalence of the black experience of God that after reading his work one is left wondering whether the strictly patriarchal, white despotic image of God as depicted by James Baldwin in his novel *Go Tell It On the Mountain* is not completely alien to black popular religion. The same problem arises for Cecil Cone who, moreover, fails to ask what relationship is to be envisaged between the Almighty Sovereign God of the black tradition and the unique Name which was confessed in Israel (cf. Deut.6.4f.).

In this connection James Cone has rightly asked whether black theology does not also have a critical function in connection with black religious experience.[61] But how can there be any question of such a function if black religion is itself the only source of knowledge? In that case, from where does black theology get the critical norm? By what standard can particular religious expressions be tested?

James Cone has also put these questions to Gayraud Wilmore, who, in contrast to Mitchell and Cecil Cone, does have an eye for the ambivalence and oppressive side of black religion. In the first edition of *Black Religion and Black Radicalism* (1972) Wilmore mentions three sources from which black theology must draw: 1. the black community itself, and especially the cultural, religious and political forms of expression in the lowest strata of this society; 2. the writings, sermons and addresses of prominent black preachers and other black leaders like Sojourner Truth and W.E.B.DuBois; 3. the traditional African religions. It is striking that in this summing up Wilmore does not mention the biblical writings and the tradition of the early church – and for this he is told off by James Cone. The reason is that Wilmore is particularly cautious about a systematic or dogmatic approach by black theology which is orientated on Rome, Wittenberg and Geneva, and makes use of white theological categories. A theology of this kind may be able to achieve respectability in the ecumenical world and in the university, but the price that it pays for that is that it is alienated from the 'street people', from ordinary black people. Wilmore is looking for a theology which has a feeling for, which speaks the language of, men and women who have been softened up by the hopelessness of their struggle against the system, or who in their vital urge for survival have become hard and cynical, who have sought and found their salvation in the numerous sects and cults or in the rapidly growing black Pentecostal communities. But Wilmore also wants to hold on to the gospel of Jesus. In the second, revised edition of *Black Religion and Black Radicalism* (1983), so as to avoid misunderstanding, in his summing up of the three sources Wilmore has explicitly added that he presupposes the 'critical importance of Scripture and the witness of the early church'.[62] However, it still remains unclear precisely how the hermeneutical process in which this critical importance is achieved comes about.

We get the impression that the complex relationship between black theology and black religion is a hermeneutical minefield in which most black theologians prefer to run around with a bow. That in itself is not surprising. On the one hand there is the intellectual world of the theological discourse, still dominated by the disputes from the first half of this century: Barth, Bultmann, Tillich and Reinhold Niebuhr. On the other hand there is the world of black culture and religion, with its own language, music, dance and narrative art, born in the daily struggle for survival against poverty and racism. One world is separated from the other by a gigantic gulf. Can one accept the rules of systematic theology and at the same time do justice to the specific mood of the blues people? Or is there not a risk here that the black theologian may be alienated in two directions? How can a discipline like systematic theology or dogmatics, in which the written word is uppermost, give expression to the specifically oral tradition of black culture and religion? If black theology uses the language and thought of academic theology (even if only to criticize what goes on in it), is it then still relevant for Wilmore's 'street people'? But if it articulates the religious experience of ordinary black people in their own language, can it still gain a hearing in the theological faculties or in ecumenical dialogue?

Given the roots of theology in European culture and history, it is understandable that Charles Long thinks that a discipline like the history of religions is in a better position than theology to investigate black religion.[63] At all events the historian of religion is always bound to leave his own tradition and convictions as far outside his investigation as possible. However, so far the history of religions, too, has been a predominantly Western academic affair and, just as much as theology, it too needs to see whether the religious imagination of marginalized peoples and cultures can be expressed in the language of intellectuals.[64] Of course there is an essential difference between the task of the historian of religion and that of the black theologian. If the work of the former is predominantly descriptive, the latter does not avoid raising normative questions which have to do with the critical and educative function which it seeks to fulfil in the black church. In order to be able to reflect critically on the praxis of proclamation in the black church, the black theologian needs a deep knowledge of the situation, history and culture of the black community. To achieve this he or she is pointed towards, among other things, the results of historical investigation, and there is no way in which these may be treated arbitrarily and one-sidedly. But on the other hand the renewing power of the Spirit in the praxis of the black church and community calls for ongoing reflection on the sources in which the messianic praxis of the Jew Jesus of Nazareth is documented. Everything here depends on the way in which the relationship between the two elements – black experience and biblical witness – is given a hermeneutical basis and is worked out methodologically – unconfused and undivided![65] Whether black theology does as much justice to the universal dimension of faith as to the particularity of the black experience depends on the hermeneutical, methodological starting point. Here the maxim *methodus est arbitraria* applies.[66]

To bring us now to the heart of the question, I would propose the following thesis: *the hermeneutical foundation of the relationship between the biblical witness and black experience must be sought in pneumatology; the hermeneutical, methodological process that connects the liberating praxis of Jesus of Nazareth with black history and culture is therefore a pneumatological obligation.*[67]

That the praxis of Jesus, his life, death and resurrection, become a living reality for his community is attributed in Christian tradition to the work of the holy Spirit. It is the Spirit which calls people and incorporates them into the messianic movement of the kingdom of God. In the established churches this article of faith is often no more than a dead letter – and the blossoming of the Pentecostal movement in this century can be seen as a justified reaction to the lack of the fire of the Spirit, even if it is not above suspicion. It is no coincidence that it was a black preacher, W.J.Seymour, whose activities in Los Angeles in 1906 gave the impetus to the world-wide charismatic movement of our time, in which speaking with tongues, prophecy and healings have a central place. So if I argue for a pneumatological basis for the hermeneutical process that connects the historical praxis of Jesus with the black situation and experience, this is also on the basis of the specific spirituality of the black tradition of faith.

It is well known that in traditional African religions human life is dominated by a wide range of spirits which act as intermediaries between the Supreme Being and humanity. In the conversion of Afro-American slaves to Christianity, according to Henry Mitchell in *Black Belief*,[68] 'spirit possession' underwent a deep metamorphosis:

Those who had once been healingly possessed by a variety of deities were now overshadowed by the one but triune God, in his person as Holy Ghost or Holy Spirit. The music and speech which once induced possession were quite similar to the rhythm repetition, and mass-hypnotic phenomena which accompany much of Blackamerican shouting even today.

The truly surprising new element of the Christian gospel was that the Supreme Being had assumed human form in the person of Jesus. It was, however, through the mediation of the Spirit that the presence of this liberator and redeemer was actually experienced. Mitchell writes:

> The name by which the possessing Spirit was referred to in direct address, however, was the second person of the Trinity, according to his earthly or human name, Jesus. Nowhere was the doctrine of God's immanence more evident than in the folksy way slaves talked to Jesus.

When the black slaves on the plantations of the Old South met together after sundown at the agreed secret place, the Spirit came upon them and took possession of their soul and body. In ecstatic rapture they participated in the other, heavenly reality of which they sang in their spirituals. It was the creative, justifying power of the Spirit which gave a new name to those without a name, which lifted up the humiliated and the downtrodden from the dust, and raised the dead (God struck me dead) to life. It was the healing power of the Spirit, bringing the community into being, which incorporated the individual believer through baptism into the community of the exalted Christ and thus made a new life possible. The presence of the Spirit, finally, ensured that in this community the gospel did not become fossilized doctrine but remained a liberating event in the oppressive, racist world. Down to the present day the enthusiasm and the proverbial emotionalism with which believers celebrate the Sunday service is a sign that the Spirit is present among them. The way in which the Spirit moves believers can differ from church to church; the established churches of the black middle classes in the suburbs do in stylized, controlled form what happens in the Holiness churches and the Pentecostal communities by means of glossolalia, dance and rapture. But however civilized the proceedings may be, there remains a direct, tangible difference from liturgical celebration in the white churches. Thus old insights of the Christian tradition come to life in a very special way in black experience and one cannot but wonder that generally speaking the black theologians have paid little attention to the pneumatological dimension of black spirituality. A pneumatological foundation of black hermeneutics offers the possibility and the obligation of a *critical* intervention in church praxis. Obviously, in the black churches not only the power of the Spirit but also the spirit of power is alive. Within the black community it is the black churches which form the sphere in which the struggle between the Spirit of life and the idols of death take shape most clearly. James Cone in particular has roundly criticized the uncritical acceptance of capitalism and anti-communism, the quest for status and prestige, and the power-play of church politics.[69] In the churches there are manifestations not only of the living power of African ancestors which in fact converges to a surprising degree with the creative power of the Spirit of which the Christian tradition speaks, but also the overpowering presence of the destructive, deadly spiritual powers which in American society – and not only there – constantly block the way to justice and humanity. The black churches display two faces: on the one hand they keep alive the liberating power of the black experience of faith and on the other they form the opening through which the powers of domination can take possession of black spirits. The emotionalism and enthusiasm in the black community are an expression both of liberating protest and revolutionary élan and of escapism and alienation.

It makes no sense to deny this ambivalence in black religion, as do Cecil Cone and Mitchell. On the contrary, black theology can only pursue its function within the black church and community if it can make a sharp distinction here. For that, a hermeneutical process is necessary in which a historical analysis of black experience is critically related to careful biblical exegesis. Two insights can serve as guidelines here.

1. The third article of faith is concerned with the Holy Spirit, in other words with the Spirit of God. God's Spirit and the human spirit cannot be confused or identified with each other. That has never been simple in the Christian tradition. O.Noordmans has clearly indicated why this distinction is so difficult: 'Because he seems to stand completely on our side over against Father and Son, whose work he appropriates for us, he seems to be one with our heart. He prays in us and it is our prayer; he works faith in us and it is our faith. So the Holy Spirit can easily be seen as a gift (which he also is) but also as a thing, a pledge, a possession.' [70] Particularly

with regard to the black tradition of faith there is a great temptation
to explain the charismatic gift as a specific human gift or possession,
because there is everything to be said for connecting this gift with
spirit possession in the African religions – just as there is also
everything to be said for seeing the emotionalism of black religion
as the 'longing of the oppressed creature, the feelings of a heartless
world, as it is the spirit of spiritless circumstances' (Karl Marx).

But it is of vital importance for black theology to maintain that
the Spirit in all circumstances remains God's Spirit, which cannot
be appropriated by human beings – even by oppressed human beings
– and is not under human control. 'The wind blows where it wills,
and you hear the sound of it, but you do not know where it comes
from and where it is going; so it is with everyone who is born of the
Spirit' (John 3.8). The working of this Spirit cannot be explained by
black theology on the basis of cultural, social or psychological
factors. The empirical fact of the black historical experience can at
any rate also be interpreted in another way – for example in the
direction of William R.Jones's question whether God is not a white
racist.

In hermeneutical and methodological terms the critical importance of scripture and the witness of the early church, of which
Wilmore spoke, lies in the fact that here, in contrast to later church
history, the work of the Spirit is not limited to the church or the
individual but is seen in its salvation-historical dimension. 'When
later in the church, until the present day, the redemptive facts came
to be regarded as having an end with the ascension of Jesus, after
which the Spirit only "applied" them, we are miles removed from
the New Testament vision which sees the activity of the Spirit as the
historical presence of God that builds the bridge from the first fruits
to the coming consummation.' So writes H.Berkhof in his *Christian
Faith*.[71] This vision gives black theology its hermeneutical authoriz-
ation to begin from the effective presence of God's Spirit in black
history. It cannot itself be the foundation of this real presence. On
the contrary, this presence is its foundation and is its *raison d'être*.
Precisely the fact that black theology here leaves the freedom of the
Spirit as a historical power intact in turn gives it freedom not just to
seek traces of the Spirit within the framework of the institutional
church. The black experience in its totality is here its sphere of
activity, the blues as much as the gospel songs, the folk tales as much

as the sermons, the work of Malcolm X as much as that of Martin Luther King Jr.

2. If in the first perspective all the emphasis is on the freedom of the Spirit, over which people have no control, we must now directly stress the dialectical opposite to this truth and say that in all circumstances the Holy Spirit is and remains the Spirit of Jesus Christ. Here the concrete, contextual aspect of the work of the spirit is illuminated. In Luke 4.16-21, the *locus classicus* of black theology, Jesus reads in the synagogue at Nazareth from the prophecy of Isaiah: 'The Spirit of the Lord is upon me because he has anointed me to bring the gospel to the poor...' In the New Testament the relationship between them is presented in two ways. It is the Spirit who begets Jesus (Matt.1.18; Luke 1.35), who descends upon him at his baptism . . . who inspires and guides Jesus . . . On the one hand the Spirit creatively precedes; he is greater than Jesus and controls him. Jesus is the work of the Spirit. On the other hand the Spirit is the work of (the risen) Jesus.'[72] On the basis of this unity and connection the Spirit cannot but share in the partisan love of Jesus for the poor and the handicapped. The historical power of the Spirit is the same as the anti-power which Jesus demonstrated on his way to the cross.

The freedom of the Spirit as God's Spirit therefore does not mean any lack of commitment or any randomness. The Spirit commits itself to the poor. That is sealed once and for all by the career of Jesus, who paid for his partisan love with a criminal's death and who gave his life as a ransom for many. That means that we do not meet the Spirit of the Risen One all over history as a kind of universal fluid, but that he is present in that liberating sub-current of history where the poor and the oppressed rise up and rebel. The Spirit which goes out from Jesus Christ the Risen One manifests himself in their hopes and longings, their cares and anxieties, as an effective creative power which does not abandon people to the fate that higher powers have resolved for them. It is no coincidence – see the quotation above from Mitchell – that the black slaves could converse with Jesus as with a familiar friend.[73]

> Jesus is our friend
> He'll keep us to the en'
> And a little talk with Jesus
> Makes it right.

From a hermeneutical perspective there is a relationship of

reciprocal verification between the praxis of Jesus and black experience. That the black slaves – very much against the desire and intention of the white missionaries – understood the gospel of Jesus Christ as a subversive story of liberation from slavery is a verification of the biblical witness to the praxis of Jesus and the power of the Spirit. Only a completely privatized and spiritualized understanding of salvation can pass by the power of this historical testimony. On the other hand, in their turn scripture and the witness of the early church form the verification of the black experience with Jesus. They establish the truth-content of this experience.

But there is a difficulty. The reciprocal verification would do if it were unambiguously clear what were the contents of black experience and scriptural witness. However, not only are there very different readings of the stories of Jesus but, as we have seen, the black experience is heterogeneous and ambivalent. Therefore what I said above about reciprocal verification is valid only within the framework of a hermeneutical process in which bible-reading and black experience mutually clarify one another. Careful investigation of the Bible is then constantly necessary to provide an answer to the normative question what in the black experience really bears witness to Jesus Christ the liberator. Conversely the black experience creates an eye for dimensions in the biblical writings which traditional (white) exegesis has overlooked. This leads to a creative hermeneutical interplay which is a guarantee of the vitality of black theology as critical reflection on the praxis of the black church.

It must, however, be clear that this process starts from and rests on a pneumatological foundation: the Spirit of the humiliated and exalted Son of Man is the life-giving, creative power in black history and experience. It is not the black theologian who makes the connection between the praxis of Jesus and black experience. This connection is made by the work of the Spirit. In the last resort, therefore, the provocative statement 'Christ is black' is a pneumatological confession. It says that in the context of white racism Jesus Christ identifies himself with the victims through the effective presence of his Spirit. Only in this specific context does the confession of Christ's blackness hold. In other contexts other statements would have to be made. Thus the mobility of the Spirit calls for a mobile, flexible theological reflection which is constantly aware of its contextuality. And conversely, the discovery of the contextuality of all theological thought and language makes theological reflection on the third article of faith the highest priority. The way to a black christology cannot avoid pneumatology.

It is therefore a pity that in the work of James Cone, who has occupied himself more than anyone with the hermeneutical problems of the relationship between the biblical witness and black experience, pneumatology does not really make an appearance. That is all the more remarkable because Cone's theology, at least in my view, tends towards a pneumatological christology. His book *God of the Oppressed*, which appeared in 1975, offers an extended hermeneutical approach in which Cone speaks of the interdependence and convergence of Jesus Christ and the black experience. This convergence is the significance of the incarnation.[74] 'Because God became man in Jesus Christ, he disclosed the divine will to be with humanity in our wretchedness. And because we blacks accept his presence in Jesus as the true definition of our humanity, blackness and divinity are dialectically bound together.'[75] The word 'dialectical' must serve here to avoid the suspicion of a 'blood and soil' theology. Cone in fact will hear nothing of a natural propensity of blacks to be mediators of revelation. The confession 'Christ is black' is not based on a black cultural or psychological need, and it is not to be misunderstood in an exclusive sense. It rests exclusively on the free will of Christ really to enter the world of blackness, with all the humiliation and pain that that involves.[76]

However, the problem is that Cone has a tendency to relate God's incarnation in the Jew Jesus of Nazareth, as an unrepeatable event limited by place and time, directly to black history. Ascension and Pentecost are passed over. But Christ's real presence in the world of blackness cannot be exclusively based in theological terms on Col.1.15ff.;[77] the work of the Spirit must be involved here: it is the Spirit which incorporates men and women into the messianic community of the exalted Christ. If that does not happen, or happens insufficiently, then a remarkably unhistorical element enters into the dialectical connection between incarnation and blackness which arouses the suspicion that a dialectical pattern is being imposed on the text of scripture and the context of black experience from outside.

God of the Oppressed is written from the discovery of the contextual determination of all theology. In *Black Theology and Black Power* and *A Black Theology of Liberation* contextuality had not yet explicitly come up as a hermeneutical problem. Insight into the need to challenge the pseudo-universality of theological argument – and the non-intellectual factors[78] which are involved in it! – leads Cone to stand further away from Tillich, Barth and Moltmann and to recognize the depths of the black story, the history of the black people which at the same time is his own personal history. *God of the Oppressed* is the most important study that Cone has written so far. But a key hermeneutical concept like 'convergence' indicates that he has not really left behind the Tillichian method of correlation which he used in *A Black Theology of Liberation*. As a result the hermeneutical, methodological substructure is characterized by a degree of obscurity which cannot be masked by a frequent use of the word dialectical. At least in my view, a next step must be to connect contextuality as a hermeneutical problem with much-needed reflection on the third article of faith.

Hermeneutical-methodological considerations on the relationship of the biblical story to black experience have led us to the conclusion that a black christology must be a pneumatological christology. But does this also provide an answer to the urgent methodological question raised by William Jones in *Is God a White Racist?* When black theologians talk about the liberating action of God in black history, does that not need historical and empirical verification? How is the holocaust of the black experience to be reconciled with the confession of God's goodness and justice? The prophets in Israel could point to the exodus from Egypt and the gift of the land of Canaan. But blacks in America are still a people without land. What exaltation-liberation event can black theologians point to? What verification can they give of their assertion that God is on the side of the oppressed?

I spoke above about the reciprocal verification of the black experience and the praxis of Jesus. In so doing I tried to answer Jones's methodological question about historical verification. But this answer would certainly not satisfy the author of *Is God a White Racist?*, because it begins from something which first needs to be demonstrated. My answer presupposes the reality and the effectiveness of the resurrection. Only for those who are gripped by this (hi)story is the verification of which I have spoken valid. By contrast Jones seeks a historical verification *remoto Christo*; he regards neither the biblical narratives of Easter and Pentecost nor the liberating experience which emerged in black experience with these stories as historical facts.

It is beyond question that this view represents a substantial reduction of the black experience. Jones, as James Cone has shown, cannot establish his claim that he is practising internal criticism.[79] But the greatest difficulty in his theodicy question is that it has to be answered on an impossible level, namely that of the intellect. In any theological or philosophical argument non-intellectual factors play their part and determine its outcome and nature. These non-intellectual factors are closely connected with what we understand by faith. One can try to be as aware as possible of these non-intellectual factors – and that is precisely where the concept of contextuality comes in – but one cannot get rid of them. For Jones these factors play just as much of a role as for Cone, Roberts or Washington. Therefore the contrast between Jones' black humanism and black theology is not that between reason and faith but between one faith and another – which does not of course mean that both parties could not join forces in the struggle for a society without racism.

A book like Jones's makes it clear to us that the black experience of religious history is heterogeneous. Jones rightly points out that black theology deals selectively with this experience. Thus pie-in-the-sky eschatology is rejected outright, though this view of faith occurs in the history of the black church. But does that not also hold for the experience of God's absence, impotence and superfluity which is expressed by William Jones? What does black theology make of the last chapter of Benjamin Mays' *The Negro's God*, which contains texts about 'Ideas of God Involving Frustration, Doubt, God's Impotence and his Non-Existence'?[80] Where was God during the unsuccessful slave revolts, the rapes of black women, the whippings and the lynch parties? In *Black Christ*, Countee Cullen (1903-1946) writes:

> God, if He was, kept to His skies,
> And left us to our enemies.[81]

These strophes, too, are part of black experience! On what basis does black theology claim God's effective presence in the ghettoes, in the quiet misery of lifelong unemployment, slavery to drink and the vain use of aggression? How can a history in which failure, suffering and hopeless expectation are so clear be the basis for a theology of liberation? Are not the bare facts of black history in themselves a criticism of religion that is more incisive than any theory?

Is God a White Racist? caused a great deal of discussion among black theologians but did not produce any solutions. That is not surprising, since theodicy is not in the last instance a question for discussion. But the question remains: are not blackness and theology mutually exclusive? Is theology, whether or not provided with the explicative genitive 'of liberation', the appropriate way of giving expression to all that blackness means in terms of oppression, suffering and otherness?

Here we must return to the work of the historian of religion Charles Long. In an article which appeared in 1983 Long stressed the relationship in the Christian church between theology and power. 'Theologies are specific modes of religious discourse that have become overwhelmingly predominant within the Christian Church. Theologies are about power, the power of God but equally about the power of the specific form of discourse about power.'[82] In the tradition of Western Christianity this demonstration of power has implicitly or explicitly led to an image of the divine as being white or transparent, so that it has justified and hallowed a power structure which has subjected countless people and different cultures economically and by force of arms and, as Long puts it, has made them transparent to the West. For Long transparency is a key concept. It is derived from the symbolic significance of the term Enlightenment and as such is an indication of a cultural orientation which is concerned to see through, make transparent, human life and nature. Modern theology, too, is permeated by this ideal of knowledge. In this connection Long quotes a significant passage from Paul Tillich's *Systematic Theology* in which Christ is described as the man in whom God becomes transparent – here the crucifixion is regarded as the definitive manifestation of this transparency![83]

Over against this legacy of the Enlightenment, as we have seen at the beginning of this chapter, Long sets the opacity of the experience of oppressed peoples and cultures. The tendency of Western cultures to subject peoples, reducing the other to a transparent object,[84] clashes with the hard corporeality of blackness, the symbol of opacity. Because of their bodies blacks were not only regarded as valuable workers, but these bodies were also the locus of the ideologies which justified their slavery. 'These bodies of opacity, these loci of meaninglessness... were paradoxically loci of a surplus of meaning, meanings incapable of universal expression during the period of oppression.'[85]

Long puts the recent rise of black theology and other forms of theology which recognize colour, like *God is Red* by the Indian author Vine Deloria, in the context of this dialectical reversal.[86] He calls these forms of theology 'theologies opaque'. But according to Long they suffer from an internal ambivalence; here he is thinking in particular of the work of James Cone. They seek to break with theology as a demonstration of power that overshadows people and cultures, but to achieve this they move on to the opponent's ground in order to attack him. In so doing, however, they run the risk of getting involved in the same power structure and repeating the destructive course of events. The 'theologies opaque' must therefore not seek to occupy the theological arena. Their task is the demolition of theology as a demonstration of power. The sources of this break lie in the stories and traditions of marginalized people and cultures. The 'theologies opaque' must make common cause with folklorists, poets, novelists and many others who are occupied in a non-theological way in recovering the silent history and cultures of countless nameless people. Although it is not always precisely clear towards what Long is feeling his way, we can safely assume that Cone's christological interpretation of the black experience is far too transparent for him. Cone in turn is afraid that Long is caught up in 'cultural survival' without the political implications of a return to African culture becoming clear.[87] Therefore Cone keeps to the theme of liberation and criticizes Long for a lack of social theory. However, the underlying question in the discussion between the two seems to me to be this: is a christology possible which does justice to the experience of opacity in black history? Or, to put the same question in a different way, can the dialectic of master and slave – the dialectical reversal – which Charles Long as a historian of religion identifies in the depths of black experience, be interpreted christologically without illegitimate transgressions of boundaries and violations of the historical reality of people's religious experience?

The answer depends on further internal discussion between Long, Cone and others, and it is not for us to anticipate that. However, it seems to me very important that the Kampen dissertation of the black South African theologian Takatso A.Mofokeng should be brought into this debate. This christological study, entitled *The Crucified among the Crossbearers*, has as its context the struggle against apartheid, and more particularly the black consciousness movement.[88] In order to be able to develop the already existing christological approaches of Manas Buthelezi, Allan Boesak and Zephaniah Kameeta, Mofokeng has been deeply concerned with the christologies of Karl Barth and Jon Sobrino. Here I am concerned above all with some important insights which Mofokeng derives from Sobrino, who is at work in Central America (El Salvador).[89]

Both locate their christological outline in a conflict situation which cries out for change. It is not a matter of interpreting reality, i.e. making it transparent, but of changing it. From 'the historical praxis of liberation' they seek 'the historical praxis of Jesus'. Sensitive to the way in which concepts, ideas and dogmas tend to veil social conflicts, they want to go back to the (hi)story of Jesus' life.[90] Christological dogmas, as they have developed in church history, have a history behind them and cannot be understood without tracing the historical course which led to their origin. If the confession that Jesus is the Christ is the end-point of christology, then the starting point lies in the affirmation that this Christ is the historical Jesus who lived to the uttermost as a human being in Roman-occupied Palestine in the midst of the oppositions and conflicts of his time. J. Sobrino in particular puts strong emphasis on the paradigmatic character of this life. A development takes place in Jesus' life: in the service of the kingdom of God this life goes from crisis to crisis, but through the defeats and crises Jesus becomes increasingly aware of his own task and destiny. In human terms his life ends in complete failure. The crucifixion seals the definitive failure and is the historical consequence of a life in the service of justice.

According to Sobrino,[91] Jesus dies in complete discontinuity with his life and the cause for which he strove. The crucifixion compels us to revise our conceptions of God. The cross does away with any image of God, any form of natural theology. It raises the question whether God's love is impotent in the face of evil in history.[92] On the cross we find no transparency – to use Long's terminology – but simply opacity. 'On the cross God does not show up as one who wields power over the negative from outside; rather, on the cross we see God submerged within the negative.'[93]

For Sobrino and Mofokeng the cross is therefore not a transitional phase to the resurrection as the definitive manifestation of God's power and Christ's triumph. There is no continuity between abandonment by God on the cross and God's presence in the resurrection. The conflict between God's absence on the cross (Mark 15.34) and his presence (II Cor.5.19f.) makes it impossible to speak (mono)theistically about God; it is only possible to speak – or, better, stammer or sing – about God in trinitarian terms as Father, Son and Holy Spirit. According to Sobrino the abandonment on the cross is an expression both of God's judgment on human history and of his deep solidarity with human life. The opacity of the cross raises the question of God not in terms of theology (argument about God) but of theodicy (the justification of God). 'On the cross theodicy is historicized.'[94] Jesus was not killed through natural disasters but through what people do to one another in history as free beings. The dialectic of cross and resurrection is not detached from history; on the contrary it is history, it makes history. The way to knowledge of this dialectic is the way of historical participation – participation by becoming a companion of those who are the special objects of the love of the Son of Man.

However, if we say that the dialectic of cross and resurrection is not a matter of theological speculation but history, and through the life-giving power of the spirit makes history – must we not go further and say that we make this history an abstraction unless we can connect it with the real history of what people share in, experience and do to one another? Is it then possible to see the dialectic of master and slave indicated by Charles Long in the opacity of black history apart from the event of cross and resurrection? Is it really forbidden to see here a verification of the fact that Golgotha is not the last word in the history of Jesus and in the history of all innocents who are killed and tortured? And if in fact traces of the Spirit of the humiliated and exalted Messiah are present in black history and culture, must it then not be possible to arrive at a christology which does justice to the reality of blackness?

5 · Context

Black Theology in Dialogue with Other Forms of Contextual Theology

1. Kairos *and context*

To friends who wanted to go on seeing him as the great prophet who proclaims the *kairos*, in 1927 Barth used an attractive image. Looking back on the course he had followed he compared himself to someone feeling his way up the dark steps of a church tower and by chance getting hold of the bell-rope instead of the hand-rail. To his amazement he hears the great bell beginning to ring out in a way which he and others cannot possibly miss.[1]

This image makes it clear that for Barth the writing of *Romans*, however intrinsically necessary it was in the situation after 1914, was an action the consequences and implications of which he could not completely foresee. In a sense one can say that the whole of his further work, which was also determined by the constantly changing circumstances of the time, was a further working out and thinking through of what moved him in 1914 to break with the then liberal and orthodox theological world.

Something of the kind in fact happens wherever the *kairos* brings people to break with what hitherto has been valid and authoritative. James H.Cone did not write *Black Theology and Black Power* for his own amusement but because he could do no other. Only afterwards did it become clear that he was putting into words what was also the experience of others. But this book and the first joint declaration on black theology in 1969 are really not much more than programmatic announcements. The hermeneutical implications of this prophetic dedication and approach were hardly recognized. Only as things progress do the real problems of content and structure begin to become evident. In the previous chapter we followed the intense discussion about the relationship between black experience and black theology as a theology of liberation and we saw how this discussion is far from achieving adequate clarity and agreement. The same applies to the problems that we shall now be considering.

If the previous chapter was concerned with liberation as the content of black theology, we are now concerned with contextuality as its structure. From the moment that the expression 'black theology' came into circulation it was clear that this was a way of doing theology which was rooted in a specific spirituality and experience which arose in a specific situation of dispute, and in the first instance was intended for a specific group of people. This made black theology from the beginning a contextual theology. In the first part of this study (above all ch.1, section 2 and ch.2, section 2) I indicated what the discovery of the contextual character of theological reflection signifies – theology as the second element, the hermeneutical priority of the specific struggle of the poor as the locus of God's presence, a rejection of the autonomy of the thinking subject and of the dualism of thought and action, a recognition of the social and cultural determination of all theological thought as a condition of practice in 'seeing' the O(o)ther, recognition of one's own limitations as a condition for ecumenical thought and action. In describing these decisive elements I tried to incorporate as many insights as possible as these have arisen in different situations and in different parts of the world. But if we look at the earliest phase of black theology we must note that an understanding of the structural and methodological significance of contextual theology is present at most in embryonic form. Awareness of problems is clearly lagging behind what is already in fact being done.

This is evident, for example, from Cone's *A Black Theology of Liberation*, the first attempt to systematize black theology. Although this theology with its fierce attack on all – white – theology which does not recognize its social and cultural conditioning is *ipso facto* itself a 'situated' theology, this does not work through sufficiently into its structure and method, as we saw earlier. The method of correlation borrowed from Paul Tillich by which Cone brings the gospel of Jesus Christ and the black struggle as closely together as possible, has a schematic character which blocks rather than furthers contextuality as a hermeneutical and methodological problem.

It says much for the vitality of black theology that in a relatively short time the methodological insights which have developed especially in Latin American theology have been grasped and worked out in a distinctive way. Five years after *A Black Theology of Liberation* Cone produced a book, *God of the Oppressed*, the main theme of which is the social and cultural determination of any theological language. The way in which Cone expresses the fact that the story, the black story, determines not only the content but also the structure of black theology makes the book an impressive model of contextual theology.

Along with Wilmore's *Black Religion and Black Radicalism*, *God of the Oppressed* is in my view the most important book that black theology has produced so far. But it is not the last word. Pressing questions remain open, especially that of the place and function of the analysis of power relationships within society. In this chapter I am concerned to do two things. First I want to show that the peripheral ecumene – the contacts wth feminist theologians and representatives of Spanish-speaking and other ethnic minorities at a national level, and with African, Asian, Latin American and Caribbean theologians at an international level – was of decisive significance for the development of black theology as a contextual reflection in the field of tension between particularity and universality. Secondly I want to investigate what the consequences are of the discovery of contextuality for the development of a black ecclesiology.

If we look back to the publications of black theologians from the first phase, we see in them an image of America as a white monolithic block which excludes blacks. Over against this closed society militant blacks can attempt two things. They can try to break open this society – the means of doing this are legal procedures, non-violent demonstrations and possibly forms of civil disobedience – so that blacks can eventually can take their rightful place in the American democracy. The other way is that of struggling for one or another form of independence. Clear champions of integration are Major Jones, Deotis Roberts and Preston Williams. Albert Cleage and to a lesser degree James Cone by contrast support black nationalism. But both trends have one thing in common: there is no analysis of the underlying causes of racism. The historical connection between racism and capitalism is not noted, far less that between racism and sexism. Certainly the universal perspective of liberation emerges, but so little backed up by an analysis of real power relationships that it is legitimate to say that – to return to a distinction made earlier – in its initial period black theology was more a survival theology than a liberation theology.

Black theology at a later stage does not lack self-criticism in respect of this first period. In his sketch of a radical Afro-American philosophy of religion, *Prophesy Deliverance!*, Cornel West, the younger colleague of James Cone in Union Theological Seminary in New York, sums up the shortcomings of earlier conceptions of black theology:

> 1. Its absence of a systematic social analysis, which has prevented black theologians from coming to terms with the relationships between racism, sexism, class exploitation and imperialist oppression.
>
> 2. Its lack of social vision, political program, and concrete praxis which defines and facilitates socio-economic and political liberation.
>
> 3. Its tendency to downplay existential issues such as death, disease, dread, despair, and disappointment which are related to, yet not identical with, suffering caused by oppressive structures.[2]

In his latest book, *For My People*, Cone gives a similar list of sins and mentions as shortcomings the negative over-reaction to white racism, a lack of social analysis, a lack of economic analysis and a lack of insight into sexism.[3]

It is not difficult to give some reasons for these shortcomings. Those who oppose injustice done to them tend, at any rate in the first place, to turn to what causes them most pain, to what is most tangible and visible – and perhaps white racism is the most visible of all mechanisms of oppression in modern society.[4] Class conflicts, for example, certainly in contemporary American society, are more concealed and call for an analytical tool that can cut through myths like free market and free world to the real power systems. That is not to say that the causes of racism are easier to analyse. The opposite is the case. Precisely this visible aspect of racial oppression can block a view of underlying causes. It is no coincidence that only at the end of their lives did both Martin Luther King and Malcolm X associate racism with economic conditions of exploitation without in so doing overlooking the fact that racism as an ideological force has a dynamic and a logic of its own. In addition, for a scientific, rational analysis of this phenomenon victims of racism must go over to their opponents' ground – because the discipline is in the hands of white scholars, sometimes well-meaning and sometimes not, who with their definitions and categories define what may be accounted racism and what may not. By contrast victims know what racism is through their daily experience, and this experiential knowledge mistrusts any form of analysis from outside which cannot be derived directly from their own experience.

All these factors explain why black theologians in the first instance did not feel any need to develop a social theory and concentrated on investigating the black religious experience. It was above all the critical questions of Latin American and feminist theologians which led black theology to leave behind the image of America as a closed society, as a white monolithic block, and to have an eye for racism as a power complex which is deeply entangled in other systems of domination, which manifest themselves not only outside but also within the black community, systems which include sexism and the widening gulf between the black middle class and the hopeless situation of the black underclass. It has been the encounters in the peripheral ecumene which has made black theologians see that integration into existing American society means extending the present power systems in the world.

This is not the place to describe the history of these encounters, fascinating though it is in itself. For that one can go to James Cone, who has written a good deal about them.[5] Two organizations have given structure to peripheral ecumenism. One is Theology in the Americas, which began in 1975 in Detroit; a sub-division of this is the Black Theology Project, which at present is directed by the historian Howard Dodson.[6] The other is the Ecumenical Association of Third World Theologians (EATWOT), which in 1976 held its first conference in Dar es Salaam and since then has held five inter-continental conferences in Ghana (1977), Sri Lanka (1979), Brazil (1980), India (1981) and Switzerland (1983). It is true of both organizations that their weakness is at the same time their strength: although a relatively small number of people meet with some regularity at the different conferences and these people all too often occupy only a marginal position in their own land or church, the very fact that this is a limited group of people means that over the years a far-reaching process of mutual recognition and correction has taken place.

In the years preceding the establishment of EATWOT some meetings with African theologians took place which did not run very smoothly. If North American black theology found a warm welcome among the rising Black Consciousness movement of black students in South Africa, among other Africans it came up against opposition. When it came to paternalism, the missionary history of the Afro-American churches on the African continent was not very different from that of the white churches. There was therefore a certain antipathy to American black theologians who exported their theology to Africa. Moreover many African theologians thought that black theology put too much emphasis on socio-political and economic liberation. In a notorious article John Mbiti claimed that the thought of black theologians grew out of hatred and bitterness.[7] However, in the context of EATWOT there was an unmistakable process of reciprocal convergence: African theologians began to sense the inadequacy of programmes of indigenization; black theologians put more stress on the religious and cultural dimensions of the process of liberation.

This last development took place also as a result of fruitful contacts with Asian Christians. Asian theological reflection confronted black theologians not only with the problem of the overwhelming poverty but also with the liberating potential that is present in Asian religions and cultures for challenging this poverty on a material and spiritual level.

However, it was Latin American liberation theology which caused black theologians most difficulty. It is too simplistic to explain the sometimes harsh confrontations in terms of the opposition between class struggle and race struggle. There is more to it than that. The Latin Americans made two contributions in Detroit 1975 and later within EATWOT: 1. a methodology in which commitment comes first and theological reflection follows; 2. a coherent model of social analysis which interprets global economic and political relationshps in terms of centre and periphery, domination and dependence. From this position they asked black theologians about the praxis of their struggle: what was the context of black liberation, capitalist or socialist? What was the relationship between the struggle for racial equality within America and the struggle which was being waged in Third World countries against the economic interests, the propaganda and the violence of American imperialism?

In any case the Latin American criticism was the occasion for some black theologians to reflect on 1. the need for a social theory as an essential part of the hermeneutical process; 2. more specifically the relationship betwen class conflicts and racism. An intense reciprocal discussion arose over the need for Marxist analysis and the tenability of the paradigm of equality which dominated the black struggle for so long. When in 1980 the second conference of Theology in the Americas took place in Detroit, Jualynne and Howard Dodson had the following to say about the ideal of equal rights and equal opportunities:

> The pursuit of equality of access and equality of opportunity has been framed with concepts that are part and parcel of the United States' particular kind of capitalist exploitation. For example, under current definitions, Black People, Asians, Hispanics, Native Americans, and even women are fighting each other for the resources which will allow us the opportunity to be integrated into existing educational institutions, professional organizations, employment... The point is, we are striving for equal opportunity but the model of things and situations that define equality were created from the exploitation and deprivation of some people, usually Third World people.[8]

However, the problem is that even in the socialist alternative there are presuppositions which make the ideal of equality dubious. Does the abolition of the gulf between rich and poor and of the class struggle in fact of itself lead to the disappearance of the inequality between sexes, races and cultures? Is not socialism as the new economic order problematical because it must be regarded as a kind of social panacea?[9]

In this respect black, African and Asian theologians have found one another united in common criticism of the rigidity and the dogmatism of Latin American theology. They did not want to go back on what they had learned from the Latin Americans about the analysis of economic conditions, and their hermeneutical and methodological insight into what was already being done. But they missed an adequate affinity to the values of indigenous cultures and traditional religions, while moreover they noted a suspicious silence over the struggle against racism and sexism. Gustavo Gutiérrez and other Latin Americans involved in the world of EATWOT tried at the 1980 Brazil conference to counter this criticism by approaching the struggle of women, black population groups and Indians in the light of Gramsci's notion of the 'organic and permanent character of the crisis' of capitalism at the periphery.[10] But the very person among the black theologians who was most involved in the work of Gramsci, Cornel West, said at the conference that the Latin American theology was too occupied in producing Marxist theory and paid too little attention to the experience that could be contributed by representatives of women's groups, blacks and Indians. The Marxist analysis is indispensable when it comes to examining the power of capital, but its Achilles heel is the culture and identity of ethnic and racial communities. West sees as the cause of this the fact that Karl Marx wrote in a society, England, which was homogeneous ethnically and racially, and in the nineteenth century, when social identity was determined by its place in the work process. But in heterogeneous societies, marginalized ethnic and racial minorities derive the means for self-preservation and the quest for identity from their religion and culture. Any analysis which passes over the need for this cultural self-establishment is suspect.

> When Marxists are preoccupied with an analysis that downplays or ignores the liberating aspects of degraded and oppressed cultures, it suggests that such Marxists share the ethos – not of the degraded and oppressed minorities – but of the dominant European culture.[11]

Here we come to the crucial question: can the black struggle for liberation be reconciled with Marxist theory? Is a version of this theory possible which can do justice to the liberating potential of black religion and culture? Or is Marxism, in whatever version, so much part of the ethnocentrism of European culture that it is unsuitable as an instrument of liberation for blacks?

There are different views about these questions within black theology. Charles Long gives the impression[12] that for him a liberation theology which works with a Marxist analysis *ipso facto* stands in the world of the Enlightenment, which has forced out the opaqueness of history. By contrast, James Cone has come to the conclusion, especially as a result of the discussions within EATWOT, that Marxist theory is indispensable for the analysis of capitalism and class relationships. Cornel West in turn sees in the concept of hegemony developed by Gramsci the possibility of on the one hand holding fast to the autonomous place of religion and culture and on the other of combining their own dynamic with the power in society.[13] In *Prophesy Deliverance!* West argues for an alliance betwen prophetic Christianity and progressive Marxism. A black philosophy or theology may not simply be based on Afro-American history and experience, but should also take up and incorporate modernity into itself.[14]

In his book, however, West does not make it clear whether in the alliance between prophetic (Afro-American) Christian thought and progressive (left-wing) Marxism there is still a role for the black church – not as an idea but as an entity which really exists, made up of different denominations and organizations. As West himself has made clear,[15] the black church and Marxist thought form two separate worlds – despite the example of Reverend George Washington Woodbey (San Diego, California) who at the beginning of this century was a prominent socialist leader. Does West write off the black church, apart from some prophetic marginal phenomena, as an essential factor in the process of liberation? But can political organizations like the National Black Independent Political Party ever establish a broad base in the black community if they do not gain wide support in the black church? If this last question is fair, then the crucial question for black theology becomes: what strategy can the religious bulwark formed by the black church mobilize for a messianic community?

If it is already difficult enough to establish the right relationship between racism and class analysis, the practical and theoretical problems become even greater when the struggle over sexism is also involved. Just as Latin American liberation theology put critical questions to black theologians (and vice versa), so too white feminist theologians had their hesitations about the work of Cone and his colleagues (and here, too, the reservations were mutual). In itself that is not surprising. Although it is clear that in modern society sexism and racism are structurally interwoven in a linked system of white patriarchal domination,[16] precisely this interweaving also creates tensions which are described by Rosemary Radford Ruether in her book *New Woman/New Earth: Sexist Ideologies and Human Liberation*, which appeared in 1975, as follows:

> This interstructuring of oppression by sex, race, and also class creates intermediate tensions and alienations – between white women and black women, between black men and white women,

and even between black men and black women. Each group tends to suppress the experience of its racial and sexual counterparts. The black movement talks as though blacks meant black males. In so doing it conceals the tensions between black males and black females. The women's movement fails to integrate the experience of black and poor women, and so fails to see that much of what it means by female experience is confined to those women within the dominant class and race.[17]

This tendency indicated by Ruether to make a monolithic picture of one's own experience of oppression is precisely the reason why peripheral ecumenism is of vital importance for any form of liberation theology. Anyone who adds 'of liberation' as an explicative genitive after the term theology is exceeding his or her competence. The term cannot be more than a declaration of intent. Who can guarantee that the liberation striven for does not mean the continued oppression of those who get overlooked? Only a permanent *metanoia* (conversion) can prevent people being caught up in the mechanism of division and domination in existing power systems without being aware of it – and even that is no guarantee. The process of exchanging experiences, of confrontation and mutual recognition, which takes place in organizations like EATWOT and Theology in the Americas between representatives of oppressed groups and popular movements, is therefore extremely necessary for the constant adjustment of strategy and analysis.

The first declaration on black theology from 1969 ends with the proud and virile words of Eldridge Cleaver: 'We shall have our manhood. We shall have it or the earth will be leveled by our efforts to gain it.'[18] Cleaver, like some other Black Power leaders, was notorious for his macho comments about women: for him rape was a political action. Manhood was at stake in the struggle for freedom. Although women often occupied important positions in the various organizations and did much of the dirty work, they seldom got any publicity. In the historical account of the struggle for civil rights and Black Power only the names of Rosa Parks and Fannie Lou Hamer crop up with any regularity.[19]

The quotation from Cleaver is symptomatic of the first phase of black theology. Any reference to sexism or to the specific experience of black women is lacking. In this respect black theology is a reflection of the power relationships in the black church. Here, despite the fact that women make up more than seventy per cent of the membership they seldom attain positions of leadership and constantly come up against opposition when performing official functions in the church.

That black women still hardly appear in either black theology or in feminist theology is a direct result of the structural interweaving of racism and sexism which they experience in body and soul. But one cannot say that black women have not made their voice heard. In the nineteenth century the black women's struggle developed in the context of abolitionism. Sojourner Truth, Harriet Tubman, Ida B.Wells-Barnett, Mary Church Terrell and many others were in the forefront of the fight for the rights of black women.[20] In the period of the civil rights struggle and Black Power, however, militant black women opted for the 'movement', rejecting the American women's movement as white and middle class. According to James Cone,[21] it was not until the play by Ntozake Shange, *For Colored Girls...*(1967), and the book by Michele Wallace, *Black Macho and the Myth of the Superwoman* (1979), that black feminism became the subject of intensive discussion in the black community. It makes one think, however, to note that black theology and feminist theology, both with their explicit claims to liberation, have shown and still show so much ideological narrowness towards the specific experiences and problems of black women. One has to accept that Jacquelyn Grant is right when she says:

> It is my contention that if Black Theology speaks of the Black Community as if the special problems of Black women do not exist, it is no different from the White Theology it claims to reject precisely because of its inability to take account of the existence of Black people in its theological formulations.[22]

It was not until 1976 that James Cone broke the silence – he was the first black theologian to do so – with a lecture on 'New Roles in the Ministry: A Theological Appraisal'.[23] Since then Cone has begun to speak in an ever more articulate way about the need for a black feminist theology. However, the problem is that there are only a few feminist theologians to develop the fallow ground.

What needs to be done is first of all to examine the specific faith-experience of black women, and secondly to see what this historical faith still means for their present situation and struggle. A conversation with Katie Cannon, one of the women doing pioneer work here, was published some time ago in the monthly *Wending*. What she says there about her still unpublished investigation into the work of black women writers at all events gives a first impression of the content of this faith-experience: 'The overriding theme of my work is that virtue has nothing to do with abstractions like goodness or beauty. Virtue is the art of living in the midst of the most acute tensions. It is the capacity to make life valuable in a loveless situation in order to have the feeling "I am someone" when someone says to you, "You have no right to exist".'[24] The three virtues which constantly recur in black women writers are 'quiet grace' as the capacity to survive through the experience of God's love; 'unsheltered courage' as the courage to live in the midst of existential uncertainty, and 'invisible dignity' as the worth and perseverance which women show without being aware of it. So according to Katie Cannon black women have created an ethic and a theory of virtue of their own out of their religious tradition and the life which they lead.[25] A question which is of real importance for the future of black feminist theology is to what degree these values and virtues are still alive today among the majority of black women, who belong to the lowest class in American society.

2. Towards a black ecclesiology. The dialectic of particularity and universality

What is the significance of the discovery of the complex structural interconnection of different forms of oppression for a theology which, like black theology, is born out of the struggle against one particular power complex? Is its original commitment not weakened and does not its focus become vaguer? What remains of the *kairos* which brought it to life?

Without doubt there is a risk that in the course of development the prophetic élan may be lost. A realization of the complexity of power relationships can also have a paralysing effect, particularly in times of conservatism and economic recession. But another development is also possible. We have seen that in its initial phase black theology tended more to be a survival theology than a real theology of liberation. Granted, the term 'survival' here has absolutely no pejorative connotations. Why should survival, in whatever form, not come first for a people which has had to undergo so many traumas? Who has the right to pass a negative judgment here? However, it is an unmistakable fact that the black struggle for survival has never been without a wider vision, one extending to total liberation in a world without tears. From the beginning this inclusive dimension was also present in black theology. Especially thanks to experiences in peripheral ecumenism this dimension has become more visible. Black theology now moves in the field of tension between particularity and universality, *kairos* and context. The *horizontal* polarity of particularity and universality means that black theology seeks to combine its commitment towards the black community with an active connection with the struggle for marginalized groups, peoples and cultures elsewhere in the world. The *vertical* polarity of *kairos* and context means that it does not lose its prophetic élan, but seeks to deepen it through a sober analysis and assessment of specific power relationships.

However, this polar structure must have a place where it can manifest itself. Otherwise it remain abstract. Here we arrive at the question of the hermeneutical *locus* of black theology. Earlier, in Ch.2, section 2, I called ecumenism the place where the tension between particularity and universality becomes visible. There is no need to retract this statement in connection with black theology as a specific form of liberation theology, but it needs further qualification. The place of black theology cannot only be the black church. That this does not contradict what I have already said should be clear by the end of this chapter.

By black church I understand in the first instance the visible church, both the different black church denominations and the black Christians in predominantly white churches. However frustrating the conservatism, fundamentalism and moralism of this church may be at times, however much its leaders may seem to be concerned simply to maintain their own institutions and organizations, if black theology does not function critically within this church, it does not function anywhere. The view which Gayraud Wilmore expressed at the second conference of Theology in the Americas in Detroit 1980, that there can be no élitist transcendence of this church, is correct.[26] In fact, as Wilmore says elsewhere, the black church is, paradoxically enough, both the most reactionary and the most radical of all black institutions, the most pervaded by the mythology and values of white America, and at the same time the institution which is the most self-aware and independent (in financial terms, too) in the black community.[27]

However, if black theology seeks to function critically within this visible church, it may never identify this church with the messianic community, with what Karl Barth calls the 'earthly-historical form of existence of Jesus Christ'.[28] The church is only and exclusively church by virtue of the life-giving power of the Holy Spirit. Any form of sacralization of the black church or the black people is completely ruled out here. But on the other hand this emphasis on the work of the Spirit does not amount to any spiritualization of the concept of the church. We may recall what was said in the previous chapter about God's Spirit who binds himself in freedom to the poor; and regardless of what people seem to think in the Vatican, the poor are a political category. Therefore I agree with James Cone when in his lecture 'New Roles in the Ministry: A Theological Appraisal', he comments:

> The only way to encounter God's Spirit is to have one's religious consciousness formed in a political context. The social and political context of the victims is indispensable for hearing our true calling, a vocation that is always bound up with the liberation of victims from servitude. It is not possible for anyone to hear the divine Spirit's call into the Christian ministry, and at the same time derive his or her perception of that ministry from an ecclesiastical structure that oppresses women.[29]

The visible church becomes church, *ecclesia*, when it in fact lives by the expectation of the kingdom of God which is at hand, and in so doing, by virtue of the presence of the Spirit, gives shape in a provisional, fragmentary way to the existence of the church of the poor. So the church is on one hand the place where the *kairos*, the fulfilled time of radical reversal, is experienced, and on the other hand the place where, precisely on the basis of this expectation, the social context is taken with complete seriousness. In other words, the church is the place where the polarity of *kairos* and context, particularity and universality, takes shape. For the critical functioning of black theology within church institutions as they in fact are, this means that there must be a constant remembrance that these institutions have a twofold task: they are the place where black identity is found and the nursery of the beloved community.

Particularity and contextuality are expressed in the church as the place where black identity is found. It is of vital importance for the survival of the black community and of individual black men and women that they should continue to remember the black experience. The black church is the place dedicated to keeping alive the subversive memory of the history of slavery and segregation. In pastorate, diaconate and worship blacks can hear who they are, where they come from and where they get the power which has enabled them to survive the terrors of white supremacy.

But in the last forty or fifty years the black church has gradually become a middle-class instiutuion – and precisely among this class there is a strong tendency not to want to be reminded of slavery and the ghetto existence which, by making enormous efforts, they have left behind. These facts cannot and may not be ignored. In his honest and pastoral book *Black and Presbyterian: The Heritage and the Hope*, Gayraud Wilmore comments:

> We are no longer preaching on Sunday mornings to a group of poor, oppressed Black people who may not have had a decent meal on Saturday. Whether Baptist, Methodist, Presbyterian or Congregational, we are ministering to people who, after certain adjustments for the difference between Black and white norms, belong to that great and growing company of taxpayers who enjoy what is called the middle-class American Way of Life. We may not be happy about that, and there are some things we need to do about it, but that is the case today and we need to face it squarely in order to understand who we are and where we are going.[30]

However, *Black and Presbyterian* shows by a true and representative story that among many women and men who belong to the black middle class there is a deep underlying crisis of identity. Wilmore's book is therefore intended to be a summons to find a new life-style by going back to the roots of black history and experience and on the basis of its subversive memory to learn to distinguish between the Spirit of the living God, who calls non-persons by name and raises up those who are bowed down, and the un-spirit of a society which lets the poor go to the dogs. The subversive memory arouses the black church again to be the church of the poor. In contrast to many white churches, it has not yet lost contact with the lowest classes in society.

In the black community the black church is probably the only institution which is in a position to bridge the growing gap between blacks who have 'made it' and the poor blacks. The circumstances in which the latter must live have grown much worse over past years. Of the total black population, thirty-five per cent live below the official poverty line. Complete demoralization, suicide and slavery to drink and drugs are steadily on the increase. More and more women have to care for their children by themselves because an increasing number of husbands have left their families in the lurch.[31] This disastrous situation is a test case for the black church – and also for the critical function of black theology within this church. If pastorate and diaconate fail here, if black worship no longer fulfils its healing, therapeutic function here, the black church is neither the place where black identity is to be found nor the nursery of King's vision of the beloved community.

There is a dialectical connection between these two elements. If in the one there is a stress on pastorate and diaconate, in the other the apostolic function of the church comes to the fore. If in the place where black identity is found the accent is on survival, in the black church as the nursery of the beloved community the concept of liberation attains its full dimension. Historically the second element is rooted in the spirituals, in the visionary witness of David Walker and Henry Highland Garnet, and in the dream of Martin Luther King. At the present juncture this element must take shape at the three levels of ecumenical activity which I discussed earlier in ch.2, section 2: black ecumenism, peripheral ecumenism and ecumenism as polemic (or missionary ecumenism). Black ecumenism is concerned with the communal rooting of black church denominations in black history and experience, and with the question of the significance of this historical experience for the work of the beloved community. In peripheral ecumenism the conviction takes shape that the exchange of various experiences and a sense of mutual alliance are vitally necessary in the common struggle for another world. Finally, missionary ecumenism does not avoid conflict with white churches and theologians – but the polemic is not an end in itself but a means of making liberation possible for both black and white.

6 · Ideology

Black Theology in Dialogue with White Theologians

1. The reciprocal charge of ideology

The rise of black theology did not leave the feelings of white theologians untouched. Although the reactions to the polemical wrath of James Cone were for the most part negative, and silence was the means most used to express this repudiation, there were also those who recognized their duty to a tradition which excluded blacks *de facto*. This recognition made possible a conversation which, like the other forms of black ecumenical activity, was dominated by a specific problem: if in black ecumenism the main theme is the relationship between black experience and liberation as the content of the gospel (Ch.4); if conversation over the relationship with other forms of opposition and oppression is concentrated in the peripheral ecumene (Ch.5); the debate with white theologians is dominated by the reciprocal charge of ideology. On the one hand the black criticism unmasks the dominant theological traditions as forms of white ideology because of their silence on black experience, their pseudo-universality and dualism; on the other hand the white conversation-partners are concerned that the struggle of blacks for human worth and freedom tends to be so identified with God's will and word that the gospel is reduced to political ideology.

I shall begin this last chapter with an account of the critical questions put by Paul Lehmann and Helmut Gollwitzer. There is a survey of the total response to black theology by James Cone in the collection *Black Theology: A Documentary History, 1966-1979.*[1] Lehmann's article 'Black Theology and Christian Theology' and Gollwitzer's 'Why Black Theology?' both date from the beginnning of the 1970s: they are reactions to a lecture by Cone entitled 'Black Theology on Revolution, Violence and Reconciliation'. I have chosed to limit myself to these two lectures because both express a concern over black theology which is still widely prevalent and this makes them representative of the white response; what is certainly not representative of the moderate white reaction is the constructive, far-reaching way in which the conversation with black theology is being carried on here – to this degree both essays are a cheering demonstration that 'incommunication'[2] between black theology and white theologians is not inevitable.

From the side of black theology the most extensive discussion of theology and ideology is to be found in the fifth chapter of James Cone's *God of the Oppressed*. It is a pity that as far as I can see no other prominent black theologians have put their views of the ideology problem into writing. So we have to limit ourselves to Cone, although that does not do justice to the diversity of black theology.

In the second part of this chapter I want to investigate what contribution discussion of the reciprocal charge of ideology makes to what in the sub-title of this book is called 'the hermeneutical challenge of black theology as a theology of liberation'. The issues that I shall raise there are meant to be a continuation and accentuation of what was said in the first part of this study about 'Theology as ideology and ideological criticism' (Ch.1, section 3) and 'Chalcedon as a condition of a liberating hermeneutics' (Ch.1, section 4).

Helmut Gollwitzer begins his article by noting that black theology challenges the white theologian to submit to criticism of his ideology.

> Ideology critique as self-criticism is now required of him, but not merely as an individual; the tradition itself in which he stands and which he tries to develop further is being questioned as a whole. This is happening not just in the programmatic sense in which, under the aegis of the scripture principle, tradition-criticism has long been part of the theology evolving from the Reformation, but through the rejection which reaches his whole world, the world of the white man, from another segment of humankind. It is a rejection on theological grounds in the name of the gospel.[3]

The *metanoia* for which black theology calls involves learning to see one's own world with the eyes of another, from outside, and asking oneself how far theology and its tradition are perhaps the expression of one's own world, the world of the dominant race. Next Gollwitzer goes deep into the history of slavery and colonialism and into the complicity of Christianity in the exploitation, conquest and annihilation of alien peoples and cultures. Only when one has become aware of this history and has undergone a practical *metanoia* by becoming black – in other words by actually showing solidarity with the victims of the struggle against racism and imperialism – only then can there be a real conversation with black theology in which people support one another mutually by means of critical questioning.

The method which Gollwitzer uses in his essay is particularly important. By going so extensively into history he not only puts the dialogue with black theology in a historical context; at the same time he expresses the fact that not only black theology but also his own theological tradition is determined by the history of which it is a part. To recognize this determination is a condition for going further in systematic theology or dogmatics.

However, if we look at the critical questions which Gollwitzer presents to Cone, we may ask ourselves whether he has drawn the consequences of his methodological insight sufficiently. Gollwitzer wants to avoid theological thought simply being a reflection of a particular situation. If theology is to transcend being bound to its direct context, then it must reflect on the critical distance of the Word of God from any situation. The theological way of knowing leads from God's revelation to our needs and wants and not vice versa. With Karl Barth Gollwitzer wants to hold on to the doxological element of the worship of God for the sake of God himself; 'God' is not an expression or function of interpersonal relationships and human longings or needs.[4] In this respect Gollwitzer feels that Cone has failed to think through the theological significance of the cross adequately. It is precisely the power of the message of the cross that compels us to take into account the difference between God's struggle for liberation and our initiatives for liberation. The criticism of the cross preserves the awareness of being chosen by God from hybris, and avoids black self-consciousness being dominated by resentment (in Nietzsche's sense) or simply being a repetition of white contempt for skin of another colour.[5] Not only whites need conversion, but also blacks:

Even though the balance of guilt may weight whites more than blacks, that does not change the fact that the *metanoia* to which God's grace calls all men is no smaller and no easier with blacks than with whites, although its concrete form may be different. God's partisanship for the oppressed is not a Yes to everything they do in various enterprises...[6]

The heart of Gollwitzer's perceptive criticism is clear: the significance of the cross lies in the fact that God's judgment is given upon all human beings, both black and white; if black theology does not remember this, it functions as political ideology.

As a theologian, Gollwitzer is in fact schooled in the German Church Struggle. It was there that he learned the hard lesson which – in critical solidarity – he now offers to his black colleagues, and especially James Cone. But at the beginning of his article he has made it clear that the world of blackness is a different world from the one in which he himself lives and works. Is it *a priori* certain that the lessons which were learned in the German Church Struggle can be applied without further ado – in other words without close analysis of the difference in historical context – to the completely different situation of black Christians in the United States? Does insight into the historical and social determination of theological arguments not also mean that their ideological function can only be judged in connection with their involvement in the context in which they appear?

In his response to black theology John C.Bennett makes the important comment that to a certain degree all theologies are strategic arguments and that this is particularly true of Cone's black theology.[7] The strategy determines what accents are placed in the interpretation of the biblical message. In one situation particular words and concepts function quite differently from the way in which they do in another. However, Gollwitzer does not get as far as the question of the *Sitz im Leben* of *Black Theology and Black Power* and *A Black Theology of Liberation*. As a result his criticism remains that of an outsider who has insufficient awareness of the effect that theological notions like the criticism of the cross have on people who have borne the cross for centuries.

In his article 'Black Theology and Christian Theology', Paul Lehmann, too, shows his concern that black theology may risk becoming political ideology. He does not for a moment deny that black theology is Christian theology, but he does recognize that it should be 'Christian' theology – the quotation marks here indicate the distance between any given theology and the truth to which it is bound.[8] Theology has an indicative function: it points to the freedom and priority of the truth which precedes thought, and it is aware of its provisional and experimental character. For Lehmann the difference between theology and ideology lies in the way in which it points beyond itself (transcendence) and the humility of theology:

> Professor Cone has made it plain that in the United States today, Christian theology cannot be 'Christian' except as black theology. But it must also be made plain that black theology cannot be 'Christian' theology except as the liberation which it proclaims includes also the transcendence and humility which set free black theology, as indeed every theology, from the temptation and practice of ideology and the idolatry implicit in them.[9]

Lehmann can go a long way with what Cone says about violence and reconciliation. But in his view there is a dimension in the gospel which escapes Cone – and that is the dimension which Lehmann has worked out further in his book *The Transfiguration of Politics*.[10] According to Lehmann, the gospel is the good news of a God who heals through liberating and liberates through healing. He condemns the oppressors and gives power to the oppressed. But this statement is not the last word in the gospel. The Bible knows of a God who strengthens those whom he condemns by giving them the gracious gift of hope, and who curbs those to whom he gives power by the gracious gift of compassion.

> Meanwhile, under the gospel, oppressors and the victims of oppression can and must continually pray that they may be forgiven as they forgive.[11]

This notion is very important for Lehmann's theology and ethics. It would be worth going into further, but that would take us too far. However, given that Lehmann is right, does this mean that Cone has wrongly neglected this dimension in his books and articles? Is there indeed a blind spot in his theological thought?

In order to discover this, a far deeper methodology was needed than that which underlies Lehmann's article. The specific strategic position of Cone's *Black Theology and Black Power* and other publications needs to be analysed more sharply. Words like transcendence and humility point to a dimension which goes deeper than what can be expressed in a given text. They point to an attitude of faith, a theological existence. They therefore call for an investigation of the *Sitz im Leben*, of the connection of text and (historical, biographical) context, of theory and praxis. Anyone who does not take account of the total hermeneutical process of the commitment of faith, the interpretation of scripture and tradition, social vision and strategy, is not in a position to judge whether humility and transcendence are or are not present. Lehmann cannot be blamed for not doing this. But one can ask where he gets the right to suppose that Cone is deficient at this point. So his criticism, like that of Helmut Gollwitzer, remains that of an outsider, directed at a number of provocative comments by Cone, but without giving a complete account of their strategic and therapeutic function.

It sounds like a direct reaction to the critical questions asked by Paul Lehmann when in *God of the Oppressed* Cone asks himself the following questions:

> Who decides when the speech of the oppressed has lost its authentic humility or proper openness? Who decides when theology is ideology? Who decides when the oppressed are truly listening and hearing the Word of God as he invades the brokenness of their situation? As a black theologian who has experienced the dehumanizing effects of white theological reflections, I do not care to rest the future of black humanity upon the judgment of white theologians here or abroad. The decision about these critical questions must rest with those who are struggling for liberation as they encounter the eventful presence of the One who is the source of their fight for freedom.[12]

God of the Oppressed is Cone's attempt to do justice to the element of truth in the criticisms of Gollwitzer, Lehmann and others without, however, making concessions to his deep conviction that in the context of a white racist society God is black. Gollwitzer is right that the way of theological knowledge does not begin with the struggle and the longing of the poor but with God's revelation in Jesus Christ. 'God' is not a cipher for human aspirations and needs. Therefore a distinction must be made between God's Word and our words, between his will and our desires, his Spirit and our spirit. Any theological reflection which is not aware of the way in which it is contextually determined – and therefore of its limitations and finitude – is guilty of blasphemy and is an ideological distortion of the gospel. Lehmann is right here, in that in fact any theological talk of God is vulnerable and ambiguous, so that humility and openness are called for.

But dialectically there is another side to this truth. God became man – or, to put it more strongly, he assumed the form of a slave (Phil.2.7). In so doing he identified himself with the weak and humiliated in order to liberate them from their oppression – and thus make possible the liberation of all human beings. On the basis of this it can be said that God's Word is not an abstract object but the liberating subject in the life of the poor. In all circumstances God's Word remains his word, and not that of the oppressed. But according to Cone, God is free to choose the words of the oppressed as the divine Word, and in so doing to free them for a new existence.[13] The statement that the struggle of the oppressed is God's struggle is not conditioned by psychological needs nor is it religious projection. It is based on historical experience. Both Israel and later the black community – it is striking that Cone mentions the two in the same breath – take history seriously and continue to test the validity of their belief by history. It was not on the basis of inner experience or mystical meditation, but through a believing interpretation of history, that Israel and the black community came to believe that God took the side of the exodus and Jesus to make broken humanity whole again.[14]

According to Cone, on the basis of God's initiative and his option for the humiliated and downtrodden, it is reserved for this category of people to show where theology becomes ideology. Where theology does not function in their struggle for freedom and human worth, but is at the service of the interests of the privileged minority, it is ideology. Any interpretation of the biblical witness which suggests that the exodus story, the prophetic accusations and Jesus' dealings with prostitutes and tax-collectors are only incidentals is ideological. So, too, is that way of thinking which *a priori* acts as a barrier to the partisan truth of the biblical narrative. If God is in fact a God of the oppressed, then they are those who are mentally predisposed to hear and do the will of God which is unfolded in their midst.[15] By this Cone does not mean to say that all the poor also in fact hear the Word and put it into practice. They have often internalized the values of those who rule over them and in so doing have shut themselves off from the liberating events in their history. However, James Cone insists that the social determination which is necessary for belief in God's liberating presence in Jesus Christ is present in the social existence of poor people in a way in which it is not among rich people.

I have tried as best I can to sketch out what Gollwitzer and Lehmann on the one hand and James Cone on the other have to say about the relationship between theology and ideology within the framework of the reciprocal charge of ideology. However, it is my view that both sides have made things too easy when it comes to distinguishing between theology and ideology.

Gollwitzer looks for a basis to the distinction in the notion of God's freedom as the dialectical opposite to his love. Theology which does not keep in mind the distance between God's truth and our truths – which are always provisional – between God's revolution and our revolution, loses the capacity to transcend the existing realities and then irrevocably becomes ideology. Therefore theology, too, must reflect that like any other human language it stands under the judgment of the cross. Only as *theologia crucis* can it avoid turning into interests determined by human situations. But does not Gollwitzer here fall short of the insights which he has developed elsewhere about the connection between theory and praxis? Is a theological argument in which the qualitative distinction beween God's Word and human words is stressed *a priori* less ideological than one in which that is not the case? At all events, is it not necessary here to look at the praxis of which this argument forms a part? Is not the history of the Barmen theses in post-war Germany an illustration of the way in which a text which confesses the freedom of God's word over against any form of ideology can at the same time become the object of 'situational interests'? To repeat Cone's question: 'Who really decides when theology becomes ideology?'

Gollwitzer and Lehmann give the impression that in their approach to black theology they want to prevent the eschatological dimension of the gospel being usurped by the aspirations of a group, people, race or class. Here 'ideological' is a term applied to thought which is subordinated to the interests of a group or class. Over against this Gollwitzer stresses the freedom of God's Word over against any situation and Lehmann in turn stresses the need for transcendence and humility. However, both tend to put the decisive element which distinguishes theology from ideology within the theological argument itself. At all events they suggest that if Cone would only stress God's freedom and transcendence more strongly and God's identification with Black Power less, he could avoid the danger of ideology. But is this really the case? In order to determine that, is it not important also to consider the context and the praxis in which Cone is involved?

Cone himself has in one way or another recognized the weakness in the position of his conversation partners. The weakness lies in their idealistic view that the guarantee against ideological distortion can be produced in the argument itself. Therefore Cone has taken the deciding factor whether the theological argument does or does not have an ideological function out of the argument itself, and put it in a social category: the poor or oppressed. But at the last moment Cone also introduces a qualification: the decisive element lies with those who struggle for liberation in so far as they experience the active presence of God who is the source of their struggle for freedom. However, with this qualification Cone betrays the fact that he himself does not come out of this well. Who determines the active presence of the living, liberating God? When is he really present and when not? The historical experience of the black community is much too heterogeneous and ambivalent to provide certainty in this respect.

In my view, for both Lehmann and Gollwitzer, as for Cone, the difficulty lies in their definition of ideology. For all three the word has a negative significance and is largely an indication of that thinking which is distorted by being led astray by situational interests.[16] Now the word ideology is used with such different meanings that in itself it is difficult to raise objections to such a content. However, it is suspicious that this definition raises those who use the word - whether unconsciously or not - above ideology. The charge of ideology always affects the other side. The one making it believes he or she has found particular guarantees of transcending ideology. In so doing, however, he or she gives his or her own position a particular advantage over the other side: for Cone this lies in his speaking in the name of an oppressed people; for Gollwitzer in his insight into God's freedom; and for Lehmann in his concept of the need for humility and transcendence.

Would it not be better to drop this term ideology, including Karl

Mannheim's distinction between ideology and utopia? Is it not better to say that theology, like the Christian belief to which it relates, has no more possibility of appropriating God's freedom than Baron von Münchhausen had of getting out the mud by his own bootstraps, so that in this earthly vale of tears it will never cease to be and to produce ideology? In that case we see ideology, as we did earlier, as the way in which people envisage their reality,[17] as the imaginary relation of human beings to the conditions in which they really live. In that case ideology is not a false awareness of power relationships (though it can be that), but that which precedes and determines consciousness. Christian faith, as a human possibility and choice, lives in ideology and not outside it. The same is true of theology. Cone's theological commitment is involved in ideology and his struggle, like that of Gollwitzer in the context of the Federal Republic of Germany, is connected with the opposing views of men and women about their relationship to the conditions of existence in which they really live.[18] But does this not represent an enormous relativizing of the struggle of liberation theologians? On the contrary, it only means that the struggles between the idols of death and the God of life – the title of a recent collection from Latin America[19] – is not the struggle between ideology and faith but that between 'faith' and 'faith'.

In fact in this way I am trying to do justice to the insight from the Christian tradition that faith is a gift of the Holy Spirit. It is the Spirit which shows men and women the way, the truth and the life. But this knowledge of faith remains a gift; it is not something which is at the disposal of human beings in order to play off their faith or the knowledge they derive from it against those who do not have it. When it comes to the point, theologians, too, stand with empty hands and can claim no higher knowledge. Certainly, theologians can do everything possible to keep up the hermeneutical circulation of their theology, but whether this theological circulation is really vital depends on the response to the *Veni Creator Spiritus*.

2. Towards a hermeneutic of black narrative. The dialectic of love and power

James Cone ends his survey of black theology and ideology with some pages which in fact contradict what he stressed earlier about the relationship between black theology and ideology. He writes:

If someone asks me, 'Jim, how *can you* believe that? What is the *evidence* of its truth?', my reply is quite similar to the testimonies of the Fathers and the Mothers of the Black Church: let me tell you a story about a man called Jesus who was born in a stable in Bethelehem and raised in an obscure village called Nazareth. When the time had come, he was baptized by John the Baptist. After John's death he went throughout the region of Galilee preaching that the Kingdom is coming, repent and believe the gospel. The Kingdom is the new creation where the hungry are fed, the sick healed, and the oppressed liberated. It is the restoration of humanity to its wholeness. This man Jesus was killed because of his threat to the order of injustice. But he was resurrected as Lord, thereby making good God's promise to bring freedom to all who are weak and helpless. This resurrection is the guarantee that Jesus is the Christ who is with us now in our present and will be with us forever and ever.[20]

When asked for evidence for the truth in which he believes, Cone replies with a story. Neither Cone nor anyone else can 'prove' the truth of this story.[21] Even as a representatitve of an oppressed people Cone cannot claim any higher knowledge here. He does not have more means than anyone else for showing that this story is more than a subjective, situationally determined vision of reality, more than one of the many stories which make the human consciousness a consciousness 'entangled in stories'.[22] In fact here Cone breaks out of the scheme of his earlier argument, for by falling back on the story which holds him in its grasp and supports him as man and theologian he abandons the task of refuting the charge of ideology and puts the burden of proof that he is speaking as a theologian and not as an ideologist elsewhere than he did earlier, in the story itself.

What Cone writes about the black story amounts to the best pages of *God of the Oppressed*. He recognizes that finally the theologian can speak only as a witness, as someone who is part of a community in which the story goes the round which gives this community its specific identity. Any people, any community, lives by stories. The power of these stories is that they cannot be reduced to a private possession, but remain the property of the community. As a result of this they are capable of taking people outside their social context. So according to Cone if I understand the truth as story, I am more open to listen to the stories which others tell about themselves.

Through them I am challenged to leave my own subjectivity behind and enter into another domain of thought and action. The same thing happens to others when I tell my story.[23]

Imprisonment in ideology can be overcome by listening to what people of another colour, sex or culture have to say about themselves. If one is not prepared to or in a position to do that, then the other's otherness is suppressed and there is inevitably an ideological distortion in which one's own partial experience of reality is taken to be the whole truth. Although Cone does not use the expression, we might think here of what Charles Long descried as 'functional otherness'.[24] This functional otherness makes people 'strangers', 'wild', 'primitives', and excludes them from what are regarded as the culture and rules of behaviour of their own environment. History teaches us that, especially when economic interests – uranium mining, building new roads, housing speculation and so on – are involved, 'functional otherness' implies that people without proper representation can be driven out of or uprooted from their land. Aborigines from Australia, blacks in South Africa, Indians on the Amazon or in Canada, foreign workers in Western European countries know what it means to be condemned to functional otherness: people do not listen to their story.

James Cone sees the biblical story in particular as a means of attacking that way of thinking which distorts reality by keeping it trapped within one's own subjectivity. Theologians must become aware that however indispensable the formation of concepts and analysis, argumentation and abstract summary may be, the story is the basic material and basic structure of theological reflection. Here, however, according to Cone,[25] one must begin from the fact that the biblical story exists independently of our stories and that it makes a claim on our present existence. It therefore leads us to leave our own subjectivity behind us and listen to the Word that we do not possess. However, if we accept this Word as truth in faith, then it takes possession of our existence and is indissolubly bound up with the story of our personal life.

Thus on the basis of the narrative basic structure of the gospel Cone makes it clear that in Christian faith subjectivity and objectivity have a dialectical connection with each other. The objective element implies the need to leave behind us the subjectivity of our own story, not only by allowing the biblical story to come into its own but also by confronting ourselves with the way in which the church fathers, the Reformers, David Walker and Sojourner Truth dealt with this story in the struggle of their days. For ideology can only be avoided or lessened by listening to the stories of others outside our own time and situation – and here Cone emphatically includes adherents of other religions in Africa and Asia.[26]

But Cone does not avoid a certain dualism in his argument. On the one hand he gives the story a trans-subjective element, that can take people out of their ideological determination. On the other hand he concedes that neither he nor anyone else can claim to speak the truth. In my view this ambivalence is the consequence of the concept of ideology that he uses. By in fact reducing ideology to holding distorted ideas he can bring the story to bear as an ideological weapon, in so doing suggesting that the stories by which people identify themselves and others are more than ideology. But does this not strongly idealize the function of stories in human life? Do not stories in fact make or break people? Is it not the case that it is in stories that people come to hear who they are, what is or what is not expected of them as citizens, as wives, as old people? Do not the myths, the folk tales, the history lessons at school, the popular television series tell people – not abstractly, but very concretely and tangibly – what 'life' is, how it goes on and how roles are distributed?

Anyone who understands ideology as the product of thought determined by interests and concerns and therefore distorted, makes a connection in an almost deterministic way between the ideas which people have and the political and economic interests of the class to which they belong. However, ideology is much more subtle. It is the stories which go the rounds in a society and which derive their vitality and power of conviction from the fact that they are an active part of the way in which this society has organized itself in economic, political, military and legal terms: it is those (hi)stories which precede the individual consciousness and make the individual a subject, in both senses of the word, who, to use Althusser's term,[27] 'inserts' himself or herself into the existing order.

Now Althusser's theory of ideology has been criticized for being a 'theory of insertion', while there is no 'theory of extraction'.[28] Cannot stories change existing circumstances? And is that not precisely the case with the biblical stories? Is not the exodus story *par excellence* a story of 'extraction'? Is it not impossible to insert the proclamation of the nearness of God's kingdom into existing social conditions? That may be the case, but church history shows that it is quite possible to allow the witness of apostles and prophets to function as a story which inserts people into the existing social order. What for Nat Turner and David Walker was a story of radical 'extraction', was for the pious and upright Charles Colcock Jones, preacher and slaveholder, a story of 'insertion' into the existing slave society.

Evidently the biblical narrative shares in the fate of all stories – of being vulnerable to misuse and manipulation. Stories do not exist apart from the way in which they are transmitted and told, and a story performs one function when told by one person and another when told by someone else. Although in itself the question how far biblical stories and stories in general are to be related is a complex one – so that, for example, it could be said that biblical stories intensify the narrative dimension of experience[29] – it is difficult to deny that the witness of prophets and apostles enters history in the same way as all other stories, subject to the mechanisms by which people appropriate stories to themselves or hold them at bay (which in practice makes little difference). Is it an unimportant coincidence that the biblical proclamation has taken on the basic structure of a story which is always concrete and thus vulnerable, in place of the structure of dogmatic and ethical doctrines or philosophical speculation which is much more intangible because it is much more abstract? Or could it be that the narrative structure, as the form in which the gospel offers itself, is the adequate expression and reflection of its content: the mystery of the incarnation?

James Cone rightly indicates the power which this story as black story has in the life and the history of his people. The liberating power of the black story has given people the courage to 'keep on keeping on' and put them in a position to find a way where there was none. But the power of this story does not do away with its defencelessness and vulnerability to misuse and manipulation, any more than the light of the resurrection does away with the opacity of the cross. Perhaps we come closer to the mystery of the power of this story if we say: just as revelation and hiddenness, God's divinity and his humanity, his freedom and his love go dialectically together, so the power of this story lies precisely in its vulnerability. Just as we must take the humanity of the incarnate Word with complete seriousness and guard against any form of docetism, so we may not for a moment play off divine authority and inspiration against the utterly human, that is to say ideological, character of the story of

God's humanity. Just as during his lifetime Jesus was the object of the imagining of the men and women around him – 'Who do men say that I am?' – and allowed the ruling powers to determine his fate, so too the story about him is subject to the way in which people relate this story to their own imagining of reality, fitted into the subtle mechanisms by which people justify their existence, adapted to what modern men and women can 'still' believe. But we must also stress the other side: as is evident time and again, this story can cut through all the religious mechanisms of justification and adaptation and create a hearing for itself, and in so doing demonstrate an unmistakable option for those for whom Jesus was primarily concerned: the poor, the imprisoned, the blind and the afflicted. The power with which the story brings about a *metanoia* in anyone who is touched by it is none other than that of the Spirit. Where this story touches people and does not let them go there is a manifestation of the power of the Spirit. Without openness to the presence of this power in history and personal life it is impossible to hear and understand the story. I pointed earlier to the importance of a pneumatological basis for a hermeneutic of the black story.[30] Following on from this, here, where it is a matter of the way in which the power of the biblical story manifests itself in black history and experience, I want to stress two aspects which belong together but which can be distinguished: (*a*) the power of the Spirit as an expression of God's freedom, and (*b*) the power of the Spirit as an expression of God's love.

(*a*) Cone distingishes two dimensions in the black story:[31] a collective one and a personal one. The former is concerned with the interweaving of the biblical story into the history and and experience of black people, the latter with those who have come to know the story of Jesus as the personal story of their life, as the hope by which they live. In both cases there is a danger that secretly a change of power will take place, an exchange of subject and object: the believing people or the individual believer become the subject of the story in place of the free power of the Spirit. That happens, for example, when blacks are supposed to have a natural predisposition for the gospel. It also happens when the power of Immanuel, God with us, is subtly transformed into the autonomous we-with-God, and authentic otherness – 'God as the specific reality over against us' (Schellong) – is transformed into the functional otherness against which Gollwitzer rightly protests. Gollwitzer's plea for praise of

God for God's own sake is founded on the notion of God's freedom, which cuts out any functionalism. It is important that Cone also stresses that we ourselves do not possess the story that takes possession of us. However, we must maintain more consistently than Gollwitzer or Cone that God's freedom is the freedom of his love of humanity, which shares in the vulnerability of any human story. That means that the power of the Spirit does not free us from our finitude and from the limits that are set to our knowledge – we see through a glass darkly, in riddles (I Cor.13.12) – and does not therefore elevate us above ideology but calls us to choose a position in ideology, against resignation, fatalism, pessimism and cynicism, and for a radical optimism that finds its basis in the expectation of the messianic kingdom. The old Reformation insight into the *simul iustus ac peccator* here becomes topical in an unprecedented way; the one who is justified remains a sinner and a beggar. That does not mean that human action is doomed in a way which would justify historical pessimism. It means that the believer is as much one who has nothing as all those others who have nothing. To put it even more strongly, the confession of faith given by the illumination of the Spirit who is and remains the subject of this knowledge is the basis for solidarity with those who have nothing. The power of the Spirit as an expresion of God's freedom makes any escape from the opacity of human history impossible.

(*b*) Mention of the much-misused word solidarity brings us to the next aspect, that of the power of the Spirit as an expression of God's love. That God's freedom may never be separated from his love of humanity shown in Christ means that this freedom is the opposite of the sovereign power with which potentates impose their will on their subjects. There is no denying the fact that the way in which notions like 'omnipotence' and 'sovereignty' have functioned in Christian tradition have largely contributed to the absolutizing of power which is characteristic of the doctrines of state security in Latin American countries and elsewhere.[32] As an understandable reaction to this some people try to arrive at a theology and ethics of kenosis and powerlessness. But, José Miguez Bonino rightly asks, 'Do they not in turn derive from an implicit acceptance of the same notion of power, so that they are the other side of the coin, its opposite, but not a criticism of it?'[33]

Power is a relational concept, and it depends on the relationship whether the power is legitimate or not. Even where power is understood as the courage to be', as it is by Cone and Allan Boesak,[34] power is a relational concept, because in their view this power is a given power, given by the creative power of the Spirit which makes human beings in the image of God and puts them in a position in their relationships with others to give form to the messianic community in which one person no longer dominates another. The criterion for power in the biblical sense is whether in one way or another it is an expression of its basis, *agape*. In *Stride Toward Freedom*, Martin Luther King wrote:

> *Agape* is disinterested love. It is a love in which the individual seeks not his own good, but the good of his neighbour (I Cor.10.24). *Agape* does not begin by discriminating between worthy and unworthy people, or any qualities people possess. It begins by loving others for their sakes.[35]

For King *agape* is both an eschatological and an ethical notion. The object of his struggle is the beloved community in which people are no longer judged on the basis of the colour of their skin but on the basis of their character. Here King fights against the power mechanisms and procedures which exclude people because of their bodies, make them invisible, condemn them to 'functional otherness' and a 'state of transparency' (C.Long). In this struggle he opts for non-violent resistance, not out of an ethical preference for powerlessness, as a widespread misunderstanding would have it, but out of his conviction that powerlessness is a form of effective power which can conquer functional otherness.

We have seen that in the historical circumstances of 1966 a number of black church leaders felt compelled to resist the pressure, above all from the white side, to condemn Black Power and propagate non-violence as the only possible ethical option for Christians. That in all circumstances love in the biblical sense means turning the other cheek was unacceptable to these leaders. In their 1966 Black Power Declaration power became the central element and in fact made *agape* subordinate as the feature which must preserve the formation of power from misuse and corruption.[36] However, this was to throw the baby out with the bathwater: with the rejection of non-violence in principle the vision of the beloved community also vanished from sight.

That is why the black story, as this was put into words and handed down in its initial phase, was more a story of survival than of liberation, focussed more on the particularity of blackness than on the universality of the beloved community. With the ebbing away of the 'movement' in the 1970s, however, changes began to take place. Above all as a result of an increase in dialogue in peripheral ecumenism, after 1975 a development began to emerge – most clearly in James Cone – in which the question of the possibility of integration into a capitalist society was answered in the negative. Here the need for forming coalitions and alliances with movements, groups and parties who also want to bring about real social change becomes evident. However, if blacks do not want for the umpteenth time in history to become the victims of the alliances into which they enter,[37] they can no longer make themselves dependent on the good will of others but must operate from a position of power, of power in economic and political spheres as far as that is possible, but above all of ideological power. Black history and experience is about this last, and the subversive memory which lies in it. Without the past there is no future. Adaptation to existing circumstances is possible only to those who forget the ideals for which Martin Luther King, Malcolm X and many before them lived and died. In the way in which they both supplemented and criticized each other, King and Malcolm X, as we heard from Gayraud Wilmore, embody the total spectrum of black experience and black religion. Malcolm X represents the survival line in black history and Martin Luther King the liberation line – but the lines cross!

This last comment could be a decisive statement about the hermeneutical challenge confronting black theologians. As an outsider I am not, of course, in a position to prescribe to black theologians what their hermeneutical challenge must be. Nor is that my intention. But if we allow ourselves to be affected by what black theology says to us through its various representatives, then we are forced to conclude that the dialectical connection of love and power is of vital importance for a hermeneutic of black narrative. At all events, from a theological perspective black power cannot be other than the power given by God's Spirit, and this Spirit in turn cannot be other than the Spirit of God's *agape*. So it is possible to remain faithful to the historical context in which black theology arose by combining King's vision of the beloved community as eschatological reality with the historical reality of black power as a power given by the Spirit on the basis of the resurrection of the crucified one.

Here black theology must not give up King's view of *agape* as the basic ground of our existence. Love is more, at least in the biblical-theological sense, than the controlling element in power! But love needs power in order to become effective, and this power is the power of God's Spirit in history, which incorporates men and women people into the messianic community and puts them under the promise of the coming kingdom. It is this Spirit which enlightens the human spirit to discern the signs of the times and to discover where the lines of conflict run in history in the struggle between the living God and the idols of death. The *kairos* which is evoked here inspires us to begin to think and act 'contextually' – by practising seeing with the eyes of the O(o)ther while remaining aware of our own limitations.

For a white theologian to read and study the work of black theologians is practice of this kind. Black theology is important because in its way it bears witness to the black story, the story of the struggle for human dignity and freedom in the midst of the opacity of history. In the story of these 'stepchildren of Western culture' (C.Long[38]) we realize the otherness of the O(o)ther, embodied in blackness, with all that this term implies in terms of hurt, shame, defilement, anxiety and guilt-feelings in a centuries-long history of white supremacy.

When blacks confess Jesus as the black messiah, this title is not 'just' a symbol. Brought from Africa because of their physical value as manual workers, in their physicality the object of the lust of white masters, these strangers and outcasts in the New World paradoxically enough felt accepted in that physicality by the God who allowed himself to be nailed to the cross. In the context of racism and slavery, his self-emptying is his blackness.

Confrontation with this black messiah is a confrontation with the darkness of barely conscious anxiety and guilt. But anyone who sees the confrontation as a challenge to enter the world of blackness and listen to the stories that are told there will discover, surprisingly, that there is still room at the table of the beloved community.

NOTES

1. Challenge

1. Hugo Assmann, *Theology for a Nomad Church*, Orbis Books, Mary-knoll 1976, 111-19.

2. William Jones, 'Toward an Interim Assessment of Black Theology', *Christian Century* 89, 3 May 1972, 513-17: 'To put the issue in another way: It appears to many black theologians that any external criticism now is simply a covert form of racism whereby the critic comes to his evaluation with a prior conclusion of the inherent superiority of the truth or ultimacy of the established – i.e. nonblack – theologies.'

3. James Baldwin, *Notes of a Native Son*, Bantam Books, New York 1972 and Corgi Books 1973, 4.

4. This last comment must be read against the background of studies like that of Dieter Schellong, *Bürgertum und christliche Religion*, Theologische Existenz heute 187, Munich 1975. In this compact book Schellong starts from Hegel's analysis of bourgeois society in *Outlines of the Philosophy of Right*. He sums up the thoughts of Hegel on the bourgeois principle as follows: 'It is a fact that the individual and his needs are a personal end in themselves over against which the other individuals represent an alien body, and indeed are nothing, but are used and exploited as a means. To this degree individualization is as much a principle of bourgeois society as a general mutual dependence. Both are essentially abstract, and thus in tendency revolutionary and in reality full of devastation. Hegel was able to see that because he already had sufficient experience.'

5. James H.Cone, *A Black Theology of Liberation*, Lippincott, Philadelphia 1970, 28.

6. Dietrich Bonhoeffer, *The Cost of Discipleship*, SCM Press and Macmillan, New York 1959, 43.

7. Eberhard Bethge, in *Werken met Bonhoeffer*, Baarn 1979, 84f.

8. By this I mean particularly discussions of terms like 'theology in context', 'conciliar fellowship' and 'church of the poor'.

9. Bruno Chenu, *Dieu est noir*, Paris 1977; 'Point de vue d'un théologien européen', *Lumière et Vie*, Lyons, November-December 1974, 73-81; Henri Mottu, 'Noirs d'Amérique et opprimés du Tiers Monde à la recherche d'une théologie de la libération (James Cone et Rubem Alves)', *Bulletin du Centre Protestant d'Etudes*, Geneva, March 1972; id., 'Le contexte historique et culturel de la théologie noire', *Lumière et Vie*, Lyons, November-December 1974, 10-28; Peter Hodgson, *Children of Freedom*, Fortress Press, Philadelphia 1974; id., *New Birth of Freedom: A Theology of Bondage and Liberation*, Fortress Press, Philadelphia 1976; Helmut Gollwitzer, 'Why

Black Theology?', in Gayraud S. Wilmore and James H. Cone (eds),*Black Theology: A Documentary History 1966-1979*, Orbis Books, Maryknoll 1979, 152-173.

10. These are indeed theological movements. It is therefore a misunderstanding for E.Schillebeeckx to call his gripping paper of 13 October 1978 on this question 'Liberation theologies between Medellin and Puebla' ('Bevrijdingstheologieën tussen Medellin en Puebla', in *Bevrijding en christelijk geloof in Latijns-Amerika en Nederland*, Baarn 1980, 18-34). It is not a matter of liberation theologians in the plural but of liberation theology. In saying this I am not of course denying that there are different insights within this movement. However, these do not function as they do in our academic theology. A good example of this different way of functioning is the common strategy which liberation theologies have adopted over the important conference of the Latin American bishops in Puebla; on this see T.Witvliet, Miguel Cabrera et al., *Het onmogelijke verenigen? Werkboek rond Puebla, de derde algemene vergadering van het latijns-amerikaanse episcopaat*, Amersfoort nd (1981), 27f.

11. I have taken this term from G.Casalis, *Correct Ideas Don't Fall from the Skies*, Orbis Books, Maryknoll 1984, 16-19.

12. Gustavo Gutiérrez, 'Bevrijdingstheologie als het recht van de armen om te denken', in *Bevrijding en christelijk geloof in Latijns-Amerika en Nederland*, 83.

13. Id., *A Theology of Liberation*, Orbis Books and SCM Press 1974, 15.

14. Id., 'Theology from the Underside of History' (1977), in Gustavo Gutiérrez, *The Power of the Poor in History*, Orbis Books, Maryknoll and SCM Press 1983, 169-221.

15. Op.cit., 204. This text contains in extended form the account that Gutiérrez gave in Dar es Salaam. The original version appeared in French translation in *Théologies du tiers monde, Du conformisme à l'indépendance, Le Colloque de Dar es Salaam et ses prolongements*, Paris 1977, 138-80. The quotation is on 176. The English translation is slightly different: 'All liberation theology originates among the world's anonymous, whoever may write the books or the declarations articulating it', *The Emergent Gospel*, ed. Sergio Torres and Virginia Fabella MM, Orbis Books, Maryknoll 1978, 250.

16. Id., 'Bevrijdingstheologie als het recht van de armen', 93.

17. Cf. id. *The Power of the Poor in History*, 55-61, 201-6.

18. Choan-Seng Song, *Third-Eye Theology*, Orbis Books, Maryknoll and Lutterworth Press 1979, 96. On the same page: 'Theological particularity is the basis for doing theology with Asian spirituality or, for that matter, with any kind of spirituality.'

19. In the address which Mgr Oscar Arnulfo Romero gave in Louvain shortly before his death (2 February 1980) he said: 'The structures are sin because they produce the fruits of sin: the death of Salvadorans – the swift death brought by repression or the long drawn out but no less real death from structural oppression... No matter how tragic it may appear, the church through its entrance into the real socio-political world has learned how to recognize, and how to deepen its understanding of, the essence of

sin', Oscar Romero, *Voice of the Voiceless*, Orbis Books, Maryknoll 1985, 183.

20. Gutiérrez, op.cit., 55-8; see also 'Praxis of Liberation, Theology and Proclamation', *Concilium 10.6*, June 1974, 65 (though this article was written at a time when Concilium was not appearing in English); *We Drink from our Own Wells*, Orbis Books, Maryknoll and SCM Press 1984, 35f.:'When we insist that theology can be done only from within the context of praxis, we are saying that people can understand and appreciate the Jesus who sends the Spirit only if they live a life in accordance with that Spirit.'

21. This is the central position of James H.Cone, *God of the Oppressed*, Seabury Press, New York 1975, 15.

22. Henri Mottu puts this crudely but not necessarily wrongly: 'The dominant characteristic of our theology is in fact that it has no connection with the religion of the people', 'Theologische Kritik der Religion und Religion des Volkes', *Genf '76. Ein Bonhoeffer-Symposion*, Munich 1976, 71.

23. Clodovis Boff makes the following comment on the relationship between the intellectual and the people in an article 'Gegen die Knechtschaft des rationalen Wissens', which is included in *Befreiungstheologie als Herausforderung*, ed. Horst Goldstein, Düsseldorf 1981, 138: 'The exchange between intellectual knowledge and popular wisdom is an uninterrupted process which makes it necessary for one to question the other constantly. So it may not be the case that the people assimilates wisdom as though this were something finished once and for all, nor may it be that the culture of the people is protected as though it were completely perfect and healthy.' Boff, who teaches systematic theology in Petropolis and Rio de Janeiro, spends five months a year in a basic community of rubber plantation workers and Indians in the state of Acre, in north-west Brazil (op.cit., 220).

24. Cone, *God of the Oppressed*, 253: 'Either Black Theology is a theological expression of the hopes and dreams of black people, or it is an articulation of the intellectual interests of black professors. If the former, as I think it must be, then its meaning must be decided by the people about whom it claims to speak.'

25. That this liberation can be a deep emotional experience is evident from a reference by Cone to the time when he wrote his first book: 'The writing of *Black Theology and Black Power* (during the summer of 1968) was a deep emotional experience for me. It was a cleansing experience because I endeavoured to purge myself of any direct dependence upon my white theological mentors' ('The Gospel and The Liberation of the Poor', in *Christian Century*, XCVIII, no.5, 18 Feb 1981, 164). See also James H.Cone, *My Soul Looks Back*, Abingdon Press, Nashville 1982, 47f.

26. Cf. Allan Boesak, *Farewell to Innocence*, Ravan Press, Johannesburg and Orbis Books, Maryknoll 1977.

27. Leendert Oranje, 'Althusser en de Theologie', in *Wending* 36. 3, March 1981, 180.

28. Ernst Käsemann, *Jesus Means Freedom*, SCM Press and Fortress Press 1969, 133.

29. Adolf von Harnack, *What is Christianity?*, Harper Torchbooks 1957,

56. The saying of Augustine to which allusion is made in this quotation was very dear to von Harnack. In 1922 he compiled an anthology of the work of Augustine which began with the well-known pasage from the *Soliloquies* *(Augustin. Reflexionen und Maximen,* Tübingen 1922, 3): 'He devoted long years of work and great skill to the translation of this work. His confession, like that of Augustine, was 'I desire to know God and the soul, nothing else' (Agnes von Zahn-Harnack, *Adolf von Harnack,* Berlin 1936, 516).

30. It would be worth making a careful investigation of the possible parallels between the religious socialism of the beginning of our century and Latin American liberation theology. I have the impression that there are tendencies in liberation theology which show an affinity with the thinking above all of Ragaz. For example if the basis communities are seen by some theologians as forms of society which are qualitatively different from what happens in both the capitalist world and the socialist world, we are reminded of the 'socialistic life' of Ragaz.

31. Karl Barth, *Church Dogmatics* IV.3,1, 274-367.

32. José Miguez Bonino, *Doing Theology in a Revolutionary Situation,* Fortress Press, Philadelphia and SPCK 1975, 61.

33. H.Assmann, *Onderdrukking en Verzet,* Baarn 1975, 9.

34. H.Gollwitzer, *Befreiung zur Solidarität,* Munich 1978, 38.

35. Gutiérrez, *Theology of Liberation,* 6-20.

36. Cf. Cone, *God of the Oppressed,* 152: 'Liberation then is not merely a thought in my head; it is the sociohistorical movement of a people from oppression to freedom – Israelites from Egypt, black people from American slavery. It is the mind and body in motion, responding to the passion and the rhythm of divine revelation, and affirming that no chain shall hold my humanity down.'

37. Cf. Jon Sobrino, *Christology at the Crossroads,* 230: 'The *u* of utopia becomes real through the cross... the more deeply we experience the "against hope" of the cross, the more deeply we live the "hope" of the resurrection.' The christology of Sobrino is more convincing on this point than that of L.Boff, *Jesus Christ Liberator,* Orbis Books, Maryknoll 1978, 135.

38. Cone, *A Black Theology of Liberation,* 160.

39. Id., *God of the Oppressed,* 146.

40. Gutiérrez, op.cit., 137.

41. The concluding document of the Third Assembly of the Latin American Episcopate in Puebla (1979) frequently speaks of integral liberation (e.g. 166, 173, 189, 321). This expression has a polemic slant, directed against liberation theology, which it suspects of reducing the liberation of Christ to its historical and social implications. However, those who introduced the expression give the impression that they are reducing the impact of liberation by spiritualizing the concept and removing its political implications. See Gutiérrez, *The Power of the Poor in History,* 144-8, and Witvliet and Cabrera et al., op.cit., 46-9.

42. Albert Cleage, pastor of a black community in Detroit, is one such exception in the context of black theology; see the criticism by Allan Boesak, *Farewell to Innocence,* 116–21.

43. *Theology in the Americas*, ed. Sergio Torres and John Eagleson, Orbis Books, Maryknoll 1976, 289.

44. According to Hugo Assmann, the concept of praxis used by Latin American theologians relates to 'something quite evident that they have experienced along with the people, though it is clear that the experiences of the people are rather more brutal than the experiences of those who have written down the peoples' cause' (Hugo Assmann, 'Das Evangelium des Technologismus', in *Befreiungstheologie als Herausforderung*, ed. Horst Goldstein, 52f.).

45. 'Human liberation often seems to be a grim and joyless struggle. The Magnificat shows otherwise. And I exult in the fact that this Asian woman, this Mary, upon her encounter with God bursts out into this great song of thanksgiving and joy given to God, who liberates through the oppressed themselves,' Marianne Katoppo, *Compassionate and Free*, WCC, Geneva 1979, 24.

46. But when Gutiérrez differentiates three levels in the process of human liberation of which the second relates to the creation of a new humanity in the course of history, does his vision not include an organic process of growth in history? In fact Gutiérrez' book has led to misunderstanding on this point. At least before drawing over-hasty conclusions it is important to study the crucial section on faith, utopia and political action (232-50, see especially 235f.). There it is evident that Gutiérrez thinks that the second level is necessary above all to avoid an uncritical combination of faith and politics and in this way to remove the dangers of political and religious messianism. Here it emerges that the second level is that of utopia, the level of imagination, and according to Gutiérrez utopia is characterized by three things: 1. by its relation to present historical reality; 2. by its verification in practice, in historical action; 3. by its rational nature. From this characterization of the term utopia it is evident that the second level of the process of liberation in Gutiérrez is meant to be something complete different from a speculative philosophy of history or optimistic belief in progress.

47. C.Boff has some illuminating things to say about the experiential wisdom of the people, op.cit., 125-30.

48. 'One of the gravest obstacles to the achievement of liberation is that oppresive reality absorbs those who live in it and thereby acts to submerge men's consciousness', Paulo Freire, *Pedagogy of the Oppressed*, Penguin Books 1972, 27.

49. For liberation theology as hermeneutics of the hope which the poor themselves experience in the heart of their struggle see G.Gutiérrez, *We Drink from Our Own Wells*, 38. See also Gutiérrez, 'Reflections from a Latin American Perspective. Finding our Way to Talk about God', in *Irruption of the Third World*, ed. Virginia Fabella and Sergio Torres, Orbis Books, Maryknoll 1983, 222-34.

50. Elisabeth Schüssler Fiorenza, 'Feminist Theology as a Critical Theology of Liberation', in *Mission Trends No. 4*, ed. Gerald H.Anderson and Thomas F.Stransky CSP, Eerdmans 1979, 201-4, writes of Gal.3.28 as the '*magna carta* of Christian feminism'.

51. Song, op.cit., 175.

52. Sobrino, op.cit., 221, 370.
53. Ibid., 222.
54. Ibid., 223f., 349f., 371.
55. William R.Jones, *Is God a White Racist?*, Anchor Press, Garden City 1973.
56. The term existence is used here deliberately: both in South Africa and in various Asian and above all Latin American countries there is a great personal risk that identification with this praxis can involve intimidation, imprisonment, torture and even death.
57. J.B.Metz, *Faith in History and Society*, Burns and Oates and Seabury Press, New York 1979.
58. Ibid., 51f.; cf. 59f.
59. Ibid., 73.
60. Ibid., 76.
61. Ibid., 4.
62. Ibid., 76.
63. The dilemma that I think that we can find in *Faith in History and Society* is of course connected with the political and church situation in Western European countries. The more specific the form of the basic church which Metz is looking for becomes – and in that connection a good deal has happened since the publication of *Faith in History and Society* – the more he will be in a position to use his reflection in the service of a demonstrable praxis. However, just how close Metz has come to the limits of the academic and church world (at least the institutional church world) is evident from the fact that in the summer of 1979 obstacles were put in the way of his moving to the chair of fundamental theology in Munich. While Metz is still within the bounds of academic theology, many of his pupils stand outside it. In a collection written by them entitled *Theologisch-politische Protokolle*, Tiemo Rainer Peters says, 'This theology has opponents whose deliberate and effective resistance is directed particularly against its disciples, especially in the college sphere' (*Theologisch-politische Protokolle*, ed. Tiemo Rainer Peters, Munich and Mainz 1981, 12).
64. José Miguez Bonino has expressed this hermeneutical movement very clearly in the structure of his book *Doing Theology in a Revolutionary Situation*: the first part describes the praxis in its historical and socio-political context while the second part contains theological reflection on questions which are evoked by this praxis.
65. 'Theory serves primarily to enlighten those to whom it is addressed about the position that they hold in an antagonistic social system and the interests of which they must become conscious in this situation as being objectively theirs,' Jürgen Habermas, *Theory and Practice*, Heinemann Educational 1974, 32. In the view of liberation theology theological reflection does not fall outside but within the general functional description of theory given here by Habermas.
66. In *A Black Theology of Liberation*, 1970, Cone can still write: 'Christian theology cannot afford to be an abstract, dispassionate discourse on the nature of God in relation to man, as if such an analysis has no ethical implications for the contemporary forms of oppression in our society' (45);

the difficulty in this formula is that it suggests that first of all there is a theory which then also seems to have ethical implications; in that case the theory itself is not situated and can be applied to all situations.

67. K.H.Miskotte, *Om het levende Woord*, The Hague 1948, 75.

68. Calvin, *Institutes* I,6,2; see Karl Barth, *Church Dogmatics* I.1, 18 and above all IV.1, 846-72 (*The Act of Faith*). See also Gollwitzer, op.cit., 34. However, it should be realized that the part of the *Institutes* in which this sentence occurs deals with the authority of scripture. Without quoting Calvin, but on the basis of a study of a number of biblical passages, Bonino comes to the conclusion that 'Obedience is not a consequence of our knowledge of God, just as it is not a pre-condition for it: obedience is included in our knowledge of God. Or, to put it more bluntly: obedience is our knowledge of God. There is not a separate noetic moment in our relationship to God' (*Christians and Marxists. The Mutual Challenge to Revolution*, Hodder and Stoughton 1976, 40).

69. Cf. ch. 4, section 3 and ch. 6, section 2.

70. Miskotte, op.cit., 108.

71. This and similar comments are quoted by Mechal Sobel, *Trabelin' On*, Greenwood Press, Westport 1979, 126.

72. 'Only the one who takes part in a historical situation in its depths can speak of a *kairos*. Such a participation concerns the one who experiences it in all his being... He himself is an element in the total situation. That marks the fundamental difference between the prophet and the mere observer', Paul Tillich, *Auf der Grenze*, Siebenstern Taschenbuch 3, 1965, 124.

73. See Gollwitzer, op.cit., 40ff.

74. Miskotte, op.cit., 109.

75. We find the same basic notion that appears in the quotations from Miskotte given above in Barth's postscript to the selection from Schleiermacher made by Heinz Bolli (Siebenstern Taschenbuch 113/114, 1968, 311); here Barth considers the possibility of a theology of the Holy Spirit and among other things raises the question: 'Is God – the God made known to his people through his revelation in the covenant and to be proclaimed as such in the world – not Spirit all along the line (John 4.24; I Cor.3.17) – i.e. the God who makes himself present *and applies himself* in the freedom, power, wisdom and love which are his own (my italics)?'

Clodovis Boff, *Theologie und Praxis. Die erkenntnistheoretischen Grundlagen der Theologie der Befreiung*, Munich and Mainz 1983, makes a basic study of the problem of necessary mediations from the perspective of the Latin American theology of liberation. Boff draws a distinction between the social-analytic mediation which applies to the relationship between theology and the social sciences and the hermeneutical mediation which is concerned with the relationship between theology and holy scripture, and the practical mediation of faith which is concerned with the relationship between theology and praxis. The book by Boff, a study originally written in French, by which the author qualified as a lecturer at the Catholic University of Louvain in 1976, is an extremely acute and careful attempt to think through the epistemological foundations of liberation theology and –

more in general terms – of a 'theology of politics'. However, it must be said that his approach differs from mine in a number of points. In Boff's comments Thomistic theological epistemology certainly undergoes a metamorphosis, but its basic structure is still maintained. By contrast I try to show that there is a convergence between Barth's and Miskotte's theological epistemology on the one hand and the epistemological logic of liberation theology on the other. It would take us too far afield to enter into an extended discussion with Boff at this point. Differences in confessional and theological background also unmistakably play a part here. So Boff can assert (27f. n.13) that only since the 1930s has theology begun to be theologically interested in earthly realities *qua* earthly; he then distinguishes two trends, an Anglo-Saxon one which began with Gogarten and Bonhoeffer and leads up to the 'death of God theology', and a Francophone one which began with Teilhard de Chardin and G.Thils and was continued in *Gaudium et Spes*, the Vatican II pastoral constitution on the church in the modern world and in the Medellin documents. This leaves out not only liberal Protestant theology from Schleiermacher to Troeltsch but also religious socialism and the work of Barth.

76. In all these controversial, perplexing, fascinating images of reality Miskotte is constantly in search of the ultimate decisive contrast: that between the pagan acceptance of fate, resignation in fatality and the alliance against fate, the militant expectation of a world of peace and justice. But see here the comments by Rinse Reeling Brouwer, 'Teksten Godsdienstkritiek II', *Eltheto* 62, 1980, 168f.

77. Tillich, op.cit., 124.

78. 'It simply does not accord with the truth to assert that the distinctive feature of the theological method of these circles of committed Christians consists in the fact that they took over a particular, e.g. Marxist method to analyse reality... The methodological root of the theology of liberation consists in identification with the struggle of the people over its fundamental rights to life. Everything else comes as an addition', Assmann, op.cit., 53.

79. 'Concerning Feuerbach,' in Karl Marx, *Early Writings,* ed. Lucio Colleti, Penguin Books 1975, 423.

80. Ibid., 422.

81. Clarification here is given by José Miguez Bonino, *Doing Theology in a Revolutionary Situation*, 88.

82. Jean Paul Sartre, 'Matérialisme et révolution', in *Situations* III, Paris 1967, 181.

83. Ibid., 181: the formulation is meant polemically, and is only comprehensible as such. Still, if thought is equated with action, how then must the theoretical activity be distinguished from deliberate and purposive intervention into external reality?

84. Assmann, op.cit., 53.

85. Jean-Paul Sartre, op.cit., 182: 'It must be noted that the thought of the philosophers from the ruling class is also action... But its inferiority to revolutionary thought derives from the fact that the philosophy of oppression seeks to hide its pragmatic character... It envisages society and nature from the point of view of pure knowledge without accepting that

this attitude tends to perpetuate the present state of the universe by persuading one that one can know it rather than change it, and that at least if one wants to change it one must first know it.'
86. Sobrino, op.cit., 221f., 349, 370.
87. The question how far the concept of ideology used by James Cone is adequate for his purposes will be discussed in the last chapter of this book.
88. The way in which the term conscientization is used in the West at training centres and conferences has been sharply condemned by Freire. Real conscientization only comes about in a revolutionary process: 'Hence conscientization, whether or not associated with literacy training, must be a critical attempt to reveal reality, not just alienating small-talk. It must, that is, be related to political involvement. There is no conscientization if the result is not the conscious action of the oppressed as an exploited social class, struggling for liberation' (Paulo Freire, 'Education, Liberation and the Church', *Risk* 9,2, 1973, 36. See also Hans Achterhuis, *Filosofen van de derde wereld*, Baarn 1975, 63).
89. A short but good sketch of this 'knowing' of the negro in the old South is given by J.W.Schulte Nordholt in his book about the struggle for civil rights, *In de schaduw van een groot licht*, Deventer 1971, 35-42 (see especially 41).
90. For discussion of the report and the text see Lee Rainwater and William Yancey, *The Moynihan Report and the Politics of Controversy*, Harvard Univerity Press, Cambridge, Mass. 1967. The complete title of the report is *The Negro Family in America: The Case for National Action*.
91. Stanley M.Elkins, *Slavery*, Chicago University Press [3]1976. This book, which appeared in 1959, was the occasion for a fierce discussion: see *The Debate over Slavery, Stanley Elkins and his Critics*, ed. Ann J.Lane, University of Illinois Press [2]1975. The black historian John W.Blassingame comments on the Sambo image as follows: 'Like a man whistling in the dark to bolster his courage, the white man had to portray the slave as Sambo. This public stereotype only partially hid a multitude of private fears, which reached the proportion of mass hysteria at the mere mention of the word rebellion... If whites really believed that a majority of slaves were Sambos, how could they also believe that these pathetically loyal and docile blacks would rise up and cut their throats' (John W.Blassingame, *The Slave Community*, Oxford University Press 1979, revised and enlarged edition).
92. Hegemony is one of the central concepts in the thought of Antonio Gramsci; see *Approaches to Gramsci*, ed. Anne Showstack Sassoon, Writers and Readers Publishing Co-operative Society, London 1984, 94-126; Christine Buci-Glucksmann, *Gramsci and the State*, Lawrence and Wishart 1980 (especially Part Two), and the good introductory account by Gabriël van den Brink, 'Ideologie en hegemonie bij Gramsci', *Te Elfder Ure* 24.1, Nijmegen 1978, 10-57.
93. 'At the center of the tangle of pathology is the weakness of the family structure... It was by destroying the Negro family that white America broke the will of the Negro people' (*The Moynihan Report*).
94. Cf. van den Brink, op.cit., 22f.; ideology can be described by Gramsci as a 'view of life which is implicitly expressed in art, in law, in economic

action, in all expressions of individual and collective life' (Antonio Gramsci, *Marxisme als filosofie van de praxis*, introduced and collected by Yvonne Scholten, Amsterdam 1971, 26).

95. A number of spirituals reflect the pain of slave existence in a very direct way. Without doubt the most famous of them is 'Motherless Child'. W.E.B.DuBois must have been thinking of these songs when he described spirituals as sorrow songs in *The Souls of Black Folk*, Dodd, Mead, New York 1967 (first impression 1903), 181-91.

96. Opaqueness or opacity is stressed by the black historian of religion Charles Long as a central element in black experience. 'The opacity of our experience which has been revealed carries its own internal history and logic. It did not occur yesterday or even the year before: it is our total past; it is our present and our future. It was a-borning at least since the slave trade, and then, its roots go deeper into Africa itself' (Charles Long, 'Structural Similarities and Dissimilarities in Black and African Theologies', in *Journal of Religious Thought* 33 (Fall-Winter 1975), 21. For Long's relationship to black theology see James Cone, in *Black Theology: A Documentary History, 1966-1979*, 615f., and J.Deotis Roberts, *Roots of a Black Future: Family and Church*, Westminster Press, Philadelphia 1980, 18f. We shall return to Long's work in Chapter 4.

97. *Another Country* is the title of the novel by James Baldwin which appeared in 1960; for the significance of this novel see A.C.Zijderveld, 'James Baldwin', *Wending* 19, October 1964, 464ff.

98. James H.Cone, 'Een zwart perspectief op Amerika; zwarte theologie en het tweede eeuwfeest', *Wending* 31, October 1976, 404f.

99. The term necrophily comes from Erich Fromm, *The Heart of Man* (1964), Harper and Row, New York 1971, Chapter 3, 'Love of Death and Love of Life', 35-69. It has been taken over by Paulo Freire, *Pedagogy of the Oppressed*, 50f. and by a number of Latin American theologians.

100. Wyatt Tee Walker, a fellow-worker of Martin Luther King and now preacher at the Canaan Baptist Church of Christ in New York, published a book on black sacred music and social change under this title, Judson Press, Valley Forge 1979.

101. DuBois, op. cit., 16f.

102. 'Such prophetic perspective does not represent an escape into a world of unattainable dreams. It demands a scientific knowledge of the world as it really is. For to denounce the present reality and announce its radical transformation into another reality capable of giving birth to new men and women, implies gaining through praxis a new knowledge of reality', Paulo Freire, *Education, Liberation and the Church*, 45.

103. For these two sides of Western mission see the impressive speech given by M.M.Thomas at the World Conference on Mission and Evangelization in Bangkok, 1972/73: this speech is printed in M.M.Thomas, *Towards a Theology of Contemporary Ecumenism*, CLS Madras 1978, 175-90 (see above all 182f.).

104. 'Black Power and the American Christ' originally appeared in *The Christian Century*, 4 January 1967; it was reprinted in *Black Power. A Documentary History, 1966-1979*, 35-42; 'The Religion of Black Power'

appeared in *The Religious Situation: 1968*, ed. Donald R.Cutler, Beacon Press, Boston 1968, 3-38.

105. In a retrospective survey of developments in the 1960s Gayraud S.Wilmore says: 'Harding, a Mennonite historian and the director of the Institute of the Black World in Atlanta, was a perceptive critic of the early developments of the NCNC (the National Committee of Negro Churchmen, later the National Conference of Black Churchmen) and a lay theologian whose writings have had a profound impact upon those who tried to think theologically about the meaning of Black Power between 1966 and 1979' (*Black Theology; A Documentary History, 1966-1979*, 18). See also Gayraud S.Wilmore, *Black Religion and Black Radicalism*, Orbis Books, Maryknoll [2]1983, 212f.

106. 'Black Power and the American Christ', 37.

107. Ibid.

108. Ibid., 36.

109. 'The Religion of Black Power', 31.

110. Ibid.

111. Ibid., 22.

112. This advertisement stands at the beginning of the development which led to the rise of black theology. The text has been reprinted several times, e.g. in *Black Theology: A Documentary History, 1966-1979*, 2-30; and in Warner R.Traynham, *Christian Faith in Black and White*, Parameter Press, Wakefield, Mass. 1973, 66-72.

113. Harding, op.cit., 25.

114. Ibid., 26.

115. 'If Wright (the reference is to Dr Nathan Wright, president of the first National Black Power conference and author of *Black Power and Urban Unrest*, Hawthorn 1967) and the other black churchmen put any serious stock in the life and teachings of Jesus of Nazareth as the clearest possible window to the face of God, then one must at least examine another way of power', ibid.; however, Harding also puts critical questions to Martin Luther King at the end of his article (32-7).

116. Wilmore, *Black Religion and Black Radicalism*, 212.

117. Francis Houtart, 'Südafrikas Schwarze Theologie in sociologischer Sicht', in *Theologie im Konfliktfeld Südafrika, Dialog mit Manas Buthelezi*, Studien zur Friedensforschung 15, Stuttgart and Munich 1976, 180.

118. In 1974 John Mbiti published an article in which he stated: 'the concerns of Black Theology differ considerably from those of African Theology... Black Theology hardly knows the situation of Christian living in Africa, and therefore its direct relevance for Africa is either nonexistent or only accidental' (*Black Theology: A Documentary History, 1966-1979*, 481). African theologians like E.W.Fashole-Luke, Harry Sawyerr and Gabriel M.Setiloane distanced themselves from Afro-American black theology. Meanwhile over the past few years a fruitful dialogue has come into being. The short history of relations between black theology and African theology has been summed up by J.Cone in *Black Theology: A Documentary History, 1966-1979*, 447-50. An important encounter was the Pan-African conference of Third World Theologians; the documents of this

conference were published in *African Theology en Route*, ed. Kofi Appiah-Kubi and Sergio Torres, Orbis Books, Maryknoll 1979.

119. I go more deeply into these problems in Chapter 5.

120. These three Kantian questions form the starting point for the way in which Jon Sobrino discusses the hermeneutics of rebellion in his christology (op.cit., 236-58).

121. Thus in *A Black Theology of Liberation*, 17, James Cone describes black theology as 'a rational study of the being of God in the world in light of the existential situation of an oppressed community, relating the forces of liberation to the essence of the gospel, which is Jesus Christ'.

122. C.Eric Lincoln, 'Black Church', in *Christianity and Crisis* XXX,18, 16 November 1974, 144f., cf. also 138: 'One of the classic strategies of racism is to deliberately organize social and personal perception in such a way that the practical oblivion of the proscribed subject is consistently accomplished... White Western theology has contributed significantly to the involuntary invisibility of Black people – to Black oblivion.'

123. Juan Luis Segundo, SJ, *The Liberation of Theology*, Orbis Books, Maryknoll 1976, 8.

124. Bonino, op.cit., 91.

125. Segundo, op.cit., 9: 'Firstly there is our way of experiencing reality, which leads us to ideological suspicion. Secondly there is the application of our ideological suspicion to the whole ideological superstructure in general and to theology in particular. Thirdly there comes a new way of experiencing theological reality that leads us to exegetical suspicion, that is, to the suspicion that the prevailing interpretation of the Bible has not taken important pieces of data into account. Fourthly we have our new hermeneutic, that is, our new way of interpreting the fountainhead of our faith (i.e. Scripture) with the new elements at our disposal.'

126. Ibid., 25-34. Vital theology is not, however, in itself any guarantee of its truth content: 'The hermeneutical circle itself merely proves that a theology is alive, that it is connected up with the vital fountainhead of historical reality' (25).

127. As far as I can see, the expression 'hermeneutical circle' used by Tillich, Bultmann and others comes from Martin Heidegger, who in *Being and Time* (ET SCM Press and Harper and Row 1962) raised the question in para. 32: 'Understanding and Interpretation' (188-95), 'But if interpretation must in any case already operate in that which is understood, and if it must draw its nurture from this, how is it to bring any scientific results to maturity without moving in a circle, especially if, moreover, the understanding which is presupposed still operates within our common information about man and the world?' (194). George Casalis develops his view about hermeneutical circulation in *Correct Ideas don't Fall from the Skies*, 61-77.

128. Cone, op.cit., 117.

129. See chapter 3, section 3.

130. Segundo, op.cit., 39f.: 'It is the fact that the one and only thing that can maintain the liberative character of any theology is not its content but its methodology. It is the latter that guarantees the continuing bite of theology, whatever terminology may be used and however much the existing

system tries to reabsorb it into itself.' In *Theologie und Praxis*, 30, Clodovis Boff quotes Nietzsche's *Antichrist*: 'The methods, it must be said ten times, are the essential, also the most difficult thing, also that which has for the longest time had custom and laziness against it.'

131. Karl Barth, *CD* I.2, 860.

132. Cornelis Castoriadis, *L'institution imaginaire de la société*, Paris 1975.

133. See n.21 above.

134. See n.27 above.

135. Gollwitzer, op.cit., 42.

136. Ibid., 40.

137. Silvano Burgalassi, 'Towards a Theology of Man as Worker', *Concilium* 131, 1980, 103-16, gives a concise sketch of the problem.

138. 'Evidently theology as such has no value for human emancipation. In the last resort everything depends on its relationship to its conditions of production', Houtart, op.cit., 178.

139. Gollwitzer, op.cit., 44.

140. Cf. Oranje, op.cit., 184.

141. From the perspective of Latin American liberation theology and philosophy the autonomous subjectivity of thought has been criticized above all by the historian, philosopher and theologian Enrique Dussel, who was born in Argentina (*Para una ética de la liberación latinoamericana*, 3 vols, Buenos Aires 1973-75; *Método para una filosofía de la liberación*, Salamanca 1974; *Ethics and the Theology of Liberation*, Orbis Books, Maryknoll 1977); a short account of his philosophical insights is given by L.Schuurman, *Bevrijding en geweld*, Kamper Cahiers 32, Kampen 1977, 11-16. It is interesting to see how here Dussel goes back to the phenomenological thought of Martin Heidegger and in particular of Emmanuel Levinas; however, both are read in the context of Latin America, and that means that for Dussel it is the oppressed, marginalized Latin American people who give specific content to the category of 'the other' which is so central for Levinas (though kept too general): the poor represent otherness, real otherness. For Heidegger and the problem of the *cogito* see also Paul Ricoeur, *The Conflict of Interpretations*, Northwestern University Press 1974, 223-35.

142. Bonino, op.cit., 145.

143. Ibid., 144-9.

144. J. Moltmann, *The Crucified God*, SCM Press and Harper and Row 1974, 329.

145. Bonino, op.cit., 148.

146. Ibid., 149. In *Evangelische Kommentare* 14, August 1981, 8,444, Bonino writes that even those European theologians who actually had influence on Latin American theology were motivated by another interest and commitment: 'In their academic work these theologians, above all in Europe, have been challenged at decisive points by philosophical questions and problems which have led them to enter into dialogue with neoidealistic, existentialist and Marxist forms of thought... The difference between the two approaches... includes a deep epistemological gulf. In the one case

truth is understood as an intellectual formulation which can then be applied in and to actions, whereas in the other case knowledge is thought of as a total act which cannot hover above commitment and action, just as on the other hand it cannot be without theory and understanding.'

147. Bonino, *Doing Theology in a Revolutionary Situation*, 149.

148. This letter first appeared in *Christianity and Crisis*, 29 March 1976. The discussion was continued in October 1977 in Mexico; see Jorge V.Pixley and Jean-Pierre Bastin (eds.), *Praxis Cristiana y produción teológica*, Salamanca 1979.

149. Juan Luis Segundo, 'Capitalism-Socialism, A *crux theologica*', *Concilium* 10.6, June 1974, 109ff.

150. Moltmann, op.cit., 337; cf. 211f.

151. Bonino, op.cit.,149. For this point see also the questions from Markus Barth to Moltmann in *Diskussion über Jürgen Moltmanns Buch, Der gekreuzigte Gott*, ed. Michael Welker, Munich 1979, 161.

152. Bonino, op.cit., 149. In connection with this idealism Dorothee Sölle points out the thought-pattern 'beyond...' which constantly crops up in Moltmann: as a *tertium genus* belief stands beyond religion and the criticism of religion, theism and atheism, obedience and revolt (see Moltmann, op.cit., 43, 249, 252); the leap to a position *c* beyond the concrete historical and conflicting positions *a* and *b* can only be called dialectical if a real historical mediation takes place; however that is often missing. See Dorothee Sölle, 'Gott und das Leiden', in *Diskussion über Jurgen Moltmanns Buch, Der gekreuzigte Gott*, 112f.

153. Moltmann, op.cit., 338.

154. Ibid., 246.

155. Ibid., 249-52.

156. Ibid., 246, 257.

157. Ibid., 277. Daniel L.Migliore comments, 'The problem which arises here is, however, whether Moltmann's notable account of the Trinitarian history of God as an eschatological process into which the history of suffering creatures is incorporated and changed can be prevented from diverting into a speculative theodicy' (Daniel L.Migliore, 'Der gekreuzigte Gott', in *Diskussion über Jürgen Moltmanns Buch, Der gekreuzigte Gott, 41f.).

158. Moltmann, op.cit., *278.*

159. J.Moltmann, 'An Open Letter to José Miguez Bonino', *Christianity and Crisis*, 29 March 1976, 61.

160. Ibid., 60. It is not only surprising but also significant that Moltmann has nothing at all to say about the theory of dependence which affects the global framework in which the Latin American theologians of liberation try to understand their own situation. For a succinct survey of the history of this theory and its relationship with liberation theology see Gonzalo Arroyo, 'Afhankelijkheidstheorie, een geldige bemiddeling voor de bevrijdingstheologie?', in *Bevriding en christelijk geloof in Latijns-Amerika en Nederland*, Baarn 1980, 55-68. A number of significant contributions to this theory from the side of Latin American economists and sociologists have been translated into German and appear in the valuable collection,

edited by Dieter Senghaas, *Imperialismus und strukturelle Gewalt, Analysen über abhängige Reproduction*, Frankfurt am Main 1972, and *Peripherer Kapitalismus, Analysen über Abhängigkeit*, Frankfurt am Main 1974. Had he become familiar with these collections Moltmann could have been convinced that something more is involved here than quoting individual basic concepts from Marx, namely an attempt to understand the historical development of capitalism and imperialism from the perspective of the periphery.

161. Moltmann, op.cit., 62f. See also the last chapter of *The Crucified God*, esp. 336.

162. J.Moltmann, 'An Open Letter to José Miguez Bonino', 61f.

163. Ibid. Moltmann's letter contains a striking contradiction. On the one hand he says that he cannot assess what is possible or not in the Latin American situation, but on the other hand he is constantly concerned to extrapolate the concerns and irritations over his own situation to Latin America. A telling example of this is the fact that his criticism of Latin American theologians is precisely the same as his criticism of the left-wing student movement which lost contact with the people, in his view through its élitist character.

164. Ibid., 62.

165. But see Karl-Heinz Dejung, 'Vragen bij de dialoog Moltmann-Bonino', *Wending* 31.12, February 1977, 625f.

166. This sweeping and all too hasty judgment is in fact an expression of what liberation theology now rightly fights against, a lack of contextual thought.

167. Bonino, op.cit., 150.

168. The use of these terms is not fortuitous or arbitrary. In the next section we shall return in detail to the formula of Chalcedon. I think that there is much to be said for using its terms as the limits which are posed to theological speculation. See E.J.Bekker and J.M.Hasselaar, *Wegen en kruispunten in de dogmatiek 3, Christologie*, Kampen 1981, 24f.

169. Pablo Richard, 'Latin-American Theology of Liberation. A Critical Contribution to European Theology', in *European Theology Challenged by the World-wide Church*, Geneva 1976, 32.

170. Bonino, op.cit., 61.

171. In *The Trinity and the Kingdom of God*, SCM Press and Harper and Row 1981, 7, Moltmann quotes the well-known words of Gutiérrez: 'The first thing is the obligation to love and serve. Theology only comes *after* this, and is a second act' (*Theology of Liberation*, 11). The hermeneutical implications of this insight – 'our method is our spirituality' (Gutiérrez, 'Reflections from a Latin American Perspective: Finding our Way to Talk about God', 225f.; *We Drink from Our Own Wells*, 136) were, however, soon defused by the appearance of the thought-pattern in Moltmann which I indicated above (n.152): the position of Gutiérrez and his followers was reduced to position (*a*), that of the *vita activa*; over against that was set position (*b*), that of the *vita contemplativa*; both positions have their justification, but are very one-sided: 'Without the *vita contemplativa* the *vita activa* quickly becomes debased into activism, falling a victim to the

pragmatism of the modern meritocratic society'; so it is necessary that both positions be transcended in a position (*c*) which Moltmann expects from a 'change to trinitarian thought'. In the meantime there is no mention of the fact that Gutiérrez seeks to integrate theology as reflection on historical action emphatically with the classical function of theology, namely theology as *sapientia* (the spiritual function of theology) and theology as *scientia* (see *Theology of Liberation*, 5f., 13f., 203-8); similarly there is no mention of the numerous new forms of spirituality which have developed in praxis to which Latin American liberation theology relates.

172. Moltmann, *The Crucified God*, 318.

173. L.A.Hoedemaker, 'Oekumene en Paraklese', in *Leren bij het leven*, The Hague 1981, 31.

174. Cone, *God of the Oppressed*, VI.

175. Paul Tillich, 'Der Protestantismus als Kritik und Gestaltung', *Siebenstern Taschenbuch* 64, 1966, 61-5 (also reprinted in *Auf der Grenze*, 79-83).

176. *The Emergent Gospel*, ed. Torres and Fabella, 269.

177. H.B.Kossen gives some examples of this last taken from the report of Section III of the Fifth Assembly of the World Council of Churches in Nairobi, *Wending* 36.3, March 1981, 158.

178. Cf. note 123 above.

179. Cf. note 135 above.

180. This problem is discussed from the perspective of the history of religion and phenomenology of religion by J.H.Kamstra, 'Een moeilijke keuze: de godsdienst van de gewone man', *Tijdschrift voor Theologie* 20, 1980, 253-79; see also his questions put to the theology of liberation, 277.

181. How difficult this insight is to realize in practice may emerge from an anecdote told by the well-known North American theologian Robert McAfee Brown. At the 1975 Detroit Conference 'Theology in the Americas', one of the Latin American participants remarked to him: 'How is it that when you speak about our position you always talk about Latin American theology and when you speak of your position you always talk about theology?' Something had struck him which escapes us, said McAfee Brown: 'Our implicit assumption, which we would have explicitly disavowed, was that we did in fact have the normative theological position, and what was being served up from below the equator was a cultural and geographical deviant – interesting to be sure, but clearly the captive of a whole bagful of contextually conditioned assumptions, of which we were, of course, free' (Robert McAfee Brown, 'Context affects Content, The Rootedness of All Theology', *Christianity and Crisis* 37.12, 18 July 1977, 171).

182. Hoedemaker, op.cit., 31.

183. F.-W.Marquardt, *Die Entdeckung des Judentums für die christliche Theologie. Israel im Denken Karl Barths*, Munich 1967, 22.

184. The work of Michel Foucault should be mentioned in connection with this caution, see especially his *Power of Knowledge. Selected Interviews and Other Writings 1972-77*, ed. Colin Gordon, Pantheon Books, New York 1970.

185. See also Gollwitzer, op.cit.,47f.

186. G.H.ter Schegget in his attractive essay on K.H.Miskotte, 'Het gezicht van de meester', in *Indachtig*, Baarn 1981, 20.

187. Dietrich Bonhoeffer, *Ethics*, SCM Press and Macmillan, New York 1955, 171: cf. also *Letters and Papers from Prison. The Enlarged Edition*, SCM Press and Macmillan, New York 1971, 303, 345f., 381.

188. Cf. Gollwitzer, op.cit., 41.

189. 'The Humanity of God' is the title of a lecture given by Karl Barth in 1956 (see *The Humanity of God*, Fontana Books 1967, 33-64). This *retractatio* is often read as if here Barth was going back on his one-sided stress on the 'Godness of God' from the 1920s. However, there is no question of Barth here wanting to play off the Godness of God against his humanity in a quantitative 'more or less'. On the contrary, the point of his argument is precisely that earlier he had not thought radically enough about the Godness of God! 'It is precisely God's deity which, rightly understood, includes his humanity,' 42.

190. This last does not just happen in neo-orthodoxy but especially also in the liberal theology of Bultmann and most of his pupils; here faith means freedom 'from the world', a freedom which of course is not to be misunderstood in Gnostic terms but which at the same time implies 'a distance from the world and dealing with it in a spirit of "as if not"' (see Walter Schmithals, *An Introduction to the Theology of Rudolf Bultmann*, SCM Press 1968, 117).

191. Karl Barth, *CD* 1.1, 132ff. Cf. F.W.Marquardt, *Theologie und Socialismus. Das Beispiel Karl Barths*, Munich and Mainz 1972, 36.

192. G.E.Lessing, 'On the Proof of the Spirit and of Power', in *Lessing's Theological Writings*, ed. Henry Chadwick, A.&C.Black 1956, 53, 'Accidental truths of history can never become the proof of necessary truths of reason.'

193. For apostolate as transcending boundaries see Bert Hoedemaker, *Met Christus bij anderen*, Oekumene-reeks, Baarn 1978, 97-102.

194. Barth, *The Humanity of God*, 60.

195. For the limit of the apostolate see Hoedemaker, op.cit., 103-6 ('participation in suffering is the limit of the apostolate', 105).

196. See e.g. Helmut Gollwitzer, *Die kapitalistische Revolution*, Munich 1974; Dieter Schellong, 'Bürgertum und christliche Religion', *Theologische Existenz heute* 187, Munich 1975; Franz Hinkelammert, *La armas ideológicas de la muerte. El discernimento de los fetiches: Capitalismo y Christianismo*, San Jose 1977; *Christianity and the Bourgeoisie*, Concilium 125, 1979; Pablo Richard et al., *The Idols of Death and the God of Life*, Orbis Books, Maryknoll 1983.

197. Schellong, op.cit.,8.

198. Ibid., cf. n.4 above.

199. In 'A Theological Critique of the "Bourgeois World View"', *Concilium* 125, 1979, 74ff., Schellong argues that the bourgeoisie has been able to leave its mark on the world thanks to the many institutions, institutes and organizations (state, army, school, psychiatric institutions and so on) which it has called to life: 'The fact that the "socialist States" have...

strengthened rather than weakened all the "bourgeois" institutions and organizations I have mentioned is of interest and provides food for thought': the existence of all these institutions is experienced as being so completely 'natural' that the sense of that they are historical 'accidents' is hardly present at all.

200. E. Troeltsch, 'Die Mission in der modernen Welt', in *Zur religiösen Lage. Religionsphilosophie und Ethik*, Tübingen 1913, 193f. For this see in more detail T. E. Witvliet, 'Zwarte theologie en blanke theologen', *Wending* 29.4, June 1974, 194ff. It would be interesting to make an analysis of the way in which the contrast between culture and barbarism functions in a well-known correspondence between Barth and von Harnack (reprinted e.g. in Karl Barth, *Theologische Fragen und Antworten*, Zollikon 1947, 7-31); for Harnack the word barbarism denotes 'the "danger" of a proletarian revolution no less than the boundlessness of the all-German' (Carl-Jürgen Kaltenborn, *Adolf von Harnack als Lehrer Dietrich Bonhoeffers*, Berlin 1973, 21 cf. 27).

201. Cf. the quotation in n.91 above.

202. Karl Barth, *The Epistle to the Romans*, ET 1933, Preface to the Second Edition, 10.

203. See Bert Schuurman, 'Karl Barth en de bevrijdingstheologie', *Wending* 37.1, 1982, 62f.; see also id., *Bevrijding en geweld*, 12f., 25,36. Where in this last work Schuurman gives an account of the significance of the thought of Levinas for Enrique Dussel he rightly also makes a connection between the idea of exteriority and Barth's rejection of idealistic ideas of identity (God as the 'wholly other').

204. See S. R. Driver, *Notes on the Hebrew Text and Topography of the Books of Samuel*, Oxford University Press 1966, 118. Cf. also K. H. Miskotte, *Bijbels ABC*, Amsterdam 1966, second revised edition, 128.

205. D. Schellong, *Karl Barth als Theologe der Neuzeit*, Theologische Existenz heute 173, Munich 1973, 90. In 'A Theological Critique of the "Bourgeois World View"' (95) Schellong asks himself whether only the bourgeois world-view is affected by the judgment of God's reality. 'Is only the bourgeois involved in crisis when he encounters God's revelation? Should what is said not apply to everyone? Karl Barth certainly meant it to. He saw the bourgeois as the typical human being.' However, the problem is that here again the bourgeois is brought up as the representative of humanity, albeit in a negative way. Paul Tillich was not utterly wrong as far as this is concerned when he commented on Barth: 'He elevated this occasional crisis, which happens at a given time in history, into a universal crisis of the relationship between the eternal and the temporal' (*Perspectives on Nineteenth and Twentieth Century Protestant Theology*, ed. Carl Braaten, SCM Press and Harper and Row 1967, 240). Although Takatso A. Mofokeng rightly distances himself from Tillich's relativizing talk about this occasional crisis, in his study *The Crucified Among the Crossbearers. Towards a Black Christology*, Kampen 1983, 116, 193, he uses Tillich's remark to explain the fact that Barth, 'while placing Jesus Christ deeply and intimately among the poor as an effective Subject who really effects their movement, ... would not go on to think further and concretely and positively about the actual

effect of Jesus Christ's work and accord theological status which it really deserves to the communal historical praxis that arises as a result of this community's efforts' (193). With this term 'theological status' Mofokeng is referring to the pneumatology which e.g. in Barth is too little shaped by 'christological concentration' on the specific praxis of the messianic community. 'Practically, for example, Barth would have to not only bring Jesus very close to the poor as he does but also bring the poor closer to Jesus of Nazareth than he already does without, of course, identifying them with him at all times and in all situations. He would maybe have to identify their work with that of Jesus of Nazareth at particular moments and particular situations and separate them at other times and other situations' (197). For this set of problems see also Ch.3,3a and Ch.4,3 below.

206. G.C.van Niftrik, 'Het stotteren der dogmatiek', in *Maskerspel, FS W.Leendertz*, Amsterdam 1955, 121f.

207. J.B.Metz, 'A Short Apology of Narrative', *Concilium* 9.5, May 1973, 84-96; *Faith in History and Society*, 205-16; James H.Cone, *God of the Oppressed*, 53-61, 109-7; 'Sanctification, Liberation and Black Worship', *Theology Today*, XXXV,1, April 1978, 139-52 (especially 143f.); Eberhard Jungel, *God as the Mystery of the World*, T.&T.Clark and Eerdmans 1983, 299-314. The literature on narrative theology is growing rapidly and is now almost impossible to cover. Bernd Wacker, *Narrative Theologie?*, Munich 1977, is a good introduction. Mention should also be made of Harald Weinrich, 'Narrative Theology', *Concilium* 9.5, 1973, 48-57; Robert McAfee Brown, 'My Story and The Story', *Theology Today* XXXII, 1975-76, 166-73; U.Simon, *Story and Faith in the Biblical Narrative*, SPCK 1975; D.Ritschl and H.O.Jones, *Story als Rohmaterial der Theologie*, Theologische Existenz heute 192, Munich 1976; Michael Goldberg, *Theology and Narrative: A Critical Introduction*, Abingdon Press, Nashville 1982; George W.Stroup, *The Promise of Narrative Theology*, John Knox Press and SCM Press 1984; Paul Ricoeur, 'De moeilijke weg naar een narratieve theologie', in *Meedenken met Edward Schillebeeckx*, ed. Hermann Haring, Ted Schoof and Ad Willems, Baarn 1983, 80-92; also by Paul Ricoeur, *The Conflict of Interpretations* (n.14 above); 'La fonction narrative', in *Etudes theologiques et religieuses* 54.2, 1979, 209-30; 'L'histoire comme recit et comme pratique', *Esprit*, June 1981, 155-64; Paul Ricoeur et le centre de phenomenologie, *La narrativite*, Paris 1980; Paul Ricoeur, *Temps et récit* I, Paris 1983.

208. Jüngel, op.cit., 302.

209. Metz, *Faith in History and Society*, 184-97; J.M.van Veen, *Het is tijd, Verhalen rondom Jezus*, Baarn 1981, 25-37.

210. See van Veen, op.cit., 84, 93f.

211. It is worth reading from this perspective Karl Barth's polemic with Rudolf Bultmann in the preface to the Third Edition of *Romans* (16-20).

212. Jüngel, op.cit., 300.

213. Ibid., 304.

214. Ibid., 184ff.

215. Ibid., 303.

216. Ibid.

217. Jüngel discusses Marx's and Engels' criticism of Feuerbach in a footnote on p.341 and then says: 'The Marxist critique of religion could much more easily be accepted by theology than that of Feuerbach, if the latter were not presupposed by the former. At all events one can certainly integrate critically into theology the specific interest of Marx's critique or religion into theology – and in some ways it must be done. But that is the current fashion anyway, so that there is scarcely too little being done along these lines theologically. *Videant consules!*' The problem with this statement is that we cannot integrate it into the rest of Jüngel's study. Had Jüngel really taken seriously the religious criticism of Marx (not to mention critical integration) then he would not have been able to pass over in the discussion in his book about 'God' everything that suggests a historical and materialistic questioning, so sovereignly as he does.

218. Louis Althusser, 'Idéologie et appareils idéologiques d'état', *Positions*, Paris 1976, 67-125; *Essays on Self-Criticism*, New Left Books and Humanities Press 1976. For summaries of Althusser's thought on ideology see A.Callinicos, *Althusser's Marxism*, Pluto Press and Unizen Books, 1976; Henk Manschot, *Althusser over het Marxisme*, Nijmegen 1980, 285-320. Althusser's description of ideology as a presentation of the imaginary relation of people to their real conditions of existence gives ideology its own underived place which only in the last instance is determined by an economic basis. However, it is hard to say what this in the last instance actually implies. Althusser certainly situates the function of ideology in the reproduction of the conditions of production and the work force, and here he puts all the emphasis on the ideologizing of the individual as a process of insertion into existing conditions. Given this last, theology can make use of Althusser's insights only with the greatest caution; exodus, the covenant history and the life and work of Jesus amount to a practice of extraction rather than insertion. That does not do away with the fact that Althusser's revision of the Marxist theory of ideology is important to theology because he regards ideology in general as the imagination in which individuals become subjects, are called to become subjects, are given an identity, not through physical force but of their own free will. Here the idea of the free autonomous subject that can raise itself above social oppositions has become impossible. For the discussions among Dutch theologians of the value of Althusser's theory of ideology for theology see Dick Boer, 'Een fantastisch verhaal. De politieke betekenis van de lezing van de bijbel', *Eltheto* 65, Zeist 1981, 14-52; Rinse Reeling Brouwer, 'Is het marxisme een messianisme?', *Eltheto uitgave*, Zeist 1981; the contributions by H.B.Kossen and Leendert Oranje in *Wending*, March 1981, 158-63, 179-86; A.F.de Jong, *Lossen en binden, Beschouwing over een gebruikswijze van de term 'absoluut' in het werk van Louis Althusser en Emmanuel Levinas*, Amsterdam 1981; Anton van Harskamp, 'Louis Althusser relevant voor de theologie?', *Tijdschrift voor Theologie* 21, 1981, 2, 160-83, is very critical of Althusser.

219. Althusser, op.cit., 101.

220. Paul Ricoeur, *L'histoire comme récit et commme pratique*, 155,161.

221. Bonhoeffer, *Letters and Papers from Prison*, 360ff.

222. Jüngel, op.cit., 313.
223. For the question *cui bono?* see G.H.Ter Schegget, *Theologie en Ideologie*, Baarn 1981, 15-18, 108, 177.
224. K.Strijd argues for a Marxist preunderstanding in his farewell lecture, *De noodzaak van een marxistisch Vorverständnis voor de Theologie*, Amsterdam 1976.
225. H.Gollwitzer, 'Historischer Materialismus und Theologie', in *Traditionen der Befreiung* I. Methodische Zugänge, ed. Willy Schottroff and Wolfgang Stegemann, Munich 1980, 45f.
226. Wolfgang Stegemann demonstrates that children at the time of Jesus certainly belong in this context in his sociological exegesis of Mark 10.13-16, *Traditionen der Befreiung*, 114-44.

2. Response

1. Moltmann begins his introduction to *Warum 'schwarze Theologie'?*, an important thematic number of the journal *Evangelische Theologie* 34, January/February 1974, with an allusion to the notorious opening sentence of the Communist Manifesto of 1848: 'A ghost is going round Europe, the ghost of Communism.'
2. James Cone notes that by far the majority of white theologians in the US maintained a benevolent silence towards black theology 'because they contended that theology is concerned with the universal dimension in the gospel, which transcends the particularities of the Black experience. The particular concerns of Black people, they contended, were at best an ethical problem or even a pastoral problem and thus more appropriately belonged in the practical department', *Black Theology: A Documentary History, 1966-1979*, ed. Gayraud S.Wilmore and James H.Cone, Orbis Books. Maryknoll 1979, 136. Significantly enough, in the Netherlands interest in black theology from North America and Africa has been shown almost only by missiologists and ecumenists.
3. In the slave songs Jesus is often given the title 'king' or 'captain'. Both designations refer to his messianic role as liberator and redeemer of the world from the hands of Satan. As king Jesus sits on the leopard and in the imagination of the slaves he has a crown on his head and a bow in his hand (cf. Rev.6.2; 19.11). See Olli Alho, *The Religion of the Slaves*, Helsinki 1976, 73-75.
4. No less a figure than Frederick Douglass writes in his *Life and Times* 'A keen observer might have detected in our repeated singing of

O Canaan, sweet Canaan,
I am bound for the land of Canaan,

something more than a hope of reaching heaven. We meant to reach the North, and the North was our Canaan', *Life and Times of Frederick Douglass*, Collier-Macmillan 1962 (following the revised edition of 1892) 159.

5. Jean-Paul Sartre, 'Matérialisme et révolution', *Situations* III, Paris, 188f.

6. Sartre uses the Hegelian tripartite division for his analysis of *négritude* in *Black Orpheus* (Panther House 1971), a magisterial essay which originally appeared as the introduction to Léopold Sedar Senghor's *Anthologie de la nouvelle poésie nègre et malgache* (Paris 1948) and later in *Situations* III, 229-86. Franz Fanon, *Black Skin, White Masks*, Grove Press, New York 1967, 132-8, made important criticisms of this essay; see also T.Witvliet, 'Sartre en de strijd tegen racisme', *Wending* 35.9, September 1980, 501-11.

7. For this see above all Gayraud S.Wilmore, *Black Religion and Black Radicalism*, Orbis Books, Maryknoll ²1983, 135-52.

8. See Wilmore, op.cit., 174-91, and his lecture 'Martin Luther King Jr. – 20th Century Prophet', in *Asians and Blacks*, Bangkok 1973, 64-75, cf.73-75; the same line is taken by Allan Boesak, *Coming in out of the Wilderness*, Kamper Cahiers 28, Kampen nd.

9. There are no indications that in the last months of his life King went back on his method of non-violent resistance, nor did Malcolm X revoke his 'by any means necessary' strategy.

10. When one of the white students commented to King in Berkeley in 1967 that the autobiography of Malcolm X was having great influence on black and white students, King reacted with the words: 'That is what we call the power to become, the ability to go on in spite of. It was tragic that Malcolm was killed, he was really coming around, moving away from racism. He had such a sweet spirit. You know, right before he was killed he came down to Selma and said some pretty passionate things against me, and that surprised me because after all it was my own territory down there. But afterwards he took my wife aside, and said he thought he could help me more by attacking me than praising me. He thought it would make it easier for me in the long run', David Halberstam, 'When "Civil Rights" and "Peace" Join Forces', in *Martin Luther King Jr, A Profile*, ed. C.Eric Lincoln, Hill and Wang, New York 1970, 211.

11. See Louis Lomas, 'When "Nonviolence" meets "Black Power"', in *Martin Luther King Jr, A Profile*, 179.

12. Wilmore, *Asians and Blacks*, 73; *Black Religion and Black Radicalism*, 191.

13. See Wilmore, op.cit., 11; for mission and evangelization in the old South see Erskine Clarke, *Wrestlin' Jacob*, John Knox Press, Atlanta 1979; Winthrop D.Jordan, *White over Black*, University of North Carolina Press, Chapel Hill 1968; Donald G.Mathews, *Slavery and Methodism*, Princeton University Press 1965; id., *Religion in the Old South*, Chicago University Press 1977; Milton C.Sernett, *Black Religion and American Evangelism*, Scarecrow Press, Metuchen, NJ 1975; H.Shelton, *In His Image, But...*, Duke University Press, Durham, NC 1972.

14. In Afro-American culture there is no absolute distinction between church music and secular music: 'A Black Baptist preacher's daughter named Aretha Franklin can get loose and celebrate as well in one context as the other' (Henry M.Mitchell, *Black Belief*, Harper and Row 1975, 146).

15. That powerlessness is a Christian virtue is a misunderstanding which

is current above all among those who are not in this position. 'Powerlessness breeds a race of beggars', says the declaration on Black Power by a number of black church leaders in the New York Times of 31 July 1966 (*Black Theology: A Documentary History, 1966-1979,* ed. Wilmore and Cone, 23). That powerlessness is as corrupting as power and can lead to forms of extreme violence is demonstrated by Rollo May in his fascinating psychoanalytical study *Power and Innocence,* Norton 1972.

16. Joseph R.Washington gives a number of telling examples of the moralism, individualism and materialism in the black churches in his book *Black Religion. The Negro and Christianity in the United States,* Beacon Press, Boston 1964. The central idea in this sociological study is that because of the strict segregation in the South and the discrimination in the North, after the First World War the black churches were in fact deprived of theology; the black preachers spent their time on problems of organization and church-political disputes. 'In that era of decline in the quest for freedom the Negro minister remained the spokesman for the people with this difference – faced by unsurmountable obstacles, he succumbed to the cajolery and bribery of the white power structure and became its foil. Instead of freedom he preaches moralities...' (35). This book by someone from their own circle caused a vigorous discussion among black church leaders and theologians, and in this way it made an important contribution to the origin of black theology. Although Washington later shifted his insights, Cecil W.Cone still found in necessary in 1975 to go at length into black religion (*The Identity Crisis in Black Theology,* Abingdon Press, Nashville 1975, 73-80). For a balanced evaluation of *Black Religion* see Wilmore, *Black Religion and Black Radicalism,* 144f., and James H.Cone in *Black Theology: A Documentary History, 1966-1979,* 609-11, and *For my People,* Orbis Books, Maryknoll 1984, 8-10.

17. 'Every person becomes somebody, and one can see the people's recognition of their new found identity by the way they walk and "carry themselves". They walk with a rhythm of an assurance that they know where they are going, and they talk as if they know the truth about which they speak. It is this experience of being radically transformed by the power of the Spirit that defines the primary style of black worship', James H.Cone, 'Sanctification, Liberation, and Black Worship', *Theology Today* XXXV.1, April 1978, 41.

18. 'Black Theological reflection takes place in the context of the authentic experience of God in the Black worshipping community', *Black Theology in 1976. Statement by the Theological Commission of the National Conference of Black Churchmen,* reprinted in *Black Theology: A Documentary History, 1966-1979,* (340-344) 341.

19. Wilmore, *Asians and Blacks,* 54.

20. That liberation is always more than the socio-political and ideological emancipation of a people, group or class, also emerges clearly from the way in which Gutiérrez distinguishes three levels (see ch.1, section 1). We find the same dialectic between universality and particularity in Mary Daly's well known programmatic formulation of *Beyond God the Father,* Beacon Press, Boston 1973 and The Women's Press, 1986, 6: 'The women's

revolution, insofar as it is true to its own essential dynamics, is an ontological, spiritual revolution, pointing beyond the idolatries of a sexist society and sparking creative action in and toward transcendence. The becoming of women implies universal becoming. It has everything to do with the search for ultimate meaning and reality, which some would call God.'

21. For the origin and influence of this declaration, which was produced by, among others, H.J.Deotis Roberts, J.Cone and G.Wilmore, see *Black Theology: A Documentary History, 1966-1979*, 252f.; the quotation comes from p.343.

22. See Chapter 1, n.38.

23. Wolfgang Huber, *Der Streit um die Wahrheit und die Fähigkeit zum Frieden*, Munich 1980, 58. Huber rightly points out: 'Even academic theology in the European sense, which so far has often made a claim to universal validity, is a particular theology from a particular perspective; it only becomes ecumenical theology through dialogue' (60). Unfortunately Huber has a tendency to trivialize the difference between a theology of liberation and progressive European theologies: 'Pablo Richard has asserted that the transition to the theology of liberation – and he includes black theology in this – is a change of theological method in a radical sense. I cannot follow him here; the methodologial proximity of the liberation theologians in particular to European theology seem to me rather to be manifest' (78). The 'Self-enlightenment about the conditions of one's own production' which Huber supports might perhaps be of service in clarifying the essential difference here.

24. See A.Boesak, *Farewell to Innocence*, 26f.; see also Manas Buthelezi, 'African Theology or Black Theology?', in *Black Theology: The South African Voice* (US title *The Challenge of Black Theology in South Africa*), essays collected with an introduction by Basil Moore, C.Hurst and John Knox Press, 3–9; and *Theologie im Konfliktfeld Südafrika – Dialog mit Manas Buthelezi*, ed. Ilse Tödt, Stuttgart and Munich 1976, 111-32.

25. Reflection on contextual theology may learn much from 'Hermeneutische Vorerwägung zum theologischen Reden von Israel', which F.-W.Marquardt gives in the first chapter of his study *Die Entdeckung des Judentums für die christliche Theologie*, Munich 1967, 17-32, esp. 22ff.

26. That theological dialectic and living dialogue have an intrinsic connection is something which according to Marquardt is insufficiently thought about by modern theology. Here in particular he refers to Bultmann's pupils; this has to do with the fact that '*The de-objectivizing of God with which modern theology has detached itself from the metaphysical tradition has not led at the same time to a deobjectivizing of humanity or to a deobjectivizing of one's fellow human being*' (his italics), op.cit., 29.

27. It is no coincidence that the discussion about contextuality has come up in an ecumenical context. Here I am thinking particularly of the work of the Theological Education Fund (now rechristened the Programme on Theological Education of the World Council of Churches) which was directed by Dr Shoki Coe of Taiwan. See *Ministry in Context*, TEF, Bromley 1972; *Learning in Context*, TEF, London 1973. Coe's essay 'Contextualizing Theology', in Gerald H.Anderson and Thomas F.Stransky (eds.), *Mission*

Trends No.3, Paulist Press, New York and Eerdmans, Grand Rapids 1976, 19-24, has already become a classic. However, L.A.Hoedemaker is right in pointing out that the question of contextual theology arose in Third World situations where alienation from one's own culture was felt deeply when he says: 'Thus contextualization has a polemical structure: it is a question from below, against forms which constantly threaten to dominate and to alienate, against forms which in fact break the structures which have grown up in history and support patterns of separation' ('Conciliare gemeenschap of Kerk van de armen?', in *Praktische Theologie, FS P.J.Roscam Abbing*, ed. C.P.van Andel Azn, A.Geense and L.A.Hoedemaker, The Hague 1980, 184).

28. 'Cheap ecumenism' is an expression of Philip Potter's, formed by analogy with Bonhoeffer's talk of 'cheap grace', *From Uppsala to Nairobi*, ed. David E.Johnson, SPCK 1975, 20.

29. *Black Theology. A Documentary History, 1966-1979*, 342.

30. Ibid., 34f.

31. Ibid., 342.

32. James H.Cone and Gayraud Wilmore, 'Black Theology and African Theology: Considerations for Dialogue, Critique and Integration', *Pro Veritate*, 15 January-15 February 1972, reprinted in *Black Theology: A Documentary History, 1966-1979*, (463-76) 476.

33. For the contacts of black theology with theological movements in the Third World see above all the survey article by James Cone in *Black Theology: A Documentary History, 1966-1979*, 445-62. For the difficulties and possibilities of collaborating with other minority groups in the US see the account by Gayraud S.Wilmore of the workshop on racial and ethnic minorities on the occasion of the fiftieth anniversary of the Riverside Church in New York, 'The New Need for Intergroup Coalition', *The Christian Century* 99.5, 17 February 1982. Cf also Chapter 5.1.

34. The report of the Detroit conference is *Theology in the Americas*, ed. Sergio Torres and John Eagleson, Orbis Books, Maryknoll 1976; for the significance of this meeting for black theology see Gayraud S.Wilmore, 'The New Context of Black Theology in the United States', in *Black Theology. A Documentary History 1966-1979*, 602-8 (it appeared earlier in *Mission Trends No.4*, ed. Gerald H.Anderson and Thomas F.Stransky, Paulist Press, New York and Eerdmans, Grand Rapids 1979, 113-22).

35. The text of the Black Manifesto has been reprinted many times, e.g. in Arnold Schuchter, *Reparations. The Black Manifesto and its Challenge in White America*, Lippincott 1970, 191-202, and in *Black Theology: A Documentary History, 1966-1979*, 80-9; in Wending 24.7, September 1969, 56-63, H.Hoekendijk provides a commentary under the title 'Kerk op de korrel; het zwarte manifest'. The declaration *Black Theology* by the National Committee of Black Churchmen, 13 June 1969, supports the demand for reparations (see *Black Theology: A Documentary History, 1966-1979*, 101).

36. Karl Barth, *Der Römerbrief* (first edition, 1919, which was never translated into English), Zurich 1963, 266. For Barth as a polemicist see F.-W.Marquardt, *Verwegenheiten, Theologische Stücke aus Berlin*, Munich

1981, 424ff. (M wrongly locates the sentence quoted in the second impression of *Romans*, 425.)

37. Karl Barth, *Church Dogmatics* II.2, 213f.

38. Ibid., *Römerbrief*, 268.

39. Ibid.

40. Ibid. Cf.also *Romans*, second edition, Oxford University Press 1933, 337.: 'Nothing but the honour of God can make any sense whatever of anti-clerical propaganda. Attacks on the Church which proceed upon the assumption that its enemies possess some superior knowledge or some superior method of justifying and saving themselves are – non-sense. Consequently, when the prophet raises his voice to preserve the memory of eternity in himself and in the Church, he will always prefer to take up his position in hell with the Church – and this is applicable to the study of Theology – rather than to exalt himself with the pietists – whether they be crude or refined, old-fashioned or modernist, is irrelevant – into a heaven which does not exist.'

41. What is said above about the connection between dialectic and dialogue can be sharpened in the following way: 'Because dialectical theology in its most living form was polemical theology, it proved to be a theology of understanding between human beings', F.W.Marquardt, *Die Entdeckung des Judentums für die christliche Theologie*, 23.

42. See Ch.1, n.25.

43. James Cone describes his experiences as follows: 'The theological blindness of White professors in relation to the Black experience did not mean that they were consciously and intentionally racist. Only a few were blatantly racists; most were cordial and considerate. Some were even genuinely sympathetic to this black concern but were confused about what to do concerning it', *Black Theology: A Documentary History, 1966-1979*, 135.

44. For parallel experiences see Catharina J.M.Halkes, *Met Mirjam is het begonnen*, Kampen 1980, 73-86.

46. C.Eric Lincoln, *The Black Church Since Frazier*, Schocken Books, New York 1974, 138, where he describes the 'theology of benign neglect' as 'the theology which has operated on the principle that the white man's understanding is sufficient and proper for all men and all conditions of man and that the Black man's understanding could be improved by leaving him conveniently alone'.

46. Cone, op.cit., 136f.

47. Wilmore, *Asians and Blacks*, 62.

48. David E.Jenkins, *The Contradiction of Chistianity*, SCM Press 1976, 9.

49. Ibid., 10.

50. Ibid., 9.

51. J.Moltmann, *The Church in the Power of the Spirit*, SCM Press and Harper and Row 1977, 127ff.; Hoedemaker, op.cit., 180.

52. The Black Mennonite Hubert L.Brown notes in his book *Black and Mennonite*, Herald Press, Scottdale, 1967 91: 'Black History and Black theological thought have some of the same elements as Anabaptism.' It

would be interesting to investigate these elements more closely. In my view the most important agreement lies in the fact that in both traditions the work of the Holy Spirit is given a large place. For Baptists see A.F.de Jong, 'Geest en toekomst', in *Doopsgezinde Bijdragen*, nieuwe reeks 6, 1980, 26ff. For black religion see ch. 4, section 3.

53. James Baldwin, 'White Racism or World Community', *The Ecumenical Review*, Vol.XX, 1968, 371.

54. J.H.Oldham, *Christianity and the Race Problem*, SCM Press 1924.

55. See Neville Richardson, *The World Council of Churches and Race Relations : 1960 to 1969*, Frankfurt am Main and Bern 1977, 23-7; J.C.Adonis, *Die afgebreekte skeidsmuur weer obgebou*, Amsterdam 1982, 109-15.

56. Baldwin, op.cit., 375.

57. See John Vincent, *The Race Race*, SCM Press 1970, 42-8; Elisabeth Adler, *A Small Beginning. An Assessment of the First Five Years of the Programme to Combat Racism*, Geneva 1974, 11ff.

58. Norman Goodall (ed.), *The Uppsala Report. Official Report of the Fourth Assembly of the World Council of Churches*, Geneva 1968, 241.

59. The text of the declaration is printed in Barbara Rogers, *Race: No Peace without Justice*, Geneva 1980, 95-8; for the reports of working parties see 99-132.

60. Stokely Carmichael and Charles Hamilton, *Black Power*, Random House 1967.

61. In *A Place in the Sun*, SCM Press and Orbis Books 1985, 44-8, I went in detail into the problem of the quest for a definition of racism. Although I am aware of the dangers of a definition, there I opted for the following description: 'Racism is the specific ideology which organizes and regulates the exploitation and dependence of a particular "race" (group, people) on the basis of the supposed cultural and/or biological inferiority of this "race" and in this way perpetuates and deepens already existing differences of power' (47). See also T.Witvliet and Hans Opschoor, 'De onderschatting van het racisme', *Wending* 38. 9, 1983, 554-64.

62. See Ernst Lange, *De oekumenische utopie*, Oekumene reeks, Baarn 1974, 164; original edition *Die Ökumenische Utopie, oder Was bewegt die ökumenische Bewegung?*, Stuttgart 1972. An abridged English edition, *And Yet It Moves. Dream and Reality of the Ecumenical Movement*, is published by Christian Journals Ltd, Belfast and World Council of Churches, Geneva 1979.

63. Ibid., 164

64. Ibid., 131; *And Yet It Moves...*, 89.

65. Ibid., 51-4.

66. Ibid., 147f.

67. Huber, op.cit., 120.

68. See Hoedemaker, op.cit., 174: 'In Orthodox circles conciliar community is preferred as a description of the immanent trinitarian life of God and thus as an expression of the mystery of the eucharistic community; and a Roman Catholic theologian calls it "the specific realization of the

economy of salvation", in which the local eucharistic community is the focal point of specific discipleship in community and in praxis.'

69. Huber, op.cit., 125.

70. Cf.Hoedemaker, op.cit., 174ff.

71. *Racism in Theology and Theology against Racism, Report of a Consultation*, Geneva 1975, 9.

72. Lange, op.cit., 260; *And Yet It Moves...*, 166

73. For the idea of the church of the poor see the three studies edited by J.de Santa Ana: *Good News to the Poor*, Geneva 1977; *Separation Without Hope?*, Geneva 1978; *Towards a Church of the Poor*, Geneva 1979.

74. *Racism in Theology and Theology against Racism*, 9.

75. Hoedemaker, op.cit., 181-5.

76. *Racism in Theology and Theology against Racism*, 5f.

77. Rogers, op.cit., 121.

78. Hoedemaker, op.cit., 182.

3. Break and Continuity

1. 'We need a theology as well as a sociology of the Black church... We are in great need of a theology to undergird the worship and service of black Christians in fellowship': thus J.Deotis Roberts, 'A Black Ecclesiology of Involvement', *The Journal of Religious Thought* 32, Spring 1975 (36-4) 36; the different beginnings which have so far been made call for still further development.

2. An example of such an approach is W.Dantine, *Schwarze Theologie: Eine Herausforderung der Theologie der Weissen?*, Freiburg, Basle and Vienna 1976. This Viennese theologian approaches black theology in principle in a positive way. His view is that black theology cannot be dismissed because of its particular social and political starting points (16-22) but he also notes the danger that black theology might become racism in reverse (22-31). Dantine argues for recognition of the right of other forms of independent theology to exist alongside Western theology (98-105): 'However, it is possible to talk about an indepedent theology only when an independent development in doctrine is actually implemented which is able to shape the central doctrines of God as Creator and Redeemer or a theological anthropology and a Christian eschatology and last but not least an independent ecclesiology' (108). But this is where the difficulties begin! What the criterion of 'independent doctrinal development' means for him in practice is all too clear from the shortcomings which he thinks he has to point out in black theology and which particularly relate to soteriology – in the threefold ministry of Christ the *munus sacerdotale* is almost forgotten, the equality of all human beings is not seen sufficiently as a gift of God's grace, and black theology is fixated on its own needs, it has no self-criticism and penitence, and so on (80ff.). The problem in these critical questions is that the critic's own tradition continues to function as the norm by which the independent development of doctrine in black theology is measured. The existence of black, African and Latin American theology *alongside*

normative Western theology is in fact his subject of discussion; his own theological framework forms a starting point which is not open to further discussion.

3. Black theology counts as what Barth has called 'irregular dogmatics' as opposed to 'regular dogmatics'. According to Barth 'irregular dogmatics' is marked by the fact that 'in one respect or another, or even in many or all respects, it will be, and will mean to be, a fragment' (*CD* I.1, 277). A difficult problem, on which there has still been too little reflection, is what the discovery of contextuality means for the future of regular dogmatics.

4. Cf. ch. 1, section 2, and ch. 2, section 2.

5. J.Deotis Roberts, *A Black Political Theology*, Westminster Press, Philadelphia 1974, 47.

6. The term Black Power was used for the first time in an essay by the writer Richard Wright in the 1950s; in 1966 the slogan was already used before Carmichael and his supporters by Adam Clayton Powell in a lecture at Howard University. This information is taken from Manning Marable, *Blackwater; Historical Studies in Race, Class Consciousness and Revolution*, Challenge Press, Dayton 1981, 98.

7. Martin Luther King Jr, *Where Do We Go From Here? Chaos or Community?*, Harper and Row 1967 (British title, *Chaos or Community?*, Penguin Books 1969), 30; David L.Lewis, *Martin Luther King. A Critical Biography*, Allen Lane: The Penguin Press 1970, 325f.

8. See Chapter 1 n.112.

9. Gayraud S.Wilmore and James H.Cone (eds.), *Black Theology: A Documentary History, 1966-1979*, Orbis Books, Maryknoll 1979, 18.

10. Within the framework of this study I shall limit myself to an attempt to sketch out the specific dynamics of the historical movement in which black theology came into being. For a detailed historical survey of and insight into the civil rights movement see above all J.W.Schulte Nordholt, *In de schaduw van een groot licht*, Deventer 1971 (the book ends with the events of 1966). Of literature in English I would mention the outstanding survey by the historians August Meier and Elliott Rudwick, *From Plantation to Ghetto*, Hill and Wang ³1976, 271-313; the same authors also wrote the history of *CORE: A Study in the Civil Rights Movement 1942-1968*, Oxford University Press, New York 1973; the early history of SNCC is described by Howard Zinn, *SNCC: The New Abolitionists*, Beacon Press, Boston 1964; August Meier, Elliott Rudwick and Francis L.Broderick (eds.) *Black Protest Thought in the Twentieth Century*, Bobbs Merrill 1971, discusses the changes in the nature of the struggle for civil rights from the beginning of this century: good documentation for this period is also provided by John Hope Franklin and Isidore Starr, *The Negro in Twentieth Century America. A Reader on the Struggle for Civil Rights*, New York 1967, and Henry Steel Commager, *The Struggle for Racial Equality. A Documentary Record*, Peter Smith 1967; an admirable political and economic analysis is given by Frances Fox Piven and Richard A.Cloward in their study *Poor People's Movements*, Pantheon 1977, 181-263; there are good interviews with black leaders from the 1960s in Robert Penn Warren, *Who Speaks for the Negro?*,

Random House 1965; for literature by and about Martin Luther King see n.57 of this chapter.

11. Benjamin Mays, *Born to Rebel*, Scribner 1971, 149.

12. For the term caste in an American context see Gunnar Myrdal, *An American Dilemma*, Harper and Row 1944, 667ff.

13. C.Vann Woodward, *The Strange Career of Jim Crow*, second revised edition, Oxford University Press, New York 1966, 67ff., 97ff.

14. Schulte Nordholt, op.cit., 37.

15. James Weldon Johnson, *The Autobiography of an Ex-colored Man*, Knopf 1960, 76: he adds: 'I am sure it would be safe to wager that no group of Southern white men could get together and talk for sixty minutes without bringing up the "race question". If a Northern white man happened to be in the group, the time could be safely cut to thirty minutes': cf. Schulte Nordholt, ibid.

16. Schulte Nordholt, op.cit., 38, 41f.

17. Gunnar Myrdal, op.cit., 587: 'Sexual association itself is punished by death and is accompanied by tremendous public excitement; the other social relations meet decreasing degrees of public fury. Sex becomes in this popular theory the principle around which the whole structure of segregation of the Negroes – down to disfranchisement and denial of equal opportunity on the labor market – is organized.'

18. Gunnar Myrdal comments on this cult of purity: 'The fixation on the purity of white womanhood, and also part of the intensity of emotion surrounding the whole sphere of segregation and discrimination, are to be understood as the backwashes of the sore conscience on the part of white men for their own or their compeers' relations with, or desires for, Negro women. These psychological effects are greatly magnified beause of the puritan milieu of America and especially of the South', op.cit., 591.

19. Winthrop D.Jordan, *White over Black*, University of North Carolina Press, Chapel Hill 1968, 153f.; *The White Man's Burden*, Oxford University Press 1974, 80f. (the latter book is a summary of the more detailed *White over Black*).

20. Jordan, *White over Black*, 158: *The White Man's Burden*, 82. In *From Sundown to Sunup. The Making of the Black Community*, Greenwood 1972, 127-333, George P.Rawick brings out the idea – following studies by Michel Foucault, Philippe Ariès and E.P.Thompson – that these sexual projections are connected with the deep changes in life pattern and human psychology which follow the rise of European capitalism; the process of work calls for regulation and discipline – a new element in the history of a hitherto prevalently agrarian society, in which the alternation of seasons had determined the rhythm of life; the rhythm of the new methods of production called for rationalization which progressed at the expense of the non-rational; sexual urges and longings were restricted and suppressed. We can understand the vigorous reactions of the northern Europeans, and especially the English, to encounters with West Africans in the sixteenth and seventeenth centuries, if we remember that the West African mode of living of this period in many respects resembled the pattern of life which Western Europeans were trying to rise above; work was intertwined with

ceremonial and religious practices; people lived in small and compact communities, and attitudes towards sexuality and the non-rational were relatively non-repressive: 'The Englishman met the West African as a reformed sinner meets a comrade of his previous debaucheries' (132). In order not to fall back into the old way of life which he had abjured, in his imagination the European created an enormous gap from those whom he had formerly resembled – and he projected the sexual fantasies which still kept arising on to others. Thus it could come about that fantastic stories could go the round (and were accepted as true facts) about Africans as an exceptionally lustful people among whom one could find women openly copulating with apes.

21. Jordan, *White over Black*, 154f.; *The White Man's Burden*, 81. Of crucial importance here were the sociological and psychological insights and intuitions of Franz Fanon in Chapter 6 of *Black Skin, White Masks*, Grove Books. New York 1968; comparing negrophobia with antisemitism, Fanon says: 'No antisemite, for example, would ever conceive of the idea of castrating the Jew. He is killed or sterilized. But the negro is castrated. The penis, the symbol of manhood, is annihilated, that is to say, it is denied. The difference between the two attitudes is apparent. The Jew is attacked in his religious identity, in his history, in his race, in the relations with his ancestors and with his posterity; when one sterilizes a Jew one cuts off the source: every time that a Jew is persecuted it is the whole race that is persecuted in his person. But it is in his corporeality that the negro is attacked' (162f.).

22. Walter Benjamin, *Illuminationen*, Frankfurt 1977, 255.

23. Leon F.Litwack, *North of Slavery*, Chicago University Press 1965: Ira Berlin, *Slaves Without Masters*, Pantheon 1975.

24. The Black Codes which were promulgated in 1865 by the provisional governments of the Southern states and repealed again by the Reconstruction contain regulations by which blacks could be hired out to their former masters, so that they were forbidden to rent or to lease land, and so on. For liberation from slavery and the subsequent period up to 1867 see the comprehensive study by Leon F.Litwack, *Been in the Storm So Long*, Knopf 1979.

25. The classic work on this period remains W.E.B.DuBois, *Black Reconstruction in America*, Atheneum 1971, which originally appeared in 1935.

26. Eugene D.Genovese, *The World the Slaveholders Made*, Vintage Books 1971, 111f.

27. Schulte Nordholt, op.cit., 40.

28. As well as *The Strange Career of Jim Crow*, C.Vann Woodward, who himself came from the South, wrote a number of other standard works about Southern history like *Origins of the New South*, La State University Press, Baton Rouge 1951, and *The Burden of Southern History*, revised edition, La State University Press, Baton Rouge 1968.

29. The political significance for the civil rights movement of *The Strange Career of Jim Crow* could be found in two things: 1. Vann Woodward shows that even after the start of reconstruction there was a period with possibilities

for reconciliation between white and black; only when the powers which restrained extreme racism began to weaken as a result of economic depression, political frustration, indifference in the North and decisions from the Supreme Court of Justice, the segregation laws were gradually introduced between 1890 and 1910; in contrast to the current conviction that laws cannot create *mores*, the specific 'folkway of Southern life' (that permanent pattern of life in the South to which the white Southerner was so fond of referring) was the direct consequence of the introduction of these laws; the political implication of this historical view is clear: what is introduced by laws can also be done away with by legislation. 2. Despite everything Populism had demonstrated the real possibility of a confederation between white and black; it is probable that in this short-lived movement, 'Negroes and native whites achieved a greater comity of mind and harmony of political purpose than ever before or since in the South' (64). In his well-known address on the march from Selma to Montgomery in 1965 Martin Luther King referred to *The Strange Career of Jim Crow*. However, the crisis in the civil rights movement after 1965 cast doubts on the optimism of this historical view; for criticism see e.g. Lawrence J.Friedman, *The White Savage*, Prentice Hall, Englewood Cliffs, NJ 1970; Robert L.Allen, *Reluctant Reformers*, Doubleday 1974, 51-83.

30. William Julius Wilson, *The Declining Significance of Race*, Chicago University Press 1978, 9: 'When I speak of racial belief systems I am referring to the norms or ideologies of racial domination that reinforce or regulate patterns of racial inequality.'

31. Donald L.Noel, in *The Origins of American Slavery and Racism*, ed.id., Charles E. Merrill Publishing Co. 1972, 155. One of the most sophisticated definitions along these lines is given by Pierre L. van der Berghe, *Race and Racism, A Comparative Perspective*, Wiley [2]1978: 'Racism is any set of beliefs that organic, genetically transmitted differences (whether real or imagined) between human groups are intrinsically associated with the presence or absence of certain socially relevant abilities or characteristics, hence that such differences are a legitimate basis of invidious distinctions between groups socially defined as races.' We have already looked at the problem of defining racism in Chapter 2.3, in connection with the WCC consultation in Noordwijkerhout, 1980. There is a close connection between the way racism is defined and how it is evaluated as a historial phenomenon in the modern world. So the consultation at Noordwijkerhout observes that racism in the modern world is on the increase, while in the introduction to the second impression of his study Van den Berghe comes to the conclusion that racism, at any rate in its Western form (!), is on the way out (XXXI)! We also come across this latter view in a recent article by John Rex, an English sociologist who is an authority in the sphere of race relations, in *Racism and Colonialism*, ed. Robert Ross, The Hague, 1981, 218; for the USA see also Wilson, op.cit. See also T.Witvliet and H.Opschoor, 'De onderschatting van het racisme', *Wending* 38.9, 1983, 154-64.

32. *Slavery in the New World*, ed. P.Foner and E.D.Genovese, Englewood Cliffs NJ, 244.

33. See Ch.1, n.94.

34. Genovese, *The World the Slaveholders Made*, 95-102, 131, 199.

35. As an acute observer, Frederick L. Olmsted did not miss this contradiction on a ship in which he sailed as a passenger; in his journal he writes: 'It is difficult to handle simply as property, a creature possessing human passions and human feelings, ...while, on the other hand, the absolute necessity of dealing with property as a thing, greatly embarrasses a man in any attempt to treat it as a person' (quoted by Kenneth M.Stampp, *The Peculiar Institution*, Knopf 1965, 193). See also David Brion Davis, *The Problem of Slavery in Western Culture*, Cornell University Press 1966, 62, and *The Problem of Slavery in the Age of Revolution*, Cornell University Press 1975, 82: 'In summary, then, slavery has always embodied a fundamental contradiction arising from the ultimately impossible attempt to define and treat men as objects.'

36. Eric Williams, *Capitalism and Slavery*, University of North Carolina Press, Chapel Hill, NC 1944, 4: 'Slavery was not born of racism; rather, racism was the consequence of slavery.'

37. Ibid., 19.

38. In 1847 – note the year! – Karl Marx wrote: 'Direct slavery is the cornerstone of bourgeois industry, as are machines and so on. Without slavery no cotton; without cotton no modern industry. Only slavery has given the colonies their value; the colonies have created world trade; and world trade is the condition of major industry. So slavery is an economic category of supreme importance. Without slavery North America, the most advanced country, would turn into a patriarchal country. Wipe North America off the map of the world and you have anarchy, the complete collapse of trade and modern civilization. Let slavery disappear and you wipe America off the map of nations' ('The Poverty of Philosophy', in *Karl Marx: Selected Writings*, ed. D. McLellan, Oxford University Press 1977, 203f.). For slavery as an archaic means of production see above all, Genovese, op.cit., 21-26, 112f.

39. Genovese, op.cit., 110.

40. Ibid., 105.

41. Transatlantic slave trade was of great importance in this respect: 'It was the capital gained from the slave trade which fertilized what became the Industrial Revolution', C.L.R.James, 'The Atlantic Slave Trade and Slavery: Some Interpretations of their Significance in the Development of the United States and the Western World', *Amistad* 1, New York 1970, 123.

42. Genovese, op.cit., 111.

43. Ibid., 111f.

44. The description of ideology used here is a free paraphrase of Louis Althusser, *For Marx*, Random House, New York and Verso Editions 1979, 230-43: 'It is enough to know very schematically that an ideology is a system (with its own logic and rigour) of representations (images, myths, ideas or concepts depending on the case) endowed with a historical existence and role within a given society' (238); 'So ideology is the expression of the relationship of men to their "world", that is to say the (overdetermined) unity of their real relationship and their imaginary relationship to their real conditions of existence' (240).

45. The black writer Ralph Ellison, author of *Invisible Man*, observes in his collection of essays *Shadow and Act*, Secker and Warburg 1967, 28: 'Color prejudice springs not from stereotype alone, but from an internal psychological state; not from misinformation alone, but from an inner need to believe. It thrives not only on the obscene witchdoctoring of men like Jimmy Byrnes and Malan, but upon an inner craving for symbolic magic. The prejudiced individual creates his own stereotypes, very often unconsciously, by reading into situations involving Negroes those stock meanings which justify his emotional and economic needs.'

46. The description of the civil rights movement as 'the Second Reconstruction' originally comes from C.Vann Woodward: it was taken over by the black historians and activists who wanted to investigate and further the conditions for the Third Reconstruction still to come; see Marable, op.cit., 187-208.

47. Vincent Harding, *The Other American Revolution*, Center for Afro-American Studies, Los Angeles and Atlanta 1980, XIV.

48. The March on Washington Movement was also already strongly influenced by the strategy of Gandhi in India, see Meier and Rudwick, *From Plantation to Ghetto*, 272f.

49. Ibid., 277; 'Ironically, it was the NAACP's very successes in the legislatures and the courts that more than any other single factor led to this revolution in expectations and the resultant dissatisfaction with the limitations of the NAACP's program.'

50. Harding, op.cit., XV.

51. James Baldwin, *The Fire Next Time* (1962), Dell 1978, 127.

52. According to the 1910 census three-quarters of the black population lived in rural areas and nine-tenths in the South; see Meier and Rudwick, op.cit., 232. In their study *Poor People's Movements*, Piven and Cloward suggest that this migration caused by economic necessity released the black population in the agrarian South from the rigid caste system in which they had had to live hitherto: 'By mid-century, southern ghettos were... swollen with displaced agricultural poor. Protest had become possible; victories had become possible. Except for freedom from caste relations, all of the structural developments essential to a protest movement that were present in the northern ghettos were also to be found in the southern ghettos; the economic base formed by a wage laboring class; the consequent occupational and institutional expansion and diversification; the volatile underclass produced by unemployment and underemployment' (208).

53. In their analysis Piven and Cloward pay considerable attention to the way in which the civil rights movement could allude to the division and the electoral instability of the national Democratic party. The appearance of King and his followers brought a substantial sharpening of the polarization which was already present between conservative southern Democrats on the one hand and white liberals and blacks from the North on the other; the only way that the leaders of the party saw of recouping electoral losses was that of gradual political reforms in the South: 'By this time there was no other way that the profound conflicts dividing the northern and southern wings of the party could be lessened. Nor, except by enfranchising blacks

and incorporating them in the southern wing of the party, could Democratic strength in the South be regained' (183f.). It is, however, very regrettable that in Piven and Cloward's work an excellent analysis of economic and political factors does not pay equal attention to the ideological struggle. What takes place at that level as far as they are concerned is no more than a reflection of what takes place in the economic and political sphere. Against that I would say: 1. the race struggle has a specific dynamic of its own as compared with the class struggle; however much maximal economic exploitation is ultimately the occasion for and consequence of racial oppression, in the first instance we have racism as ideology, in other words as a specific view of reality which involves the complete disregard of the humanity of the black; 3. black liberation therefore primarily means a struggle to establish one's own identity; 4. therefore the struggle on the level of consciousness – in other words on the level of religion and culture – is not fortuitous, but the condition for political and economic liberation.

54. Harding, op.cit., XV; the sentence is in brackets – sometimes people say the most important things in passing.

55. James H.Cone, *Black Theology and Black Power*, Seabury Press 1969, 7; Allan Boesak, *Farewell to Innocence*, 50: 'The power to be, the courage to establish one's human dignity, must inevitably lead to the transformation of structures to fulfil its search for completion and wholeness.'

56. The text of King's famous speech in Washington in 1963 of which the quotation forms the end is printed in Franklin and Starr, op.cit., 143-7. For the use of the Hegelian triad see Chapter 2.1 (n.6): of course it is not my aim to express the historical dynamic of the black struggle for liberation in a pattern of thought; I am using the triad simply as a way of clarifying a particular historical dynamic.

57. The classic biography of King is David L.Lewis, *King. A Critical Biography*, Allen Lane: The Penguin Press 1970; Coretta Scott King, *My Life with Martin Luther King, Jr*, Holt, Rinehard and Winston and Hodder and Stoughton 1969, is certainly also an important document. One of the best biographies is Stephen B.Oates, *Let the Trumpet Sound: The Life of Martin Luther King*, Harper and Row 1982. In addition mention must be made of Kenneth L.Smith and Ira G.Zepp Jr, *Search for the Beloved Community: The Thinking of Martin Luther King Jr*, Judson Press, Valley Forge 1974, and a collection of essays by different authors, *Martin Luther King Jr, A Profile*, ed. C.Eric Lincoln, Hill and Wang 1970. The most important publications of King himself are: *Stride toward Freedom, The Montgomery Story*, Harper and Row and Gollancz 1958; *Strength to Love*, Harper and Row and Hodder and Stoughton 1963; *Why We Can't Wait*, Harper and Row 1964; *Where Do We Go from Here?* (see n.7 above), and *Trumpet of God*, Harper and Row and Hodder and Stoughton 1968, which appeared posthumously. The study by John J.Ansbro, *Martin Luther King Jr: The Making of a Mind*, Orbis Books, Maryknoll 1982, offers an attractive introduction to the thought world of King; however, from the black side the criticism has been made that while Ansbro rightly has paid much attention to the influence that particular theologians and philosophers had

on King, he overlooks the most important influence: the spirituality of the black church; see James H.Cone, 'Martin Luther King Jr, Black Theology – Black Church', in *Theology Today*, Jan.1984, 409-20, esp. 414.

58. 'I was not a follower of Dr Martin Luther King. I respected him, but very early in his ministry, I differed with him in his approach to the problems of black people,' Albert B.Cleage Jr, *The Black Messiah*, Sheed and Ward 1968, 206.

59. Ibid., 211.

60. August Meier, 'On the Role of Martin Luther King', in *Martin Luther King Jr, A Profile*, 146; also reprinted in *The Making of Black America*, ed. A.Meier and E.Rudwick, II, Atheneum 1974, (353-61) 355; cf. also Meier and Rudwick, *From Plantation to Ghetto*, 297f.

61. Harding, op.cit., 212, relates: 'Early in the 1970s, one of King's closest and best known co-workers reflected on the direction his friend and leader had been taking in those last perilous years of his life. He said, "In a way, it was probably best for many of us who worked with Martin that he was killed when he was, because he was moving into some radical directions that few of us had been prepared for." The man paused. Then he added, "And I don't think that many of us would have been ready to take the risks of life, possessions, security, and status that such a move would have involved." Then another pause,and the final reflection: "I'm pretty sure I wouldn't have been willing."'

62. King, *Trumpet of Conscience*, 59f. Cf. *Where Do We Go from Here?*, 130, where King could still write: 'The American racial revolution has been a revolution to get in rather than to overthrow.'

63. Cheryl Benard, *Die geschlossene Gesellschaft und ihre Rebellen*, Frankfurt 1981, 19.

64. That King was only concerned with integration and that his dream was therefore little more than rhetorical decoration is a thought which can easily arise when one reads his statements about the black struggle as a struggle to be taken up in the mainstream of American society, in education and so on. In that case, however, there is no explanation of (*a*) his part in the rise of the revolutionary situation of the 1960s, (*b*) the radical development which took place in him in the last two years of his life. This latter can only be explained if we assume that King himself only gradually – after the fires in Detroit and the nightmares of Vietnam made him aware of the depth of the gulf between dream and reality – realized the radical nature of his vision of the future. The paradox of King's career lies in the tension between his moderate political and economic views and ideas on the one hand and the radical ideological effect of his strategy and rhetoric on the other; King began to recognize this tension more sharply, and in the last two years of his life it brought him to a deep spiritual crisis and a proces of radical reorientation which was broken off in an untimely way by his death.

65. Franklin and Starr, op.cit.,144.

66. For an analysis of the style of King's sermons and addresses see Hortense J.Spiller, 'Martin Luther King and the Style of the Black Sermon',

in *The Black Experience in Religion*, ed. C.Eric Lincoln, Hill and Wang 1974, 75-98.

67. Warren, op.cit., 149.

68. Quoted in Schulte Nordholt, op.cit., 149.

69. King, *Where Do We Go from Here?*, 64.

70. Franklin and Starr, op.cit., 144.

71. Ibid.

72. King, *Strength to Love*, 100.

73. Paul Tillich, 'Auf der Grenze', *Siebenstern Taschenbuch* 3, 1965, 124. For the term *kairos* see Ch.1, 2 above.

74. Vincent Harding, *There is a River*, New York 1981, XXIII (this passage, too, is in brackets).

75. For King and Black Consciousness cf. also Allan Boesak, *Coming in out of the Wilderness*, Kamper Cahiers 28, Kampen nd., 47f. Outside America black consciousness, introduced by the black student organization SASO, has become above all a key term in the black struggle for liberation in South Africa; see the contributions by Steve Biko and Nyameko Pityana in *Black Theology in South Africa*, ed. Basil Moore, 17-27, 37-43. When Biko describes black consciousness as an expression of 'group pride and the determination by black to stand and to attain the envisaged self' (62), then here too it is the case that black self-awareness lives from hope.

76. We can also find the thought that a people without a past has no future in a saying of Marcus Garvey which serves as a motto for the LP *Survival* by Bob Marley and the Wailers: 'A People without the knowledge of their past history, origin and culture is like a tree without roots.'

77. Lewis, op.cit., 292

78. Gayraud S.Wilmore, *Black Religion and Black Radicalism*, Orbis Books, Maryknoll ²1983, 174-83; *Asians and Blacks*, Bangkok 1973, 64f., 70.

79. King, *Stride toward Freedom*, 73-83.

80. See also Boesak, op.cit., 31-3, for a summary of the way in which King based his non-violent resistance on his conception of *agape*. John J.Ambro gives the most extensive exposition in the first chapter of his book *Martin Luther King Jr: The Making of a Mind*, 1-36. Inspired by Tillich's study *Love, Power and Justice*, King writes in his dissertation *A Comparison of the Conceptions of God in the Thinking of Paul Tillich and Henry Nelson Wieman*: 'Love is the ontological concept. Justice has no independent ontological standing. Justice is dependent on love. It is part of love's activity' (quoted by Ansbro, op.cit., 8). We shall be considering the relationship between *agape* and power in ch.6, section 2.

81. Karl Jaspers, *Von der Wahrheit*, Munich 1958, 933.

82. Paul Tillich, *Auf der Grenze*, 120, writes: 'No prophetic word is ever fulfilled in terms of its own expectations. And yet at the same time: no prophetic word has ever remained unfulfilled.'

83. Nordholt, op.cit., 216.

84. Ibid., 217.

85. Paul Lehmann, *The Transfiguration of Politics*, SCM Press and Harper and Row 1974, 191.

86. For King's own interpretation of events see *Why We Can't Wait*, Chs.3-6.

87. When Ansbro, op.cit., 330 says of Cleage's remark, 'Cleage refused to see that one could not be King's follower if one resorted to violence,' he misses the point. Cleage does not mean an agreement which there should be in thought and strategy, but the social and dynamic effect of King's strategy.

88. Lewis, op.cit., 196.

89. Cf. Lehmann, op.cit., 191f.

90. King, op.cit., 87, '...I am further convinced that if our white brothers dismiss as "rabble rousers" and "outside agitators" those of us who employ non-violent direct action, and if they refuse to support our non-violent efforts, millions of Negroes will, out of frustration and despair, seek solace and security in black-nationalist ideologies - a development that would inevitably lead to a frightening racial nightmare.'

91. Bernard, op.cit., 26, cf. 129f.

92. See above all ibid., 119-25, 129-40: 'Although certain patterns can be recognized and stages isolated in the conduct and experiences of dominated groups in the USA it must be presupposed that there can be no model for this. Nevertheless connections can be described which seem useful for understanding contemporary situations' (119). Marable, op.cit., 175f., can write: 'The Black Movement articulated questions in both its content and practice with which other latently dissident sectors of American culture and society could identify... It was only with the rise of Black Power that militant white women began to popularize the term "sexism" and imitated the organization and style of previous black protest formations in practice... Even gay men and lesbians used tactics (e.g. street demonstrations), slogans ("Gay Power") and legal strategies calling for affirmative action and anti-discrimination leislation which evolved directly from the legacy of the Civil Rights and Black Power movements.' See also Harding, op.cit., 205f.

93. Benard is here arguing with Oscar Negt, who regrets the neglect of non-academic groups, ethnic minorities and women by Marxism, but does not go on to consider the underlying causes of this: 'The standpoint of those whose goal is not to renew Marxism but to understand their own lifestyle and express their view of life, who therefore want to be subjects of their own thought patterns and not objects of a completed theory, is still ignored' (188).

94. In her book the following biographical details are given: Cheryl Benard was born in New Orleans in 1953 and is associated with the Institute of Political Science in the University of Vienna.

95. Cf. the quotation of Luce Irigaray by Cheryl Benard, op.cit., 22.

96. Ibid., 190.

97. Ibid., 187.

98. Ibid., 26.

99. Ibid., 26, cf.72.

100. Ibid., 137, 189. In connection with the word 'black' J.Deotis Roberts, *A Black Political Theology*, 23, tells the following story: 'While in Atlanta during June, 1973, a group of black scholars in religion paid a visit to

Ebenezer Baptist Church. We viewed the grave site of Martin Luther King, Jr and then entered the church, where we were greeted by Martin Luther King, Sr, affectionately referred to as Daddy King. In the course of our conversation the word "black" came up. We were involved in a worship session in the Society for the Study of Black Religion. Daddy King immediately informed us that he was not black. Looking us straight in the eyes, he asked: "Are you black?" One brave brother among us said frankly but politely: "Yes, sir!" We were all shocked by the challenge but shared the experience with the larger fellowship. Whereas we all were united on the terms of black awareness, we realized that Daddy King represents a large segment of powerful black churchmen for whom black theology has no real meaning.'

101. Benard, op.cit., 24-26: 188f.

102. Ibid., 190.

103. Ibid.

104. Quoted by Thomas L.Blair, *Retreat to the Ghetto*, Hill and Wang 1977, XXI. Integration can be distinguished from assimilation; in the latter case the image used is that of the melting pot; in the case of integration there is talk of the salad bowl and a pluralistic society.

105. A short survey of the different elements and attempts at definitions is given by Alphonso Pinkney, *Red, Black and Green, Black Nationalism in the United States*, Cambridge University Press 1976, 1-7; see also John H.Bracey, August Meier, and Elliott Rudwick (ed.), *Black Nationalism in America*, Bobbs Merrill 1970.

106. Eugene D.Genovese, *Red and Black*, Allen Lane: The Penguin Press 1971, 58: 'Black nationalism arises from two sources: a community of interest in a virulently racist society; and a particular culture that has itself been a mechanism for survival as well as for resistance to racist oppression.'

107. Sterling Stuckey, *The Ideological Origins of Black Nationalism*, Beacon Press, Boston 1972, 26.

108. The terms nationalism and separatism are often interchanged; however one can only speak of black separatism if the struggle for one's own country or state is predominant.

109. Stuckey, op.cit., 2; he challenges the view that black nationalism only begins with the appearance of Martin Delany, cf. his polemic with Harold Cruse, 10.

110. Ibid., 28.

111. 'As came John the Baptist, of old, to spread abroad the forthcoming of his master, so alike are intended these words, to denote to the black African or Ethiopian people, that God has prepared for them a leader, who awaits but for his season to proclaim to them his birthright.' The text of the manifesto is printed in Stuckey, op.cit., (30-38) 36f.

112. 'We have as much right biblically and otherwise to believe that God is a negro, as you buckra or white people have to believe that God is a fine looking, symmetrical, and ornamented white man' (Bracey, Meier and Rudwick, op.cit., 175); cf. also Edwin S.Redkey, *Respect Black: The Writings and Speeches of Henry McNeal Turner*, Arno Press, New York 1971.

113. See Wilmore, *Black Religion and Black Radicalism*, 110; Wilmore finds the same notion in Marcus Garvey, see 149. Chapter 5 of Wilmore's book *Black Religion and Black Nationalism* gives an excellent survey of the life and thought of Delany, Crummell, Blyden and Turner, whom he regards as black theologians *avant la lettre*. For Delany, see further Victor Ullman, *Martin R. Delany: The Beginnings of Black Nationalism*, Beacon Press, Boston 1971.

114. In *The Condition, Elevation, Emigration, and Destiny of the Colored People of the United States*, dated 1852, Delany is still thinking of emigration on the American continent itself (though in the appendix he discusses East Africa); however, when in 1859 he paid a visit to West Africa he had become a warm advocate of 'Africa for the Africans'.

115. Wilmore's position is that the black church, as the preeminent institutional expression of the black religious consciousness, gave political and theological foundations to black nationalism and pan-Africanism: 'Not only did it provide the organizational skills requisite for mass movements in the twentieth century, it provided also the spiritual inspiration and philosophical rationale – building blocks for the structure of African and Afro-American solidarity as it developed from the early DuBois to Malcolm X' (op.cit., 133f.).

116. Ibid., 126-33, cf.155f. The champions of missionary emigrationism constantly return to the prophetic biblical text Ps.68.31: 'Princes shall come out of Egypt, and Ethiopia shall stretch forth her hands unto God' (Wilmore, op.cit., 112f., 121); this text is also extremely important for the Rastafarian movement of our days.

117. Marable, op.cit., 96, writes: 'Throughout Afro-American history, the élite has been overwhelmingly integrationist and anti-nationalist, while the majority of working class and rural blacks have more often been mobilized to support nationalist ideas and movements.'

118. In *From Plantation to Ghetto*, 204, however, August Meier and Elliott Rudwick comment: 'Booker T. Washington's public image as an accommodator was one thing; his covert behind-the-scenes activity was another. Privately he appeared to contradict his public stance... Overtly he might urge blacks to acquiesce in the separate-but-equal doctrine; privately he had entrée to white social circles in the North and abroad that few Southern whites could enter, and secretly he aided the fight against railroad segregation.'

119. For these reasons Washington's nationalism was termed 'economic and educational nationalism'.

120. Cf. Marable, op.cit., 96; the best known studies of the Nation of Islam are E.U. Essien-Udom, *Black Nationalism: A Search for Identity in America*, Chicago University Press, 1962, and C. Eric Lincoln, *The Black Muslims in America*, Beacon Press, Boston 1961.

121. In *The Fire Next Time* James Baldwin gives an impressive account of his encounter with the Nation of Islam and Elijah Muhammad. He sees power as a central theme in the nationalism of the Black Muslims: 'Power was the subject of the speeches I heard. We were offered, as Nation of Islam doctrine, historical and divine proof that all white people are cursed,

and are devils, and are about to be brought down... But very little time was spent on theology, for one did not need to prove to a Harlem audience that all white men were devils. They were merely glad to have, at last, divine corroboration of their experience, to hear – and it was a tremendous thing to hear – that they had been lied to for all these years and generations, and that their captivity was ending, for God was black' (Dell Edition 1978, 70f.).

122. After his death in 1975 Elijah Muhammad was succeeded by his son Wallace Deen Muhammad. He very soon changed the name to 'World Community of Islam in the West', took over the most orthodox doctrinal positions of Islam, gave up the ideal of a separate state and declared the organization open to whites. This drastic turn-around led to great internal tensions. At the beginning of 1981 Louis Farrakhan announced a return to the principles of Elijah Muhammad. According to Manning Marable the widespread popularity of Malcolm X who left the Nation in 1964 was one of the causes of the decline of the Black Muslims: 'Malcolm's great prestige, which was upheld uniformly by every tendency of the new Black Power and Pan Africanist Movements, placed the Nation in an extemely difficult position' (op.cit., 113).

123. J.W.Schulte Nordholt, *Het volk dat in duisternis wandelt*, Arnhem 1957, 213. Garvey's thought world can best be explored through Amy Jacques Garvey, *The Philosophy and Opinions of Marcus Garvey*, Atheneum 1974. See further Edmund D.Cronon, *Black Moses*, University of Wisconsin Press 1964: Theodore G.Vincent, *Black Power and the Garvey Movement*, Pathfinder Press of New York 1971; Tony Martin. *Race First: The Ideological and Organizational Struggles of Marcus Garvey and the Universal Negro Improvement Association*, Greenwood Press, Westport, Conn.1976.

124. Cf. Pinkney, op.cit., 287f.

125. Wilmore, op.cit., 148.

126. Richard Leter in August Meier, Elliott Rudwick and Francis L.Broderick (eds.), *Black Protest Thought in the Twentieth Century*, Hill and Wang ²1971, 469-84.

127. Cone, *Black Theology and Black Power*, 8.

128. Stokely Carmichael and Charles V. Hamilton, *Black Power. The Politics of Liberation in America*, Random House 1967, 4-6, 22.

129. Ibid., 2-32; Robert L.Allen, *Black Awakening in Capitalist America*, Doubleday 1969, 7ff., 52-5; James Boggs, *Racism and the Class Struggle*, Monthly Review 1970, 136ff., 154ff.

130. George Breitman, *The Last Year of Malcolm X, The Evolution of a Revolutionary*, Pathfinder Press of New York 1967, 68: 'Malcolm was beginning to think about the need to replace capitalism with socialism if racism was to be eliminated. He was not sure if it could be done, and he was not sure how it could be done, but he was beginning to believe that that was the road to be traveled.' For a first survey of the life and work of Malcolm X see *The Autobiography of Malcolm X*, Grove Press 1965 and Hutchinson 1966. See also Peter Goldman, *The Death and Life of Malcolm X*, Harper and Row 1973; George Breitman (ed.), *Malcolm X Speaks*,

Grove Press 1966; George Breitman (ed.), *By Any Means Necessary; Speeches, Interviews and a Letter by Malcolm X*, Pathfinder Press of New York 1970.

131. In an interview published shortly after his death in 1965, Malcolm X says: 'It is impossible for capitalism to survive, primarily because the system of capitalism needs some blood to suck... As the nations of the world free themselves, then capitalism has less victims, less to suck, and it becomes weaker and weaker. It's only a matter of time in my opinion before it will collapse completely' (Breitman, *Malcolm X Speaks*, 199).

132. Nathan Wright, *Black Power and Urban Unrest*, New York 1967, 62.

133. Allen, op.cit., 130-2, cf. 43, 55ff., 161f.

134. Ibid., 178: 'The theory was that such a class would ease ghetto tensions by providing living proof to black dissidents that they can assimilate into the system if only they discipline themselves and work at it tirelessly.' Cf. also Paul A.Baran and Paul M.Sweezy, *Monopoly Capital* (1966), Pelican Books 1977, 266f.

135. Allen, op.cit., 179ff.: automation and economic recession are the main causes for the failure of the approach, 190f. From the figures which William Julius Wilson gives in The *Declining Significance of Race*, 88-92, it appears that in fact the relationship between black and white unemployment in the period after the Second World war has constantly remained the same: the black population has twice as many unemployed, despite the civil rights movement and Black Power. For example in 1966 the percentage of whites out of work was 3.3 and that of blacks 7.3; in 1969 the ratio was 3.1 to 6.2; in 1972 5.0 to 10.0. In the 1970s unemployment among black young people assumed gigantic proportions and grew in relationship to the percentage of unemployed white youth. The unfavourable developments in the 1970s therefore have, according to Wilson, partly to do with the growth of corporate enterprises: 'The growth of the corporate sector has resulted in the expansion of industrial technology and thereby in an increase in the number of workers victimized by technological unemployment... In the face of the decreasing demand for labor and the more rigorous prerequisites for higher levels of employment, teenagers and other workers entering the labor market for the first time find it increasingly difficult to obtain employment in the corporate sector. Blacks constitute a sizable percentage of both corporate sector workers who have become redundant because of advancing technology and the new job-seekers locked out of this sector of the economy' (97).

136. See Philip S.Foner (ed.), *The Black Panthers Speak*, Lippincott 1970; Bobby Seale, *Seize the Time: The Story of the Black Panther Party and Huey P.Newton*, Random House 1970.

137. See Ch.2, n.35.

138. Carmichael and Hamilton, op.cit., 44.

139. Richard M.Nixon was not wholly wrong when on 25 April 1968 he declared: 'What most of the militants are asking is not separation, but to be included in – not as supplicants, but as owners, as entrepreneurs – to have a share of the wealth and a piece of the action.' And Nixon continued

with the view that government policy must move in this direction: 'It ought to be oriented toward more black ownership, for from this can flow the rest – black pride, black jobs, black opportunity and yes, black power, in the best, the constructive sense of that often misapplied term...' (Allen, op.cit., 193).

140. Harding, op.cit., 202f.
141. Ibid., 204.
142. Ibid., 202.
143. Cited by Marable, op.cit., 106.
144. Ibid., 106.
145. Pinkney, op.cit., 122-6.
146. Marable, op.cit., 110.
147. Ibid., 114.
148. See n.46 above.
149. Marable, op.cit., 190.
150. See Ch.2, n.1.
151. Breitman, *The Last Year of Malcolm X*, 111.
152. See T.Witvliet, 'Verzwegen geschiedenis van een zwart volk', *Wending* 34.2, 2, February 1979, 100-7.
153. Pinkney, op.cit., 127; cf Ch.1 n.93.
154. *The Autobiography of Malcolm X*, 179.
155. Lehmann, op.cit., 194ff.
156. Pinkney, op.cit., 129ff., 140ff.
157. King, *Where Do We Go From Here?*, 37; for this section see also Boesak, *Farewell to Innocence*, 52-6.
158. King, op.cit., 38.
159. If King was a pastmaster in demonstrating the contradictions of the existing order, with his great rhetorical gifts Malcolm X did precisely the same thing in a more aggressive way. One example of this is the way in which he speaks about the use of violence in his famous 'Message to the Grass Roots': 'If violence is wrong in America, violence is wrong abroad. If it is wrong to be violent defending black women and black children and black babies and black men, then it is wrong for America to draft us and make us violent abroad in defense of her. And if it is right for America to draft us, and teach us how to be violent in defense of her, then it is right for you and me to do whatever is necessary to defend our own people right here in this country' (*Malcolm X Speaks*, ed. George Breitman, 8).
160. King, *Why We Can't Wait*, 93f.; *Where Do We Go from Here?*, 64.
161. Vincent Harding, 'The Religion of Black Power', in Donald R.Cutler (ed.), *The Religious Situation*, Beacon Press, Boston 1968, 21f.
162. *The Autobiography of Malcolm X*, 220. Cf. 200, 241f., 368ff.
163. In black nationalism this tendency towards assimilation was often connected with the difference between house niggers and field niggers; the slaves who worked inside the house were far more exposed to the white life-style and inclined to imitate it than the slaves on the land. Thus LeRoi Jones (Imamu Amiri Baraka), *Blues People*, William Morrow 1963, 33, thinks: 'The house Negroes, who spent their lives finding new facets of the white culture that they could imitate, were the first to adopt Christianity.

And they and their descendants, even today, practice the most European or American forms of Christianity. The various Episcopal and Presbyterian churches of the North were invariably started by the black freedmen, who were usually the sons and daughters of "house niggers".'

164. The classic work on the black bourgeoisie is that by the black sociologist E.Franklin Frazier, *Black Bourgeoisie*, Free Press of Glencoe, Illinois 1957; according to Franklin Frazier the black bourgeoisie was dominated by pressure for social status and to that end it made itself a world of make-believe. 'This world of make-believe, to be sure, is a reflection of the values of American society, but it lacks the economic basis that would give it roots in the world of reality. In escaping into a world of make-believe, middle-class Negroes have rejected both identification with the Negro and his traditional culture. Through delusions of wealth and power they have sought identification with the white America which continues to reject them. But these delusions leave them frustrated because they are unable to escape from the emptiness and futility of their existence' (237).

165. The great migration from the South to the North and West took place during the First World War as a result of a combination of circumstances; whereas as a result of the war situation there was a growing need in the industrial North for unskilled or semi-skilled workers, in the agrarian South many blacks were driven off the land by the plague of the boll weevil, by great floods in Mississippi and Alabama, and more generally, by advances in agricultural technology which put many black landworkers out of their jobs. See John Hope Franklin, *From Slavery to Freedom, A History of Negro Americans*, Knopf [3]1969, 471-5; Meier and Rudwick, *From Plantation to Ghetto*, 212-19.

166. Cf. Cone, *Black Theology and Black Power*, 105.

167. 'Negro Churches (in the USA)', *Encyclopaedia Britannica* [15]1974, 938.

168. See Lawrence N.Jones, 'The Black Churches. A New Agenda?' *The Christian Century*, 18 April 1979, 434.

169. Ibid., 436; Wilmore, op.cit., 161.

170. Cf. Boggs, op.cit., 23; Baran and Sweezy, op.cit., 257-62.

171. The social gospel movement did not entirely pass by the black churches between the two world wars. Wilmore, op.cit., 160f., mentions in this connection great urban communities like R.C.Ransom's Institutional AME Church in Chicago, H.H.Proctor's Congregational Church in Atlanta and Adam Clayton Powell Sr's Abyssinian Baptist Church in New York.

172. Wilmore, op.cit., 162; for a concise survey of all three factors see 160-66.

173. As one example I quote a passage in which the power of the Spirit speaks clearly: 'On Sunday mornings the women all seemed patient, all the men seemed mighty. While John watched, the Power struck someone, a man or a woman; they cried out, a long, wordless crying, and, arms outstretched like wings, they began the Shout. Someone moved a chair a little to give them room, the rhythm paused, the singing stopped, only the pounding feet and the clapping hands were heard; then another cry, another dancer; then the tambourines began again, and the voices rose again, and

the music swept on again, like fire, or flood, or judgment. Then the church seemed to swell with the Power it held and, like a planet rocking in space, the temple rocked with the Power of God' (Corgi Books 1963, 15f.).

174. For a description of the different cults, see Joseph R.Washington, *Black Sects and Cults*, Doubleday 1972; Arthur H.Fauset, *Black Gods of the Metropolis*, University of Pennsylvania Press 1944; cf. also C.Eric Lincoln (ed.), *The Black Experience in Religion*, Doubleday 1974, 195-272.

175. See Chapter 2 n.35.

176. Wilmore, op.cit., 172; however, he notes: 'Despite the dechristianization process I have described, the separation of black radicalism from Christian roots was never completely achieved during the 1960s. Even the Muslims were affected by patterns of church life by former Christian ministers who crossed over into their ranks with vestiges of their old faith still clinging to their preaching, and particularly by the fact that these followers of Allah continued to make an important place for Jesus. In a negative way their anti-Christian diatribe backed them into a grudging esteem for authentic Christianity'(188).

177. The text of the declaration is included in Wilmore and Cone (ed.), *Black Theology: A Documentary History, 1966-1979*, 23-30, and in Warner R.Traynham, *Christian Faith in Black and White: A Primer in Theology from the Black Perspective*, Parameter Press, Wakefield, Mass 1973, 66-72. For explanation and commentary see Wilmore, op.cit., 195-8, and Vincent Harding, 'No Turning Back', *Renewal* X, 7, October-November 1970; see also the recent book by James H.Cone, *For My People. Black Theology and the Black Church*, Orbis Books, Maryknoll 1984, 10-14.

178. A sociological investigation by Gary T.Marx comes to the following conclusion: '...the greater the religious involvement, whether measured in terms of ritual activity, orthodoxy of religious belief, subjective importance of religion, or the three taken together, the lower the degree of militancy.' See Gary T.Marx, 'Religion: Opiate or Inspiration of Civil Rights Militancy among Negroes',in Meier and Rudwick, *The Making of Black America* II, 364; cf.id., *Protest and Prejudice*, Hill and Wang 1969, 94-105.

179. Wilmore, op.cit., 233, describes Jackson like this: 'Jackson represented the old-style, Bookerite leadership, essentially survivalist in character but certainly not against racial progress. This element of black Baptist leadership was rather committed to a nonconfrontational, conservative amelioration of the racial *status quo*.' Joseph H.Jackson's political and theological views are well summmed up by Peter J.Paris, *Black Leaders in Conflict*, Pilgrim Press 1978, 44-70, 176-83, 227-35. For his criticism of black theology see also Wilmore and Cone, *Black Theology: A Documentary History*, 257-61. In autumn 1982 Jackson was succeeded as president of the National Baptist Convention USA by the more progressive T.J.Jemison.

180. For the significance of Black Religion in the origin of black theology see ch.2 n.16.

181. Joseph R.Washington, *Black Religion*, Beacon Press, Boston 1964, 141.

182. See Dorothy Sterling, *Freedom Train: The Story of Harriet Tubman*,

Doubleday 1954, and Jacqueline Bernard, *Journey Toward Freedom: The Story of Sojourner Truth*, Dell 1967.

183. See Wilmore, op.cit., 195f.

184. Ibid., 195ff. Dr Benjamin Payton was executive of the Commission on Religion and Race of the American Council of Churches. The contrast between the North and the South comes into the relationship of NCNC to SCLC. NCNC consisted of mainly northern church leaders who were very familiar with the living conditions of blacks in the ghettos. However, the fact that the majority of them belonged to predominantly white church denominations explains why NCNC had little influence on the leadership of the black churches.

185. Wilmore, op.cit., 199, writes: 'It was the black folk of Watts, Newark, Detroit, and hundreds of other communities across the nation and the young men and women of the SNCC and northern-based nationalist groups who convinced black ministers that the church was expendable if it proved unwilling to immerse itself in the vortex of the black power movement.'

186. Wilmore and Cone, op.cit., 23; cf. ch.2 n.15.

187. Ibid., 26.

188. Ibid.

189. Cf. Boesak, *Coming in out of the Wilderness*, 48.

190. Harding, op.cit., 26; see the quotation in ch.1 n.115.

191. Wilmore and Cone, 25: also 'Our beloved country', 23.

192. According to Wilmore, op.cit., 197-200, King did not react to the 13 July 1966 advertisement; however, at the end of 1967 he changed his attitude and sought to collaborate with the setting up of cadre training for clergy in some strategically important cities. Some of his closest collaborators joined the NCBC.

193. This declaration interprets the outbursts of violence in the ghettos as riots – the term which was used by the media. By contrast militant blacks spoke of insurrections.

194. It is not completely clear when the expression 'black theology' came into vogue. There seems no doubt that Cone's first book gave the term general currency. But before 1969 the expression was already being used in NCBC circles; Wilmore speaks on different occasions of 'black theology' in his report on the activities of the NCBC theological commission which appeared in the autumn of 1968, cf. Traynham, op.cit., 83-96. For the origin of the term see Wilmore and Cone, op.cit., 67, and Cone, *For My People*, 19-24.

195. For the logic which underlies the epistemological break see ch.1, 3 (especially 3b. Second Phase. Break and Continuity). See also Witvliet, *A Place in the Sun*, ch.2. The phrase 'epistemological break' derives from the French philosopher Gaston Bachelard, who in his epistemology uses the term 'rupture' to indicate the shift from non-scientific knowledge to scientific knowledge; Althusser speaks of an epistemological caesura (*'coupure'*). The first declaration of the Ecumenical Association of Third World Theologians (EATWOT) of 1976 mentions readiness for a 'radical break in epistemology' (see Witvliet, op.cit., 31, 35-42).

196. Washington, op.cit., 143.

197 Cone, *My Soul Looks Back*, Abingdon Press, Nashville 1982, 36f.: 'It is revealing to note that during my nearly six years of residence at Garrett-Northwestern, not one text written by a black person was ever used as a required reading for a class... Equally problematic for my stay at Garrett was the absence of the discussion of racism as a theological problem. For a black person who was born in the South and whose church came into being because of racism, the failure to discuss it as a central problem appeared strange and racist to me.'

198. J.Deotis Roberts, op.cit., 85.

199 Cited by Dr Paul Kraemer, at that time on the staff of the Urban Training Centre, in his Chicago Journal, which he wrote for the monthly journal *Wending* 23.3, March 1968, 218.

200. Wilmore stresses that black theology was in fact born in the ghetto pastorate when he says: 'A few theological professors participated in the movement from the beginning, but it was men like Albert B.Cleage, Jr, Lawrence Lucas (a Harlem Roman Catholic priest) and Calvin Marshall (an AME Zion minister in Brooklyn) who were preaching every Sunday in the ghettos of the nation and hammering out the first tenets of a Black Theology on the anvil of their experience' (Wilmore and Cone, op.cit., 67f.).

201. A second book by Cleage is *Black Christian Nationalism*, William Morrow 1972.

202. Harding, *No Turning Back?*, 7ff.: cf. Cone, *For My People*, 88-92.

203. James Cone observes, op.cit., 91: '...although the NCNC and black caucuses attacked white religion on the basis of black power philosophy, their organizational existence depended on money from the white churches that they attacked. Black independent churches did not involve themselves in the attack on white religion and thus did not provide much financial support for the NCC. NCBC support came from the pressure that black executives applied to their white constituencies.'

204. Thus the Black Power declaration, 31 July 1966, by NCBC, Wilmore and Cone, op.cit., 27.

205. Wilmore, op.cit., 199.

206. See the important report by Wilmore on the activities of the commission, in Traynham, op.cit., 83-96.

207. Wilmore, op.cit., 215.

208. Wilmore and Cone, op.cit., 101.

209. Ibid., 100.

210. Ibid., 101, on the effect of the demand for reparations on the setting up of the special fund for the Programme to Combat Racism by the World Council of Churches, see Wilmore, op.cit., 206, 267, and John Vincent, *The Race Race*, SCM Press 1970, 42-8.

211. Cone, op.cit., 11, mentions among others the Alamo Black Clergy of the San Francisco Bay area, Black Methodists for Church Renewal (BMCR), the Interreligious Foundation for Community Organization (IFCO), and the Philadelphia Council of Black Clergy. Roman Catholic clergy were also affected by black theology from the beginning. See above

all Lawrence Lucas, *Black Priest/ White Church*, Random House 1970, and Edward K.Braxton, *The Wisdom Community*, Paulist Press, New York 1980. Cone, op.cit., 51, comments: 'As a black Protestant who looks at the Catholic Church from the outside, the immensity of the task of trying to challenge the tradition of Catholic theology and also to remain inside the church is so great that it overwhelms me. But despite the extent of the task and because of the foundation laid in the 1960s there are young Catholics (priests, sisters, and lay persons), who are determined to develop a black theology that is accountable to their experience in both the black and Catholic communities.'

212. Cf. ibid., 17, 24, 102.

213. Cone, op.cit., 99, writes of the place of the black church: 'Beginning in the late eighteenth century and continuing to the present, it has been the oldest and most independent African-American organization. Its importance is so great that some scholars say that the black church is the black community, with each having no identity apart from the other. Even if some will deny this claim, no informed person can deny the centrality of the black church in the black community.'

214. See Wilmore in Wilmore and Cone, op.cit., 4ff., and Cone, in Cone, op.cit., 24-8.

215. Cone, op.cit., 25f.; see also *Theological Education* VI.3, Spring 1970, and the supplement.

216. The beginning of this third phase is marked by the declaration *Black Theology in 1976*, which I discussed in chapter 2, sections 1 and 2.

217. It is clear how stubborn this misunderstanding is from the question which James Cone claims to have been asked most over the last ten years: 'How do you reconcile the separatist and violent orientation of black theology with Martin Luther King's emphasis on integration, love and non-violence?', see James H.Cone, 'Martin Luther King Jr, Black Theology – Black Church', *Theology Today*, January 1984, 410.

218. For a criticism of *Black and White Power Subreption* see Allan Boesak, *Farewell To Innocence*, 74f. For a bibliographical survey of black theology between 1966 and 1979 see the annotated bibliography by Vaughn T.Eason in Wilmore and Cone, op.cit., 624-37, though this does not mention *Black and White Power Subreption*, Beacon Press, Boston 1969 (another omission is Henry Mitchell, *Black Preaching*, Westminster Press, Philadelphia 1970).

219. For the differences between Albert Cleage and Cone see James H.Cone, *For My People*, 225f.

220. See J.Deotis Roberts, *Liberation and Reconciliation: A Black Theology*, Westminster Press, Philadelphia 1971, cf. 23, 72, 117, and *A Black Political Theology*, 205-222. James Cone, *God of the Oppressed*, Seabury Press, New York 1975. 239-46, and in Wilmore and Cone, op.cit., 612ff.

221. Preston N.Williams, 'James Cone and the Problem of a Black Ethic', *Harvard Theological Review* 65, October 1972, 483-4.

222. Ibid., 438.

223. Ibid., 494. Cone's answer is in *God of the Oppressed*, 203-6.

224. James Cone writes in *For My People*, 18: 'Although I wrote the first two books on black theology and have been at the center of many of the debates regarding its meaning, it was Wilmore's theological expertise and imagination that laid the foundation for the early development of black theology. He is the one most responsible for the positive response of the NCBC to my writings and those of Preston Williams, J.Deotis Roberts, and C.Eric Lincoln. He has also been our most creative critic.'

225. Wilmore, op.cit, 214.

226. Karl Barth, Postscript in the *Schleiermacher Auswahl* by Heinz Bolli, Siebenstern Taschenbuch 113/114. 1968, 294.

227. On the significance for theology of the outbreak of the First World War in Autumn 1914 see above all Dieter Schellong, 'Theologie nach 1914', in *Richte unsere Füsse auf den Weg des Friedens*, ed. Andreas Baudis, Munich 1979, 251-68.

228. As is well known, for Barth the epistemological break was caused in particular by the manifesto of the ninety-three German intellectuals who identified themselves with the war aims of Kaiser Wilhelm II. In the Postscript, 293, Barth writes: 'A whole world of theological exegesis, ethics, dogmatics and preaching which hitherto I had regarded as basically credible was shaken to the foundations as a result , and with it the rest of what one read in German theologians.' See also Eberhard Busch, *Karl Barth*, SCM Press and Fortress Press 1976, 81-3.

229. Barth, 'Postscript', 294: 'It was Thurneysen who once quietly whispered to me in confidence, "What we need for preaching, teaching and pastoral care is a wholly other theological foundation".'

230. In the preface to the second edition of *Anselm; Fides Quaerens Intellectum*, SCM Press and John Knox Press 1969, 11, Barth says: 'Most commentators have completely failed to see that in this book about Anselm I am working with a vital key, if not the key, to an understanding of that whole process of thought that has impressed me more and more in my *Church Dogmatics* as the only one proper to theology.'

231. James H.Cone, *God of the Oppressed*, 6.

232. James H.Cone, *The Spirituals and the Blues*, Seabury Press, New York 1972, 1ff.

233. Quoted by Cone, *The God of the Oppressed*, 7.

234. Cone, *My Soul Looks Back*, 23.

235. Ibid., 19-23, 50, 57.

236. In an intriguing footnote in *A Black Theology of Liberation*, 28, Cone writes: 'When I say that white theology is not Christian theology, I mean the theology which has been written without any reference to the oppressed of the land. This is not true of Karl Barth and certainly not true of Dietrich Bonhoeffer. Even Reinhold Niebuhr's *Moral Man and Immoral Society* moves in the direction of blackness.' The fact that blackness here serves as another word for oppressed – in *Black Theology and Black Power*, 151, he can say, 'Being Black in America has very little to do with skin color' – is connected with the fact that in this period he did not yet feel that his dependence on Barth and Bonhoeffer was a problem.

237. In *God of the Oppressed*, 7, Cone writes about his first books:

'Reflecting on thse books I realized that something important was missing. They did not show clearly enough the significance of Macedonia A.M.E.Church and the imprint of that community upon my theological consciousness.'

238. Klauspeter Blaser, *Wenn Gott Schwarz wäre...*, Zurich and Freiburg 1972, 285. Unfortunately this suggestion is not sufficiently developed.

239. Cone, *My Soul Looks Back*, 45.

240. In *Black Theology and Black Power*, 89, Cone writes...: 'The black revolution is the work of Christ.' See also 37. 'If the gospel of Christ, as Moltmann suggests, frees a man to be for those who labor and are heavily laden, the humiliated and abused, then it would seem that for twentieth-century America the message of Black Power is the message of Christ himself.' See further 38, 48, 61, 112.

241. Blaser, op.cit., 290.

242. Helmut Gollwitzer, 'Why Black Theology?', in Wilmore and Cone, *Black Theology. A Documentary History*, 165.

243. This lecture is included in Karl Barth, *The Word of God and the Word of Man* (1928), reissued Harper Torchbooks 1957, 51-96 (see esp. 80f.). The remarkable thing about this lecture is, among other things, that it has striking analogies to what Dietrich Bonhoeffer was later to write in his *Letters and Papers from Prison* about worldliness and the *disciplina arcana*, see B.E.Benktson, 'Christus und die mündiggewordene Welt. Eine Studie zur Theologie Dietrich Bonhoeffers', *Svensk teologisch Kvartalskrift* 40, 1964, 2.

244. Ibid., 68.

245. Ibid., 69.

246. Ibid., 76.

247. Dieter Schellong has referred to this in his essay 'Theologie nach 1914', 455.

248. See Ch.1 n.206.

249. Schellong, op.cit., 455.

250. Quoted in Gollwitzer, op.cit., 164.

251. See *Black Theology and Black Power*, 103-15, and *A Black Theology of Liberation*, 236f. (see also 186-96).

252. Quoted by Cone, *The Spirituals and the Blues*, 53; *God of the Oppressed*, 112.

253. See n.236.

254. See above all Cone, *My Soul Looks Back*, 81, and Wilmore and Cone, op.cit. 453, where Cone mentions the Cuban theology of Sergio Arce Martínez as a theology which more than Latin American liberation theology takes the Bible as a starting point and consequently has a great affinity with black theology.

255. See Cone, A Black Theology of Liberation, 47-81.

256. Cone, *Black Theology and Black Power*, 38.

257. Ibid., 69; cf. also *A Black Theology of Liberation*, 218f.: 'The importance of the concept of the Black Christ is that it expresses the concreteness of Christ's continued presence today.'

258. Although in *Black Theology and Black Power*, 6, Cone can describe

black power in general terms as 'complete emancipation of black people from white oppression by whatever means black people deem necessary', for him black power is in the first place an event which takes place at the level of the human psyche, cf. 8, where black power is seen as an attitude, 'an inward affirmation of the essential worth of blackness', and 28, where Cone says, 'Freedom is what happens to a man on the inside.' This strong emphasis on the inward, psychological side of the process of liberation becomes understandable when we remember that black slavery and racism involved the total destruction of the humanity of the black. For that reason alone one cannot therefore reduce racism to a derivative of the class struggle. Therefore Cone, 7, can use Tillich's analysis of 'the courage to be' in order to understand black power as the courage 'to affirm one's being by striking out at the dehumanizing forces which threaten being'. This 'courage to be' is not only a condition for the struggle against racism but at the same time an essential ingredient of it. When Cone see Black Power as the work of Christ one needs to remember that for him in the last instance black power involves no less than the becoming human of the black person.

259. Cone, *A Black Theology of Liberation*, 62.

260. Theodor W.Adorno, *Negative Dialectics*, Routledge and Seabury Press 1973, 28.

261. Dr L.Schuurman has pointed to the difference between this onto-logical thought and the stress on the factical in Barth in a regrettably unpublished lecture on Barth and liberation theology. Cf. also Witvliet, *A Place in the Sun*, 131-47.

262. Karl Barth, *Church Dogmatics* I.2, Edinburgh 1956, 429.

263. Cone, *A Black Theology of Liberation*, 27.

264. Paul Tillich, *Systematic Theology* I, Chicago University Press 1951, reissued SCM Press 1978, 239f.

265. In *Theology of Culture*, Oxford University Press 1959, 59, Tillich says: 'Religious symbols are taken from the infinity of material which the experienced reality gives us. Everything in time and space has become at some time in the history of religion a symbol for the Holy. And this is naturally so, because everything that is in the world we encounter rests on the ultimate ground of being. This is the key to the otherwise extremely confusing history of religion.'

266. Tillich, *Systematic Theology* I, 34.

267. Ibid., 34-68.

268. Ibid., 52.

269. Tillich, *Systematic Theology* III, Chicago University Press 1963, reissued SCM Press 1978, 4: Cone, op.cit., 62.

270. J.Sperna Weiland, 'Theologie als dialoog', *Wending* 20.4, June 1965, 240.

271. Cone, op.cit., 61.

272. Ibid., 62.

273. Ibid., 69; in this connection Cone cites John Macquarrie, *Principles of Christian Theology*, SCM Press and Scribner 1966, 8.

274. Ibid., 80.

275. Cone, *Black Theology and Black Power*, 120.

276. Wilmore, op,cit., 217f., puts his concern like this: 'It is appropriate to ask whether black theology is simply the blackenization of the whole spectrum of traditional or classic Christian theology, with particular emphasis upon the operation of the oppressed, or is it singular, or is it something else? In other words, does it find in the experience of the oppression of blacks in the Western world, as black, a singular religious meaning?'

277. Cone, op.cit., 31; cf. also Ch.1 n.66. Although Cone's theology even in his first books inclines towards a pneumatological christology in which the situation is a sphere that is clearly at the disposal of the creative event of God's living Word, numerous formulations show that methodologically he is still in the old schema in which the gospel and the situation are two independent entities which must be brought together by the one who does theology.

278. See ch.1, section 2.

4. Liberation

1. Cf. the excursus in Chapter 1. See also Theo Witvliet, 'De verzwegen geschiedenis van een zwart volk', *Wending* 34.2, February 1979, 100-7.

2. Vincent Harding, 'The Uses of the Afro-American Past', in Donald R.Cutler (ed.), *The Religious Situation 1969*, Beacon Press, Boston 1969, 829f.

3. Cited by Lawrence W.Levine, *Black Culture and Black Consciousness*, Oxford University Press, New York 1977, XIII.

4. W.E.B.DuBois, *The Souls of Black Folk* (1903), Dodd, Mead, New York 1967, 16f. See also Chapter 1, 49.

5. Gayraud S.Wilmore, *Black Religion and Black Radicalism*, Orbis Books, Maryknoll ²1983, 218.

6. Ibid., 234; cf. also 219, 223.

7. Cecil Wayne Cone, *The Identity Crisis of Black Theology*, Abingdon Press, Nashville 1975, 24.

8. Ibid., 141ff.

9. Gayraud S.Wilmore, *The Union Seminary Quarterly Review* XXXI,1, 1976, 56-8.

10. James H.Cone, 'Epilogue: An Interpretation of the Debate Among Black Theologians', in Gayraud S.Wilmore and James H.Cone (eds.), *Black Theology: A Documentary History 1966-1979*, Orbis Books, Maryknoll 1979, 620.

11. William R.Jones, *Is God a White Racist? A Preamble to Black Theology*, Anchor Press, Garden City 1973, Part 3, esp. 196f. A summary article by him had appeared earlier in the *Harvard Theological Review* 64, 1971, 541-57, under the title 'Theodicy and Methodology in Black Theology. A Critique of Washington, Cone and Cleage'. Cf. also Warren McWilliams, 'Theodicy according to James Cone', in *The Journal of Religious Thought* 36.2, Fall-Winter 1979-80, 45-54.

12. William R.Jones, 'The Case for Black Humanism', in Calvin R. Bruce

and William R.Jones (ed.), *Black Theology II. Essays on the Formation and Outreach of Contemporary Black Theology*, 230f.

13. Charles H.Long, 'Structural Similarities and Dissimilarities in Black and African Theologies', *The Journal of Religious Thought* 33, Fall-Winter 1975, 19. Other important works by Long are: 'The Black Reality: Toward a Theology of Freedom', *Criterion*, Spring-Summer 1969, 2-7; 'Perspectives for a Study of Afro-American Religion in the United States', *History of Religions*, Vol.2, 1971, 54-66; 'The Oppressive Elements in Religion and the Religions of the Oppressed', *Harvard Theological Review* 69, 1976, 397-412; 'Freedom, Otherness and Religion: Theologies Opaque', *The Chicago Theological Seminary Register* LXXIII, Winter 1983, 13-24.

14. Long, 'Structural Similarities and Dissimilarities', 20, 22f. Here Long refers to the philosophical phenomenology of Paul Ricoeur, who in the second part of his *Philosophie de la volonté* which deals with *Finitude et Culpabilité* devotes a whole book to the symbolism of evil in which he points to *soillure, péché* and *culpabilité* as primary symbols. What intrigues Long in Ricoeur's analysis is that Ricoeur sees the symbol as a structure of meaning in which a direct, primary, literal meaning points to an indirect, secondary, hidden one: 'The symbol, the originative source of all human meaning and expression, is not transparent but opaque: one cannot see through it; one could almost say that the symbol is black' (22). For a description of symbol in Ricoeur see above all *The Conflict of Interpretations*, Northwestern University Press 1974, 28f.

15. Ibid., 21.

16. Long refers to the dialectic of lordship and bondage at greatest length in 'The Oppressive Elements in Religion and the Religions of the Oppressed', 408-12; see also 'Freedom, Otherness and Religion: Theologies Opaque', 22. Long's reference to Hegel is somewhat indirect; he quotes from the last chapter of David Brion Davis, *The Problem of Slavery in the Age of Revolution*, Cornell University Press 1975; Davis regards Hegel's analysis as 'the most profound analysis of slavery ever written' (558). However, Davis' work is in turn based on the French Hegel interpretation of the 1930s, when Alexandre Kojève interpreted Hegel's phenomenology at the École Pratique des Hautes Études to a group of students which included Sartre, Merleau-Ponty, Weil and Levinas. In 1947 Raymond Queneau edited these lectures under the title *Introduction à la lecture de Hegel*, Paris 1979. This interpretation by Kojève, which is sometimes described as Marxist, is controversial. For Hegel a reversal comes about in the dialectical movement: the master, who has subjected the slave to his will, finally proves to be the prisoner of his own power; he has robbed the slave of all independence and as a result has reduced him to a thing or an animal – except that he can now no longer be recognized as being master, since true recognition comes about only through self-awareness. According to Kojève, he thus arrives at an 'existential impasse' which he cannot escape. By contrast, the servant/slave, who for fear of death surrendered his selfhood and has become the possession of his master without a will of his own, has nothing to lose and as a result can develop an independent consciousness; he has an interest in radical change. His awareness comes

about through the work that he does in the service of his master: 'Granted, this work does not of itself bring about liberation. But while he changes the world through this work, he changes himself and thus creates new objective conditions, which put him in a position to wage the liberating struggle for recognition which in the first instance he rejected because of his fear of death' (Kojève, op.cit., 34).

The question is, however, whether in his *Phenomenology of Spirit* Hegel sought to give a paradigm of specific social relationships. But even if this should not be the case, it is nevertheless remarkable that David Brion Davis and Charles Long should see the dialectic of lordship and bondage described by Hegel as a theoretical model of the historical dynamic of black slavery. One might ask whether in Hegel history is not so much *a priori* taken up into the movement of the Spirit that justice is not done to its opaqueness. Perhaps, however, Davis is right when he says, 'It was Hegel's genius to endow lordship and bondage with such a resonance of meanings that the model could be applied to every form of physical and psychological domination' (564).

17. Long, 'Freedom, Otherness and Religion: Theologies Opaque', 22.

18. Levine, *Black Culture and Black Consciousness*, 5.

19. Mechal Sobel, *Trabelin' On*, Greenwood Press, Westport 1979, 148.

20. Donald G.Mathews, *Religion in the Old South*, University of Chicago Press 1977, 13. My description of evangelical faith owes much to Mathews's study.

21. Ibid., 42. Mathews adds: 'Perhaps even more intimate than ritualistic touching, however, was public confession of sin and sharing with others the deepest, most private thoughts about oneself and his relationships with other people and with God.'

22. For a more extended account of the ambiguous attitude of the churches to black slavery see my *A Place in the Sun*, SCM Press and Orbis Books, Maryknoll 1985, 53-63.

23. Mathews, op.cit., XVII and ch.3.

24. In addition to slaves, white women were also attracted by the evangelization movement, often much to the discontent of their husbands. Mathews writes: 'Women's conversion could very easily be interpreted as an independent action and a personal determination to develop oneself through a new ideology, even against the wishes of one's husband – or perhaps especially against the wishes of one's husband. The intimate bonds of the religious community must have provided some women with care, sense of worth, and companionship they did not receive from husbands' (op.cit., 105). If evangelical faith on the one hand gave women psychological and social space, on the other it developed a model of the ideal woman which was stifling: 'Evangelical women – endowed by the ideal with a unique capacity to sense religious and moral truth – were expected to personify the church itself in refined manners and pious attitudes' (120).

25. Sobel, op.cit., 101.

26, Eugene D.Genovese, *Roll, Jordan, Roll*, Oxford University Press, New York 1974, 211f., 246f., 274f., 278f.

27. Ibid., 246.

28. Cited in ibid., 254.

29. Donald G.Mathews, 'Religion and Slavery: The Case of the American South', in Christine Bolt and Seymour Drescher (eds.), *Anti-Slavery Religion and Reform*, Folkestone 1980, 230.

30. *The American Slave: A Composite Autobiography*, Vol.19, *God Struck Me Dead*, ed. George P.Rawick, Greenwood Press, Westport 1974, 85.

31. Olli Alho, *The Religion of the Slaves*, Helsinki 1976, 185.

32. Sobel, op.cit., XIXf., 14, 108f., 112f.

33. Ibid., 114.

34. Ibid., 115.

35. We see what happens by contrast if a 'conversion experience' is set in the context of a black feministic process of awareness from Ntozake Shange, *For Colored Girls Who Have Considered Suicide*: 'i was missing somethin/ somethin so important/ something promised/ a layin on of hands.../ makin me whole/... / i wanted to jump outta my bone and be done wit myself leave me alone and go on in the wind it waz too much i fell into a numbness til the only tree I could see took me up in her branches held me in the breeze made me dawn dew that chill at daybreak the sun wrapped me up swinging rose light everywhere... i waz cold/i waz burnin up/a child/ and endlessly weavin garments for the moon wit my tears i found god in myself and i loved her/ i loved her fiercely' (quoted in Cheryl Benard, *Die geschlossene Gesellschaft und ihre Rebellen*, Frankfurt am Main 1981, 32).

36. Cone, op.cit., 52.

37. Genovese, op.cit., 284.

38. George P.Rawick, *From Sundown to Sunup*, Greenwood Press, Westport 1972, 42-5, sees the upturned pot or kettle as a survival from Africa: he points out that in West Africa and the Caribbean such vessels were used for carrying water and sacred objects in religious ceremonies. For other possible explanations see Albert J.Raboteau, *Slave Religion*, Oxford University Press, New York 1978, 215f., 360.

39. Levine, op.cit., 33.

40. Marguerite Yourcenar, who has translated a large number of black spirituals, writes about them as follows: 'Seen as a whole, the texts of negro spirituals seem in fact to have emerged from the old store of the metaphors and formulae of Protestant hymnody. However, what is so miraculous about them is that the ornate and oratorical poetry of the Wesleyan and Methodist hymns of the eighteenth century or the emphatic and flat pietism of more recent hymns have ended up on black lips as these lyrical and dramatic marvels, these poems whose vivacious or solemn piety has rediscovered over the centuries something of the naked emotion of Villon or the tenderness of Franciscan poetry. Paradoxically, it is the primitivism of the newly converted negro, his instinct for rhythm, his profound sense of the sacred brought from black Africa, which has led him to retranslate the Christian drama with the fervour of the pious mediaeval peasant or of catechumens from the times of the catacombs', *Fleuve profound, sombre rivière* (1966), Paris 1980, 38f.

41. For the historical problems of interpreting the religions of illiterate peoples see J.H.Kamstra, 'Een moeilijke keuze: de godsdienst van de gewone man', *Tijdschrift voor Theologie* 30, 1980, 258-62.

42. Alho, op.cit., 233.

43. Levine, op.cit., 50.

44. Quoted in ibid., 50.

45. Quoted in Alho, op.cit., 79.

46. Levine, op.cit., 37.

47. Genovese, op.cit., 251.

48. Levine, op.cit., 35.

49. Quoted in Genovese, op.cit., 263.

50. Wilmore, op.cit., 48-52.

51. Ibid., 51.

52. See ibid., 53-73. The classical work on the slave revolts is Herbert Aptheker, *American Negro Slave Revolts*, International Publications, New York 1974 (new edition); but see also Marion D. de B.Kilson, 'Towards Freedom: An Analysis of Slave Revolts in the United States', in August Meier and Elliott Rudwick (eds.), *The Making of Black America* I, Atheneum Publications, New York 1971, 165-78. See also Gerald W.Mullin, *Flight and Rebellion. Slave Resistance in Eighteenth-Century Virginia*, Oxford University Press, New York 1972; John Lofton, *Insurrection in South Carolina: The Turbulent World of Denmark Vesey*, Kent State University Press 1964; Herbert Aptheker, *Nat Turner's Slave Rebellion*, Humanities Press, New York 1966; and Stephen B.Oates, *The Fires of Jubilee: Nat Turner's Fierce Rebellion*, Harper and Row 1975.

53. See the previous chapter, 1 (e).

54. Henry H.Mitchell, *Black Belief*, Harper and Row 1975, 120.

55. Wilmore, op.cit., 227-34.

56. Quoted in Alho, op.cit., 133f.

57. James H.Cone, 'Epilogue: An Interpretation of the Debate Among Black Theologians', in Gayraud Wilmore and James H.Cone (eds.), *Black Theology: A Documentary History, 1966-79*, Orbis Books, Maryknoll 1979, 618.

58. In his article 'Liberation Theism', in *Black Theology* II, ed. Calvin Bruce and William R.Jones, 239, J. Deotis Roberts comments: 'James Cone imposes ready-made theological structures in this material, and they do not fit.'

59. See especially the recent 'Freedom, Otherness and Religion: Theologies Opaque', in *The Chicago Theological Seminary Register*, 20f.

60. Mitchell, op.cit., 142, and 'Theological Posits of Black Christianity', in Bruce and Jones, *Black Theology* II, 129f.

61. Cone, op.cit., 619.

62. Wilmore, op.cit., 234f. For Cone's criticism see James H.Cone, *God of the Oppressed*, Seabury Press, New York 1975, 252f.

63. This is the way in which Long's position is described by James Cone in his book *My Soul Looks Back*, Abingdon Press, Nashville 1982, 60.

64. See Kamstra, op.cit., 254, 270-8.

65. See ch.1, section 4.

66. See ch.1, section 3.

67. The expression 'pneumatological obligation' is used in connection with theological methodology by Takatso A. Mofokeng, *The Crucified among the Crossbearers*, J.H.Kok, Kampen 1983, 66-8.

68. Mitchell, *Black Belief*, 136-52 (quotations 139, 141).

69. See James H.Cone, *Black Theology and Black Power*, Seabury Press, New York 1969, 103-15; *My Soul Looks Back*, 64-92; *For My People*, Orbis Books, Maryknoll 1984, 99-121.

70. O. Noordmans, Herschepping, Amsterdam 1959, 169.

71. H. Berkhof, *Christian Faith*, Eerdmans 1984, 329.

72. Cf. ibid., 324 cf. 326.

73. A contemporary example of this concrete, 'materialistic' and familiar way of conversing with Jesus is the impressive film *Woza Albert*, directed by Barney Simon, in which two black actors investigate (by means of interviews) and act out how black children, women and men react to the return of Jesus in black South Africa today.

74. Cone, *God of the Oppressed*, 35; see also 'The Content and Method of Black Theology', *The Journal of Religious Thought* 33, Fall-Winter 1975, 102f.

75. Ibid.

76. Cone, *God of the Oppressed*, 136.

77. Cone, op.cit., 34, and 'The Content and Method of Black Theology', 102f.

78. Cone, *God of the Oppressed*, VI.

79. Ibid., 267f., and Wilmore and Cone (eds.), *Black Theology. A Documentary History, 1966-1979*, 621f.

80. See Jones, 'The Case for Black Humanism', in Bruce and Jones (eds.), *Black Theology* II, 224, 226.

81. Cited in Benjamin Mays, *The Negro's God*, Negro University Press, New York 1969, 227, 229.

82. Long, op.cit., 20.

83. Paul Tillich, *Systematic Theology* 1, University of Chicago Press 1951, reissued SCM Press 1978, 134; see also Long, 'Structural Similarities and Dissimilarities in Black and African Theologies', 19.

84. Long, 'Freedom, Otherness and Religion: Theologies Opaque', 19, quotes in this connection the following sentence by the Indian writer Vine Deloria: 'Sometimes when people ask me what tribe I belong to, I am tempted to say Others.' With this and similar comments Deloria means to show the way in which American language and culture have assigned the original inhabitants to the category of 'a functional otherness' and to 'a state of transparency' (Long).

85. Long, op.cit., 22f.

86. Vine Deloria, *God is Red*, Dell 1973.

87. See Wilmore and Cone (eds.), *Black Theology: A Documentary History, 1966-1979*, 616.

88. Mofokeng, op.cit., 6-19.

89. The critical questions raised by Mofokeng on Sobrino are less important for our concerns, see op.cit., 108-11, 216-18.

90. Mofokeng makes the following comment on the differences between this interest in the life of Jesus and the nineteenth century quest of the historical Jesus: 'There is no attempt here to penetrate behind the gospel accounts of the story about Jesus of Nazareth with the intention of constructing a biography of Jesus that is verifiable by means of tools of historical criticism. There is no preoccupation here with the intellectual demands of man in the climate of the first stage of the Enlightenment in relation to what could be known about the historical data concerning Jesus' (op.cit., 69).

91. Jon Sobrino, *Christology at the Crossroads*, Orbis Books, Maryknoll and SCM Press 1979, 218.

92. Ibid., 215.

93. Ibid., 221.

94. Ibid., 371, cf. 224.

5. Context

1. Karl Barth, *Die christliche Dogmatik*, Munich 1927, IX.

2. Cornel West, *Prophesy Deliverance! An Afro-American Revolutionary Christianity*, Westminster Press, Philadelphia 1982, 106.

3. James H.Cone, *For My People. Black Theology and the Black Church*, Orbis Books, Maryknoll 1986, 86-98.

4. Cf. James H.Cone, *My Soul Looks Back*, Abingdon Press, Nashville 1982, 115.

5. See Gayraud S.Wilmore and James H.Cone (ed.), *Black Theology: A Documentary History, 1966-1979*, Orbis Books, Maryknoll 1979, 445-62; Cone, *My Soul Looks Back*, 93-113; *For My People*, 140-74; Sergio Torres and John Eagleson (eds.), *The Challenge of Basic Christian Communities*, Orbis Books, Maryknoll 1981, 265-81; Virignia Fabella MM and Sergio Torres (ed.), *Irruption of the Third World*, Orbis Books, Maryknoll 1983, 235-45.

6. Other projects of Theology in the Americas are the Hispanic Project, Asian-American Project, Indigenous Peoples' Project, Women's Project, Church and Labor Dialogue, Theologians' Task Force and Alternative Theology Project. See Cone, *For My People*, 161-74; Sergio Torres and John Eagleson (eds.), *Theology in the Americas*, Orbis Books, Maryknoll 1976; Cornel West, Caridad Guidote and Margaret Coakely (eds.), *Theology in the Americas. Detroit II Conference Papers*, Orbis Books, Maryknoll 1982.

7. John Mbiti, 'An African Views American Black Theology', in Wilmore and Cone (eds.), *Black Theology. A Documentary History, 1966-1979*, 477-82.

8. West, Guidote and Coakley, *Theology in the Americas*, 119.

9. Ibid., 119f.

10. For the discussion over this conference see Berma Klein Goldewijk, 'Derde Wereld Theologen ontgrenzen Gramsci', *Wending* 39.3, 1984, 169-75.

11. Cornel West, in Torres and Eagleson, *The Challenge of Basic Christian Communities*, 256.

12. Cf. Charles Long, 'Freedom, Otherness and Religion: Theologies Opaque', *The Chicago Theological Seminary Register* LXXIII, Winter 1983, 20.

13. See West, *Prophesy Deliverance!*, 118f. It is not completely clear how this evaluation of Gramsci relates to what West, who is not afraid of wild statements, writes on p.137: 'Gramscianism is to Marxism what neo-orthodoxy is to Christianity: an innovative revision of dogmas for dogmatic purposes.'

14. Ibid., 24: 'Afro-American philosophy expresses the particular American variation of European modernity that Afro-Americans helped shape in the country and must contend with in the future.'

15. See Cornel West, 'Black Theology and Marxist Thought', in Wilmore and Cone, *Black Theology. A Documentary History, 1966-1979*, 552-67.

16. Cf. Rosemary Radford Ruether, *New Woman/New Earth. Sexist Ideologies and Human Liberation*, Seabury Press, New York 1975, 115-33.

17. Ibid., 166.

18. Wilmore and Cone, *Black Theology. A Documentary History, 1966-1979*, 102.

19. On this see Cone, *For My People*, 127-32.

20. Ibid., 123-7.

21. Ibid., 132.

22. Jacquelyn Grant. 'Black Theology and the Black Woman', in Wilmore and Cone, *Black Theology. A Documentary History, 1966-1979*, 428.

23. Quoted in ibid., 389-97.

24. Trudi Klijn, in a conversation with Katie Cannon, *Wending* 39.3, 1984, 131.

25. Ibid., 134f.

26. West, Guidote and Coakley, *Theology in the Americas*, 90-6.

27. Gayraud S.Wilmore, *Black Religion and Black Radicalism*, Orbis Books, Maryknoll 1983, X.

28. Karl Barth, *Church Dogmatics* IV.2, T.&.T.Clark 1958, 727-840.

29. Wilmore and Cone, *Black Theology. A Documentary History, 1966-1979*, 391.

30. Gayraud S.Wilmore, *Black and Presbyterian. The Heritage and the Hope*, Westminster Press, Philadelphia 1983, 77.

31. See J.Deotis Roberts, *Roots of a Black Future: Family and Church*, Westminster Press, Philadelphia 1980, 23-8, 110-35.

6. Ideology

1. Gayraud S.Wilmore and James H.Cone, *Black Theology: A Documentary History, 1966-1979*, Orbis Books, Maryknoll 1979, 135-43. Paul Lehmann's lecture is reprinted on pp.144-51, and that by Gollwitzer under the title 'Why Black Theology?', on pp.152-73.

2. In May 1973 a symposium on black theology and Latin American

liberation theology was organized by the World Council of Churches in Geneva. The intention was to introduce these forms of theology to European theologians. The course of this symposium was the occasion for giving the title 'Incommunication' to the special number of *Risk*, WCC, Geneva 1975, which was devoted to it. See also the preface to this book.

3. Gollwitzer, 'Why Black Theology?', 152.

4. Ibid., 164.

5. Ibid., 167.

6. Ibid., 164f.

7. John C.Bennett, ' Theology of Liberation', in *Black Theology. A Documentary History*, 179: 'All theologies are to some extent strategic theologies. They give emphasis to the questions of a particular time and place and they seek to counteract what are believed to be the errors that are most tempting at the time of writing.'

8. Paul L.Lehmann, 'Black Theology and Christian Theology', in *Black Theology. A Documentary History*, 145f.

9. Ibid., 147.

10. Paul L.Lehmann, *The Transfiguration of Politics*, SCM Press and Harper and Row 1974.

11. Lehmann, 'Black Theology and Christian Theology', 151.

12. James H.Cone, *God of the Oppressed*, Seabury Press 1975, 101.

13. Ibid., 95.

14. Ibid., 100.

15. Ibid., 94f.

16. Cone, op.cit., 91, writes in connection with Mannheim's sociology of knowledge: 'Simply put, ideology is deformed thought, meaning that a certain idea or ideas are nothing but the function of the subjective interest of an individual or group.'

17. See ch.1, section 4.

18. For bibliography see ch.1 n.219.

19. Pablo Richard et al., *The Idols of Death and the God of Life. A Theology*, Orbis Books, Maryknoll 1983.

20. Cone, op.cit., 106f.

21. Ibid., 102,107.

22. Eberhard Jüngel, *God as the Mystery of the World*, Eerdmans and T.& T.Clark 1983, 310. See ch.1, section 4.

23. Cone, op.cit., 102f.

24. Charles Long, 'Freedom, Otherness and Religion: Theologies Opaque', *The Chicago Theological Seminary Register* LXXIII, Winter 1983, 19.

25. Cone, op.cit., 103f.

26. Ibid., 104.

27. For the approach to a theory of ideology by Louis Althusser, see ch.1 n.219.

28. See Dick Boer, 'Een fantastisch verhaal. De politieke betekenis van de lezing van de bijbel', *Eltheto* 65, Zeist 1981, 21.

29. Paul Ricoeur, 'De moeilijke weg naar een narratieve theologie', in *Meedenken met Edward Schillebeeckx*, ed. Hermann Haring, Ted Schoof

and Ad Willems, Baarn 1983, 87-92, gives four reasons for doubting whether one can say that the biblical narratives and narratives generally show this form of continuity. In Cone, op.cit., 102-7, it remains unclear how far the biblical narrative and black stories generally have any continuity.

30. See ch.4, section 2.

31. Cone, op.cit., 105-7.

32. José Miguez Bonino, 'Fundamentele levenservaring als een factor van theologiseren', *Gereformeerd Theologisch Tijdschrift* 83, 1983, 155.

33. Ibid., cf. also id., *Toward a Christian Political Ethics*, Fortress Press and SCM Press 1983, 94-9.

34. James H.Cone, *Black Theology and Black Power*, Seabury Press, New York 1969, 7; Allan Boesak, *Farewell to Innocence*, 48-50.

35. Martin Luther King, *Stride Toward Freedom: The Montgomery Story*, Harper and Row and Victor Gollancz 1958, 104f.

36. See ch.3, para 2.

37. See Robert L.Allen (with the collaboration of Pamela P.Allen), *Reluctant Reformers. Racism and the Social Reform Movements in the United States*, Doubleday, Garden City 1975.

38. Long, op.cit., 22.

INDEX